# German Philosophy of Language

# German Philosophy of Language

*From Schlegel to Hegel and Beyond*

Michael N. Forster

OXFORD
UNIVERSITY PRESS

# OXFORD

**UNIVERSITY PRESS**

Great Clarendon Street, Oxford OX2 6DP

Oxford University Press is a department of the University of Oxford.
It furthers the University's objective of excellence in research, scholarship,
and education by publishing worldwide in

Oxford New York

Auckland Cape Town Dar es Salaam Hong Kong Karachi
Kuala Lumpur Madrid Melbourne Mexico City Nairobi
New Delhi Shanghai Taipei Toronto

With offices in

Argentina Austria Brazil Chile Czech Republic France Greece
Guatemala Hungary Italy Japan Poland Portugal Singapore
South Korea Switzerland Thailand Turkey Ukraine Vietnam

Oxford is a registered trade mark of Oxford University Press
in the UK and in certain other countries

Published in the United States
by Oxford University Press Inc., New York

© Michael N. Forster, 2011

British Library Cataloguing in Publication Data
Data available

Library of Congress Cataloging in Publication Data
Data available

Typeset by SPI Publisher Services, Pondicherry, India
Printed in Great Britain
on acid-free paper by
MPG Books Group, Bodmin and King's Lynn

ISBN 978-0-19-960481-4

1  3  5  7  9  10  8  6  4  2

To the memory of Michael Frede (1940–2007)

# Acknowledgments

Together with its companion volume *After Herder: Philosophy of Language in the German Tradition*, this volume is dedicated to the memory of Michael Frede, who, shortly after retiring from the Chair in the History of Philosophy at Oxford University in 2005, died tragically while swimming in the sea near Delphi in the summer of 2007. Together with Raymond Geuss, Michael supervised my doctoral dissertation on Hegel's reception of ancient skepticism at Princeton University in the early 1980s. He was an intellectually inspiring and generous teacher, as well as a constant source of inspiration and support throughout the rest of his life.

This book also owes much to many other individuals and institutions. As an undergraduate at Oxford University in the late 1970s, I had the good fortune to learn about German philosophy from Patrick Gardiner, Peter Hacker, Alan Ryan, Peter Strawson, Charles Taylor, and Ralph Walker. At Princeton University in the early 1980s, I benefited greatly from the teaching and publications of Michael Frede, Raymond Geuss, Saul Kripke, and Richard Rorty (together with Michael, Raymond deserves especially warm thanks in this connection). I also owe a debt of gratitude to Hans Friedrich Fulda, who generously hosted and judiciously advised me during a year I spent at Heidelberg University in 1984–5. I would also like to thank Klaus Vieweg and Wolfgang Welsch for generous hospitality and rich intellectual stimulation during several visits I have paid to the Friedrich-Schiller University in Jena (the original home of much of the philosophy discussed in this volume). This volume also owes a huge debt to the university at which I have taught for the past twenty-five years, the University of Chicago. I would especially like to thank the following colleagues past and present: Arthur Adkins, Dan Brudney, Ted Cohen, Arnold Davidson, Dan Garber, Charles Larmore, Jonathan Lear, Brian Leiter, Leonard Linsky, Ian Mueller, Martha Nussbaum, Bob Richards, Howard Stein, Lina Steiner, Josef Stern, George Stocking, and Bill Tait. I would also like to thank the following students past and present (many of whom have now gone on to successful professional careers): Stephen Engstrom, Susan Hahn, Jim Kreines, Sheela Kumar, Alison Laywine, Stephen Menn, Nathana O'Brien, Gregg Osborne, Erich Reck, Tim Rosenkoetter, David Sussman, and Rachel Zuckert. This project also benefited greatly from the encouragement and generosity of the Dean of the Humanities Division, Martha Roth, and from a research fellowship I received for 2008–9 at the University's Franke Institute for the Humanities, ably directed by Jim Chandler. So warm thanks to them as well. Other individuals who have contributed to the development of this project in one way or another, and whom I would like to thank, include: Karl Ameriks, Andreas Arndt, Fred Beiser, Anne Birien, Paul Boghossian, Rüdiger Bubner, Thomas Erikson, Eckhart Förster, Kristin Gjesdal, Rolf-Peter Horstmann, John Hyman, Michael Inwood, Mark Johnston, John McDowell, Michael Rosen, Richard Schacht, Hans Sluga, Stelios Virvidakis, Pirmin Stekeler-Weithofer, Michael Williams, Allen Wood, and John Zammito. Institutions which have supported this project by hosting presentations of parts of it, or closely related material, include the following: the Aristotle University in Salonica, the University of Athens, the University of California at Berkeley, the University of Chicago, Columbia University, the University of Crete, Drew University, the University of Georgia, Harvard University, the Humanities Institute of Osaka, the University of Illinois at Champaign–Urbana, the Internationale Hegel Gesellschaft, the Internationale Hegel Vereinigung, James Madison University, Johns Hopkins University, McGill University, the University of Michigan at Ann Arbor, New York University, the University of Notre Dame, Oslo University, the University of Patras, Princeton University, Temple University, and the University of Washington in Seattle. Finally, I would also like to thank Oxford University Press and in particular its Philosophy editor Peter Momtchiloff for bringing this project to fruition. Peter's support and advice during the development of the project were essential.

Several of the essays in this volume have been published before in some form. I would therefore like to thank the publishers and editors of the following essays for allowing me to re-publish them here: "Hegel and Some (Near-) Contemporaries: Narrow or Broad Expressivism?" *Das Interesse des Denkens: Hegel aus heutiger Sicht*, ed. K. Vieweg and W. Welsch (Wilhelm Fink, 2003); "Hegel and Hermeneutics," *The Cambridge Companion to Hegel and Nineteenth-Century Philosophy*, ed. F.C. Beiser (Cambridge University Press, 2009); "Language," *The Cambridge History of Philosophy in the Nineteenth Century*, ed. A.W. Wood (Cambridge University Press, 2011); "Hermeneutics," *The Oxford Handbook of Continental Philosophy*, ed. B. Leiter and M. Rosen (Oxford University Press, 2008).

Last but not least I would like to thank my family for their love, support, and patience: my wife Noha, my daughter Alya, and my parents Michael and Kathleen.

# Contents

The present volume is preceded by a companion volume *After Herder: Philosophy of Language in the German Tradition* whose contents are:

Introduction

## Part I: Herder

## Part II: Hamann

## Part III: Schleiermacher

*Select Bibliography*

# Abbreviations

DGS      Wilhelm Dilthey, *Gesammelte Schriften* (Stuttgart: B.G. Teubner and Göttingen: Vandenhoeck and Ruprecht, 1914– )

FSSW      *Friedrich Schleiermacher's sämmtliche Werke* (Berlin: G. Reimer, 1835– ), references to division, volume, and page

G      *Johann Gottfried Herder Werke*, ed. U. Gaier et al. (Frankfurt am Main: Deutscher Klassiker Verlag, 1985– )

KFSA      *Kritische Friedrich Schlegel Ausgabe*, ed. E. Behler et al. (Munich: F. Schöningh, 1958– )

S      *Johann Gottfried Herder Sämtliche Werke*, ed. B. Suphan et al. (Berlin: Weidmann, 1877– )

WHGS      *Wilhelm von Humboldts Gesammelte Schriften*, ed. A. Leitzmann et al. (Berlin: B. Behr, 1903– )

All references are to volume and page unless otherwise stated.

# Introduction

In the Anglophone world the philosophy of language has for some time now enjoyed something like the status of "first philosophy," having displaced in that central position such previous occupants as metaphysics and epistemology. But where did the philosophy of language begin? Michael Dummett claims that Frege is "the father of 'linguistic philosophy,'"[1] and Anthony Kenny similarly maintains that "Frege gave philosophy its current linguistic turn."[2] Assuming, as seems reasonable, that the expressions "linguistic philosophy" and "[philosophy's] linguistic turn" here refer mainly to the two doctrines that (1) thought is essentially dependent on and bounded by language, and (2) meaning consists in the use of words, then these historical claims are false. Long before Frege, a series of important German thinkers, including Herder, Hamann, Schleiermacher, Friedrich Schlegel, Wilhelm von Humboldt, and Hegel, had already espoused versions of these doctrines. And far from introducing them, Frege actually reacted *against* them, backing off the bold claim that thought is *essentially* dependent on and bounded by language and substituting for it the weaker claim that the dependence in question is only a contingent feature of the thought of human beings, as well as rejecting any equation of meaning with the use of words in favor of a Platonism about meaning, or "sense" (see Essay 8).[3] The present volume and its companion volume *After Herder: Philosophy of Language in the German Tradition* explore the *real* beginnings of modern philosophy of language, namely in the earlier German tradition just mentioned. One of their aims is thus to correct a mistake and fill a lacuna in Anglophone philosophy of language's knowledge of its own origins, and hence in its self-understanding. In doing this, *After Herder* was mainly concerned with Herder, Hamann, and Schleiermacher. The present volume by contrast mainly focuses on Friedrich Schlegel, Wilhelm von Humboldt, and Hegel.

In addition to the controversial historical claim just stated, these volumes also make a number of further controversial historical claims. One of these is that it was *Herder* who played the most fundamental role within the earlier

German tradition in question. It seems to me that Coseriu sums up the situation pretty well in the following isolated aperçu:

Herder famously (or: as should be famous) stands at the beginning of classical German philosophy of language not only chronologically; he is at the same time the "main source," so to speak, and the constant, even if only implicit, reference point of the philosophy of language. Fichte, Friedrich and A. W. Schlegel, Schleiermacher and Schelling, Hegel and Humboldt all take over, directly or indirectly, explicitly or tacitly, ideas of Herder's. That many of these ideas often appear in these authors much more elaborated and better proven than in Herder himself should not be allowed to obscure the fact that they are already to be found in Herder at least in a seminal form and that Herder in many respects simply made the beginning.[4]

Accordingly, one of the things I attempt to do in *After Herder* and the present volume is in effect to provide a detailed vindication of this aperçu. In *After Herder* I was especially concerned to make a case that three important revolutions which occurred towards the end of the eighteenth century in the philosophy of language (now understood stricto sensu), the theory of interpretation (or "hermeneutics"), and the theory of translation were all deeply connected; that these revolutions were mainly the work, not of the philosophers who have tended to receive most of the credit for them, namely Hamann and Schleiermacher, but of Herder, who achieved them first and then passed them on to Hamann and Schleiermacher; and moreover, that his versions of them were to a great extent philosophically superior to theirs. The present volume continues the task of vindicating the claim of Herder's fundamental role, but this time mainly in relation to Friedrich Schlegel, Wilhelm von Humboldt, and Hegel.

Another controversial historical claim made in these volumes is that, besides laying the foundations for modern philosophy of language, hermeneutics, and translation-theory, Herder also laid the foundations for such entire new disciplines (intimately related to those fields) as cultural anthropology and linguistics. The case of anthropology was mainly discussed in *After Herder*.[5] The present volume mainly discusses the case of linguistics (see Essay 4).

Those are some of the more dramatic historical claims championed in these two volumes. However, the purpose of these volumes is not *only* historical, but also to a considerable extent systematic; they aim not only to set the historical record straight, but also to rescue and champion a tradition of thought about language which, in my opinion, gets many important things right that more recent philosophers of language have tended to get wrong. For example, *After Herder* in effect made a case that—in sharp contrast to recent Anglophone philosophers of language such as Quine and especially Davidson, who have erroneously sought to undercut or minimize the claim that radical intellectual diversity occurs across historical periods and cultures, and who have only developed theories of "interpretation" and "translation" of a highly abstract and dubious sort, with little potential value for people actually engaged in such activities—Herder and his tradition correctly embraced that claim, and consequently undertook the task of thinking through its fundamental implications for the methodologies of interpretation and translation in ways which are both philosophically profound and of enormous relevance for actual practice. Similarly, the present volume sketches a case in defense of a thesis of the fundamental diversity of grammars which Herder and Schlegel originally developed against Chomsky's more recent contrary thesis of a "universal grammar" (Essay 4). And it also sketches a case in defense of Herder and Schleiermacher's insistence in their theories of interpretation on the need to avoid a pervasive pitfall of assimilating the interpreted Other's viewpoint to one's own against Gadamer's recent championing of such assimilation (Essays 7 and 9).

Part of what is so interesting and admirable in this earlier German tradition as compared with more recent philosophy of language is thus its sheer philosophical *depth*, the fact that its ideas are often superior to those that later came to dominate philosophy of language in the twentieth century. This depth is not altogether surprising on reflection, for the following reason. To put it a bit pointedly, compared with most recent philosophers of language, the thinkers in this earlier tradition *knew a lot* about language. In particular, they all had an impressive knowledge, not only of their native German and other modern European languages, but also of ancient languages (for example, they all had good Latin, Greek, and Hebrew, and several of them also knew Sanskrit), and in some cases culturally distant living languages as well (for example, Humboldt knew a number of these). Moreover, they were all deeply engaged in, and skilled at, the tasks of interpreting and translating texts, including not only texts in other modern European languages but also ones in historically-culturally distant languages. This intimate, skilled acquaintance with a broad range of languages and linguistic tasks could hardly but lend depth to their theoretical ideas about language.

In addition to sheer depth, another striking virtue of this earlier tradition's ideas about language is their *breadth*, which contrasts sharply with the narrowness of most recent Anglophone philosophy of language. For example, in addition to such foundational questions in the philosophy of language as those concerning the relation between thought and language and the nature of meaning, these thinkers were also deeply interested in such further questions as the following: the extent of linguistic-conceptual variation across historical periods and cultures; the nature of interpretation, and how to accomplish it; the nature of translation, and how to accomplish it; the nature of expression in non-linguistic arts like sculpture, painting, and music, and how to interpret it; the role of genre in both linguistic and non-linguistic art; a range of ethico-political questions concerning language; and many other fascinating questions as well.

One sometimes hears Anglophone philosophers today sounding the death-knell of philosophy of language as the central core of the discipline of philosophy. This is not too surprising given the largely misguided and severely impoverished stock of ideas that currently constitute philosophy of language in the Anglophone world. One of my more ambitious hopes for these two volumes is that they may help to revive philosophy of language in the Anglophone world by re-injecting into it some of the depth and breadth of the Herderian tradition.

Like the essays in *After Herder*, the essays in the present volume were in many cases originally written as discrete pieces rather than as parts of a whole, and I have attempted to preserve rather than to erase their original autonomy in putting them together here. Consequently, they do not form a continuous narrative, and they sometimes overlap.[6] Nonetheless, by arranging them in a certain order and including introductory encyclopedia-style essays on each of the main thinkers covered, I have endeavored to produce something that at least approximates a continuous narrative. Consequently, an energetic reader might want to read through the essays in sequence from beginning to end. Alternatively, since each essay has sufficient autonomy to be read by itself, he or she might prefer to "dip" selectively according to interest.

The essays in these two volumes make no claim to exhaust the wealth of the tradition they explore. However, it is my plan to complement them with further essays in the future, and my hope that they may also encourage other philosophers to venture into this extraordinarily rich and underdeveloped territory.

## Notes

1. M. Dummett, *Frege: Philosophy of Language* (Cambridge, Mass.: Harvard University Press, 1981), p. 683.
2. A. Kenny, *Frege* (London: Penguin, 1995), p. viii.
3. This is not to deny that Frege made any important contributions to the philosophy of language. He did—for example, his clear sense/referent distinction.
4. E. Coseriu, "Zu Hegels Semantik," *Kwartalnik neofilologiczny*, 24 (1977), p. 185 n. 8.
5. See *After Herder*, Essay 6.
6. For example, Essays 6 and 7 overlap, as do Essays 7 and 9.

# PART I
# Schlegel

# 1

# Friedrich Schlegel

Friedrich Schlegel (1772–1829) was—together with his almost equally important, albeit less original, older brother, August Wilhelm Schlegel (1767–1845)—
the main founder of German Romanticism. In addition, he made seminal
contributions to hermeneutics, the theory of language, and general aesthetics
(as well as other fields). In all of these areas—Romanticism, hermeneutics, the
theory of language, and general aesthetics—he was strongly influenced by
Herder. Friedrich Schlegel is an "ideas man" rather than a systematic thinker; he
frequently changes his mind, and is sometimes inconsistent even at a particular
period. But the brilliance and the influence of his ideas make him a thinker of
great importance. This essay will give an overview of Schlegel's thought under
the following headings:

1. Intellectual Life
2. The Idea of Romanticism
3. Hermeneutics
4. Translation-Theory
5. General Aesthetics
6. Theory of Language
7. Epistemology and Metaphysics
8. Political Philosophy
9. The Later Schlegel

## 1. Intellectual Life

Friedrich Schlegel (1772–1829) was born in Hanover in 1772. His father, Johann
Adolf Schlegel (1721–93), was a Protestant pastor and literary theorist, whose
ideas are of some significance for his son's development (for example, he held
the interestingly radical view that the number of literary genres that were possible was infinite). Friedrich had several older siblings, but was closest to August
Wilhelm, who supported and mentored him in his youth, and was his main
intellectual ally thereafter.

After being largely home-schooled by his older brothers (especially August Wilhelm), Friedrich was for a short time apprenticed to a banker, but soon gave this up. In 1788–9 he devoted himself to an intensive reading of Plato in the Greek—a step that proved of great consequence for his subsequent career, both developing his extraordinary talent for languages and introducing him to a philosopher who would have a lasting impact on him. In 1790 he went to Göttingen and then Leipzig in order to study law, but subsequently left law for literature. In 1792 he met Schiller (with whom his relationship would be difficult) and Novalis (with whom he would have an enduring close friendship).

In 1793 Caroline Böhmer, the married daughter of the philologist Michaelis, began to play a large role in the life of Friedrich and his brother August Wilhelm. She had moved to Mainz in 1792, lived there with the radical Georg Forster and his wife, participated in the Mainz rebellion, and had an affair with a French officer. After the collapse of the rebellion she had been imprisoned for her political involvement, and found herself pregnant. August Wilhelm, who had been in love with her before these events, came to the rescue, setting her up in a village near Leipzig for the duration of her pregnancy, where Friedrich visited her regularly, himself becoming enthralled by her. August Wilhelm would eventually marry her in 1796, but she subsequently left him for Schelling (the marriage had broken down by 1800, divorce followed in 1803).

In 1794–6 Friedrich lived in Dresden, where he began an intensive study of Greek literature and visited the city's (reproductions of) ancient sculptures, which had a powerful impact on him. In the winter of 1796 he spent some time in Halle working with the classical philologist F.A. Wolf. In the summer of 1796 he moved to Jena, the great intellectual center of the period, where his brother August Wilhelm and his new wife Caroline settled at about the same time. Friedrich stayed in Jena until the summer of 1797, teaching as a *Privatdozent*. While in Jena he got to know Fichte, Goethe, and Schelling personally, as well as renewing his acquaintance with Schiller, with whom, however, he and his brother soon fell out.

During the period 1788–97 Friedrich complemented his classical and literary studies with an extensive study of contemporary philosophy, including Kant's *Critique of Judgment* (1790), Fichte's subjective idealism, Schiller's *Letters on the Aesthetic Education of Mankind* (1794/5), and Schelling's philosophy of nature. He also wrote and published. To this period belongs his important essay *On the Study of Greek Poetry* (mostly written in 1795, but only published in 1797), a work that constitutes a sort of pivot between his early classicism and his eventual romanticism: in its main body he champions the classical against the merely "interesting" (i.e. the romantic), but in a preface written later under the intervening influence of Schiller's *On Naive and Sentimental Poetry* (1795) he tends to reverse that assessment, according the "interesting" (or romantic) equal legitimacy and value. Other significant pieces from this period include *On Diotima* (1795), an essay in a feminist spirit which gives a very favorable inter-pretation of the depiction of women in Greek literature; the *Essay on the Concept of Republicanism* (1796), a work in political philosophy which champions a radi-cal form of republicanism; and the two "characteristics," *Georg Forster* and *On Lessing* (both 1797).

In the summer of 1797 Schlegel moved to Berlin, where he lived until 1799. There he became the center of a literary-philosophical group that also included Schleiermacher, Dorothea Veit, and Tieck, thereby in effect establishing German Romanticism as a school (though the name "Romanticism" was not used by the group itself). Especially important for his own intellectual development was the fact that he met and became close friends with Schleiermacher, even shar-ing rooms with him for a time. This relationship expanded his philosophical horizon to include Schleiermacher's early synthesis of Kant's critical philoso-phy with Spinoza's monism; gave birth to a joint project of translating the works of Plato (a project which Schlegel did not follow through on, but which Schleiermacher eventually brought to fruition); and after a time encouraged Schlegel to accord more importance to religion, as Schleiermacher did. Less intellectually, but no less personally, important was Schlegel's encounter with Dorothea Veit, daughter of the philosopher Moses Mendelssohn and wife of a banker. Schlegel began an affair with her that led to her divorce in 1799. They would eventually marry in 1804, and their relationship lasted for the rest of Schlegel's life. He also at this time met and began to encourage the then still relatively unknown poet Tieck.

This period produced some of Schlegel's most important writings and publications. These included materials on literary theory, hermeneutics, and translation-theory that were not published until the twentieth century—especially, the *Philosophy of Philology* (1797) and the *Literary Notebooks* (1797–1801). They also included the *History of the Poetry of the Greeks and Romans*, an unfinished but impressively original and learned treatment of its subject published in 1798, which responded to a challenge Herder had issued for someone to do for the history of Greek literature what Winckelmann had already done for the history of Greek art.[1] They also included contribu-tions to the journal *Lyceum*, followed by even more important contributions to the journal *Athenaeum* (1798–1800), a journal which Schlegel founded and wrote for in cooperation with his brother August Wilhelm, Schleiermacher, Novalis, and Tieck. The *Athenaeum* published many of his most important fragments on literary, hermeneutic, and philosophical themes, as well as sev-eral of his longer pieces on such themes, including the *Dialogue on Poetry* and

*On Incomprehensibility* (both 1800). The journal also essentially established German Romanticism as a literary-philosophical movement. Another piece that belongs to this period is Schlegel's main literary work, *Lucinde* (1799)—a novel based on his contemporaneous affair with Dorothea Veit, and notable for its feminist agenda as well as for its (at the time) scandalously frank treatment of sexuality.

In 1799 Schlegel moved back to Jena, where most of the Romantics were now together for a time: besides himself, also August Wilhelm, Caroline, Dorothea, Novalis, Tieck, and Schelling (Schleiermacher was an exception). There he soon earned a doctorate and a *Habilitation* at the University of Jena, and delivered an important series of lectures on Transcendental Philosophy (1800–1). These lectures were attended by Hegel, and evidently had a major impact on the development of Hegel's distinctive version of German Idealism (especially his conception that a radical skepticism plays a fundamental role in philosophy, and his aspiration to synthesize Fichtean subjectivism with Spinozistic monism—both of which positions are anticipated by Schlegel in the lectures). However, as a public event the lectures fell flat (largely due to competition from the charismatic Schelling). This professional disappointment roughly coincided with several personal ones, including the death of Novalis in 1801, the end of Schlegel's friendship with Schleiermacher, and quarrels with his brother August Wilhelm (with whom he reconciled afterwards, but finally broke completely in 1827).

After brief stays in Berlin and Dresden, Schlegel moved to Paris with Dorothea in 1802. On the way there he stopped off in Weimar, where Goethe did him the honor of producing his romantic play *Alarcos* (a work notable for its imitation of the Spanish playright Calderón, who became increasingly important to the Schlegels as a model of romantic literature from this time on). Despite Goethe's approval and help, the play proved another public failure.

In Paris, Schlegel lectured, mainly on German literature and philosophy, and founded the journal *Europa* (1803–5). He had the good fortune to meet two wealthy brothers who were visiting from Cologne, the Boisserée brothers, to whom he began lecturing in return for payment in 1803. He also deepened his knowledge of visual art, especially through careful study of the works in the Louvre, and began publishing an important series of essays on this subject in *Europa*. In addition, he took up a serious study of Sanskrit and its literature under the guidance of the Scotsman Alexander Hamilton (who had lived in India)—a step that would pay rich dividends a few years later. He also conducted original research on Provençal literature using the manuscripts in the National Library, a subject on which he published a report in *Europa*.

In 1804, with the encouragement, and in the company, of the Boisserée brothers, he moved to Cologne, where, between 1804 and 1807, he delivered extensive lectures (some public, some private) on philosophy, history, and language and literature. The lectures on philosophy contain both a history of the subject and a system of his own. The lectures on language and literature cover topics in the philosophy of language and linguistics, as well as presenting a mature statement of his literary romanticism. While in Cologne he also continued his study of Sanskrit and its literature (as well as several other subjects). In 1808 he published *On the Language and Wisdom of the Indians*, a work grounded in his Sanskrit studies. The work has many flaws when judged from the vantage point of modern scholarship.[2] But it also made contributions of enormous importance. In particular, it essentially established Sanskrit studies as a discipline, especially in Germany, and it also established the modern discipline of linguistics (for example, by introducing the very idea of "comparative grammar" for the first time).

The period after 1808 was essentially one of intellectual decline (accompanied by a physical-moral decline that included gluttony and heavy drinking). In 1808, while still in Cologne, Schlegel formally converted to Roman Catholicism, thereby fulfilling an intention he had cherished for several years. His religious conversion went hand in hand with a shift to a much more conservative, or even reactionary, political position. In 1809, after years of failing to find secure employment and struggling with financial difficulties, he moved to Vienna, largely in the hope of finding professional and financial security there, though he was also attracted by Austria's Catholicism and *Kaisertum*, as well as by its history (in which he had developed an interest). Thanks largely to August Wilhelm's mediation, he soon assumed political posts, first as imperial court secretary to Archduke Charles (in 1809), then as Metternich's representative to the Diet of Frankfurt (1815–18). He was not successful in these posts, though his time in Frankfurt is noteworthy for agitation on behalf of civil rights for Jews. During this period he also continued to lecture, giving lectures on modern European history (1810), ancient and modern literature (1812), the philosophy of life (1827), the philosophy of history (1828), and the philosophy of language (1828–9). These lectures were delivered before prestigious audiences and were published shortly afterwards to considerable acclaim. But for the most part they lack the originality and the interest of his earlier work. During this period he also founded and edited an anti-Napoleonic newspaper (established in 1809 as part of Austria's war effort against France), as well as two new journals: the *Deutsches Museum* (1812–13) and the Catholic review *Concordia* (1820–3). His Collected Works were published in ten volumes in 1822–5. As in his early years, he became the center of a group of like-minded (which, though, now meant Catholic and conservative-reactionary) thinkers, including Adam Müller and Franz von Baader. He also developed a strong interest in the occult.

Schlegel died in Dresden in 1829.

## 2. The Idea of Romanticism

Schlegel is probably best known for having developed a conception of a type of poetry which he contrasts with "classical" poetry as "romantic [*romantisch*]," and for having championed the latter. What is the nature of this distinction, and how did he arrive at his stance towards it?

The distinction itself is already incipiently present in his early work *On the Study of Greek Poetry* (mostly written in 1795; published in 1797), in the form of a sharp contrast between the "classical," or "objective" vs. the "modern," or "interesting." Among the features which he there identifies as distinguishing the "interesting" from the "classical" are unsatisfied longing, a mixing of science and art, a mixing of genres, a reverence for genius, a rejection of what is common in form and content in favor of interesting individuality, dissonance, and rhyme. In the main body of this early work, written in 1795, he strongly valorizes the "classical" at the expense of the "interesting."[3] However, in the same year Schiller published his essay *On Naive and Sentimental Poetry* (1795), which distinguished "sentimental" from "naive" poetry in terms of a strikingly similar set of characteristics (e.g. a longing for the Infinite) but in a spirit of *defending* it as equally valid. And in a preface which Schlegel added to *On the Study of Greek Poetry* subsequently under the avowed impact of Schiller's essay, he shifted to a much more sympathetic attitude towards "interesting" poetry, according it equal validity and value with "classical." Subsequently he went on to champion this sort of poetry even more emphatically under the name of "romantic" poetry (for example, in *Athenaeum Fragments*, no. 116).

Why did Schlegel adopt this "romanticism"? The full explanation is quite complicated. Part of it clearly lies in the influence exerted on him by the fact that Schiller had drawn a very similar distinction between types of poetry but had defended the type which he had himself initially viewed negatively.[4] Another part of the explanation lies in a certain broad tendency to skepticism that came to characterize Schlegel's epistemology at this period.[5] But yet another part of it lies in the influence of *Herder*.

Schlegel already looked up to Herder as an expert on aesthetics at the time of writing the main body of *On the Study of Greek Poetry* in 1795. Indeed, he explicitly praises him there in the most glowing terms for expertise in this area ("*Herder* joins the most extensive knowledge with the most delicate feeling and the most supple sensitivity").[6] In his *Letters for the Advancement of Humanity* (1793–7) Herder drew a sharp distinction between ancient and modern poetry which turned on many of the same distinguishing features as Schlegel's "classical" vs. "interesting" distinction—including the prevalence in modern poetry of unsatisfied longing, a mixing of science and art, a mixing of genres, and rhyme. And in 1796—i.e. precisely the period of his own reversal of attitude—Schlegel wrote a review of the relevant parts of Herder's *Letters* (the 7th and 8th Collections) in which he focused on just this distinction of Herder's.[7] This review shows that Schlegel's own development of romanticism owed two large debts to Herder.

First, Herder helped Schlegel to realize that his own distinction between "classical" and "interesting" poetry was in effect a distinction between two different but equally well-defined and legitimate genres, and that it was therefore a mistake to measure the one by the constitutive standards of the other as he had initially done. This had long been Herder's standard position concerning different genres (for example, in his seminal essay *Shakespeare* [1773]). And in the *Letters* he had applied it to the distinction between ancient and modern poetry in particular. That this influenced Schlegel in the way just indicated is shown by the fact that he concludes his 1796 review with the following report on precisely that application:

The result (p. 171 and following) denies that the poetry of different times and peoples can be compared, indeed even that there is a universal criterion of evaluation.[8]

Second, when Schlegel (together with his brother August Wilhelm) went on to elaborate the basic conception of "interesting" poetry that he had already delineated in 1795 into the richer conception of "romantic" poetry, it was Herder's *Letters* that supplied him with the main elaborations.[9] The following are three examples of this: (1) Schlegel eventually came to see the romantic as distinguished from the classical not only by the features already mentioned, but also by its *Christian* character.[10] But Herder had already emphasized this as a distinguishing feature of modern poetry in the *Letters*, and Schlegel had focused on this in his review.[11] (2) Schlegel also eventually added as a distinguishing characteristic of romantic poetry a sort of fusion of a striving for a human beloved with a striving for the Infinite (God), associating this fusion with the Provençal troubadours, the Minnesinger, Dante, Petrarch, Cervantes, and Shakespeare.[12] But this whole conception again comes from Herder. For in the *Letters* Herder had prominently discussed precisely such a fusion of a striving for a human beloved with a striving for God as characteristic of precisely the same poets,[13] and Schlegel had again in his review focused on this aspect of Herder's work.[14] (3) Schlegel also eventually came to regard the novel [*Roman*]—conceived rather differently and more broadly than we would conceive it today—[15] as the distinctive romantic [*romantisch*] genre, and to see it as all-embracing in scope, in particular as combining theory with poetry and as subsuming all genres of poetry within itself.[16] But once again, Herder had already developed precisely such a conception of the novel in the *Letters*.[17]


## 3. Hermeneutics

Another area in which Schlegel makes an important contribution is hermeneutics, or the theory of interpretation. This is not a subject with which he is commonly associated—as, say, Schleiermacher is—since he did not write systematically about it. But his scattered remarks on the subject arguably add up to a contribution that is no less important than Schleiermacher's, indeed even more so. Since I discuss Schlegel's hermeneutics in detail in the following essay, my treatment of it here will be fairly brief and dogmatic.

Two German scholars, Josef Körner and Hermann Patsch, have already made cases for Schlegel's seminal importance in hermeneutics. Their cases essentially take the form of arguing—largely on the basis of evidence supplied by Schlegel's *Philosophy of Philology* from 1797, a set of notes whose composition coincided with the beginning of his close friendship with Schleiermacher in Berlin, and indeed their co-habitation there—that Schlegel anticipated and influenced key moves in Schleiermacher's hermeneutics lectures (which Schleiermacher began to deliver in 1805).

There is much truth in this argument. Schleiermacher clearly looked up to Schlegel at this early period. For example, in 1797 he wrote of Schlegel:

He is a young man twenty-five years old, of such broad knowledge that it is difficult to understand how it is possible to know so much at such a young age, with an original intellect that is far superior to everything here, despite the fact that there is much intelligence and talent here.[18]

And while it is often difficult to ascertain intellectual priority between them with any certainty given the meagerness of the available evidence and the fact that this was a period of deliberate "together-philosophy [*Symphilosophie*]," several of the doctrines in Schleiermacher's hermeneutics which Körner credits to Schlegel really do seem to have been more originally Schlegel's: in particular, that the interpreter needs to understand an author better than he understood himself; that it is important for the interpreter to identify an author's psychological development; that the interpreter should interpret the parts of a text in light of the *whole* text; and that the interpreter should reject *philologia sacra*. Moreover, the same is true of several additional doctrines which Patsch credits to Schlegel: in particular, that philology/hermeneutics is not merely a science but an art; that hermeneutics and criticism are interdependent; and that *divina-*

*tion* plays an essential role in criticism/hermeneutics. Indeed, the same seems to me true of several further doctrines as well: that interpretation typically faces the problem of a deep intellectual difference dividing the interpreter and his age from the author interpreted and his; that in interpretation misunderstanding, rather than being the exception, is the rule; and that, beyond the generic principle of identifying an author's psychological development, the interpreter of a text needs to identify, and trace the unfolding of, an author's "seminal decision [*Keimentschluß*]."[19]

Nonetheless, Körner and Patsch's *teleological* picture of Schlegel's importance for hermeneutics—their picture that this lies mainly in his having prepared the ground for Schleiermacher's hermeneutics—seems to me unfortunate. For, as I have argued elsewhere, the importance of Schleiermacher's hermeneutics itself has been somewhat exaggerated: its main claims were heavily anticipated by Ernesti and especially Herder, and to the extent that they do depart from Herder's views usually prove on inspection to be inferior to them.[20] And more fundamentally, Schlegel's *main* claim to importance in hermeneutics instead lies in certain contributions he makes which are *not* subsequently to be found in Schleiermacher.

It is this more fundamental point that I would like to develop here—by identifying five ideas (or families of ideas) in Schlegel concerning interpretation which go beyond anything in Schleiermacher's hermeneutics, and which are of great intrinsic value. These ideas are all in fact more continuous with Herder than anticipative of Schleiermacher, which is not accidental, since Schlegel from an early period looked up to Herder as an interpreter (as we recently saw from *On the Study of Greek Poetry* [1795/7]).

(1) The first of these ideas—or rather, the first family of ideas—concerns *genre*. Many of the key insights in this area had already been achieved by Herder, in such works as *Shakespeare* (1773) and *This Too a Philosophy of History for the Formation of Humanity* (1774). His insights included recognizing the following: (a) the essential role that correctly identifying genre plays in the interpretation not only of literary but also of non-linguistic art; (b) the radical historical mutability of genres; (c) the consequent frequent need for the interpreter to identify unfamiliar, new, and sometimes even uniquely instantiated genres; (d) the likewise consequent frequent need for the interpreter to resist a strong temptation to misidentify a genre by falsely assimilating it to a similar-looking genre from another time or place with which he happens already to be more familiar (e.g. to misidentify the genre of Shakespearean "tragedy" by falsely assimilating it to that of Greek "tragedy"), as well as for the critic to resist a resulting strong temptation to evaluate particular works of literary or non-linguistic art in terms of genre-purposes and -rules which they do not in fact

aspire to realize in the first place, instead of in terms of those which they do; and (e) the once again consequent need for the interpreter or critic to employ a painstaking empirical approach to the determination of genres in order to identify them correctly. A large part of Schlegel's achievement in this area lay simply in retaining these vitally important insights of Herder's. The same was true of his brother August Wilhelm.

But Schlegel (and his brother) also made two important new *applications* of these Herderian insights about genre. One of these concerned the interpretation of Greek tragedy. Before the Schlegels the understanding of Greek tragedy as a genre had been dominated by Aristotle's treatment of it in the *Poetics*, which had been considered virtually sacrosanct not only by the French dramatists and critics but also by their German opponents Lessing and Herder. With the Schlegels there emerged for the first time, in light of a more scrupulous empirical investigation of the surviving Greek tragedies themselves, a realization that Aristotle's treatment of Greek tragedy is in fact at least as much an obstacle to properly understanding it as an aid. By breaking Aristotle's undue influence on the interpretation of Greek tragedy in this way, the Schlegels made possible a recognition of its deeply unfamiliar nature and of the need to rethink this radically. They also themselves began such a rethinking, which subsequently continued with Nietzsche's *The Birth of Tragedy* and still continues today (for example, in the work of Vernant, Vidal-Nacquet, Goldhill, and Winkler)—in particular, by incorporating a new recognition of Greek tragedy's deeply religious (Dionysiac) and civic-political nature.

Another new application of Herder's insights about genre concerned the very birth of Romanticism. For, as I mentioned above, when the young Schlegel suddenly changed from his initial classicism concerning the distinction between "classical" and "interesting" (or "romantic") poetry towards a recognition of the equal legitimacy and value of the latter, this change was largely the result of his sudden recognition that the historical shift from the former type of poetry to the latter was basically an example of the sort of historical shift between different but equally well-defined and legitimate genres that Herder had already discussed, and that this precluded any simple valorization of the one at the expense of the other, in particular any negative assessment of the one in terms of the standards of the other.

Finally, Schlegel also made two further significant contributions concerning genre. First, again in continuity with Herder, he recognized that genres (e.g. tragedy) give birth to what theorists would today call genre-modes (e.g. "tragic"), which may then qualify works in other genres (for instance, one could plausibly describe Thomas Hardy's novels as "tragic novels"). Second, he recognized that genres are sometimes systematically interdependent and interdefined. This sort of situation is fairly obvious in certain cases, for example in the case of parody. But, as Schlegel and his brother August Wilhelm showed, there are also less obvious cases—for example, ancient tragedy and comedy, which (unlike their modern counterparts) are in part defined by their sharp exclusion of each other.

(2) Another important idea concerning interpretation which Schlegel introduced is that texts sometimes express meanings and thoughts, not explicitly in any of their parts, but instead implicitly through their parts and the way in which these are put together to form a whole. For example, he writes in *Athenaeum Fragments*, no. 111:

The teachings that a novel hopes to instill must be of the sort that can be communicated only as wholes, not demonstrated singly and not subject to exhaustive analysis.

He applies this point not only to novels (for example, to Goethe's *Wilhelm Meisters Lehrjahre* in *On Goethe's Meister* [1798]), but also to the philosophies of Spinoza and Fichte (in *On Lessing* [1797/1801]), and to ancient literature. Accordingly, in the last connection, he writes at *Athenaeum Fragments*, no. 325 (echoing a famous fragment of Heraclitus):

But Apollo, who neither speaks nor keeps silent but intimates, no longer is worshipped, and wherever a Muse shows herself, people immediately want to carry her off to be cross-examined.

(3) Another important contribution Schlegel made to hermeneutics concerns the role of *unconscious* meanings and thoughts in texts, and hence in their interpretation. The general idea that unconscious mental processes occur already had a long history in German philosophy by Schlegel's day: it had been a commonplace among the Rationalists, Kant had been committed to it as well, and so too had Herder, who had moreover discussed it in close connection with questions of authorship and interpretation in *On the Cognition and Sensation of the Human Soul* (1778). However, it was above all Schlegel who developed that general idea into a principle that the interpreter must penetrate beyond an author's conscious meanings and thoughts to discover his unconscious ones as well. Thus he writes in *On Goethe's Meister* that "every excellent work ... aims at more than it knows"; and at *Athenaeum Fragments*, no. 401 that "in order to understand someone who only partially understands himself, you first have to understand him completely and better than he himself does."

(4) Another important contribution that Schlegel made to hermeneutics concerns the presence of inconsistency and confusion in texts. Ernesti had already encouraged the interpreter to attribute inconsistencies and other forms of confusion to profane texts where appropriate, and Herder had extended that

principle to sacred texts as well. Schlegel accepts Herder's broader version of this principle. But he also places even greater emphasis on it and develops it further: he not only insists that confusion is a common feature of texts and should be recognized when it occurs, but also argues that in such cases the interpreter needs to seek to *understand and explain* it. Hence, in *On Incomprehensibility* (1800) he insists that confusion frequently occurs even in superior texts and needs to be recognized when it does. And as early as 1797 he argues in a note:

In order to understand someone, one must first of all be cleverer than he, then just as clever, and then also just as stupid. It is not enough that one understand the actual sense of a confused work better than the author understood it. One must also oneself be able to know, to *characterize*, and even *construe* the confusion even down to its very principles.

(5) A final important contribution Schlegel made to hermeneutics concerns the interpretation of non-linguistic art. Herder had begun his career, in the *Critical Forests*, holding that non-linguistic art does not express meanings or thoughts at all but is instead merely sensuous in nature. On such a view, the question of *interpreting* it does not even arise. But Herder had subsequently changed his mind about this, instead coming to recognize that non-linguistic art does often express meanings and thoughts, and therefore does need to be interpreted. This later position of Herder's is clearly the correct one. Schlegel deserves credit both for taking it over and for developing it in some insightful ways. (In doing so, he was strongly influenced not only by Herder but also by Wackenroder and Tieck.)

Thus, Schlegel argues unequivocally that non-linguistic art of any importance always does express meanings and thoughts. For example, in the Cologne lectures on philosophy (1804–6) he writes:

If one wished to make mere decoration and charm the purpose of art, art would be ill founded, and the objections of those people who reject it as quite useless entirely justified…But it is an entirely different matter when one makes *meaning* the purpose of art.

And he applies such a position to each of the non-linguistic arts specifically. For instance, he insists in *Athenaeum Fragments*, no. 444 that instrumental music expresses ideas. And in the pieces on visual art which he began writing in Paris in 1802 he insists that it is also visual art's function to express meanings and thoughts—in particular, that the proper function of sculpture is to express ancient myths; and that the proper function of painting and Gothic architecture is again to express meanings and thoughts, but this time ones of a religious, and more specifically Christian, character.

In addition, he develops a series of hermeneutic principles to guide the interpretation of non-linguistic art. Some of these principles are similar to ones that he applies to linguistic texts. For example, he holds that interpretation of visual art from the past faces, and needs to recognize, the problem that its subject-matter is intellectually distant from ourselves; that one of the main ways of solving this problem is through a careful study of *literature* from the visual art's period and place; that the parts of a work of visual art need to be interpreted in light of the whole work; that interpreting visual art requires correctly identifying its genre, and overcoming the obstacles that stand in the way of doing so; that it is vitally important when interpreting a work of visual art to discern its *holistic* meanings; and that the interpretation of non-linguistic art needs to include paying attention to its author's *unconscious* meanings.

But Schlegel also develops a more distinctive hermeneutic principle to guide the interpretation of non-linguistic art: a theory of a sort of *symbolism* that is distinctive of such art and by means of which it conveys its meanings and thoughts. For example (to begin with a simple case), he points out convincingly that painters such as Correggio often use light and dark colors to symbolize good and evil respectively. Again (but less simply), he argues plausibly that there is an important difference between portrait paintings which have a plain background (e.g. Holbein's) and those which have a landscape as background (e.g. Leonardo daVinci's *Mona Lisa*), since in the latter the landscape symbolically conveys (or at least clarifies) the inner state of mind of the person portrayed. Again (and more elaborately still), he cogently identifies a whole series of features of the architecture of the Gothic cathedral which symbolically convey meanings and thoughts—including, for example, the shapes of the cross and the rose, symbolic respectively of (Christ's) death and the life to come.

## 4. Translation-Theory

Another area in which Schlegel makes a relatively neglected contribution is the theory of translation. The generation before Schlegel's in Germany had already contained great translators and translation-theorists: especially Herder (an important translator, especially in his *Popular Songs* [*Volkslieder*] [1774/8], and a seminal theorist of translation in his *Fragments on Recent German Literature* [1767–8]) and Voss (the great translator of Homer). In Schlegel's own generation the greatest translators and translation-theorists were his brother August Wilhelm (who, among numerous other translations of literature from several languages, in 1797 began publishing his epoch-making series of translations of

Shakespeare, as well as theorizing deeply about translation in lectures and essays) and his friend Schleiermacher (who became Germany's great translator of Plato, as well as authoring what is arguably the most important work on the theory of translation ever written, *On the Different Methods of Translation* [1813]). However, Friedrich Schlegel himself made a significant contribution in this area as well.

After moving to Berlin in 1797 and befriending Schleiermacher, Schlegel shared equal responsibility with him for developing the project of translating the works of Plato (albeit that only Schleiermacher carried the project to fruition). In addition, some of Schlegel's fragmentary writings from this period are concerned with the theory of translation—especially, his *Philosophy of Philology* (1797) and fragments from the late 1790s now published in *Kritische Friedrich Schlegel Ausgabe*, volume 18. Furthermore, the Cologne lectures on German language and literature from 1807 contain comments concerning meter and its reproduction in another language, while *On the Language and Wisdom of the Indians* (1808) contains translations of Sanskrit texts as well as a modicum of theorizing about translation.

From these materials it is possible to reconstruct the main lines of Schlegel's own early theory of translation, as follows: (1) The modern translator usually confronts the problem of an intellectual gulf dividing him and his culture from an ancient author and his: "the immeasurable difference . . . , the quite distinctive nature of antiquity," "the *absolute* difference between the ancient and the modern."[21] The gulf in question consists first and foremost in conceptual incommensurability, but also in a sharp divergence of metrical principles.[22] (2) This makes translation extremely difficult, even to the point of being strictly speaking impossible: "Whether translations are *possible* is a question no one has worried about."[23] (3) However, the proper response to this situation is not to despair, but instead to see the task of translation as one of endless approximation: "Every translation is an indeterminate, infinite task."[24] (4) The translator who confronts an intellectual gulf of this sort faces a choice between either attempting to reproduce the original meaning and music of the source text faithfully or undertaking to transform it: "Every translation is a transplanting or a transforming or both."[25] How can translation of the former type be achieved? (5) This requires that the translator have hermeneutic (or "philological") expertise: "Translation is obviously something [philological];"[26] "Translation belongs entirely to philology, is a thoroughly philological art."[27] It also requires that he be artistic.[28] (6) In terms of specific approach, it requires that he modify the word-usages and the music features of the target language in order to approximate those of the source language as closely as possible. Thus in the *Philosophy of Philology* Schlegel remarks that "one should translate in order to mold the modern languages classically."[29] And later, in *On the Language and Wisdom of the Indians*, he argues that in translations of Sanskrit texts into German the German language should "mold itself [*sich anschmiegen*]" to the original Sanskrit and should attempt to reproduce the meters found in the latter.[30] (7) Besides its primary virtue of reproducing the original text as accurately as possible, this approach also has the virtue of enriching the target language both conceptually and musically. Schlegel implies this when he says that "one should translate in order to mold the modern languages classically." And he also makes the point in a more general way: "Each translation is actually language-creation."[31] (8) Moreover, this sort of translation elevates the translator to the rank of an artist: "Only the translator is a linguistic artist."[32]

All of these principles are both continuous with Herder's seminal theory of translation in the *Fragments on Recent German Literature* and anticipative of Schleiermacher's theory of translation in *On the Different Methods of Translation*. Given the meagerness of the relevant textual evidence, and the non-proprietorial spirit of "together-philosophy [*Symphilosophie*]" in which Schlegel and Schleiermacher worked during the relevant period, it is hard to be sure which of them adopted and developed these ideas about translation from Herder first. However, it seems likely that it was in many if not most cases Schlegel, and that to this extent much of the credit for the eventual emergence of Schleiermacher's sophisticated theory of translation in *On the Different Methods of Translation* belongs to him.

## 5. General Aesthetics

Aesthetics, in the sense of the theory of both literary and non-linguistic art, is arguably Friedrich Schlegel's (and his brother August Wilhelm's) main and best-known area of endeavor. The discussion of it that follows can therefore only be selective.

Several parts of Schlegel's aesthetic theory have already been mentioned. One consists in his basic romanticism: his conception of a sharp distinction between classical and romantic poetry, and his valorization of the latter as much as, or even more than, the former. Another part is his theory of genre, as it concerns both literary and non-linguistic art. Yet another part is his conception that, like literature, non-linguistic art expresses meanings and thoughts, and therefore requires interpretation, together with his hermeneutic principles for interpreting it. As we have seen, Schlegel's aesthetic theory is heavily indebted to Herder in all these areas.

But Schlegel's aesthetics also includes many further parts as well. One of these lies in his strong tendency until about 1800 to valorize art over other areas of culture, such as religion and philosophy. This tendency contrasts with a *religious* form of romanticism which emerged at around that time, above all in Schleiermacher's *On Religion: Speeches to its Cultured Despisers* (1799) (a work that was indeed to some extent directed against Schlegel's aestheticism), and in Novalis's *Christianity or Europe* (also written and circulated in 1799, though not formally published until 1826). However, following the composition of these two works, and under their influence, Schlegel himself shifted ground, coming to accord religion a much more important cultural position in his *Ideas* (1800), and continuing to do so thereafter. He also implicitly raised the relative cultural standing of philosophy, especially in his 1800–1 lectures on Transcendental Philosophy and his Cologne lectures on philosophy from 1804–6.

Another of Schlegel's principles in aesthetics concerns a slightly different aspect of the relationship between art and religion. In a broad sense of the term "religious," Schlegel's ideal of romantic art was arguably itself religious from the start, namely in virtue of its central principle of a striving for the Infinite.[33] Accordingly, he already writes in a fragment from the period of the *Athenaeum*: "The poetic ideal... = God."[34] And as his ideal of romantic art developed over time, it increasingly became religious in a narrower sense as well: Christian, and indeed specifically Catholic. Thus he already writes in a precocious fragment from 1799: "Art aims at the last Messiah, and is hence Catholic."[35] And this insistence on the religious, Christian, Catholic nature of romantic art is emphatic in the pieces on visual art that he began to publish in 1802.[36]

Turning to further topics: Schlegel's treatments of poetry and visual art are parallel in many ways. Beyond the ways already mentioned, such as his recognition of the role that genre plays in both, and his position that both express meanings and thoughts and hence require interpretation, the following ways are also noteworthy: Just as in poetry he comes to reject Weimar classicism, with its associated paganism and valorization of epic poetry and tragedy as genres, in favor of romanticism, with its associated Christianity and valorization of the novel as a genre,[37] so in his treatment of visual art he comes to reject Winckelmann's and Weimar's classicism (the latter represented by Goethe's *Propyläen*), with its associated paganism and valorization of the genre of sculpture, in favor of romanticism, with its associated Christianity and valorization of the genre of painting.[38] Just as in poetry he looks to poets from the medieval and early modern periods such as the Provençal troubadours, the Minnesinger, Dante, Petrarch, Cervantes, Shakespeare, and (eventually) Calderón as the main representatives of romantic poetry,[39] so in visual art he looks to painters from the medieval and early modern periods such as Correggio, Raphael, and Dürer as the main representatives of romantic visual art.[40] Just as in poetry he sees the novel as a sort of super-genre that incorporates and transcends all the others, so in visual art he posits a type of painting ("symbolic" painting) that incorporates and transcends all the others.[41]

But despite this parallelism, Schlegel also posits a sort of hierarchy of the arts which locates poetry at the top. More specifically, his hierarchy places sculpture lowest, music higher, painting and architecture higher still, and poetry highest of all. He appeals to two main criteria in order to justify such a ranking: First, it reflects an ascent from a predominance of the merely sensuous (in sculpture) to a predominance of feeling or emotion (in music) to a predominance of mean-ing (in painting, architecture, and poetry).[42] Second, unlike the other arts, poetry is a universal art that is implicated in all the others:

Poetry is alone among all the arts a, so to speak, universal accompanying art [Mitkunst] which joins together all the others.[43]

Schlegel's picture here is nuanced, though. It is not a matter of sculpture *only* being sensuous; music *only* emotional; painting, architecture, and poetry *only* meaningful. Rather, each factor is involved in each type of art, but in different proportions (hence my choice of the word "predominance" above). Thus, as we have seen, Schlegel ascribes meanings and thoughts to *all* the arts, including the lower ones in his hierarchy: sculpture expresses myths, instrumental music expresses ideas, etc. And accordingly, he sees poetry, with its meanings and thoughts, as a universal art that permeates all the other arts as well. Likewise, he understands feeling or emotion to be shared by all the arts. Hence in the *Lectures on the History of Literature* he implies that even the high art of architecture expresses emotion, and moreover that it must do so in order to be real art:

How excellent soever the style of a building may be, if it convey no meaning, express no *sentiment*, it cannot strictly be considered a creation of Art.[44]

Indeed, he develops two interesting and parallel theories positing natural cor-relations between particular sounds and particular emotions (this is relevant to both instrumental music and poetry),[45] and between particular colors and par-ticular emotions (this is relevant to painting).[46] Likewise, he would, I think, say that sensuousness is involved in all of the arts to one degree or another.

Finally, two further features of Schlegel's aesthetics also deserve mention. One of these concerns his attitude to *nature* and the *natural*. If one's conception of "romanticism" is based mainly on English models, such as Wordsworth and Coleridge's *Lyrical Ballads*, one is likely to associate romanticism with a valori-zation of the natural at the expense of the artificial. However, as Arthur Lovejoy has pointed out, this is one of the axes along which romanticism as a whole turns out to be a very contradictory movement.[47] And accordingly, *Schlegel's* romanticism in fact espouses virtually the opposite principle. Recall here that his romanticism largely had its origins in Schiller's naive vs. sentimental distinction and in Schiller's valorization of the *latter* (not the former). The same contrary spirit emerges in Schlegel's own characterizations of romantic poetry as "poetry of poetry," a set of endlessly reflecting mirrors, a fusion of poetry with philosophy or science, and so on. It also manifests itself in such positions as his rejection of the valorization of the natural that occurs in pastoral poetry and in Rousseau's theories.[48]

Finally, like several of his recent predecessors and contemporaries, Schlegel holds that true art can only come from the artistic *genius*—in the sense of someone who in an individualistic way transcends existing rules rather than following them, and who also achieves a certain sort of authenticity (the contrasting vices that Schlegel identifies here are, respectively, imitation and mannerism). In addition, he considers the historical emergence of genius to be something that is recalcitrant to explanation.[49]

## 6. Theory of Language

Schlegel is also extremely important for his contributions to the theory of language. His main work in this area is *On the Language and Wisdom of the Indians* (1808).[50] This work is profoundly indebted to Herder, both for its interest in India and for its general views about language.[51] But it also goes far beyond Herder in many ways. Let us consider its contributions roughly in order of increasing importance.

To begin with, the work contains a mildly interesting theory of the origin of language. This theory is heavily indebted to Herder's, though not identical with it. Unlike Herder, Schlegel distinguishes sharply between two kinds of languages: "organic," or inflected, languages, such as Sanskrit, and "mechanical," or uninflected, languages, such as Chinese. Again unlike Herder, he explains the latter languages' origins naturalistically in terms of animal cries and onomatopoeia. However, it is the former languages that he considers to be most important. And *like* Herder, he gives a naturalistic explanation of the origin of these in terms of their interdependence and coevalness with human awareness [*Besonnenheit*], while also imputing to them an ulterior source in God—which was precisely the account that Herder had given of the origin of *all* language in his *Treatise on the Origin of Language* (1772).[52]

A more important contribution achieved by Schlegel's work lies in the fact that it essentially founded modern Sanskrit studies, at least in Germany. Under the work's influence, Schlegel's older brother August Wilhelm went on to become Germany's first professor of Sanskrit, and Franz Bopp likewise became an eminent expert on Sanskrit. In achieving this contribution, the work built on the efforts of predecessors: It owed much on its technical side to the English Sanskrit scholar Sir William Jones. It was also heavily indebted, for its whole interest in the language and culture of India, to Herder.[53]

The work's greatest achievement, however, lies in the fact that it almost singlehandedly founded the modern science of linguistics. More specifically, its role here was basically to appropriate certain principles from Herder and turn them into a conception of a science of linguistics that would then be further developed shortly afterwards in the works of August Wilhelm Schlegel, Franz Bopp, Jakob Grimm, and Wilhelm von Humboldt (whose central work in this connection is his *On the Diversity of Human Language-Structure and its Influence on the Mental Development of Mankind* [1836]).

The Herderian principles in question are the following, all of which Schlegel took over to form the foundation of the new discipline:

(1) Thought is essentially dependent on and bounded by language—i.e. one can only think if one has a language, and one can only think what one can express linguistically.

(2) Meanings or concepts consist (not in the sorts of items, in principle autonomous of language, with which much of the philosophical tradition has equated them—e.g. things referred to, Platonic forms, or the mental "ideas" favored by the British Empiricists and others, but rather) in word-usages.[54]

(3) Mankind exhibits profound differences in language, modes of thought, and concepts, especially across different historical periods and cultures.[55]

(4) Because of principles (1) and (2), investigating the differences in the characters of people's languages constitutes a primary and reliable means for discovering the differences in their modes of thought and concepts.[56]

These Herderian principles together constituted the most fundamental rationale for the new science of linguistics that Schlegel established: since the diversity of human languages provides a sort of reliable window onto the diversity of human thought and conceptualization, in order to penetrate the latter one should empirically investigate the former.[57]

But Schlegel also built on this Herderian foundation and the fundamental project just described in some important ways, adding the following more original positions:

(a) In contrast to an impression Herder had generally still given that languages are merely aggregates of particular words/concepts, Schlegel develops a much more holistic conception of languages which sees such particular items as only possible in the context of a larger linguistic whole—a conception he expresses by characterizing languages as "organisms," "webs," or "systems."

(Schlegel restricts this observation to "organic," or inflected, languages. But Humboldt would later take it over and generalize it to cover all languages.)

(b) More specifically, Schlegel identifies as the most fundamental unifying principle of such linguistic "organisms" their *grammar*.

(c) The *early* Herder of the *Treatise on the Origin of Language* (1772) had implied at one point that grammar was inessential to language in its more original and natural forms, being a product of the late theoretical oversophistication of grammarians,[58] and at another point (rather inconsistently) that grammar was basically the same across all languages (with the exception of Chinese).[59] In sharp contrast, the *later* Herder of the *Ideas for the Philosophy of History of Humanity* (1784–91) had argued that languages differ dramatically in their grammatical structures: besides showing rich variety in other respects, "in the structure [*Bau*] of language, in the relation, the ordering, and the agreement of the parts with each other, it is almost immeasurable."[60] Schlegel rejects Herder's earlier position but continues and develops this later position, arguing that grammars differ deeply in their character from one language to another, thereby constituting deep differences in particular words/concepts as well (which may also differ for more superficial reasons).[61]

(d) Schlegel consequently identifies "comparative grammar" (an expression and concept which he virtually coins in *On the Language and Wisdom of the Indians*)[62] as the main task of the empirical investigation of languages. (Bopp, Grimm, and Humboldt would subsequently follow him in this position.)

(e) Besides the motive already mentioned above of providing a reliable window on the diversity of thought and conceptualization, another important motive behind this project of comparative grammar which Schlegel emphasizes stems from a conviction that it promises to shed more light on the genealogical relations between languages than merely lexical comparisons can do. (Here again, Bopp, Grimm, and Humboldt would subsequently follow him.)

(f) Schlegel begins the process of actually comparing different grammars in an empirically careful way. In doing so, he identifies as centrally important the contrast already mentioned above between, on the one hand, "organic," or highly inflected, languages, of which Sanskrit is his primary example, and on the other hand, "mechanical," or uninflected, languages, of which Chinese is his main example. (His brother August Wilhelm, Humboldt, and others would subsequently follow him in this position, but would also elaborate on it, especially by adding a further category of "agglutinative" or "incorporative" languages.)

(g) Schlegel also maps out and demonstrates the genealogical relations between the Sanskritic (or Indo-European) languages in a way that is superior to anything achieved before him. (In this project he would soon be followed, and improved on, by Bopp and others.)

The above moves all constitute clear and important progress. By contrast, a final move that Schlegel makes is more questionable:

(h) He also draws from this comparison between the grammars of languages certain normative conclusions concerning the relative merits of different languages as instruments of thought—in particular, arguing for the superiority of highly inflected languages such as Sanskrit and its relatives over uninflected languages such as Chinese. This is a more dubious part of his position, both factually and ethically. It is *factually* dubious in that his arguments for the superiority of the one sort of language over the other are unconvincing—largely consisting merely in sheer unreasoned wonderment at the alleged marvel of developed inflection, together with an implausible claim that this has a privileged connection with "awareness [*Besonnenheit*]" or rationality. In addition, this part of his position is *ethically* dubious in that it can easily encourage (and eventually did encourage) an invidious ranking of peoples. On the other hand, in fairness to Schlegel, it should be noted that he was himself innocent of ethnocentric, let alone xenophobic motives (indeed, a significant part of the purpose of his book was to show that Europe and Asia are "one large family"—as he actually puts it—whose literatures should be treated as a single whole; and more generally, a cosmopolitan respect for the Other is a deep and enduring feature of his outlook). Moreover, he takes considerable (albeit less than entirely successful) pains to try to forestall the inference from his normative conclusions about languages to an invidious ranking of peoples. (Not accidentally, Humboldt's position would later be strikingly similar in all of these respects.)

## 7. Epistemology and Metaphysics

Schlegel also from an early period took a serious interest in such core areas of philosophy as epistemology and metaphysics. Extensive fragments on these subjects dating from 1796 onwards have now been collected together in *Kritische Friedrich Schlegel Ausgabe*, volume 18; a set of lectures on Transcendental Philosophy that he delivered in Jena in 1800–1 also survives; and so too does an extensive set of private lectures on philosophy that he delivered in Cologne in 1804–6.

In these areas the main influence on Schlegel's thought was Fichte's *Wissenschaftslehre* (first published in 1794), together with the contemporary philosophical reactions to it in Jena. Schlegel's thought in these areas is not very systematic or stable, but it is quite bold and interesting. It also strongly influenced his work in some of the other areas that have already been discussed, including his idea of romanticism, his hermeneutics, and his general aesthetics.

Moreover, it had a major impact on such important successors as Hegel and Nietzsche. It therefore deserves careful consideration here.

The following main phases in the young Schlegel's philosophical development can be distinguished. (1) His interest in philosophy was largely sparked in the mid-1790s by Reinhold's and especially Fichte's attempts to recast Kant's critical philosophy on the basis of a single, epistemologically secure principle as its foundation, a *Grundsatz*. Schlegel's initial reaction in 1794–5 was one of sheer enthusiasm for Fichte's position. Indeed, although, as we shall see, he soon rejected Fichte's *epistemological* views, he for many years remained strongly influenced by Fichte's *metaphysical* vision, in particular his dynamic metaphysics of the self.[63]

(2) When Schlegel moved to Jena in 1796 he rejected Reinhold and Fichte's epistemology of a *Grundsatz*, instead coming to sympathize with a group of skeptically minded thinkers around Niethammer who questioned the availability of any *Grundsatz*. Thus already in a note from 1796 Schlegel declares flatly:

There are no first principles [*Grundsätze*] which could be universally effective escorts and leaders to the truth.[64]

From this time onwards, his own positive stance in epistemology was a commitment, not to a single, certain *Grundsatz*, but instead to *coherence among a multiplicity of fallible principles*—what he called a "reciprocal proof [*Wechselerweis*]." Thus he already writes in 1796:

In my system the final ground is really a reciprocal proof [*Wechselerweis*]. In Fichte's a postulate and an unconditional principle.[65]

His conception of such a "reciprocal proof" largely concerns the relation between theory and experience. His thought is roughly as follows: theory cannot supply a *Grundsatz*, since it requires support from experience; but experience cannot supply a *Grundsatz* either, since it is always implicitly theory-laden, and therefore requires support from theory;[66] hence what is needed is mutual support between theory and experience. Thus he already writes in 1796:

When I appeal so often...to the confirmation of experience, I reason not only philosophically but logically. Logic and history are derived sciences from one stem. Hence there arises between them confirmation, reciprocal proof [*Wechselerweis*]. They may borrow doctrines from each other.[67]

Largely because of the essential role played within the envisaged "reciprocal proof" by experience, in all its endless variety and mutability, such a proof, despite being required, could never be fully achieved once and for all, except through some sort of illegitimate imposition of closure. This is part of the thought behind the first sentence of *Athenaeum Fragments*, no. 53: "It's equally fatal for the mind to have a system and to have none. It will simply have to decide to combine the two." But the second sentence also hints at a solution beneath its paradoxical surface: "combine the two." What does that mean? It basically means substituting for the full achievement of such a proof, or system, an endless process of approximation towards it. As Schlegel puts the thought in the lectures on Transcendental Philosophy from 1800–1: "We do not want and are not able absolutely to complete philosophy."[68]

(3) The lectures on Transcendental Philosophy from 1800–1 then constitute a new phase in Schlegel's philosophical development. For they not only strive for a more systematic presentation of the positive position just described, but also develop it further in some important ways. In particular, they add a distinctive account according to which a radical form of skepticism is necessary as a preparation for philosophy, and they espouse the philosophical ideal of combining Fichte's subjectivity with Spinoza's substance. The latter move is especially striking, since it marks a turn to a type of metaphysics that is more self-transcendent, pantheistic, or "mystical" (to borrow a term for it that Schlegel himself uses).

(4) Finally, the Cologne lectures of 1804–6 not only push the attempt at systematicity even further, but also significantly change the content of Schlegel's position: although his epistemological stance remains similar, he now modifies his metaphysics towards both a broader inclusion of Fichtean themes and an anticipation of the Catholicism to which he was by this time already strongly attracted. In addition, these lectures incorporate an extensive discussion of the history of philosophy, providing among other things a sort of genealogy of Schlegel's conception of philosophy as an endless search which traces its roots back to Plato.[69]

With this overview of the development of Schlegel's philosophical views in hand, let us now turn to consider his philosophical position in a little more depth. Since his 1800–1 lectures on Transcendental Philosophy were his most public early foray into philosophy and contain some of his most influential and interesting ideas on the subject, they will serve as our primary focus from now on. I shall briefly present and discuss a number of Schlegel's most important ideas from the lectures, beginning with the more epistemological ones before turning to those of a more metaphysical character. In doing so, I shall resist the temptation to impose more systematicity on them than Schlegel himself does.

To begin with *epistemology*: Schlegel had already been interested in, and sympathetic towards, skepticism since at least 1796. But in the 1800–1 lectures he pushes that attitude still further in certain ways. There he expresses sympathy for a very radical form of skepticism, one that even goes as far as to question the logical law of contradiction.[70] The Cologne lectures from 1804–6 contain an extensive discussion of skepticism which shows that he mainly has ancient Pyrrhonian and Academic skepticism in mind here.[71] He also argues in the 1800–1 lectures that skepticism is the beginning and the basis of philosophy: "Philosophy begins with skepticism."[72] Besides being of considerable intrinsic interest, these positions are also significant because they all reappear shortly after the 1800–1 lectures, which Hegel attended, in Hegel's seminal essay *The Relation of Skepticism to Philosophy* (1802).[73]

Another striking position in the 1800–1 lectures is that there is no absolute truth, and that all truth is relative.[74] Schlegel probably adopted this position from Protagoras, whose similar view he will have encountered while reading Plato's *Theaetetus*. Schlegel anticipates the natural objection, What about this position *itself*? He answers it with the bold assertion that this position too is relative.[75] In addition to being of intrinsic interest, these views are also noteworthy because they anticipate aspects of Nietzsche's perspectivism (for example, in *Beyond Good and Evil*, where in particular both the objection and the bold answer just mentioned recur). Nietzsche's debts to Schlegel are in general broad and deep, though it is not clear in this case what the channel of influence would have been.

Another striking position in the 1800–1 lectures, closely connected with the preceding positions, is that proof must in the end give way to assertion.[76] Similarly, in *Athenaeum Fragments*, no. 82 Schlegel says that asserting is more important than proving. This attack on the over-estimation of reason persists in his later works.[77] It is also reflected in other areas of his thought. For example, it already lies behind his interpretation in the *History of the Poetry of the Greeks and Romans* (1798) of the turn that Athenian culture took in the second half of the fifth century with Euripides and Socrates away from a fundamental reliance on bold assertion to a fundamental reliance on reasoning as a symptom of cultural *decadence*. In addition to being of intrinsic interest, this position is also important for its subsequent influence on Nietzsche, who not only took over its basic thesis but also in *The Birth of Tragedy* took over Schlegel's specific application of it to the interpretation of Athenian culture.

Another striking position in the 1800–1 lectures (already touched on above) is that philosophy should be grounded in experience.[78] Schlegel holds this view despite recognizing that human experience is always already conceptually-theoretically infused in one way or another, and hence no real epistemological foundation.[79] Accordingly, for him a philosophy's justification ultimately lies in a coherent balance of empirical and theoretical considerations (the sort of "reciprocal proof [*Wechselerweis*]" that he had already been envisaging since 1796). In consequence, philosophy inevitably has an openended, unfinished character: "We do not want and are not able absolutely to complete philosophy."[80]

Concerning, next, *metaphysics*: As I mentioned above, the 1800–1 lectures mark a turn to a more self-transcendent, pantheistic, or "mystical" metaphysics than Schlegel had held during most of the 1790s. Thus another striking position in these lectures is his commitment to a project of combining Fichte's conception of the subject with Spinoza's monistic conception of an infinite, absolute substance.[81] Schlegel's sympathy with Spinoza here is new (and indeed transient)—largely, it seems, a result of the strong influence exercised on him at this period by Schleiermacher's Spinozism. In addition to being of intrinsic interest, Schlegel's project is also significant because it evidently inspired an identical project that dominated Hegel's philosophy during his Jena period (1801–7)—as reflected, for example, in Hegel's famous remark in the preface of the *Phenomenology of Spirit* (1807) that "everything turns on grasping and expressing the true, not only as substance, but equally as subject."

This turn to a more self-transcendent, pantheistic, or "mystical" metaphysics also went through several variant formulations at around the same period. For example, Schlegel develops a similar but not identical conception in the *Dialogue on Poetry* (1800). According to this work, the whole of nature is God's poem, while human poetry is a spark of this divine poetry and consequently contains an eternal striving towards (re)attainment of the latter's compass. This conception seems to have been the main source for Nietzsche's depiction of the Absolute as a divine artist in *The Birth of Tragedy*.

Two further variants occur slightly earlier and later, respectively. Thus, another conception in a similar spirit which Schlegel already espoused a little earlier is that reality is at its deepest level *chaotic*. For example, he already writes in a note from 1798:

It is a high and perhaps the final step of intellectual formation to posit for oneself the sphere of incomprehensibility and confusion. The understanding of chaos consists in recognizing it.[82]

This conception occurs prominently in the essay *On Incomprehensibility* (1800) as well.[83] It also plays a significant role in Schlegel's theory of interpretation, since his deepest explanation of the confusion found in texts is in terms of the chaotic nature of the *reality* that texts aim to characterize. Thus he writes in *On Incomprehensibility*:

Is this infinite world [of the texts of science and art] not formed by the understanding out of incomprehensibility or chaos?[84]

Besides being of intrinsic interest and playing the important role in Schlegel's theory of interpretation just mentioned, Schlegel's conception is also significant because it would later be echoed by Nietzsche, first in his claim in *The Birth of Tragedy* that the fundamental nature of reality is a Dionysiac chaos, then later in his less metaphysically inflated but otherwise similar position that reality is at its deepest level a "chaos of sensations."

In a later variant of the same sort of metaphysical account, the Cologne lectures of 1804–6 posit as the deepest principle of reality an Infinite that is not thing-like but ever becoming and active, and to which we stand in a relationship of yearning and striving. Even more clearly than the aforementioned conceptions, this conception constitutes a sort of metaphysical underpinning for the experience of longing and striving for the Infinite which Schlegel had from the start identified as distinctive of romantic poetry.

Finally, in addition to those already mentioned in passing, there are also a number of additional features of Schlegel's literary romanticism that are closely connected with such metaphysical principles and which should be briefly discussed. One of these lies in the fact that Schlegel not only considers it to be the deepest function of both philosophy and poetry to express such a metaphysical principle, but also believes that they can only really achieve this when fused together, so that he makes such a fusion of philosophy and poetry (or science and art) part of his very conception of romantic poetry.[85]

Another central feature of his literary romanticism is his concept of *irony*. This too is closely connected to his metaphysics. As Rudolf Haym points out, his conception of irony underwent a change over the course of his early career, from an initial Fichtean subjective idealist conception of it towards an eventual mystical conception of it as the expression of an infinite chaos.[86] The former conception predominates in the *Lyceum Fragments* from 1797. The latter conception already emerges in 1798 in such remarks as that "irony is clear chaos in agility, intellectual intuition of an eternal chaos,"[87] and then continues in such subsequent texts as the *Ideas* and the *Dialogue on Poetry* (both 1800).[88]

Finally, Schlegel's development of the *fragment* as a central genre of romantic writing is largely motivated by his epistemology and metaphysics as well. He began publishing fragments in the *Lyceum* in 1797, and they continued to be one of his most important genres during the crucial period of the *Athenaeum*. His models for the fragment were partly French (especially, Chamfort) and partly German (especially, Herder, who had published works with titles such as *Fragments . . .* and *Ideas . . .*).[89] His use of the fragment is motivated by various features of his epistemology and metaphysics, including the following: his conception that assertion is more fundamental than proof; his ambition to approach a final systematicity but without purporting ever to attain it, an ambition he implements in his articulation of a loosely interconnected and expandable body of fragments which are themselves provisional mini-systems and also constitute together a larger provisional system;[90] and his metaphysical position that our condition is perforce one of trying to give limited, definite expression to what is actually an infinite, chaotic reality.[91]

## 8. Political Philosophy

German Romanticism's preoccupation with literature and art has often been interpreted as apolitical, or even as a strategy for evading politics (for example, by Madame de Staël), and its politics, such as it is, as conservative or reactionary (for example, by Heinrich Heine). However, the early Schlegel's preoccupation with literature and art—like Schiller's before him—was on the contrary from the beginning (i.e. even during his classicizing period, and then subsequently during his romantic period as well) profoundly motivated by a commitment to political ideals, especially the radical ideal of a republican-democratic community.[92]

The early Schlegel's political ideals are in general interestingly radical. Concerning international politics, he follows or agrees with Kant, Herder, Goethe, Wilhelm von Humboldt, Schleiermacher, and his own brother August Wilhelm in adopting a deeply cosmopolitan outlook.[93] Thus, Schlegel's early *Essay on the Concept of Republicanism* (1796) substitutes for Kant's cosmopolitan ideal of a federation of peoples [*Völkerbund*] the even more radical cosmopolitan ideal of a world republic [*Weltrepublik*]. And Schlegel's essay *Journey to France*, with which he introduced the journal *Europa* after moving to Paris in 1802, contains another strong statement of cosmopolitanism (especially as it concerns relations between the peoples of Europe, but also as it concerns relations between Europe and Asia).[94] This cosmopolitanism is also manifested in Schlegel's work on literature and language. Thus, another reflection of it is his general focus on world literature: his main heroes of romantic literature are not German authors (not even Goethe, despite his public championing of him in *On Goethe's Meister* and the *Athenaeum Fragments*),[95] but rather such non-Germans as the Provençal troubadours, Dante, Petrarch, Boccaccio, Cervantes, Shakespeare, and eventually Calderón. And yet another reflection of his cosmopolitanism is his exploration of Sanskrit language and literature in *On the Language and Wisdom of the Indians*, which (as I mentioned previously) is in significant part motivated by an ambition to show that Europe and Asia are "one large family."[96]

Concerning domestic politics: In the radical spirit of Herder and Georg Forster, the early Schlegel, especially in the *Essay on the Concept of Republicanism* (1796) and in his lectures on Transcendental Philosophy (1800–1), champions not only republicanism but also democracy, in particular advocating a universal franchise that includes all men and women (this goes well beyond the position espoused by Kant, who had advocated republicanism but firmly rejected democracy). He also (in a further radical revision of Kant's position) advocates a right of revolution as a means to achieving such a republican-democratic community. In addition, he strongly champions liberalism (for example, in the essay *Georg Forster* from 1797),[97] and the ideal of individuality (for example, in the *Athenaeum* fragments).[98]

Finally, in substantial agreement with Herder, Schleiermacher, and Wilhelm von Humboldt, the early Schlegel is also committed to a serious and multi-faceted feminism. As has already been mentioned, his early essay *On Diotima* (1795) discusses the treatment of women in Greek literature in a feminist spirit; his conception of romantic literature essentially includes the ideal of a fusion of a feminine beloved with the divine; and at a less exalted level he advocates that women should receive the vote. But in addition, he also argues that culture should be considered a virtue in women; that there should be a more general exchange of gender-typical characteristics between the two sexes, leading to a reduction in the difference between them (see, for example, *On Philosophy: To Dorothea* [1798] and *Lucinde* [1799]); that women should be freed from entrap-ment in stultifying marriages (see, for example, *Athenaeum Fragments*, no. 34); and that women should be liberated from prudery in sexual matters (an ideal that he champions in *Athenaeum Fragments*, no. 31 and strikingly represents in his novel *Lucinde*).[99] Closely connected with these feminist positions is an attack on the bourgeois institution of marriage in favor of less legally oppressive rela-tionships allowing for greater liberty, more individualism, and enhanced spirit-ual and sexual fulfillment.

## 9. The Later Schlegel

Just as the early Schlegel of the 1790s had taken virtually a 180-degree turn from initially supporting classicism against romanticism towards the converse, so the later Schlegel turned away from his earlier unorthodox views on religion and his radical politics towards Catholicism and political conservatism or reaction.

Even in the former case the turn was not completed all at once. The same was still truer in the latter case. Schlegel's turn to a more orthodox, indeed Catholic, religious position and to conservative-reactionary politics was in many ways already heralded as early as the turn of the century. For example, he already wrote in 1799, evidently under the influence of Novalis's Catholic work *Christianity or Europe* from the same year: "The new Christianity must, without doubt, be the Catholic one, but old Catholic, not Papism"; "Art aims at the last Messiah, and is hence Catholic."[100] And again like Novalis, he already in the 1790s began to show an interest in and sympathy with the corporate structure of society in the Middle Ages.[101] The pieces on visual art that he started writing in Paris in 1802 amplified on the message of the two notes just quoted, thus marking an even more emphatic turn to Catholicism. The Cologne lectures of 1804–6 then not only continued this turn to Catholicism but also criticized republicanism in favor of monarchy and indeed *Kaisertum*.[102] In 1808 he formally converted to Catholicism, and moved to Vienna to assume political posts at the imperial court—thus putting the final seal on this reversal of positions. From now on his scholarly work emphatically reflected his Catholicism and political conservatism/reaction. For example, his 1810 lectures on modern European history espouse the political ideal of an Austrian-style *Kaisertum* uniting the nations of Europe.[103] And his *Lectures on the History of Literature* delivered in 1812 lend his position on literary and philosophical matters a Catholic form, as well as expressing sharp opposition to the French Revolution and by contrast championing the conservative-reactionary views of de Maistre and Burke.[104]

Hand in hand with this turn came a precipitous decline in the originality and interest of Schlegel's philosophical ideas. The *Lectures on the History of Literature* still retain much of his former brilliance. But the lectures on the philosophy of life and the philosophy of language which he delivered in the late 1820s shortly before his death are extremely disappointing—full of exactly the sort of bombastic mélange of Catholic theology and conservative-reactionary politics that Heinrich Heine famously complained about in *Die romantische Schule* (1832).[105]

# Notes

1. Cf. E. Behler, *Friedrich Schlegel in Selbstzeugnissen und Bilddokumenten* (Reinbek: Rowohlt, 1966), p. 29.
2. For example, it considers Sanskrit to be the direct ancestor of the modern European languages, and it dates the Pentateuch earlier than the oldest Indian literature.
3. Cf. his similar position in a review of Jacobi's *Woldemar* from 1796, where he characterizes Jacobi's work as containing many of the distinguishing features of "interesting" literature but sharply criticizes it for this—*Friedrich*

*Schlegel 1794–1802. Seine prosaischen Jugendschriften*, ed. J. Minor (Vienna: Carl Konegen, 1882), 2:90.

4. See on this A.O. Lovejoy, "The Meaning of 'Romantic' in Early German Romanticism" and "Schiller and the Genesis of German Romanticism," in his *Essays on the History of Ideas* (New York: Capricorn Books, 1960). Cf. Behler, *Friedrich Schlegel*, pp. 38–43. F.C. Beiser has criticized this line of interpretation in *The Romantic Imperative* (Cambridge, Mass.: Harvard University Press, 2003), pp. 116 ff. But his objections work better as grounds for qualifying it than for rejecting it.

5. This is Beiser's thesis—ibid., pp. 119 ff.

6. F. Schlegel, *On the Study of Greek Poetry* (Albany, NY: State University of New York Press, 2001), p. 93. Admittedly, Schlegel's corpus also contains some more critical remarks about Herder.

7. *Friedrich Schlegel 1794–1802*, 2:41 ff.

8. Ibid., p. 48. Admittedly, in the review Schlegel still tries to resist this Herderian position. However, he evidently succumbed to its force soon afterwards. Note that Schiller (probably again under Herder's influence) had made a similar point in *On Naive and Sentimental Poetry*: "If one has previously abstracted the genre-concept of poetry one-sidedly from the ancient poets, then nothing is easier, but also more trivial, than to disparage the modern poets in comparison with them." So Schlegel was now in effect hearing Herder's point twice over.

9. Cf. H. Eichner, "Friedrich Schlegel's Theory of Romantic Poetry," *Proceedings of the Modern Language Association*, 71 (1956).

10. See e.g. Schlegel's following note from as early as 1799: "Art aims at the last Messiah, and is hence Catholic" (*Kritische Friedrich Schlegel Ausgabe* [henceforth KFSA], ed. E. Behler et al. [Munich: F. Schöningh, 1958– ], 18:398). See also the pieces on romantic visual art from the period 1802–6 in KFSA, vol. 4. Cf. A.W. Schlegel's emphasis on the Christian character of romantic poetry and art in his lectures on literature and art from the same period.

11. *Friedrich Schlegel 1794–1802*, 2:41–2.

12. See esp. F. Schlegel, *Literary Notebooks (1797–1801)* (Toronto: University of Toronto Press, 1957); the Cologne lectures on German language and literature from 1807, at KFSA 15/2:64; and the later *Lectures on the History of Literature* (1815; tr. London: Bell and Daldy, 1873). Cf. L. Tieck, *Franz Sternbald's Wanderings* (1798) for an early version of this idea. A.W. Schlegel also developed it in lectures on literature and art delivered at the beginning of the nineteenth century.

13. See esp. *Johann Gottfried Herder Werke*, ed. U. Gaier et al. (Frankfurt am Main: Deutscher Klassiker Verlag, 1985– ), 7:289–90, 409–10, 470–2, 484, 500–1. (This edition of Herder's works is henceforth abbreviated as G.)

14. *Friedrich Schlegel 1794–1802*, 2:42–5.

15. Concerning the character and breadth of the concept of the *Roman* at this period, see H. Eichner, *Friedrich Schlegel* (New York: Twayne, 1970), p. 53; cf. pp. 82–3.

16. See e.g. *Athenaeum Fragments* (in F. Schlegel, *Philosophical Fragments* [Minneapolis: University of Minnesota Press, 1991]), no. 116. Also the following passage from the Paris lectures on literature: "The concept of the novel [*Roman*]...is that of a romantic book, a romantic composition in which all forms and genres are mingled and intertwined...There are historical, rhetorical, and dialogical passages; all these styles...are mixed and combined with one another...Poetry of every kind—lyrical, epic, didactic poetry, and romances—are scattered throughout the whole work...The novel is the most original, the most characteristic, and the most perfect form of romantic poetry" (KFSA 11:159 ff.).

17. See e.g. G7:548: "No genre of poetry is of broader scope than the novel [*Roman*]; among all it is also the one capable of the *most diverse treatment*, for it contains or can contain not only history and geography, philosophy and the theory of almost all arts, but also poetry of all genres and types—in prose. Whatever interests the human understanding and the heart...can and may be included in a novel. This form of poetry allows the greatest disparities, for it is poetry in prose."

18. Behler, *Friedrich Schlegel*, p. 164.

19. This term of art is Schleiermacher's, but the thought is already in Schlegel.

20. See *After Herder*, Essays 4 and 11, and in the present volume Essays 8 and 9.

21. F. Schlegel, *Philosophy of Philology*, in "Friedrich Schlegels 'Philosophie der Philologie' mit einer Einleitung herausgegeben von Josef Körner," *Logos*, 17 (1928), pp. 16, 28.

22. In the Cologne lectures on German language and literature from 1807 Schlegel argues that the principles of ancient meter were quite different from those of modern European languages—in particular, quantitative rather than accentual—and that this makes the project of imitating ancient meters in modern European languages virtually futile (though he concedes that this may still be valid in certain cases, provided that it is modest about the measure of success it expects to achieve) (KFSA 15/2:94–9).

23. *Philosophy of Philology*, p. 42.

24. Ibid.

25. KFSA 18:204.

26. Ibid.

27. *Philosophy of Philology*, p. 47.

28. KFSA 18:71.

29. *Philosophy of Philology*, p. 50.

30. KFSA 8:324–5.

31. KFSA 18:71.

32. Ibid. Cf. the *Dialogue on Poetry* (in F. Schlegel, *"Athenäums"-Fragmente und andere Schriften* [Stuttgart: Reclam, 2005]): "The translation of poets...has become an art."

33. I here mildly disagree with Manfred Frank's claim that the early Schlegel was an atheist (M. Frank, *Unendliche Annäherung* [Frankfurt am Main: Suhrkamp, 1998], p. 935).

34. *Literary Notebooks (1797–1801)*, no. 735.

35. KFSA 18:398.

36. KFSA, vol. 4. Concerning Catholicism, note that these pieces not only focus mainly on Catholic art, but also represent the Reformation as a disaster for art, dismissing most of its results in art, such as Dutch painting, as inferior (see e.g. p. 81).

37. This does not prevent him from continuing to have very definite ideas about what is better and worse in classical literature, though. For example, he thinks Homer, Aeschylus, and Sophocles excellent, but Hesiod too grotesque in his mythology, and Euripides a decadent who misuses the chorus and succumbs to rhetoric and sophistry. See e.g. his late *Lectures on the History of Literature* (1815).

38. KFSA, vol. 4. According to Schlegel, *ancient* painting was by contrast inferior (see ibid., pp. 255–6).

39. See esp. the *Literary Notebooks* (1797–1801) as well as the later *Lectures on the History of Literature* (1815). Despite Schlegel's tendency to champion Goethe publicly, for example in *On Goethe's Meister* and the *Athenaeum Fragments*, the *Literary Notebooks* from the same era show that his private opinion of Goethe was already from an early period markedly less enthusiastic, and that it was always rather the other poets listed here who were his models for romantic poetry.

40. KFSA, vol. 4.

41. Ibid., pp. 72, 107.

42. Ibid., pp. 74 ff.

43. Ibid., p. 78.

44. *Lectures on the History of Literature*, p. 190. Emphasis added.
45. For example, he writes in the Cologne lectures on German language and literature from 1807: "There lies in the vowels themselves a certain meaning, a character and expression ... Thus the vowel *a* is strong and powerful, *u* more sad and dark, *e* more meaninglessly soundless or expresses more gravity because of its soundlessness, *o* the happiest and the fieriest, *i* the delicately inward or also the witty, the fine ... The expression of the consonants can be determined likewise. For example, *r* has something rough, hard, but *l* something light, gentle" (KFSA 15/2:103, cf. 115–16). Concerning this theory, cf. E. Fiesel, *Die Sprachphilosophie der Deutschen Romantik* (Tübingen: J.C.B. Mohr, 1927).
46. KFSA 18:172: "*Sky blue* is the color of longing, of yearning, of anguish; *indigo* probably expresses anger; *violet* hatred and despair; *red* love; *brown* force—also pleasure. Jealousy, envy perhaps *yellow*."
47. See A.O. Lovejoy, "On the Discrimination of Romanticisms," in his *Essays in the History of Ideas*.
48. *Lectures on the History of Literature*, pp. 54, 304.
49. See on this topic e.g. KFSA, vol. 4.
50. By contrast, his promising-sounding late lectures on the philosophy of language turn out to be much less significant.
51. Cf. H. Nüsse at KFSA 8:clxxxvii–clxxxviii. Schlegel in particular explicitly praises Herder's *Oldest Document of the Human Species* (1774) in the course of the work.
52. Cf. H. Nüsse, *Die Sprachtheorie Friedrich Schlegels* (Heidelberg: Carl Winter, 1962). However, Nüsse underestimates the extent of Schlegel's agreement with Herder concerning "organic", or inflected, languages. According to Nüsse, Schlegel holds that these have a divine origin whereas Herder had posited a purely natural one. But this oversimplifies both men's positions and thereby obscures their identity. In fact, Schlegel himself insists on a natural origin here, though he does *also* envisage an ulterior divine one. And Herder in his *Treatise* had likewise envisaged a divine origin beyond the natural one (considering naturalistic and divine explanations to be compatible, in the spirit of his teacher Kant's *Universal Natural History and Theory of the Heavens*). So the two philosophers' positions in this area are in fact identical.
53. Cf. H. Nüsse at KFSA 8:clxxxvii.
54. Schlegel is actually quite vague about principles (1) and (2) in *On the Language and Wisdom of the Indians* itself. However, his commitment to them is explicit in both earlier and later texts. Earlier: already in 1798–9 he writes that "each spirit has its word; the two are inseparable" (KFSA

18:289); in the Cologne lectures on philosophy from 1804–6 he insists on the dependence of reason on language (*Friedrich Schlegels philosophische Vorlesungen aus den Jahren 1804 bis 1806*, ed. C.J.H. Windischmann [Bonn: Eduard Weber, 1846], 2:28–9, 223) and says that "each concept must be a word" (ibid., 2:83); and in the Cologne lectures on German language and literature from 1807 he opens by saying that language is fundamental to all human activities because "one cannot think without words" (KFSA 15/2:3). Later: in the *Lectures on the History of Literature* (delivered in 1812, published in 1815), he says, "What is there more completely characteristic of man or of greater importance to him than language? Reason alone excepted, and even she must perforce employ the vehicle of language . . . Reason and language, thought and word, are . . . essentially one" (pp. 6–7).

55. Already in the *Philosophy of Philology* (1797) Schlegel writes of "the immeasurable difference . . . , the quite distinctive nature of antiquity" (p. 16; cf. p. 54: "absolute difference"). The Cologne lectures of 1804–6 also contain remarks on the deep differences in outlook that occur between different periods and cultures (for example, in the area of morals).

56. Concerning Herder's own commitment to this position, see e.g. his recommendation in the *Fragments* (1767–8) that one should explore the changing nature of people's moral views and concepts by carefully examining the changes that have occurred in their use of moral vocabulary (G1:322), and especially the following passage from the *Ideas for the Philosophy of History of Humanity* (1784–91): "The finest essay on the history and the diverse character of the human understanding and heart . . . would be a *philosophical comparison of languages*: for a people's understanding and character is imprinted in each of them" (G6:353).

This position is not explicit in *On the Language and Wisdom of the Indians*. However, it is the implicit foundation of the work's procedure of undertaking an investigation of the Sanskrit language in its first part as a prelude to then investigating Indian thought and conceptualization in subsequent parts.

57. Humboldt would subsequently articulate this fundamental rationale for linguistics even more explicitly than Schlegel does. See his *On the Diversity of Human Language-Structure and its Influence on the Mental Development of Mankind* (including its revealing title).

58. G1:762.

59. G1:803.

60. G6:353.

61. Humboldt would subsequently take over positions (b) and (c). However, in his case the commitment to position (c) stands in uneasy tension with a continued commitment to the much more dubious (albeit recently again fashionable) traditional idea of an implicit *universal* grammar.

62. Strictly speaking, it had already been used by his brother August Wilhelm in a review article from 1803. See on this H. Gipper and P. Schmitter, "Sprachwissenschaft und Sprachphilosophie im Zeitalter der Romantik," in *Current Trends in Linguistics*, vol. 13: Historiography of Linguistics, ed. T.A. Sebeok (The Hague/Paris: Mouton, 1975), p. 508.

63. It is striking how positively Schlegel still values Fichte in a review that he published in French in 1802–3 (KFSA 18:538–47) and in the Cologne lectures of 1804–6. Only in his later Catholic period did his enthusiasm for Fichte's metaphysics really end.

64. KFSA 18:518. Concerning the steps of development that I have described so far, cf. Frank, *Unendliche Annäherung*, esp. pp. 39, 569–93, 862 ff.; Beiser, *The Romantic Imperative*, pp. 119 ff.

65. KFSA 18:521. Cf. pp. 505, 518.

66. See *Athenaeum Fragments*, no. 226. Also, KFSA 18:396.

67. KFSA 18:505.

68. KFSA 12:104. Concerning the positive steps in Schlegel's theory just described—especially, his emphasis on coherence between a multiplicity of principles, his concept of a "reciprocal proof [*Wechselerweis*]," and his model of endless progression—cf. Frank, *Unendliche Annäherung*, esp. pp. 517 ff., 868 ff. However, certain aspects of Frank's interpretation are questionable—in particular, his ascription to Schlegel of a coherence theory of truth, and his omission from his account of the *Wechselerweis* of the important considerations about theory and *experience* just discussed. Also generally helpful in this area is F.C. Beiser, *German Idealism* (Cambridge, Mass.: Harvard University Press, 2002), pt. 3, ch. 4.

69. Concerning this conception, cf. Behler, *Friedrich Schlegel*, pp. 145–8.

70. KFSA 12:3. Cf. 18:407–10.

71. *Friedrich Schlegels philosophische Vorlesungen aus den Jahren 1804 bis 1806*, 1:183–91; cf. 255–62, 328–9, 389–91.

72. KFSA 12:4; cf. 10–11, 18, 42. Also the following remark from 1803–7: "Skepticism is the center of philosophy as such—and in this respect Greek philosophy is of great value. For the tone of Greek philosophy as a whole is skepticism" (KFSA 18:562, cf. 187–9).

73. For a discussion of Hegel's version of these ideas, see my *Hegel and Skepticism* (Cambridge, Mass.: Harvard University Press, 1989).

74. KFSA 12:91–5.

75. Ibid., p. 95.

76. Ibid., p. 24.

77. See e.g. *Lectures on the History of Literature* (delivered 1812; published 1815), where he in particular criticizes Kant and Fichte as philosophers who have accorded reason much too large a role. (At this later date Schlegel's preferred alternative was revelation.)

78. KFSA 12:101. Cf. *Athenaeum Fragments*, no. 252: "Only a man who knows or possesses a subject can make use of the philosophy of that subject; only he will be able to understand what that philosophy means and what it's attempting to do. But philosophy can't inoculate someone with experience and sense, or pull them out of a hat—and it shouldn't want to do so."

79. See e.g. *Athenaeum Fragments*, no. 226. Cf. KFSA 18:396.

80. KFSA 12:104. As I mentioned previously, in the Cologne lectures of 1804–6 Schlegel—quite plausibly—sees this model of philosophy as an endless striving towards the truth as already present in the discipline's (Socratic-)Platonic beginnings (*Friedrich Schlegels philosophische Vorlesungen aus den Jahren 1804 bis 1806*, 1:187, 309).

81. KFSA 12:5–6, 29–32.

82. KFSA 18:227.

83. In the Cologne lectures of 1804–6 Schlegel notes that the ancient Greek poet Hesiod had already depicted the world as born of chaos. So presumably Hesiod's account was already in the back of Schlegel's mind when he developed this conception.

84. *Friedrich Schlegel 1794–1802*, p. 393.

85. See for this especially the *Literary Notebooks (1797–1801)*; also the Cologne lectures on German language and literature from 1807, which in particular argue that philosophy needs to be complemented by poetry both in order to express the Infinite (since this is something that can only be achieved in images) and in order to receive a type of enthusiasm that it requires as its basis (KFSA 15/2:31, 33, 72 ff.). Cf. E. Behler, *German Romantic Literary Theory* (Cambridge: Cambridge University Press, 1993), pp. 138–40.

86. R. Haym, *Die Romantische Schule* (4th ed. Berlin: Weidmannsche Buchhandlung, 1920), pp. 550–1. Frank's discussion of irony at *Unendliche Annäherung*, pp. 944–8 fails to distinguish between these two phases.

87. KFSA 18:228. Cf. p. 128: "Irony is so to speak the *epideixis* of infinity, of universality, of the sense for the universe."

88. For example, *Ideas* (in F. Schlegel, *Philosophical Fragments*), no. 69 says that "irony is the clear consciousness of eternal agility, of an infinitely teeming chaos."

89. Cf. Behler, *German Romantic Literary Theory*, pp. 151–3.

90. Cf. KFSA 12:10: "The idea of philosophy can only be accomplished through an infinite progression of systems." Schlegel also sees this model as instantiated in the Platonic dialogues and their relations to each other, as well as in the parts of Goethe's *Wilhelm Meisters Lehrjahre* and their relations to each other.

91. Cf. Frank, *Unendliche Annäherung*, pp. 939–44.

92. See F.C. Beiser, *Enlightenment, Revolution and Romanticism*, esp. pp. 246–8 (on the early classicizing Schlegel) and pp. 259–60 (on the romantic Schlegel). As Beiser points out, the romantic Schlegel's ideal of striving for the Infinite was in essential part political: an ideal of striving for a truly republican-democratic community (a feature of his position which becomes especially clear in the lectures on Transcendental Philosophy from 1800–1). Notice that even the reactionary later Schlegel makes a point in his *Lectures on the History of Literature* of criticizing Winckelmann for having espoused an *apolitical* form of aestheticism.

93. For a good discussion of August Wilhelm's cosmopolitanism, see Haym, *Die Romantische Schule*. This finds expression, for example, in August Wilhelm's rejection of Klopstock's linguistic nationalism, commitment to the importance of world literature, and ideal of establishing Germany as a cosmopolitan center in Europe.

94. Cf. Behler, *Friedrich Schlegel*, pp. 87–9.

95. A more candid, less inflated assessment of Goethe and other German authors can be found in the *Literary Notebooks (1797–1801)* from the same period, and again later in the Cologne lectures on German language and literature from 1807, at KFSA 15/2:66–8, 129. Rudolf Haym's tendency to take Schlegel's public lauding of Goethe at face value has since been corrected by Josef Körner and Hans Eichner in light of such evidence.

96. Schlegel retains a strong cosmopolitan concern for all mankind even in his later period. For example, such an attitude is still prominent in his *Lectures on the History of Literature* (see esp. pp. 214–16), and in his agitation on behalf of rights for Jews during the Congress of Vienna (concerning which, see Behler, *Friedrich Schlegel*, pp. 124–5).

97. *Friedrich Schlegel 1794–1802*, 2:122 ff.: "Chains, walls, and dams were not for this *free* spirit . . . "

98. For a helpful discussion of these topics, see Beiser, *Enlightenment, Revolution and Romanticism*, ch. 10.

99. Cf. Haym, *Die Romantische Schule*, pp. 568 ff.; also Beiser, *Enlightenment, Revolution and Romanticism*, ch. 10. Schlegel retains a significant feminist streak even in his later, conservative period.

100. KFSA 18:398.

101. Cf. Beiser, *Enlightenment, Revolution and Romanticism*, pp. 261–3.

102. *Friedrich Schlegels philosophische Vorlesungen aus den Jahren 1804 bis 1806*, 2:333, 365, 373–4, 381, 384 ff.

103. This is a sort of autocratic variation on his earlier theme of a world republic.

104. These lectures still retain strong strands of cosmopolitanism and feminism, however. It is also worth noting that Schlegel's even later lectures on the philosophy of life, while they express a strong conservative-reactionary preference for hereditary monarchy, still show genuine respect for republicanism (though not democracy) as a form of government.

105. One of Schlegel's few really interesting new themes in these late lectures is an emphasis—continuous with Herder and Schiller—on the pathologically divided nature of modern psychological life (in contrast to an allegedly more unified, harmonious psychological life before the Fall, and the prospect of a return to this in the future). Cf. Eichner, *Friedrich Schlegel*, pp. 137 ff.

# 2

# Friedrich Schlegel's Hermeneutics

Friedrich Schlegel is something of an unsung (or at least undersung) hero in the development of hermeneutics, the theory of interpretation.

Cases for a similar *conclusion* have already been made by two German scholars: Josef Körner and Hermann Patsch.[1] But their reasons for thinking Schlegel important in this area seem to me off the mark, or at least radically incomplete.

Their cases both essentially take the form of arguing—largely on the basis of evidence supplied by Schlegel's *Philosophy of Philology*, a set of notes that he wrote in 1797, around the time he was beginning to develop a close friendship, and indeed to share rooms, with Schleiermacher in Berlin—that Schlegel anticipated and influenced key moves in Schleiermacher's hermeneutics lectures (which the latter began to deliver in 1805).

More specifically, Körner claims that Schleiermacher based the first version of his hermeneutics lectures on an actual reading of Schlegel's *Philosophy of Philology*. And he argues that the following ideas were all first developed by Schlegel before being taken over from him by Schleiermacher: that it is vitally important for interpreters to discern the inner form of a work;[2] to identify an author's psychological development;[3] to identify the structure of literary genres;[4] to develop a *science* of criticism (modeled on Fichte);[5] and to understand the author better than he understood himself.[6] Körner also hints that the same is true of two further doctrines: that it is vitally important to interpret the parts of a text in light of the *whole* text;[7] and to reject the idea of a *philologia sacra*.[8]

Patsch criticizes many of the details of Körner's account. In particular, he rejects Körner's thesis that Schleiermacher straightforwardly based the first version of his hermeneutics lectures on a reading of Schlegel's *Philosophy of Philology*; he identifies a strikingly different group of doctrines as having been first developed by Schlegel and then taken over from him by Schleiermacher; and he argues for a higher degree of modification of them by Schleiermacher in the course of his appropriation of them than Körner had envisaged. However, he retains Körner's generic picture that Schlegel's importance in this area mainly lies in his having been the first to develop doctrines which subsequently became central to Schleiermacher's hermeneutics and thereby contributed to the emergence of the latter. In this connection, Patsch himself identifies the following four doctrines as contributions of Schlegel's that were subsequently taken over (and modified) by Schleiermacher: philology/hermeneutics is not merely a science but an art;[9] hermeneutics and criticism are interdependent;[10] it is necessary in interpretation to understand an author better than he understood himself (this is the one doctrine that Patsch's list shares with Körner's);[11] and *divination* plays an essential role in criticism/hermeneutics.[12]

Although pinning down intellectual priority with confidence is difficult for this period of meager textual evidence and "together-philosophy [*Symphilosophie*]," it seems to me that there is almost certainly much truth in the generic picture shared by Körner and Patsch that Schlegel at this time developed doctrines in hermeneutics which would later become central to Schleiermacher's hermeneutics, and thereby contributed to the emergence of the latter. For it is clear that Schleiermacher looked up to Schlegel intellectually at this period.[13] Moreover, the four doctrines which Patsch identifies as contributions of Schlegel's that were subsequently taken over by Schleiermacher all seem to me plausible candidates for such a status. And so too do several of the additional doctrines identified by Körner—in particular, that it is important for interpreters to identify an author's psychological development;[14] to interpret the parts of a text in light of the *whole* text;[15] and to reject *philologia sacra*.[16]

Indeed, it seems to me probable that Schlegel deserves much of the credit for several additional doctrines in Schleiermacher's hermeneutics as well. For example, Schlegel already in the *Philosophy of Philology* emphasizes that interpretation often faces the problem of a deep intellectual difference dividing the interpreter and his age from the author interpreted and his.[17] Again, Schleiermacher's central conception that in interpretation misunderstanding, rather than being the exception, is the rule is already anticipated by Schlegel in his essay *On Incomprehensibility* (1800). Again, beyond the generic principle of identifying an author's psychological development, one can already find in Schlegel's early work something very much like Schleiermacher's more specific principle that the interpretation of a text needs to identify, and trace the development of, an author's "seminal decision [*Keimentschluß*]."[18]

However, Körner and Patsch's shared *teleological* picture of Schlegel's importance in hermeneutics, their picture that this mainly lies in his having served as a step towards the attainment of Schleiermacher's hermeneutics, seems to me unfortunate. For, as I have argued elsewhere, the importance of Schleiermacher's hermeneutics itself has been rather exaggerated: its central claims were for the most part already anticipated by Ernesti and especially Herder, and to the extent that they do diverge from Herder's hermeneutics almost always turn out to be inferior to it.[19] Moreover, and more fundamentally, Schlegel's *main* claim to importance in the development of hermeneutics, it seems to me, instead lies in the fact that he made certain vital contributions which were *not* really preserved by Schleiermacher.

It is this more fundamental point that I would like to try to establish in the present essay, namely by focusing on five (families of) ideas concerning interpretation contributed by Schlegel which all, in one way or another, go beyond Schleiermacher's ideas, and are of great intrinsic value and significance.

The ideas in question are all in fact more continuous with ones already found in Herder than anticipative of ones later found in Schleiermacher. Nor is this an accident, for Schlegel from an early period looked up to Herder as an interpreter. Thus, he already writes in *On the Study of Greek Poetry* (1795/7) that in interpreting art Herder "joins the most extensive knowledge with the most delicate feeling and the most supple sensitivity."[20] And in the *Lectures on the History of Literature* (1815) he especially praises Herder's talent for imaginatively entering into the poetry of other periods and cultures.[21]

# I

The first of the ideas (or rather, the first family of ideas) in question concerns the role of *genre* in interpretation.[22]

At least since the publication of August Boeckh's monumental *Encyclopedia and Methodology of the Philological Sciences* (1877), it has been fairly well recognized among theorists of interpretation (though not among Anglophone philosophers) that correctly identifying *genre* plays an essential role in virtually all interpretation.[23] That it does so in the interpretation of works of *literature* was already recognized by Aristotle in the *Poetics*, and reflection on this subject has a long history (including Scaliger in the sixteenth century, for example). In the eighteenth century Herder recognized that identifying genre is also essential for understanding works of *non-linguistic* art (see, for instance, his discussion of Egyptian and Greek sculpture in *This Too a Philosophy of History for the Formation of Humanity* [1774]). But Boeckh's position implies, quite correctly, that additional extensions of the point should be made as well. In particular, not only literary, or artistic, texts have genres that need to be identified if they are to be properly understood, but also *non-artistic* texts: genres include not only the epic poem, the ode, the sonnet, the tragedy, the novel, etc., but also the history book, the scientific article, the newspaper report, the newspaper editorial, the advice column, the instruction manual, the shopping list, the love letter, etc. And not only texts have genres that need to be identified if they are to be properly understood, but also *oral* uses of language: genres include, not only all the things already mentioned, but also the military command, the instruction to an employee, the confession, the paternal advice, the casual conversation, the narration of an interesting incident, the stump speech, the joke, etc.[24] Indeed, most, if not all, linguistic acts, whether artistic or not, whether written or spoken, are undertaken with an intention (however implicit or vague) that they should instantiate one genre or another, and if they are to be fully understood (or properly evaluated) by other people, it is essential that the interpreter (or critic) identify, not only their linguistic meaning and their illocutionary force (assertion, question, imperative, etc.), but also their genre.

Boeckh's theory of interpretation is for the most part heavily indebted to his teacher Schleiermacher, whom he credits generously. However, concerning the role of genre in interpretation he tends to credit a different influence instead. This is not because Schleiermacher had overlooked the subject completely; he had taken it into account to a certain extent, both in his lectures on hermeneutics and in those on aesthetics. However, he had paid it much less attention than some other theorists from the period (notably Herder and the Schlegels), had found little if anything new to say about it, and in general had not done justice either to its importance or to its difficulty.[25] Instead, Boeckh tends to credit Friedrich Schlegel and his brother August Wilhelm for elevating genre to its proper place in the theory of interpretation.[26] And some other modern theorists have implied a similar view—notably, Peter Szondi, in an essay that extols the importance of Friedrich Schlegel's theory of genre.[27]

Friedrich Schlegel's virtues as an innovator in this area actually seem to me somewhat *less* dramatic than Boeckh and Szondi imply. For one thing, as I have argued in "Herder on Genre,"[28] many of the key insights in this area had already been achieved by Herder, in such works as *Shakespeare* (1773) and *This Too a Philosophy of History for the Formation of Humanity* (1774). These included insights into: (1) the essential role that correctly identifying genre plays in the interpretation not only of literary but also of non-linguistic art; (2) the radical historical mutability of genres; (3) the consequent frequent need for interpreters to identify unfamiliar, new, and sometimes even uniquely instantiated genres; (4) the likewise consequent frequent need for interpreters to resist a strong temptation to misidentify a genre by falsely assimilating it to a similar-looking one from another time or place with which they happen already to be more familiar, for example to misidentify the genre of Shakespearean "tragedy" by falsely assimilating it to that of ancient Athenian "tragedy" (and for critics to resist a resulting strong temptation to evaluate particular works of literary or non-linguistic art in terms of genre-purposes and-rules which they do not in fact aspire to realize in the first place, instead of in terms of those which they do); and (5) the again consequent need for interpreters (and critics) to employ a painstaking empirical approach in the determination of genres in order to identify them correctly.

For another thing, some of Friedrich Schlegel's scattered and often inconsistent remarks on genre tend to contradict these profound Herderian insights, and seem in the end retrograde (Szondi correctly identifies a number of these, but treats them much too sympathetically in my view). These include remarks concerning a need to *overcome* genre in modern romantic poetry;[29] the transhistorical character of certain genres;[30] a hierarchy among genres;[31] and the need for a "deductive" approach to genres.[32]

Nonetheless, it seems to me that Friedrich Schlegel does deserve a more *qualified* form of the sort of credit that Boeckh and Szondi give him for contributions in this area. Why? Part of his achievement here simply lies in the fact that he more commonly and prominently continued both Herder's emphasis on the importance of genre and Herder's central insights concerning genre (to a degree that Schleiermacher had not). A central text for this more considered and superior side of Schlegel's thinking about genre is his Cologne lectures on German language and literature from 1807, now published in the *Kritische Friedrich Schlegel Ausgabe*, volume 15/2.[33] In particular, Schlegel normally retains Herder's insights that correctly identifying genre is essential for the interpretation both of literary and of non-linguistic art;[34] that genres are historically mutable in radical ways;[35] that the interpreter therefore often needs to identify new, unfamiliar, and in some cases even uniquely instantiated genres;[36] that he therefore also needs to resist frequent temptations to interpret (and evaluate) works in one genre by falsely assimilating them to another;[37] and that the correct identification of genres therefore requires a painstaking empirical investigation.[38]

Friedrich's brother August Wilhelm likewise (indeed, even more consistently and emphatically) continues both Herder's emphasis on the great importance of genre and Herder's specific principles concerning genre—for example, in his famous *Course of Lectures on Dramatic Art and Literature* (1809) (which is indeed in many ways just a sort of grand reworking and elaboration of Herder's seminal essay *Shakespeare*).[39]

But Friedrich Schlegel and his brother August Wilhelm also deserve credit for making two important new *applications* of the general conception of genre which they inherited from Herder. A first of these concerns Greek tragedy and Aristotle's account of it. Before the Schlegels the understanding of Greek tragedy as a genre had been dominated by Aristotle's treatment of it in the *Poetics*, which was considered virtually sacrosanct not only by the French dramatists and critics, but also by their German opponents Lessing and Herder. With the Schlegels there emerged for the first time, largely in the light of a more skilled and scrupulous

empirical investigation of the evidence supplied by the surviving ancient tragedies themselves, a realization that Aristotle's account of ancient tragedy is in fact
at least as much an obstacle to properly understanding it as an aid.

Thus, Friedrich Schlegel already attacks Aristotle's claim to be an authority
on Greek poetry in *On the Study of Greek Poetry* (1795/7)—largely on the plausible ground that Aristotle belonged to the period of its decadence, and therefore misunderstood its most important forms. In his *History of the Poetry of the
Greeks and Romans* (1798) Friedrich argues more specifically, and again plausibly,
that Aristotle assimilates the genres of epic and tragic poetry too closely (for
example, in relation to the unity of action).[40] Friedrich also correctly emphasizes the religious, and in particular Dionysiac, nature of tragedy which Aristotle
had neglected or suppressed.[41] And perhaps most impressively of all, Friedrich
implies, again plausibly, that ancient epic and tragic poetry, rather than being
intended to be fictional in historical matters as Aristotle supposes, was intended
to be historically factual.[42] August Wilhelm radically rejects Aristotle's account
as well, not only continuing most of Friedrich's points but also developing
them further. For example, in his *History of Classical Literature* (1802) and *Course
of Lectures on Dramatic Art and Literature* (1809) he argues, again plausibly (though
perhaps not in this case correctly), that Aristotle's theory that Greek tragedy's
function was the catharsis of pity and fear is false.[43] And he also argues, very
plausibly, that Aristotle had only really espoused one of the three doctrines of
the unities that are conventionally attributed to him, namely that of action, not
those of time or place; that even the doctrine of the unity of action is obscure
in its import;[44] and that the unities of time and place are in fact commonly and
quite properly violated by ancient tragedies.[45]

By thus breaking Aristotle's undue influence on the interpretation of Greek
tragedy, the Schlegels opened up the way for a recognition of the deep unfamiliarity of this genre, and for a profound rethinking of its nature. They also
themselves began such a rethinking in a positive way. Examples of this are
Friedrich's aforementioned reflections on the Dionysiac-religious purposes of
Greek tragedy and on its historically factual intentions, and August Wilhelm's
reflections on the civic-political function of the tragic chorus. This rethinking
then continued with Nietzsche's *The Birth of Tragedy* and still continues apace
today (for example, in the work of Vernant, Vidal-Nacquet, Goldhill, and
Winkler)—in particular, incorporating the Schlegels' recognition of Greek
tragedy's deeply Dionysiac-religious and civic-political nature.

A second application Friedrich and August Wilhelm make of the general
conception of genre that they inherited from Herder is less obvious, but no less
important, in that it concerns the very birth of "romanticism." As is well known,
the young Friedrich Schlegel during his early classicizing phase already drew a

sharp distinction between "classical" and "interesting" (i.e. what he would later call "romantic") poetry, identifying as distinctive of the latter such features as authorial individuality, the mixing of genres, and an unsatisfied longing, but damning it and these features for violating classical rules; and his shift from classicism to romanticism essentially took the form of ceasing to see "classical" poetry as utterly superior to "interesting" (or "romantic") poetry in this way, but instead coming to accord legitimacy and positive value to the latter. This change of attitude took place in *On the Study of Greek Poetry* (mainly written in 1795; but only published in 1797), where the classicizing main text got subverted by a preface that Schlegel added after its composition in which he began to recognize the legitimacy and positive value of "interesting" (or "romantic") poetry.

Why did his attitude change in this way? In the preface he acknowledges the profound influence recently exercised on his thinking about the "classical" vs. "interesting" distinction by the intervening publication of Schiller's *On Naive and Sentimental Poetry* (1795), with its very positive assessment of a type of poetry, the "sentimental," distinguished by several of the same features as his own "interesting" poetry. It therefore seems clear that a large part of the explanation of his change in attitude lies in the influence exerted on him by Schiller's essay.[46]

But another important part of the explanation (which to my knowledge has hitherto gone unnoticed) is that this change in attitude was also the result of a sudden recognition on his part that the historical shift from "classical" to "interesting" (or "romantic") poetry is basically an example of the sort of historical shift between different but equally well-defined and legitimate genres that Herder had already been much concerned with, and that this precludes any simple valorization of the one at the expense of the other, in particular any negative assessment of the one in terms of the standards pertaining to the other.

That this consideration played an important role is shown by the fact that in the crucial intervening year 1796 Schlegel published a fascinating review of the 7th and 8th Collections of Herder's *Letters for the Advancement of Humanity* (1793–7). In the review he focused on a sharp distinction that Herder had drawn in his work between the nature of ancient and modern poetry. Herder had represented this distinction as turning on many of the same distinguishing features as Schlegel's own "classical" vs. "interesting" (or "romantic") and Schiller's "naive" vs. "sentimental" distinctions (for example, a yearning for God or the Infinite in modern poetry). Moreover, Herder had identified as exemplars of modern poetry precisely the poets whom Schlegel (and his brother) would go on to identify as paradigmatic representatives of "romantic" poetry (especially, the Provençal troubadours, the Minnesinger, Dante, Petrarch, Cervantes, and Shakespeare). Crucially, towards the end of his review Schlegel reported on Herder's normative assessment concerning these two types of poetry, which was precisely an application of Herder's usual stance against making invidious evaluative comparisons between different genres:

The result (p. 171 and following) denies that the poetry of different times and peoples can be compared, indeed even that there is a universal criterion of evaluation.[47]

In short, an application of Herder's central ideas about genre evidently played a key role in Schlegel's very development of romanticism.

Friedrich and August Wilhelm also deserve credit for introducing, or at least developing, some important further ideas about genre more *generally*. Two of these are especially noteworthy. The first concerns what Alastair Fowler has recently called genre-*modes*. Herder had already sometimes applied genre-concepts in an adjectival way to works belonging to other genres. For example, in a draft of his essay *Shakespeare* he describes Shakespeare's plays as mixing "all the colors of the tragic, comic, etc.,"[48] and in the *Adrastea* (1801–3) he observes in a similar spirit that Shakespeare's dramas (and certain other genres) contain *idyllic* scenes.[49] Friedrich Schlegel often writes in a similar manner. For example, in *Athenaeum Fragments* (1798–1800), no. 146 he says:

Just as the novel colors all of modern poetry, so satire colors and, as it were, sets the tone for all of Roman poetry, yes, even the whole of Roman literature.

Likewise, in the Cologne lectures on German language and literature from 1807 he observes that the modes "tragic" and "elegiac" often apply to works in other genres.[50] Indeed, pushing such a position to an extreme, in some of his notes he even goes as far as to advocate *replacing* the substantival use of genre-concepts with a merely adjectival use.[51] Now Herder here already implies, and Schlegel emphasizes (even to the point of overplaying), a very important point: namely, that the basic genres (e.g. tragedy), once established, give birth to corresponding modes (e.g. being tragic), which can then qualify works belonging to other genres. This point has recently been repeated and elaborated by the most sophisticated modern theorist of genre, Alastair Fowler.[52] For example, Fowler very plausibly characterizes Hardy's novels as tragic novels (think, for instance, of *Jude the Obscure* or *Tess of the D'Urbervilles*).[53]

Another idea for which Friedrich and August Wilhelm deserve credit concerns the systematic interdependence and interdefinition of genres. Friedrich sometimes makes the point that certain genres are implicitly interdependent or interdefined.[54] This is an important point (though, characteristically, he on occasion overplays it, going to the extreme of positing a single system of all genres). There are many relatively obvious cases of an essential dependence of one genre on another—for example, parody (as in authors such as Cervantes, Swift, and Fielding). But genres also sometimes essentially depend on each other in less obvious ways. For example, as Friedrich and August Wilhelm already imply, ancient Greek tragedy and comedy are in part implicitly interdefined by their sharp exclusion of each other (a fact that can be recognized more clearly when they are compared with their modern counterparts, where by contrast "tragedies" will sometimes include comic components and "comedies" tragic ones).[55] This point about the systematic interdependence and interdefinition of certain genres has gone on to play a significant role in more recent genre theory as well.[56]

In sum, Friedrich Schlegel (together with his brother) achieves an important contribution to hermeneutics by sustaining Herder's correct emphasis on the centrality of genre to interpretation as well as Herder's more specific ideas concerning this; making two important new applications of those ideas, in connection with Greek tragedy and romanticism; and introducing, or at least developing, further insights concerning genre-modes and the systematic interdependence and interdefinition of certain genres.

## II

Let us now turn to a second important idea in Schlegel's theory of interpretation. Schlegel makes the point that texts sometimes express meanings and thoughts, not explicitly in any of their parts, but instead implicitly through their parts and the way in which these are put together to form a whole. For example, he writes in the *Athenaeum Fragments*, no. III:

The teachings that a novel hopes to instill must be of the sort that can be communicated only as wholes, not demonstrated singly and not subject to exhaustive analysis.[57]

Schlegel's famous review of Goethe's novel *Wilhelm Meisters Lehrjahre*, titled *On Goethe's Meister* (1798), attempts to apply this sort of interpretation (though one may reasonably wonder whether Schlegel does not overestimate the unity of vision in Goethe's rambling work).[58] Schlegel also applies it to the overall forms of the philosophies of Spinoza and Fichte in *On Lessing* (1797/1801):

In the case of each of these boldest and most perfect thinkers the form itself is only an expression, symbol, and reflection of the content, namely of what is essential, the single and indivisible center of the whole. Consequently the form of the one [Spinoza] is that of substance and permanence, solidity, rest, and unity, while that of the other [Fichte] is activity, agility, restless progression, in short the diametrical opposite of the first.[59]

Schlegel evidently also believes that expressing meanings and thoughts holistically is an especially characteristic feature of ancient texts. Thus in the *Athenaeum*

*Fragments*, no. 325 he writes (deliberately echoing a famous fragment of Heraclitus):

But Apollo, who neither speaks nor keeps silent but intimates, no longer is worshipped, and wherever a Muse shows herself, people immediately want to carry her off to be cross-examined.[60]

Schlegel also extends this model to non-linguistic art, in particular painting. For example, he writes in observations on painting published in 1805 that the goal of a painting should be "the meaning of the whole which all individual forms only serve and are supposed to express with themselves [*mit*]."[61]

Schlegel's fundamental point here seems to me both correct and extremely important. As far as I can see, it is not really to be found in Schleiermacher, and so constitutes a distinctive contribution of Schlegel's. In particular, it should be distinguished from certain other doctrines which Schlegel and Schleiermacher both share in some form, and with which it could be confused: the doctrine that the parts of a text need to be interpreted in light of the whole text; and the doctrine that interpretation requires identifying an author's "seminal decision [*Keimentschluß*]" and its necessary development into the whole text. Neither of these two doctrines strictly implies that the whole expresses a meaning or thought over and above that expressed by the parts. If one wanted to find a precedent for Schlegel's point a more plausible candidate might be Herder, especially in his *Critical Forests* (1769).

Schlegel's implication in the passage recently quoted from *Athenaeum Fragments*, no. 325 that ancient texts are especially committed to using this technique of holistic communication, and therefore need to be interpreted accordingly, is particularly interesting. His remark there, with its deliberate echo of the famous fragment in which Heraclitus attributes a practice of indirect communication to Apollo ("The Lord who owns the oracle at Delphi neither speaks nor hides his meaning but indicates it by a sign" [fr. 93]), contains a strong suggestion that the religious conceptions and aesthetic ideals of the Greeks encouraged them to use such a technique of communication as a central part of their literary practice, especially for the communication of their deepest messages. This suggestion strikes me as both plausible and intriguing.

Consider, for example, Homer's *Iliad*, book 1. There Homer manages to communicate, not by explicitly stating it anywhere, but instead by artfully juxtaposing and contrasting, on the one hand, the opening quarrel between the mortal rulers Agamemnon and short-lived Achilles (which Nestor attempts to mediate), with all its grandeur, passion, and seriousness, and, on the other hand, the structurally similar but parody-like quarrel at the end of the book between the immortal rulers Zeus and Hera (which Hephaistos attempts to mediate),

with all its ultimate triviality and even ludicrousness, something like the following message:

You may well have assumed that the immortality and the other apparent advantages
enjoyed by the gods would be a huge boon to any beings who possessed them, raising
their lot far above that of mere mortals like us, as indeed the gods' traditional epithet
"blessed" implies. But in fact, if you think about it more carefully, since nothing would
ever be seriously at stake for such beings as it is for us mortals (in particular, because they
cannot risk their lives, they cannot really achieve the highest virtue of honor either),
their existence would be reduced to a sort of unending triviality and meaninglessness,
so that our lot is in a very real sense the better one.

Schlegel's injunction to take account of implicit holistic meanings and
thoughts when interpreting texts certainly courts an epistemological danger of
reading in meanings and thoughts that are not really there, since the proper
criteria for attributing implicit holistic meanings and thoughts to texts are even
less clear than those for attributing explicit ones. Indeed, it seems reasonable to
suspect that some of Schlegel's own holistic readings succumb to such a danger
(for example, his reading of *Wilhelm Meisters Lehrjahre*, which arguably attributes
more overall coherence and design to the novel than is really there). And the
history of interpretations of Homer and Plato is certainly littered with ascriptions to them of implicit secret doctrines, based on overall impressions of their
works, which seem arbitrary and implausible. Still, this epistemological danger
does not seem to me so severe and unmanageable as to invalidate Schlegel's
injunction. For there are in fact various ways of distinguishing plausible from
implausible imputations of implicit holistic meanings and thoughts. For example, one relevant criterion is evidence of a broad cultural, or an individual
authorial, commitment to using such indirect forms of communication (such as
the Heraclitus fragment arguably constitutes in the case of the ancient Greeks).
Another relevant criterion is the general historical and cultural availability of
the specific meaning or thought imputed, in particular its freedom from gross
anachronism (this would preclude certain Stoic interpretations of Homer, for
example). Yet another relevant criterion is collateral evidence of a culture's or
an individual author's intention to convey the specific meaning or thought in
question. For instance, my suggestion that a message of the sort that I described
above is implicitly communicated by *Iliad*, book 1 is strongly confirmed by a
famous episode in *Odyssey*, book 5 in which the fair nymph Calypso invites
Odysseus to stay with her on her island as her consort and become immortal,
as she is, but he (the most intelligent man in all of Homer, note!) declines the
invitation, choosing instead to return to Ithaca and his aging wife Penelope as
a mere mortal and eventually to die.

It is a further question whether the implicit holistic meanings and thoughts involved *could* in principle have been explicitly linguistically expressed by the author, and/or be explicitly linguistically expressed by his interpreter, in the usual way. In the passage from the *Athenaeum Fragments* with which we began this discussion—"The teachings that a novel hopes to instill must be of the sort that can be communicated only as wholes, not demonstrated singly and not subject to exhaustive analysis"—Schlegel implies that at least in some cases they could *not*. A concluding poetical passage from his essay *On Lessing* carries the same implication:

> And because you see the divinity, you feel the sweet desire
> To form, divinely productive, the work in the likeness of the Universe.
> Blessed is the man who is able to think and to form something so great,
> To interpret which is hardly granted to mortal speech.[62]

Indeed, at the period to which these two texts belong (1798–1801), such a position was central to Schlegel's outlook, since he regarded it as the primary function of poetic art to indicate an Infinite that could not be expressed directly in language but only indirectly (he called this "allegory"—a term which he used in its strict etymological sense of "saying something other," i.e. something other than what was or could be expressed directly).[63] On the other hand, the fact that Schlegel in *On Lessing* also applies his point about the occurrence of implicit holistic meanings and thoughts, and the need to interpret them, to the forms of the works of Spinoza and Fichte shows that he recognizes that cases of the *other* sort occur as well. For in Spinoza and Fichte it is a matter of a sort of *re*-expression at the level of a philosophy's whole form of what is also its *explicitly expressed content*.

The conception that at least in some cases implicit holistic meanings and thoughts cannot be explicitly expressed in language stands in a certain tension with the Herderian doctrines, to which Schlegel usually seems sympathetic, that meaning is word-usage and that thought is essentially dependent on and bounded by language. However, it does not contradict them outright. For it could be held that even irreducibly holistic meanings are still constituted by word-usages, and that even irreducibly holistic thoughts are essentially dependent on and bounded by a capacity to express them with language. Also, it should be noted that it would be question-begging to demand a provision of clear examples in support of the conception at issue, if that meant *explicit linguistic identifications* of the implicit holistic meanings and thoughts involved. Still, it remains unclear to me whether the conception in question is actually correct. Nonetheless, whichever way that issue turns out in the end, Schlegel's more fundamental point that works sometimes express implicit holistic meanings and thoughts, and that these need to be interpreted, remains an insight of the first importance.

# III

A third vital contribution that Schlegel makes to the theory of interpretation concerns the role of *unconscious* meanings and thoughts in texts, and hence in their interpretation.

The general idea that unconscious mental processes occur already had a long history in German philosophy by Schlegel's day: it had been something of a commonplace among the Rationalists, especially Leibniz;[64] Kant had been strongly committed to it as well (for example, in his published *Anthropology*); and so too had Herder, who had moreover discussed it in close connection with questions of authorship and interpretation in *On the Cognition and Sensation of the Human Soul* (1778).

However, it is above all Schlegel who develops this general idea into a principle that the interpreter must penetrate beyond an author's conscious meanings and thoughts to discover his unconscious ones as well: "Every excellent work ... aims at more than it knows";[65] "In order to understand someone who only partially understands himself, you first have to understand him completely and better than he himself does."[66]

Schleiermacher famously uses versions of the formula of needing to "understand an author better than he understands himself" as well. However, *he* means by this something much less ambitious than Schlegel does—roughly, just that the rules of word-usage and grammar which an author usually only masters implicitly should be known explicitly by his interpreter. And Schleiermacher is in general strikingly reluctant to impute unconscious mental processes to people.[67]

Schlegel's principle seems to me extremely important.[68] One of its most interesting and plausible early applications occurs, not in his own writings, but in his brother's. In his *Course of Lectures on Dramatic Art and Literature*, August Wilhelm characterizes Aeschylus as a genius who to a great extent worked unconsciously:

[Sophocles], in speaking of Aeschylus, gave a proof that he was himself a thoughtful artist: "Aeschylus does what is right without knowing it." These few simple words exhaust the whole of what we understand by the phrase, powerful genius working unconsciously.[69]

And August Wilhelm gives a forceful example here (an example which, as it happens, not only attributes unconscious meanings to Aeschylus, but also ones

whose *subject-matter* is the contrast between the unconscious and the conscious).
He argues that in Aeschylus the contrast between the Titans and the younger
gods—in particular, the contrast between the Furies, on the one hand, and
Apollo and Athena, on the other, in the *Oresteia* trilogy—is unconsciously concerned with the contrast between unconscious mental forces (symbolized by
the former gods) and conscious ones (symbolized by the latter). Thus August
Wilhelm writes:

The Titans in general symbolize the dark and mysterious powers of primaeval nature and
mind; the younger gods, whatsoever enters more immediately within the circle of consciousness. The former are more nearly allied to original chaos, the latter belong to a world
already reduced to order. The Furies denote the dreadful powers of conscience, in so far
as it rests on obscure feelings and forebodings, and yields to no principles of reason.[70]

Another author who took up and applied Friedrich Schlegel's principle, and
also elaborated it in an impressive way, is Nietzsche. In such works as *The Gay
Science* (1882) and *On the Genealogy of Morals* (1887) Nietzsche elaborates it into
the more complex principle that beneath a person's conscious meanings there
often lie deeper unconscious ones; that the conscious meanings function as
representative-but-masking proxies for the deeper unconscious ones; that the
latter are moreover typically contrary to the former; and that the person
involved usually has motives for thus "repressing" or concealing the latter (even
from himself).[71] Furthermore, Nietzsche applies this general model in some
very powerful and interesting specific ways. For example, in *On the Genealogy of
Morals* he argues that Jesus' explicit, conscious message of love and forgiveness
in fact concealed and represented at a deeper, less conscious level quite contrary
motives of hatred and revenge which he shared with his Jewish forebears and
contemporaries (namely, ones that were directed against an oppressing Greek
and Roman imperial order).[72]

A similar approach to interpretation has, of course, also been pursued in the
twentieth century by Freud and his followers (Freud was heavily influenced by
Nietzsche here, and took over his more elaborate psychological model).
However, their pursuit of it has arguably done less to help realize its potential
than to reveal its epistemological hazardousness, its courting of an arbitrary
reading-in of meanings and thoughts due to the fact that the proper criteria for
imputing unconscious meanings and thoughts are even less clear than those for
imputing conscious ones. For example, Freud's own thesis in *The Relation of the
Poet to Day-Dreaming* (1908) that *all* poetry is motivated by wish-fulfillment is
highly implausible (as is his better known corresponding thesis concerning *all*
dreams in *The Interpretation of Dreams*). And many other Freudian readings of
literature display a similar arbitrariness.[73]

This very real danger of arbitrariness does not, in my view, warrant despair about the general approach in question, though. Rather, it just shows that great methodological rigor and tact are required in order to apply it successfully—rigor and tact of a sort that August Wilhelm Schlegel and Nietzsche arguably possessed, but Freud lacked. Nietzsche's application of this approach to the interpretation of Jesus can serve as a positive example here. For, superficial appearances to the contrary notwithstanding,[74] his interpretation of Jesus implicitly rests on an impressive convergence of a broad range of strong empirical evidence, which makes it highly plausible. The evidence in question includes the following: (1) The specific historical context in which Jesus lived, namely a Jewish community in Palestine which had been under the oppressive thumb of first Greek and then Roman imperialists for several centuries. This context already makes Nietzsche's imputation to the Jewish community of a hatred and desire for revenge directed against those oppressors plausible. (2) The strong confirmation of that imputation by many parts of the New Testament, such as the Acts of the Apostles (concerning the Greeks) and the Revelation of St John the Divine (concerning the Romans).[75] (3) The fact that Jesus' own ethical values, as articulated in such classic statements as the Sermon on the Mount, including the values of love and forgiveness of one's enemies, constitute a striking systematic inversion of the ethical values that had predominated among the Greeks and Romans since the time of Homer.[76] (Such inversions of values are a fairly common expression of resentment against perceived oppressors, documentable in other historical cases as well.) And finally, (4) the fact that Jesus makes a series of more specific remarks which betray his own hatred of the Greeks and Romans—for example, one in which he contrasts Jews and Greeks as respectively children and dogs (Mark 7:27). This impressive convergence of a broad body of strong empirical evidence towards Nietzsche's interpretive conclusion can serve to illustrate how the general approach to interpretation in question here may be properly applied.

One further issue that arises in connection with this approach should be briefly discussed as well. Like Schlegel's point that texts sometimes express irreducibly holistic meanings and thoughts, his point that they sometimes express unconscious meanings and thoughts stands in tension with the Herderian principles in the philosophy of language, to which Schlegel usually himself seems sympathetic, that meaning is word-usage and that thought is essentially dependent on and bounded by language. However, as in the former case, there is no real contradiction here. For it could be that the unconscious meanings and thoughts in question are always ones that an author has the *linguistic capacity* to express (as the contemporary French psychoanalyst Lacan indeed seems to hold).

# IV

Schlegel also makes a fourth important contribution to the theory of interpretation. Already before Schlegel, Ernesti's hermeneutics had encouraged the interpreter to attribute inconsistencies and other forms of confusion to profane texts where appropriate, and Herder had extended such a principle to sacred texts as well—a position in which he was subsequently followed by Schleiermacher. Schlegel likewise accepts Herder's broad version of the principle. But he also places greater emphasis on it and develops it further in certain ways, not only insisting that confusion is a common feature of texts and should be recognized when it occurs, but also arguing that in such cases the interpreter needs to seek to *understand and explain* it. For example, Schlegel's essay *On Incomprehensibility* (1800) is largely devoted to insisting that confusion frequently occurs even in superior texts and needs to be recognized when it does. And Schlegel already argues in about 1797:

In order to understand someone, one must first of all be cleverer than he, then just as clever, and then also just as stupid. It is not enough that one understand the actual sense of a confused work better than the author understood it. One must also oneself be able to know, to *characterize*, and even *construe* the confusion even down to its very principles.[77]

Some of Schlegel's most interesting elaborations of this position occur in connection with his application of it to the interpretation of philosophers. In *Georg Forster* (1797) he argues (with Georg Forster especially in mind) not only that it is a plain fact that philosophers sometimes commit inconsistencies, but also that it is not even clear that this is the damning vice that it is often assumed to be, since, while inconsistency may indeed be a fatal flaw in a philosophical *system*, both in daily life and in the *non*-systematic philosopher it may rather be a sign of a certain many-sidedness and intellectual integrity, whereas strict systematicity and consistency would only show one-sidedness, stubbornness, or a lack of independent-mindedness:

For a doctrinal system [*Lehrgebäude*] complete freedom even from the slightest contradictions may be the most essential main virtue. But in the individual, entire human being in active and social life this uniformity and immutability of views for the most part results only from blind one-sidedness and stubbornness, or indeed from a complete lack of an opinion and perception that is one's own and free. A contradiction destroys the system [*System*]; countless contradictions do not make the philosopher unworthy of this exalted name, unless he already is. Contradictions can even be signs of honest love of truth, and prove that many-sidedness without which Forster's writings could not be what, however, they should and must be in their kind.[78]

This is arguably a very sensible view, which applies not only to Georg Forster, but also to many other non-systematic philosophers who are prone to inconsistency on occasion, including, for example, Herder and indeed Schlegel himself.

Another interesting elaboration of the position in question lies in a more specific picture of the form that the sort of *understanding and explanation* of inconsistencies and other confusions in texts that Schlegel demands might take. In a review of a French work on Kant which he published in French in 1802–3, Schlegel indicates that at least where Kant's inconsistencies and confusions are concerned this would involve tracing Kant's development as a philosopher, and in particular observing how the positions which he eventually welded together into a system originally had their source in a number of discrete rejections of received views, adoptions of new opinions, self-criticisms, and so on, i.e. ones that were originally undertaken without any particular view to each other or to the question of their mutual consistency:

> The sole means capable of dissipating all the obscurities, and the only one that the rules of sound interpretation prescribe to us, is to study the collection of an author's ideas, to follow their thread and their successive development, and to investigate up to the point of origin the formation of his particular opinions. This is why all the good minds of Germany are fairly generally agreed that it is above all in his first essays that one must study Kant. It is there that one discovers the first germs of his theory, and that one observes his system's birth and successive development. By following this method one succeeds not only in rendering clear what previously was not, but also in discovering the cause of the apparent obscurity, which with an author like Kant is never purely a result of chance and negligence. One could rather see it as a consequence of the fact that the author has wanted to create a system out of what were originally only certain objections to received opinions, certain new views, certain attempts, certain doubts about his own opinions, in short certain detached ideas. Whence it has resulted that his ideas seem not at all to be directed towards the same point of view, but that they cross each other, aiming at several goals which are different and isolated.[79]

This again seems very sound advice, both concerning the interpretation of philosophers generally and concerning the interpretation of Kant in particular.[80]

Somewhat more debatable is a philosophically ambitious general explanation which Schlegel sometimes offers for the presence of, and the consequent need to recognize, confusion in texts, namely that this is due to the chaotic nature of the *reality* that texts aim to characterize:

> Is this infinite world [of the texts of science and art] not formed by the understanding out of incomprehensibility or chaos?[81]

It is a high and perhaps the final step of intellectual formation to posit for oneself the sphere of incomprehensibility and confusion. The understanding of chaos consists in recognizing it.[82]

This explanation is questionable to the extent that it implies that reality itself is self-contradictory.[83] On the other hand, even Anglophone philosophers no longer dismiss that idea quite as assuredly as they used to.[84] And even if it should be rejected in the end, Schlegel's explanation could easily be pruned back to say, somewhat more tamely, just that reality is complicated and confusing—which is certainly true, and certainly does constitute part of the explanation of the confusion found in texts (albeit a more obvious part).

Such further details aside, Schlegel's fundamental principle here that interpreters should be prepared to find texts inconsistent seems to me both valid and extremely important. It is especially valuable as a corrective to certain misguided notions about the need for "charity" in interpretation generally, and in the interpretation of philosophical works in particular, which have become widespread and deeply rooted in recent Anglophone philosophy. Insofar as such notions concern interpretation *generally*, they stem in part from a sort of double error: a principle, espoused by many philosophers in one version or another (including Aristotle, Kant, the early Wittgenstein, Quine, and Davidson), according to which it is impossible to think inconsistently; plus an inference from that principle to the inevitable erroneousness of imputing inconsistencies to texts. This is a double error, first, because the principle in question turns out to be mistaken,[85] and second, because even if it were true, it would only plausibly hold for *explicit* inconsistencies, whereas the inconsistencies that need to be imputed to texts are as a rule merely *implicit* ones. Insofar as the notions in question concern the interpretation of *philosophical works* in particular, they largely rest (in addition) on a dubious inference from the probably correct premise that positions which contain inconsistencies cannot possibly be true to the conclusion that any philosophy which contains them must therefore be worthless (so that if the interpreter cannot find a philosopher to be completely self-consistent, he may as well ignore him). This inference usually depends on at least one of two mistakes. Either it depends on overlooking the fact that *parts* of an inconsistent philosophy might very well still be true (perhaps including very important parts). Or it depends on making an implausible assumption that if a philosopher is guilty of an inconsistency (so that his position cannot possibly be true), then that automatically shows him to be so intellectually confused that nothing he has to say is worth paying attention to. In order to see that this cannot be right one only needs to ask oneself the following sort of question: Did the fact that Russell found a contradiction in Frege's treatment of the foundations of set theory show that Frege was so hopelessly confused that his views should simply be ignored? Obviously not. As Schlegel recognizes, a great deal depends on the particular *way* in which a philosopher is inconsistent, and certain forms of inconsistency are far from being the worst intellectual vices of which a philosopher can be guilty.

In refreshing contrast to this deeply misguided trend in recent Anglophone philosophy, some recent theorists of interpretation who have also enjoyed considerable influence in the Anglophone world and who are in substantial and commendable agreement with Schlegel in insisting on the need to recognize and explain inconsistency and confusion in texts, including philosophical texts, are A.O. Lovejoy, Quentin Skinner, and Jacques Derrida.[86]

# V

A fifth and final important contribution that Schlegel makes to hermeneutics concerns the interpretation of *non-linguistic art*—painting, instrumental music, and so on.

As I have argued elsewhere,[87] Herder began his career, in the *Critical Forests*, holding that non-linguistic art does not express meanings or thoughts at all but is instead merely sensuous in nature. On such a view, the question of *interpreting* it does not even arise. But Herder subsequently, beginning in later parts of the same work, changed his mind about this, coming to recognize that non-linguistic art does in fact often express meanings and thoughts, including ones of a religious nature, and therefore does need to be interpreted.

Schlegel deserves credit for committing himself unambiguously to a version of Herder's mature theory, and for developing it in some very rich and compelling ways. Especially important texts in this connection are his pieces on visual art (primarily painting), stemming mainly from the period 1802–6, which have now been collected together in *Kritische Friedrich Schlegel Ausgabe*, volume four.

In developing his own position, Schlegel also drew on intervening work by Wackenroder and Tieck. In continuity with Herder (and also Hamann), Wackenroder and Tieck had argued—in *Outpourings of an Art-Loving Friar* (1797), *Franz Sternbald's Wanderings* (1798), and *Fantasies on Art for the Friends of Art* (1799)—that painting and music express meanings and thoughts, including ones of a deeply religious nature.[88] But they had also developed a much more specific model concerning this which included the following additional features: a strong emphasis on the Catholic character of art (the first and last of the three works just mentioned include sympathetic representations of conversions to Catholicism); an identification of late medieval/early modern German and especially Italian painters as paradigms (in particular, Dürer in Germany and Correggio, Raphael, Michelangelo, and da Vinci in Italy); an extension of allegorical interpretation to include not only painting and music but also cathedral architecture; and a practice of serially examining individual artists and their works.[89] Schlegel took over this more specific model in its entirety.

What, then, are the main features of Schlegel's theory? He holds unequivocally and emphatically that non-linguistic art of any importance always does express meanings and thoughts. Thus in the Cologne lectures on philosophy (1804–6) he writes:

If one wished to make mere decoration and charm the purpose of art, art would be ill founded, and the objections of those people who reject it as quite useless entirely justified…But it is an entirely different matter when one makes *meaning* the purpose of art.[90]

And he also applies such a position to each of the non-linguistic arts individually. For example, already in the *Athenaeum Fragments*, no. 444 he says the following about instrumental music (in continuity with views already expressed by Herder, Tieck, and Wackenroder):

Many people find it strange and ridiculous when musicians talk about the ideas in their compositions; and it often happens that one perceives they have more ideas in their music than they do about it. But whoever has a feeling for the wonderful affinity of all the arts and sciences will at least not consider the matter from the dull viewpoint of a so-called naturalness that maintains music is supposed to be only the language of the senses. Rather, he will consider a certain tendency of pure instrumental music toward philosophy as something not impossible in itself. Doesn't pure instrumental music have to create its own text? And aren't the themes in it developed, reaffirmed, varied, and contrasted in the same way as the subject of meditation in a philosophical succession of ideas?

Similarly, that it is visual art's function to express meanings and thoughts is a central theme of the pieces in *Kritische Friedrich Schlegel Ausgabe*, volume four. Thus Schlegel argues there that the proper function of sculpture is to express meanings and thoughts, namely ancient myths;[91] that painting's proper function is to express meanings and thoughts as well, but more specifically ones of a religious character, and more specifically still ones of a Christian character;[92] and that the proper function of Gothic architecture is likewise to express meanings and thoughts ("Gothic architecture has a meaning"), in particular religious, Christian ones.[93]

Since non-linguistic art of any importance always expresses meanings and thoughts, it of course requires interpretation. Accordingly, Schlegel develops a set of hermeneutic principles to guide and facilitate this, as well as devoting considerable attention to the interpretation of specific works of art.

Some of the hermeneutic principles in question are very similar to his principles for interpreting *linguistic texts*. For example, he holds that, just like the
interpretation of linguistic texts from the past,[94] the interpretation of visual art
from the past faces, and needs to recognize, the challenge that its subject–matter
is usually intellectually distant from ourselves.[95] Again, he holds that, as in the
case of linguistic texts, one of the main ways of solving this problem in the case
of visual art is through a careful study of the *literature* of its period and place.[96]
Again, he recommends that, just like the parts of a linguistic text, the parts of a
work of visual art need to be interpreted in light of the whole work.[97] Again,
he holds that, just as a work of literature needs to be interpreted and evaluated
in accordance with its *own* genre (or individual ideal), not another,[98] so the
same is true of works of visual art.[99] Again, he insists that, as in the case of linguistic texts, it is vitally important to discern a work of visual art's *holistic* meanings.[100] Again, he implies that, just like the interpretation of linguistic texts, the
interpretation of instrumental music needs to pay attention to its author's *unconscious* meanings: "It often happens one perceives [musicians] have more ideas in
their music than they do about it."[101]

But Schlegel also here develops—and moreover, applies with great imagination and skill—a more distinctive hermeneutic principle: a theory of a sort of
*symbolism* that is distinctive of non–linguistic art and by means of which it conveys its meanings and thoughts. For example (to begin with a simple case), he
notes, convincingly, that painters such as Correggio often use light and dark
colors to symbolize good and evil respectively.[102] Again (and somewhat less
simply), he argues, very plausibly, that there is an important difference between
portrait paintings which have a plain background (e.g. Holbein's) and those
which have a landscape as background (e.g. Leonardo da Vinci's *Mona Lisa*),
since in the latter the landscape symbolically conveys (or at least clarifies) the
inner state of mind of the person portrayed.[103] Again (and most elaborately of
all), he makes a cogent case that a whole range of features of the architecture of
the Gothic cathedral symbolically convey meanings and thoughts:

Whoever the originators [of Gothic architecture were], it is evident that their intention
was not merely to pile up huge stone edifices, but to embody certain ideas. How excellent
soever the style of a building may be, if it convey no meaning, express no sentiment, it
cannot strictly be considered a creation of Art…Hence architecture generally bears a
symbolically hidden meaning, while the Christian architecture of mediaeval Germany
does so in an eminent and especial degree. First and foremost, there is the expression of
devotional thought towering boldly aloft, from this lowly earth, towards the azure skies
and an omnipotent God. Such is…the impression…on beholding the sublimity of those
vaulted arches and those fluted columns. The whole plan is indeed replete with symbols
of deep significance…The altar pointed Eastward: the three principal entrances expressed

the conflux of worshippers gathered together from all quarters of the globe. The three steeples corresponded to the Christian Trinity. The Quire arose like a temple within the Temple on an increased scale of elevation. The form of the Cross had been of early establishment in the Christian Church: not accidentally... The rose will be found to constitute the radical element of all decoration in this architectural style: from it the peculiar shape of window, door, and steeple is mainly derived... The cross and rose are, then, the chief symbols of this mystic art. On the whole, what is sought to be conveyed is the stupendous Idea of Eternity, the earnest thought of Death, the death of *this* world, wreathed in the lovely fullness of an endless blooming life in the world that is to come.[104]

One final question that remains to be considered here is this: Does Schlegel agree with Herder that the meanings which non-linguistic art expresses are always linguistically expressible as well?[105] Or does he instead agree with Wackenroder and Tieck that they are often not?[106] The answer seems to be the former. This stance can be seen from the pieces on visual art in *Kritische Friedrich Schlegel Ausgabe*, volume four. One indication there that this must be his considered position lies in the fact that he insists that the painter must be a poet, whose poetry, while it need not indeed come from poems in the usual sense, at least needs to come from one linguistic source or another:

The painter should be a poet, that is certain—though not indeed a poet in words but in colors. Let him have his poetry from any other source than poetry itself, just so long as it is poetry. The example of the old painters will best guide us here again. To be sure, only a few paintings of the old school can be called poetic if one limits this term to the poetry of words and poets... But we only mean here the poetical view of things, and this the old painters had from a position closer to the source. The poetry of the old painters was in part religion, as with Perugino, Fra Bartolomeo, and many other old painters; in part philosophy, as with the deep Leonardo; or both, as in the endlessly profound Dürer.[107]

Even more tellingly, he applies this point not only to painting but to *all* the arts: "Poetry is alone among all the arts a, so to speak, universal accompanying art [*Mitkunst*] which joins together all the others."[108] Another indication that this must be his considered position lies in the fact that when in a late piece from 1823 he undertakes to specify the overall idea at work in the painting *St. Cecilia* by Ludwig Schnorr, he unhesitatingly articulates it in *linguistic* terms:

Concerning the idea in the painting in question, it is mainly two things that specially distinguish this picture in its conception and treatment of the subject: First, that the saint has been given an angel as companion—which is to be understood in light of the legend, which this painting follows in the most exact way. The second special feature is that the saint is here represented not only as is usual with the transfigured expression of prayer or blessedness, but as looking down from the surrounding brilliance of heaven onto the earthly residence of mortals with moving compassion and a loving gaze.[109]

In short, Schlegel's considered position on this important question seems to be the same as Herder's: that the meanings expressed by non-linguistic art are always linguistically expressible as well.[110] I have argued elsewhere that this position is in fact the correct one.[111]

Schlegel's extension of meaning and interpretation into the domain of non-linguistic art, together with his principles for interpreting it, and his subtle applications of those principles, constitute yet another important contribution to hermeneutics.

Admittedly, Schleiermacher would eventually, in his late lectures on aesthetics (1819-33), make some modest moves in the same direction. In particular, he would there repeat the steps that Herder had already taken in the *Critical Forests*: starting out in the lectures with a close variant of Herder's initial theory according to which non-linguistic arts do not express meanings at all but are instead merely sensuous, but then, like Herder, coming to recognize the inadequacy of such a position and switching, albeit ambiguously, to a version of Herder's mature theory, according to which they do express meanings, but ones that are always dependent on the artist's linguistic capacity. However, whereas Herder had developed this mature theory forcefully and in convincing detail, with Schleiermacher it remained ambiguous and undeveloped.[112] Moreover, Schlegel's further elaborations of Herder's mature position, as described above—especially, his articulation of several specific principles concerning the interpretation of non-linguistic art, and his skilled application of these to particular cases—far exceed in sophistication anything to be found in Schleiermacher.[113]

# VI

In sum, Schlegel really has *two* broad claims to importance in hermeneutics rather than just one. Not only did he play a significant role in the inception and formation of Schleiermacher's hermeneutics (as Körner and Patsch already argued), but in addition, and much more importantly, he contributed five extremely valuable ideas (or families of ideas) concerning interpretation which are not really to be found in Schleiermacher: ideas concerning genre, holistic meanings, unconscious meanings, authorial confusion, and non-linguistic art.

# Notes

1. J. Körner, "Friedrich Schlegels 'Philosophie der Philologie' mit einer Einleitung herausgegeben von Josef Körner" (1928); H. Patsch, "Friedrich

Schlegels 'Philosophie der Philologie' und Schleiermachers frühe Entwürfe zur Hermeneutik," *Zeitschrift für Theologie und Kirche*, 63 (1966).

2. Körner, "Friedrich Schlegels 'Philosophie der Philologie,'" p. 7.
3. Ibid.
4. Ibid.
5. Ibid.
6. Ibid., p. 9.
7. Ibid., p. 14; cf. p. 70 n. 72. Strictly speaking, Körner only says that Schlegel anticipated and influenced *Ast* in this doctrine. But given the rest of his case, it seems that he would want to explain its occurrence in Schleiermacher in the same way.
8. Ibid., p. 67 n. 25. Strictly speaking, Körner only says that Schlegel influenced *Boeckh* to accept this doctrine. But since he holds the general view that Boeckh came to his central doctrines by absorbing them from Schlegel via Schleiermacher, the extension of this point to cover Schleiermacher seems implied.
9. Patsch, "Friedrich Schlegels 'Philosophie der Philologie' und Schleiermachers frühe Entwürfe zur Hermeneutik," pp. 446, 451.
10. Ibid., p. 448.
11. Ibid., pp. 452 ff.
12. Ibid., p. 458. In addition to the early works of Schlegel's that are most relevant to establishing his priority in this last respect, cf. his conception of the role of *divination* in the Cologne lectures on German language and literature from 1807 (KFSA 15/2:79–80).
13. For example, Schleiermacher wrote the following about Schlegel in 1797: "He is a young man twenty-five years old, of such broad knowledge that it is difficult to understand how it is possible to know so much at such a young age, with an original intellect that is far superior to everything here, despite the fact that there is much intelligence and talent here" (E. Behler, *Friedrich Schlegel in Selbstzeugnissen und Bilddokumenten*, p. 164).
14. See esp. Schlegel's emphasis on this in his report on the works of Boccaccio from 1801 (*Friedrich Schlegel 1794–1802. Seine prosaischen Jugendschriften*, 2:396), and in a review he published in French in 1802/3 (KFSA 18:541; quoted later in this essay). The doctrine is also prominent in his 1804 work on Lessing, *Lessing's Thoughts and Opinions Collected from his Writings and Explained*.

See Behler, *Friedrich Schlegel*, pp. 49–54 for a relevant discussion of Schlegel's "genetic method" (this is a term Schlegel himself uses, for example in the Cologne lectures of 1804–6). However, Behler's tracing of this method back to Fichte requires qualification. Fichte did no doubt influence Schlegel here. But Herder had already invented and named a "genetic method" in the 1760s, and Schlegel's version of the method is much more like Herder's than Fichte's, in that like the former but unlike the latter it is empirical, genuinely temporal, and genuinely historical. So Herder's influence was at least as important here as Fichte's. (Cf. H. Eichner, *Friedrich Schlegel*, p. 42.)

15. This is a constant theme in Schlegel's reviews and "characteristics" from the period 1797–1801. Most famously, it plays a central role in *On Goethe's Meister* (1798). But it also does so in *Georg Forster* (1797) and *On Lessing* (1797/1801) (see *Friedrich Schlegel 1794–1802*, 2:125, 423–4).

16. See e.g. *Philosophy of Philology*, in Körner, "Friedrich Schlegels 'Philosophie der Philologie,'" p. 24: "The nonsense of *philologia sacra*."

17. Ibid., pp. 16–17, 28.

18. Thus Schlegel already writes in a review of a French work on Kant that he published in French in 1802–3: "The sole means capable of dissipating all the obscurities, and the only one that the rules of sound interpretation prescribe to us, is to study the collection of an author's ideas, to follow their thread and their successive development, and to investigate up to the point of origin the formation of his particular opinions. This is why all the good minds of Germany are fairly generally agreed that it is above all in his first essays that one must study Kant. It is there that one discovers the first germs of his theory, and that one observes his system's birth and successive development" (KFSA 18:541).

    That the doctrine of the *Keimentschluß* should thus have had its origins in Schlegel rather than in Schleiermacher makes good sense on reflection, since it was clearly influenced by Fichte's model of tracing the self's experience back to an original act of self-positing from which it unfolded by dialectical necessity, and Schlegel was much more heavily influenced by Fichte than Schleiermacher was.

19. See *After Herder*, Essays 4 and 11, and in the present volume Essay 9.

20. F. Schlegel, *On the Study of Greek Poetry*, p. 93.

21. F. Schlegel, *Lectures on the History of Literature*, pp. 364–5.

22. The following discussion will be mainly concerned with the relevance of genre for *interpretation*. However, many normative questions arise in connection with genre as well—e.g. concerning the evaluation of particular works in light of their genre; the relative merits of different genres; and which genres, if any, should be used in future works. For the philosophers I discuss here, including Schlegel, such normative questions are very much in play alongside the interpretive question. However, I shall for the most part abstract from them here.

23. A. Boeckh, *Encyklopädie und Methodologie der philologischen Wissenschaften* (1877; 2nd edn. Leipzig: B.G. Teubner, 1886). Boeckh includes the identification of genre as one of the four essential types or aspects of interpretation that he distinguishes (the others being historical, linguistic, and individual [i.e. what Schleiermacher called psychological] interpretation).

    More recent work on the theory of interpretation that has recognized the essential role played by identifying genre includes E.D. Hirsch, *Validity in Interpretation* (New Haven and London: Yale University Press, 1967), esp. ch. 3; A. Fowler, *Kinds of Literature: An Introduction to the Theory of Genres and Modes* (Cambridge, Mass.: Harvard University Press, 1982), esp. ch. 14; T. Todorov, *Genres in Discourse* (Cambridge: Cambridge University Press, 1990); and M.M. Bakhtin, "The Problem of Speech Genres," in his *Speech Genres and Other Late Essays* (Austin: University of Texas Press, 1986).

24. Cf. Todorov, *Genres in Discourse*, pp. 9–10; Bakhtin, "The Problem of Speech Genres."

25. This was probably in large part because he associated it with *art*—a subject concerning which he was painfully aware of being less well informed and less talented than some of his contemporaries, such as Herder and especially the Schlegels, and which he therefore tended to shy away from. Compare in this respect his relative neglect of the musical features of poetry, such as meter, in his theory of translation.

26. Boeckh, *Encyklopädie*, p. 253.

27. P. Szondi, "Friedrich Schlegel's Theory of Poetical Genres: A Reconstruction from the Posthumous Fragments," in his *On Textual Understanding and Other Essays = Theory and History of Literature*, vol. 15 (Manchester: Manchester University Press, 1986). Cf. the longer discussion in P. Szondi, "Von der normativen zur spekulativen Gattungspoetik," in his *Poetik und Geschichtsphilosophie II* (Frankfurt am Main: Suhrkamp, 1974).

28. *After Herder*, Essay 5.

29. See Szondi, "Friedrich Schlegel's Theory of Poetical Genres," p. 93.

30. See ibid., p. 79.

31. See ibid., pp. 79–81, 85–9.

32. See ibid., pp. 79–81, 85–9.

33. KFSA 15/2:40 ff.

34. For example, Schlegel already writes in 1797: "It is not true that individuals have more reality than genres" (KFSA 18:24). In the *Athenaeum Fragments* (1798–1800), no. 4 he says: "The frequent neglect of the subcategories of genres is a great detriment to a theory of poetical forms" (in F. Schlegel, *Philosophical Fragments*; cf. his advocacy of a refined theory of poetic genres in the *Dialogue on Poetry* [1800]). And a similar emphasis on

the need to identify genres and sub-genres in order to understand literature is found in the Cologne lectures on German language and literature
from 1807 (KFSA 15/2:40 ff.). An analogous position concerning visual
art predominates in his pieces on that subject in KFSA, vol. 4 (though
there are also contrary remarks, for example at p. 74).

35. e.g., Schlegel writes in *Athenaeum Fragments*, no. 434: "The usual classifica-
tions of poetry are mere dead pedantry designed for people with limited
vision . . . In the universe of poetry nothing stands still, everything is developing and changing." Likewise, he says at F. Schlegel, *Literary Notebooks
(1797–1801)*, no. 1880: "All genres of poetry are originally—natural poetry—a particular, local, individual natural poetry . . . The forms are suscep-
tible of an infinite modification." Similarly, in the Cologne lectures on
German language and literature from 1807 he argues for deep differences
between ancient and modern forms of epic, tragedy, and comedy (KFSA
15/2:48–52). He makes an analogous point concerning visual art at KFSA
4:54.

36. See e.g. *On Lessing*, pp. 157 ff., where Schlegel discusses Lessing's *Nathan
der Weise* in this vein. Also, remarks quoted at Szondi, "Friedrich Schlegel's
Theory of Poetical Genres," p. 93. Schlegel's recognition that genres are
sometimes uniquely instantiated often leads him to go as far as to set aside
the notion of genre and instead focus on the individual "ideal" or "idea"
of a work. See e.g. *Literary Notebooks (1797–1801)*, no. 1733: "Criticism is
not to judge works by a general ideal, but is to search out the *individual*
ideal of every work." Cf. similar remarks concerning visual art at KFSA
4:54, 74, 263–7. However, he need not have gone quite that far. He is evidently responding here to a perception that there is a contradiction
between the notion of genre and that of unique instantiation. But as
Boeckh would later point out, there is in fact no such contradiction: the
notion of genre does indeed imply multiple instantia*bility*, but not multiple instantia*tion*. Therefore, when Schlegel recommends focusing on the
individual ideal or idea of a work, a charitable interpretation of his point
could well understand it as a recommendation to focus on the work's
uniquely instantiated genre.

37. See e.g. *Georg Forster*, p. 132: "Demand of Forster's writings each special
virtue of their genre, only not also those of all the others." Cf. similar
points concerning visual art in KFSA, vol. 4.

38. See e.g. *Literary Notebooks (1797–1801)*, no. 224: "Deduction in art must be
preceded by an empirical or historical datum that provides the basis for
classification." Also, *Athenaeum Fragments*, no. 252, where Schlegel writes
concerning a "real aesthetic theory of poetry," or "philosophy of poetry":

"Of course, to the ephemeral, unenthusiastic dilettantes, who are ignorant of the best poets of all types, this kind of poetics would seem very much like a book of trigonometry to a child who just wants to draw pictures. Only a man who knows or possesses a subject can make use of the philosophy of that subject; only he will be able to understand what that philosophy means and what it's attempting to do. But philosophy can't inoculate someone with experience and sense, or pull them out of a hat—and it shouldn't want to do so." Cf. for a similar position concerning visual art KFSA 4:79.

39. A.W. Schlegel, *Course of Lectures on Dramatic Art and Literature* (1809; tr. New York: AMS Press, 1973), esp. pp. 23, 28, 340–1.

40. Cf. KFSA 15/2:86. A.W. Schlegel in his *Course of Lectures on Dramatic Art and Literature* likewise argues for a sharper distinction between epic and tragedy, in particular incorporating a famous and illuminating sculptural analogy: epic is like the frieze but tragedy like the sculptural group. For a more recent version of Friedrich's charge against Aristotle, see S. Halliwell, *Aristotle's Poetics* (Chicago: University of Chicago Press, 1998), pp. 264–5.

41. See KFSA 15/2:48, 160–2, 183. Concerning this point against Aristotle, cf. Halliwell, *Aristotle's Poetics*, esp. pp. 146–8.

42. Friedrich already makes this point in his *History of the Poetry of the Greeks and Romans* (1798). He later repeats it in the Cologne lectures on German language and literature from 1807, where he argues that for the ancient Greeks the mythology and religion that formed the basis of their serious poetry was thoroughly mixed with true history, and that this constitutes a fundamental difference between their genres of serious poetry and our modern counterparts (KFSA 15/2:50–4; cf. pp. 54–8 where he observes that by contrast invention, or fiction, is the very essence of such modern genres as the novel and the fairy tale). He repeats it again even later at *Lectures on the History of Literature*, p. 36.

This radical thesis was and remains highly controversial. In the *Dialogue on Poetry* Friedrich himself makes one of his characters (Antonio) contradict it: "Even ancient tragedy is play, and the poet who presented a true event of serious concern for the entire nation was punished." Nor did August Wilhelm agree with it, instead holding the more conventional view that ancient tragedy was historically fictional in intention. Moreover, a great majority of scholars today would probably still reject the thesis. However, I believe the thesis to be correct. Part of the evidence for this is as follows: (1) Epic poetry was clearly conceived by the poets to contain historical fact made available to them by a divine Muse (see e.g. the openings of both Homer's *Iliad* and Hesiod's *Theogony*, and especially the

Catalogue of Ships in *Iliad*, book 2). (2) Since tragedy developed out of epic, that already warrants a default presumption that tragedy had a similar self-conception. (3) Moreover, two formidable authorities who stand much closer to the great tragedians of the fifth century both in time and in intellectual milieu than Aristotle does clearly understand tragedy to be historically factual in intention, namely Aristophanes (in the *Frogs*) and Plato (in the *Republic*, where his complaint that tragedy is guilty of historical falsehood only makes sense on the basis of such an understanding). For a little more discussion of this whole subject, see my "Herder on Genre" (*After Herder*, Essay 5) and "On the Very Idea of Denying the Existence of Radically Different Conceptual Schemes," *Inquiry*, 44/2 (1998), p. 180 n. 98.

43. Like Aristotle's theory of Greek tragedy's historically fictional intentions, which looks like an all-too-neat response to Plato's accusation in the *Republic* that tragedy is historically false, Aristotle's theory of catharsis can easily look like an all-too-neat response to Plato's accusation in the *Republic* that tragedy harmfully stirs up such emotions as pity and fear. However, I think that in this case there is probably more to Aristotle's position than August Wilhelm allows. For, once the deeply religious, and in particular Dionysiac, nature of tragedy is given its due, a version of Aristotle's theory of catharsis comes to seem quite plausible, namely because Dionysiac rite seems *generally* to have had a cathartic function.

44. August Wilhelm, having considered various natural interpretations of this doctrine and rejected each of them as an aesthetically invalid rule, does eventually come up with an interpretation of it which makes it an aesthetically valid rule (namely, that a tragedy should have a single overall *idea*). However, he does not seem to believe that this is exactly what *Aristotle* meant by it.

45. For a sophisticated recent discussion of Aristotle's supposed doctrine of the unities which basically confirms August Wilhelm's assessment, see Halliwell, *Aristotle's Poetics*.

46. See on this A.O. Lovejoy, "The Meaning of 'Romantic' in Early German Romanticism" and "Schiller and the Genesis of German Romanticism," in his *Essays on the History of Ideas*.

47. *Friedrich Schlegel 1794–1802*, 2:48. Admittedly, Schlegel immediately goes on in the review to *criticize* this application of Herder's standard position concerning different genres, as follows: "But is this proved?—Even if no faultless attempt to divide the field of poetry is yet available, does it follow that this division is therefore altogether impossible?—The method (p. 182) of considering each flower of art *without evaluation* only according to its

place, time, and kind would in the end lead to no other result than that everything should be what it is and was." However, I suggest that these rather hasty criticisms soon faded from Schlegel's mind as the force of Herder's position began to sink in.

Continuing with the subject of possible objections to the interpretation I have given here: It is also true that "classical" and "interesting"/"romantic" are extremely broad, abstract genres, and indeed that Schlegel himself sometimes even denies that romantic poetry is a genre (for example, in the *Dialogue on Poetry* [1800]). However, these facts do not undermine my fundamental point here either; at most they entail that strictly speaking it needs to be cast in terms of Schlegel having drawn from Herder a lesson concerning genres *and types which, though not strictly speaking genres, are genre-like*. In addition, note that Schlegel's change in attitude towards the two sorts of poetry in question also involves a corresponding change in attitude towards what he conceives as their paradigmatic exemplars at the level of genres more strictly so called: respectively, tragic or epic poetry (exemplary of the "classical") and the novel [*Roman*] (exemplary of the "interesting," or "romantic [*romantisch*]"). (For some further discussion of Schlegel's changing attitudes towards tragic/epic poetry and the novel, see Szondi, "Friedrich Schlegel's Theory of Poetical Genres.")

48. G2:525; cf. 520.
49. *Johann Gottfried Herder Sämtliche Werke*, ed. B. Suphan et al. (Berlin, Weidmann, 1877– ), 23:303, 305. (This edition of Herder's works is henceforth abbreviated as S.)
50. KFSA 15/2:41–5.
51. See Szondi, "Friedrich Schlegel's Theory of Poetical Genres," pp. 91 ff.
52. Fowler, *Kinds of Literature*, pp. 106 ff.
53. Ibid., p. 167. A certain interesting complication arises here which may be worth discussing briefly, however. Herder and Fowler tend to assume, somewhat naturally, that the genre must exist before any instances of its mode. However, it seems at least arguable that the necessary temporal priority of the genre to the mode only concerns *possession* of the modal concept rather than *instantiation* of it. Thus, Friedrich Schlegel already suggests, somewhat plausibly, that whereas the *Iliad* is tragic, the *Odyssey* is comic (KFSA 15/2:41: "the *Iliad* tragic, the *Odyssey* comic")—i.e. despite the fact that Homer's works (but not Schlegel!) antedate tragedy and comedy. Likewise, Richmond Lattimore has recently, with some plausibility, characterized the *Iliad* as a tragic epic—on the ground that it focuses on the tragic story of Achilles—again despite the fact that it (but not

Lattimore!) antedates the genre of tragedy. Perhaps the best solution here is a sort of compromise: while there can indeed in a *way*, or a *sense*, be instantiations of modal concepts which antedate the corresponding genre, instantiations which postdate it, and which therefore stand under its influence, are thereby able to instantiate the modal concept in a *pre-eminent* way, or a *stronger* sense.

54. See Szondi, "Friedrich Schlegel's Theory of Poetical Genres," pp. 78, 87.

55. See F. Schlegel's Cologne lectures on German language and literature from 1807, KFSA 15/2:40–2; A.W. Schlegel, *Course of Lectures on Dramatic Art and Literature*, pp. 146 ff., 342–3. For a more recent, though actually less interesting, pursuit of a similar line of thought, cf. M. Meyer, *Le Comique et le tragique. Penser le théâtre et son histoire* (Paris: Presses universitaires de France, 2003), pp. 9–62.

56. See e.g. Meyer, ibid.; C. Guillén, *Literature as System: Essays toward the Theory of Literary History* (Princeton, NJ: Princeton University Press, 1971); and Fowler, *Kinds of Literature*, pp. 251 ff.

57. Cf. no. 325. Also, Schlegel's remark in the *Dialogue on Poetry* (1800) that romantic poetry "does not manifest itself in individual conceptions but in the structure of the whole."

   That a work lends itself to this sort of interpretation is also for Schlegel an important criterion of its *value*. This point could be pursued further, but I shall set it aside here in order to stay focused on the question of interpretation.

58. Cf. R. Haym, *Die Romantische Schule*, p. 327.

59. *Friedrich Schlegel 1794–1802*, 2:426; cf. 426–8, 431. This material is all from the second half of the piece, published in 1801.

60. Cf. Heraclitus, fr. 93: "The Lord who owns the oracle at Delphi neither speaks nor hides his meaning but indicates it by a sign."

61. KFSA 4:134; cf. 23 ff., 94, 263 ff.

62. *Friedrich Schlegel 1794–1802*, 2:431.

63. Cf. M. Frank, *Unendliche Annäherung*, pp. 935–7.

64. Schlegel discusses Leibniz's commitment to it both in his Cologne lectures on philosophy (1804–6) and in his *Lectures on the History of Literature* (1815).

65. *On Goethe's Meister* (1798), in *Friedrich Schlegel 1794–1802*, 2:177.

66. *Athenaeum Fragments*, no. 401. Schlegel usually has linguistic works in mind when he makes this point, but he sometimes extends it to non-linguistic art as well. For example, he writes in no. 444: "It often happens one perceives [musicians] have more ideas in their music than they do about it."

67. *Pace* Behler, *German Romantic Literary Theory*, pp. 277 ff. The points I make here remain true despite the fact that Schleiermacher himself occasionally uses the word "unconscious" in this connection.

68. However, he also has certain specific ways of casting it which are more questionable. In particular, he sometimes conceives this situation not so much in terms of the author having unconscious meanings which he expresses in his text but rather in terms of the text itself having meanings of which the author is unaware (a position that would no doubt find favor with enthusiasts for recent French theories of "the death of the author," but perhaps not correctly). Also, he often conceives these meanings as "infinite" or divine in nature. Concerning these aspects of his position, see Patsch, "Friedrich Schlegels 'Philosophie der Philologie' und Schleiermachers frühe Entwürfe zur Hermeneutik," pp. 456–9.

69. *Course of Lectures on Dramatic Art and Literature*, p. 95.

70. Ibid., p. 88.

71. See esp. F. Nietzsche, *The Gay Science* (New York: Vintage, 1974), pars. 333, 354; *On the Genealogy of Morals* (New York: Vintage, 1967), pp. 57–8, 84–5.

72. Ibid., esp. pp. 34–5. This interpretation of Jesus is quite different from, and I think superior to, Nietzsche's later interpretation of him in *The Antichrist* (1895) as an unworldly "idiot."

73. J. Derrida has aptly criticized certain Freudian readings of literature on the score of such arbitrariness. For a helpful discussion of his criticisms, see Matthew Sharpe's treatment in *Understanding Derrida*, ed. J. Reynolds and J. Roffe (New York: Continuum, 2004), pp. 67 ff.

74. I have in mind here such things as Nietzsche's frequent carelessness about citing evidence, his rhetorical excesses, and his occasional ugly flirtations with anti-semitism.

75. One can now add here the Dead Sea Scrolls.

76. For some further details, see my *Hegel's Idea of a Phenomenology of Spirit* (Chicago: University of Chicago Press, 1998), pp. 36–7 n. 55; and "Genealogy and Morality" (unpublished).

77. KFSA 18:63.

78. *Friedrich Schlegel 1794–1802*, 2:128.

79. KFSA 18:541.

80. Some of my own interpretations of philosophers, and in particular explanations of their inconsistencies, have conformed to this model closely (incidentally, without having Schlegel in mind). See e.g. my *Kant and Skepticism* (Princeton, NJ: Princeton University Press, 2008), esp. ch. 10.

81. *On Incomprehensibility*, in *Friedrich Schlegel 1794–1802*, 2:393.

82. KFSA 18:227.

83. Concerning this implication, cf. KFSA 18:407–10; also, *Friedrich Schlegels philosophische Vorlesungen aus den Jahren 1804 bis 1806*, 1:505.

84. For a sophisticated recent defense of it in Anglophone philosophy, see G. Priest, *In Contradiction* (Oxford: Clarendon Press, 2006).

85. For an argument to this effect, see my *Wittgenstein on the Arbitrariness of Grammar* (Princeton, NJ: Princeton University Press, 2004), ch. 5.

86. For Skinner's commitment to such a principle of interpretation, see his "Meaning and Understanding in the History of Ideas," in *Meaning and Context: Quentin Skinner and His Critics*, ed. J. Tully (Princeton, NJ: Princeton University Press, 1988). Derrida is especially committed to identifying hidden contradictions in the works of philosophers, such as Rousseau and Hegel (this is the core of his method of "deconstruction"). For some specific examples of this approach at work, see his *Of Grammatology, Margins of Philosophy*, and *Writing and Difference*. (Whether his specific examples are correct is, of course, of little if any importance here.)

87. See *After Herder*, Essay 3.

88. Wackenroder and Tieck's indebtedness to Herder and Hamann here is clearest from the first and most seminal of the three works just mentioned, which includes Herder-inspired passages advocating cosmopolitanism and *Einfühlung* (W.H. Wackenroder and L. Tieck, *Herzensergießungen eines kunstliebenden Klosterbruders* [1797] [Stuttgart: Reclam, 2005], pp. 44–7), as well as Hamann-inspired passages that characterize not only art but also the whole of nature as languages through which God communicates meanings (pp. 57–60; cf. L. Tieck, *Franz Sternbalds Wanderungen*, in his *Frühe Erzählungen und Romane* [Darmstadt: Wissenschaftliche Buchgesellschaft, 1963], pp. 890 ff.).

89. Cf. Behler, *German Romantic Literary Theory*, ch. 5.

90. *Friedrich Schlegels philosophische Vorlesungen aus den Jahren 1804 bis 1806*, 2:244–5, cf. 395.

91. KFSA 4:58.

92. Ibid., pp. 15 ff., 23 ff., 57, 75–7, 134, 151, 203.

93. Ibid., pp. 180 ff. Cf. F. Schlegel, *Lectures on the History of Literature*, pp. 190–1.

94. In the *Philosophy of Philology* (1797) he remarks on "the immeasurable difference" that separates us from antiquity, and accordingly writes that "one must insist on the historicism that is necessary for philology" (pp. 16–17).

95. In the *Philosophy of Philology* he praises the art historian Winckelmann for having recognized "the immeasurable difference..., the quite distinctive

nature of antiquity," "the *absolute* difference between the ancient and the modern" (pp. 16, 28). Cf. KFSA 4:54.

96. KFSA 4:149: "The best poets of the Italians, indeed of the Spaniards, in addition to Shakespeare, indeed the old German poems that they can find, and then the newer ones which are most composed in that romantic spirit—let these be the constant companions of the young painter which could gradually lead him back into the old romantic land."

97. Ibid., pp. 263–7.

98. *Literary Notebooks (1797–1801)*, no. 1733: "Criticism is not to judge works by a general ideal, but is to search out the *individual* ideal of every work."

99. KFSA 4:54: "Let one only try to fathom as carefully as possible the individual intention of each work as the artist himself really had it in that ancient time which thought very differently from our own." Cf. pp. 74, 263–7.

100. Ibid., p. 134: "the meaning of the whole which all individual forms only serve and are supposed to express with themselves [*mit*]." Cf. pp. 23 ff.

101. *Athenaeum Fragments*, no. 444.

102. KFSA 4:23 ff.

103. Ibid., pp. 35–7. Schlegel accordingly calls the latter sort of portrait a "symbolic portrait."

104. *Lectures on the History of Literature*, pp. 190–1. Cf. KFSA 4:180 ff.

105. See *After Herder*, Essay 3 and in the present volume Essay 6.

106. See W.H. Wackenroder and L. Tieck, *Herzensergießungen eines kunstliebenden Klosterbruders* (1797), pp. 57–60, 101–2; *Phantasien über die Kunst für Freunde der Kunst* (Stuttgart: Reclam, 1994), pp. 82–3, 99, 104–7, 111.

107. KFSA 4:76. Cf. already *Athenaeum Fragments*, no. 392: "Many musical compositions are merely translations of poems into the language of music."

108. KFSA 4:78. Cf. A.W. Schlegel, *Die Kunstlehre* (Stuttgart: Kohlhammer, 1963), p. 225.

109. KFSA 4:263–4. Cf. Schlegel's unabashedly linguistic exposition of the symbolic meanings of features of the Gothic cathedral, as recently quoted from *Lectures on the History of Literature*, pp. 190–1.

110. There are, admittedly, also a few contrary statements by Schlegel. For example, in *Lucinde* (1799) the main character says at one point, "I want at least to suggest to you in divine symbols what I can't tell you in words" (KFSA 5:58). And later on Schlegel argues at KFSA 4:79 that visual art's vocation is to reveal religion's secrets more beautifully *and clearly* than words can do.

111. See *After Herder*, Essay 3 and in the present volume Essay 6.

112. Concerning these moves in Schleiermacher's aesthetics lectures, see *After Herder*, Essays 10 and 11, and in the present volume Essay 6.

113. As I mentioned in a previous note (no. 25), Schleiermacher was conscious of his inferiority to the Schlegels in the area of aesthetics, and quite rightly so. We have here yet another example of this inferiority to add to the ones already mentioned (i.e. the relative inadequacy of his treatments of genre and of the musical aspects of poetry).

# PART II
# Humboldt

# 3

# Wilhelm von Humboldt

Wilhelm von Humboldt (1767–1835) is in many ways an enigma. His personality combines elements of ruthlessness, even cruelty, with profound humanity. Similarly, his intellectual work combines the vices of derivativeness, turgidity, unclarity, and a failure to complete projects with the virtues of some extremely important ideas. Humboldt's intellectual contributions cover several fields, but he probably deserves to be remembered above all for his work in developing the discipline of linguistics and for his political and educational philosophy. This essay will attempt to provide an overview of Humboldt's life and thought under the following headings:

1. Intellectual Life
2. Philosophy of Language and Linguistics
3. Hermeneutics
4. Translation-Theory
5. Anthropology
6. Aesthetics
7. Political Philosophy
8. Philosophy of Education
9. Philosophy of Religion

## 1. Intellectual Life

Wilhelm von Humboldt (1767–1835) was born at Potsdam. His ancestors had originally been middle class but had risen to the nobility in 1738. His younger brother Alexander von Humboldt was a famous intellectual as well (indeed, during their lifetime, a more famous one), known mainly for his work as an explorer and natural scientist.

Wilhelm became a Prussian statesman of considerable importance. He was also a broad humanist, whose fields of inquiry included philosophy, literature, anthropology, political thought, education, and, above all, language. He was fluent in German, French, English, Italian, and Spanish. In addition, over the course of his career he studied, and wrote about, more than two hundred different languages from all over the world.

He knew most of the leading intellectuals of his time personally, including not only the leading figures of the Berlin Enlightenment, but also Herder, Goethe, Schiller, Friedrich and August Wilhelm Schlegel, Heyne, Georg Forster, Fichte, Jacobi, F.A. Wolf, Madame de Staël, and Coleridge.

His early education was by private tutors, who included several of the leading thinkers of the Berlin Enlightenment (for example, Campe, Klein, Dohm, and Engel). This education covered a broad range of subjects, with special emphasis on the classics. Together with his brother Alexander, he also attended the vibrant Berlin literary salon of Markus and Henrietta Herz as an adolescent. He went on to study at the uninspiring University of Frankfurt an der Oder for a year (1787), but then transferred to the University of Göttingen (1788–9), which was probably the best German university of the time. At Göttingen he mainly studied classical philology, natural science, and Kant's philosophy. (Thus began a lifelong influence of Kant's thought on his own. However, the view taken by Haym, Spranger, Cassirer, and others that this influence was predominant is wide of the mark.[1])

In 1789, shortly after the start of the French Revolution, he visited Paris, keeping a travel journal. As his decision to go to Paris at that time already suggests, his reaction to the Revolution was generally optimistic. Indeed, it remained so even during the Terror of 1793. However, it was also cautious and ambivalent—his reservations stemming partly from a conviction that political reform should preserve continuity with existing institutions rather than prescribing new ones ex nihilo on the basis of reason alone, and partly from an aristocratic aversion to some of the Revolution's more extreme egalitarian tendencies. 1789 was also the year in which he produced his first significant philosophical essay: *On Religion*.

In 1791 he married the wealthy and well-connected Karoline von Dacheröden, to whom he would stay married until her death in 1829. Their marriage was unconventional (especially for the time), since it was sexually open and involved long periods of separation. But it was also intimate, both emotionally and intellectually, among other things generating a rich correspondence. The year 1791 was also the year in which Humboldt wrote his main work in political philosophy: *Ideas towards an Attempt to Fix the Limits of the State's Operation*. This work makes a case for a radical form of liberalism. It was not published during Humboldt's lifetime. However, he did publish a series of journal articles on social and political philosophy closely connected with it in 1792. The work itself was eventually published posthumously in Germany in 1851. Its impact in

Germany itself was (unfortunately) modest, but it had a much bigger impact in Britain, where it strongly influenced both John Stuart Mill and Matthew Arnold.

In 1792 Humboldt stayed near Jena, where he became friends with Schiller and Goethe—thus beginning a lifelong interest in and involvement with their work, as well as an equally enduring preoccupation with aesthetic questions.

In 1793 he wrote one of his most forceful expressions of his classicism, i.e. his profound admiration for the cultures of ancient Greece and Rome, and especially for that of ancient Athens: *Concerning the Study of Antiquity, and of Greek Antiquity in Particular*.

In 1794 he actually settled in Jena for a time, taking an active role in the town's literary life (in collaboration with Schiller and Goethe), and also engaging in some scientific research. In the latter connection, he participated in work on comparative anatomy at the University of Jena, which contributed to his composition of the fragmentary *Plan of a Comparative Anthropology* (1795–7). In 1795 he published two articles on gender difference in a broadly feminist spirit in Schiller's journal *Horen*. To this general period belongs also the fragmentary essay *The Eighteenth Century*, which was an attempt to provide a characterization of Humboldt's own age. Finally, it is likely that the important short essay *On Thinking and Speaking* belongs to this period as well (Humboldt's main editor Leitzmann dates it to 1795–6, though this dating has been disputed). This is Humboldt's first theoretical work on language. Under the evident strong influence of Herder (and in some degree also Fichte), the essay already lays out such fundamental principles of Humboldt's future work on language as the principle of the dependence of thought on language.

During the period 1797–1801 Humboldt lived in Paris. While there he met, and held (largely frustrating) discussions with, some of the leading French intellectuals of the day, including the "Ideologues," as well as studying French theater, literature, and philosophy. This period of his life also included two visits to Spain for the purpose of studying the unique Basque language and Basque culture. Humboldt's work on this subject enabled him to refute existing theories concerning the origin and nature of the Basque language, and to accumulate much new data about it (which he eventually published in 1821). This early research on the Basque language (and culture) was an important step in his development as a linguist.

In 1799 he published his main work in aesthetics, *Aesthetic Essays I: On Goethe's "Hermann and Dorothea"* (a projected second part was never written). He also published a separate version of some of its main ideas in French.

Humboldt had already joined the Prussian civil service in 1790, thus beginning what was to become a long, demanding, and rather illustrious career of government service. However, shortly after joining the civil service he had taken a leave of absence. During the period 1803–8 by contrast he served as Prussian envoy to the Vatican in Rome. His official duties did not prevent him from continuing his intellectual work: while there he did much translation from classical Greek; wrote essays on ancient Greece and Rome; composed his best known poem, the elegy *Rome*; and befriended the head of the Jesuit missions in the Americas, Lorenzo Hervás, a renowned linguist, whose extensive studies of Native American languages he thereby acquired. He subsequently continued his study of the Native American languages, writing the substantial *Essay on the Languages of the New World* in 1812, and going on to explore them further in later years. His work in this area laid the foundations for important work on the Native American languages done later in the nineteenth century, and early in the twentieth, by Brinton, Boas, and others.

In 1808 Humboldt was appointed to the section of the interior ministry in Berlin that dealt with religion and education. His responsibility for religion caused both consternation and amusement among his contemporaries in light of his known coolness towards the subject. However, his main focus was on education. He radically reformed the entire Prussian educational system. This included playing the leading role in the founding of the University of Berlin (now the Humboldt University) in 1810. He based the University on the ideal of a never-ending search for new knowledge, and on the principle of combining research with teaching within a single institution. He thereby established the model for the modern research university in Germany, and indeed in the West generally. He also attempted to make the University financially independent, in order to guarantee its freedom from state interference. However, this led to quarrels with opponents, which eventually forced him to resign.

From 1810 onwards, he served as Prussia's ambassador in Vienna. Following the military defeat of Napoleon, he played a leading role in the complex negotiations that culminated in the Congress of Vienna (1814–15). His role in these negotiations involved much *Realpolitik* (the harder side of his personality should not be underestimated; it also manifests itself in a certain callousness about war, for example). But it also had more idealistic dimensions. In particular, he succeeded in defending Jewish rights, and he also tried, albeit unsuccessfully, to win a liberal constitution for the German confederation based on a *Grundgesetz* that would have guaranteed the rights of the smaller German states and of all citizens.

During the period 1817–18 he served as Prussia's ambassador in London. But in 1819 he returned to Berlin in order to participate in drawing up a new constitution for Prussia. He again tried to achieve a liberal constitution (with a constitutional monarchy), but his attempt again failed. He also tried to resist the repressive Karlsbad decrees that instead came into force at this time, but as a result was dismissed from public service by King Friedrich Wilhelm III. This virtually ended his life in public service (though he would return to royal favor and to less important governmental functions in later years).

He spent most of the rest of his life on his family estate at Tegel near Berlin, devoting his time to study, especially the study of languages. As early as 1820 he presented a plan for a new discipline of comparative linguistics to the Berlin Academy: *On the Comparative Study of Language in Connection with the Various Epochs of the Development of Language*. During this last period of his life he added to his knowledge of particular languages, eventually acquiring familiarity with a huge number (well over two hundred), concerning many of which he wrote special studies. He accomplished this feat largely thanks to an extensive correspondence with other researchers, both in Germany and around the world (for example, Pickering and Duponceau in North America). He also presented a series of further important addresses to the Berlin Academy on the subject of language, including *On the Emergence of Grammatical Forms and Their Influence on the Development of Ideas* (1822), *On the Grammatical Structure of the Chinese Language* (1826; this is a shorter version of a famous long letter that he wrote to the French scholar Abel-Rémusat on the same subject in the same year), *On the Dual* (1827), and *On the Languages of the South Sea Islands* (1828). In addition, he delivered important addresses on other subjects, including *On the Task of the Historian* (1821) and two presentations concerning the Indian poem *Bhagavad-Gita* (1826).

In 1829 his wife Karoline died, which left him emotionally distraught. However, in 1830 he published two substantial pieces on the literature of Schiller and Goethe, thereby continuing his lifelong engagement with their work and with aesthetic matters.

The rest of his life was mainly devoted to a monumental study of the Kawi language of Java. The study considered the Kawi language in the context of the Austronesian family of languages as a whole, and included a famous "introduction" that discussed general principles of linguistics. He completed this "introduction" and the rest of volume one (this material was published in 1836, the year after his death). Two further volumes were edited and published posthumously (appearing in 1838–9). The famous "introduction" was also republished in a slightly modified form as a self-standing work in 1836, at the request of his brother.

Humboldt had died near Berlin in 1835.

## 2. Philosophy of Language and Linguistics

Humboldt's earliest theoretical statement on language, the short essay *On Thinking and Speaking* (probably 1795–6) is strongly influenced by Herder, especially by Herder's *Treatise on the Origin of Language* (1772).[2] The essay is especially noteworthy for its championing of a doctrine, clearly taken over from Herder's *Treatise*, that reflection, or the awareness of objects as distinct from ourselves and our desires, is coeval with our development of language.

Humboldt's mature philosophy of language, as articulated in the famous Kawi-introduction and elsewhere, contains many further borrowings from Herder as well. For example, Humboldt basically subscribes to the naturalistic account of the origin of language that Herder had given in his *Treatise*, according to which language, while it is partly rooted in the "cries of sensation" which human beings share with animals, is also interdependent and coeval with a distinctively human type of "awareness [*Besonnenheit*]."[3] Again, like Herder in his *Treatise*, Humboldt holds that language is essential to the very existence of the human being. Again, like Herder in his *Treatise*, Humboldt holds that language fundamentally and essentially consists in heard sounds. Again, like Herder in his *Treatise*, Humboldt holds that the verb is the most original and fundamental part of language. Again, Humboldt advances a version of the striking doctrine which Herder had first adumbrated in the *Treatise* and then articulated more emphatically in *On the Cognition and Sensation of the Human Soul* (1778) that language—and consequently, also thought, human mental life more generally, and indeed the very self—is fundamentally *social* in nature. Again, Humboldt espouses a doctrine from Herder's *Ideas for the Philosophy of History of Humanity* (1784–91) and other works to the effect that linguistic reference to particulars never takes place directly, but is always mediated by general concepts.[4] Again, Humboldt even espouses the doctrine from Herder's *Ideas* that human language and rationality are intimately dependent on human beings' upright posture.

However, more important than any of the aforementioned debts that Humboldt owes to Herder are four further principles in the philosophy of language which he borrowed from Herder and which then formed the foundation for his own conception of linguistics:

(1) He espouses a version of Herder's doctrine that thought is essentially dependent on and bounded by language—i.e. that one can only think if one has a language and one can only think what one can express linguistically.[5]

(2) He espouses a version of Herder's doctrine that concepts or meanings are constituted—not by referents, Platonic forms, mental "ideas," or whatnot, but—by word-usages.[6]

(3) He also espouses a version of Herder's doctrine that mankind exhibits deep linguistic and conceptual-intellectual diversities, especially between historical periods and cultures, but even to some extent between individuals within a single historical period and culture.

(4) He also espouses a version of Herder's doctrine, stated most explicitly in the *Ideas*, that because of (1) and (2) the investigation of the varying characters of people's modes of thought and conceptualization should primarily take the form of an investigation of the varying characters of their languages.[7]

For Humboldt's greatest contribution to the theory of language, and indeed arguably his greatest intellectual contribution *tout court*, lay in helping to establish the modern discipline of linguistics on the foundation of these four Herderian principles. In doing so he was to a great extent anticipated and influenced by Friedrich Schlegel's seminal work *On the Language and Wisdom of the Indians* (1808).

Let us therefore consider this project further. As has been mentioned, in 1820 Humboldt presented to the Berlin Academy his plan for a new discipline of comparative linguistics: *On the Comparative Study of Language in Connection with the Various Epochs of the Development of Language*. This piece argues that languages constitute concepts and thought, that different languages embody a "diversity in worldviews," and that there is therefore a need to complement the philosophy of language with an empirical investigation of languages. This basic position recurs in Humboldt's best known and most influential work on general linguistics, the famous introduction to his massive study of the Kawi language, also published separately under the revealing title *On the Diversity of Human Language-Structure and its Influence on the Mental Development of Mankind* (1836).

Let me attempt to describe in a little more detail how Humboldt helped to found empirical linguistics on the four Herderian principles recently mentioned. Like Schlegel before him, but to an even greater degree, Humboldt is explicitly committed to those four principles. He argues that it is mainly because of them, and especially (4)—namely, the resulting fact that an investigation of the diversity of languages promises to provide a sort of reliable window onto the diversity of human thought and conceptualization—that one should undertake the empirical investigation of languages. This constitutes his main rationale for the new science of linguistics.

Building beyond that theoretical foundation and beyond Herder, but still broadly following Schlegel, Humboldt adds the following positions:

(a) Contradicting an impression that Herder had usually still given (in continuity with Enlightenment predecessors) that languages are fundamentally aggregates of particular words/concepts, Humboldt embraces a more holistic conception of languages which sees such particular items as only possible in the context of a larger linguistic whole. He often expresses this conception by characterizing languages as "organisms," "systems," or "webs." (Schlegel had already made this move, but only in relation to a subset of languages, namely inflected languages. Humboldt extends it to cover all languages.)

(b) More specifically, he identifies *grammar* as the most fundamental unifying principle of such linguistic "organisms."[8]

(c) Again in contrast to the early Herder—who in his *Treatise* had said that grammar is basically the same across all languages (except for the anomalous case of Chinese)—but in continuity with the later Herder—who in the *Ideas* had instead held that grammatical structure varies greatly across languages—Humboldt sees grammars as differing deeply from one language to another, and as thereby also constituting deep differences in the natures of the particular words/concepts employed within a language (which may also differ for more superficial reasons).

(d) Humboldt consequently identifies the comparative study of grammar as the main task of an empirical investigation of languages.

(e) Besides the fundamental motive already explained of providing a reliable window on the diversity of thought and conceptualization, another important motive behind undertaking comparative grammar which Humboldt emphasizes lies in his conviction that it promises to shed more light on the genealogical relations between languages than merely lexical comparisons can do.

(f) Humboldt greatly advances the process of actually comparing different grammars in an empirically scrupulous way. Schlegel had already taken steps in this direction. But Humboldt goes much further. During the course of his career, he considers well over two hundred languages. These include (Indo-) European languages—among them, ancient Greek, Latin, Sanskrit, the Romance languages, English, Basque (whose modern study Humboldt founds), Old Icelandic, Lithuanian, Polish, Slovenian, Serbo-Croatian, Armenian, and Hungarian; Semitic languages—in particular, Hebrew, Arabic, and Coptic (on which Humboldt writes a grammar); Asian languages—among them Chinese, Japanese, Siamese, Tamil, and the Kawi language of Java (which Humboldt analyzes in his massive three-volume study); the native languages of America; and the languages of the Pacific—in particular, East African languages, Hawaiian, and the languages of the South Sea Islands.

(g) In the course of doing this, Humboldt also complicates the twofold distinction that Schlegel had drawn between, on the one hand, "organic," or inflected, languages (such as Sanskrit), and on the other hand, "mechanical," or uninflected, languages (such as Chinese). Humboldt divides the latter category into two: "isolating" languages (such as Chinese) and "agglutinative" languages (exemplified by some of the native languages of America). Inflected languages work by means of suffixes, prefixes, or stem-modifications which do not by themselves have semantic content; isolating languages lack inflection, and indeed most forms of grammatical marking, instead working mainly by means of word order and context; agglutinative languages function mainly by means of a compounding of elements which (unlike inflecting suffixes, prefixes, or stem-modifications) are independently meaningful (as in the case of the English word "doghouse," for example). For Humboldt these are basically three different linguistic techniques, which may sometimes be found together within a single language, the classification of a whole language as belonging to the one type or the other being a matter of which of these techniques predominates within it.

The principles just described are arguably all correct, and constitute great progress beyond their Herderian starting-point, though only modest progress beyond Schlegel. However, Humboldt also follows Schlegel in embracing an additional principle which is of more questionable value:

(h) Like Schlegel, he draws from his comparative investigation of the grammars of different languages certain strong normative conclusions about the relative merits of different languages as instruments of thought. In particular, he argues for the superiority of highly inflected languages, such as Sanskrit and its relatives, over "isolating" languages, such as Chinese, and "agglutinative" languages, such as those in America. This normative project constitutes yet a third motive behind his enterprise of comparative grammar (in addition to the motives of providing a reliable window on thought and determining the genealogical relationships between languages). However, this part of his position seems very questionable, not only factually but also ethically.[9] On the other hand, it should be noted in his defense that (like Schlegel before him), he was a sincere cosmopolitan, and went to considerable lengths to try to forestall any inference from his differential ranking of languages to an invidious ranking of peoples.

Humboldt also adds another dubious principle, this time one *without* precedent in Schlegel:

(i) Despite his commitment to the principle that there are deep differences between the grammars of different languages (principle (c)), he is also committed to a principle which stands in sharp tension with it, namely that there is a *universal* grammar shared by all languages. Here Humboldt is ultimately influenced by seventeenth-century theories of universal grammar, in particular that of the Port Royal *Grammaire*, and proximally by more recent versions of such theories with which he was familiar, such as Sacy's *Principes de grammaire générale* (1799) and Bernhardi's *Sprachlehre* (1801–3). Humboldt has recently been praised for this side of his position by the linguist Noam Chomsky in his influential book *Cartesian Linguistics*. However, it seems very doubtful that he *should* be praised for it.[10]

Finally, two further principles of Humboldt's general linguistics which again go beyond Schlegel should also be mentioned:

(j) Humboldt famously holds that language is not an *ergon* (a work) but rather an *energeia* (an actualization). What exactly this means is obscure and has been much debated in the secondary literature.[11] But one important aspect of it evidently derives from Fichte's conception that action is prior to things or facts, as a transcendental condition of the possibility of experience (Humboldt was already attracted to this Fichtean conception in his Paris notebooks of 1798). In Humboldt's version of this conception, language plays the role of a transcendental condition of the possibility of a person's experience (it is constitutive of his "worldview"), and its fundamental nature is that of an activity.

(k) Humboldt also holds that every language has a certain "inner form" (involving its grammar and concepts) as well as a certain "outer form" (involving its phonetics). This doctrine is again somewhat obscure, and has again occasioned considerable discussion in the secondary literature.[12] Humboldt evidently models the distinction on Kant's famous distinction in the *Critique of Pure Reason* between the "form of inner intuition" (time) and the "form of outer intuition" (space). A large part of Humboldt's purpose in drawing on that Kantian model is to emphasize that, just as for Kant time and space are wholes which have a certain priority over particular times and places and are not reducible to the latter, so that any knowledge of the latter presupposes knowledge of the former, likewise, a language's whole grammatical/conceptual system and its whole phonetic system are in a sense prior to the particular grammatical/conceptual and phonetic features in which they are manifested, not reducible to them,[13] and the latter can only be properly grasped in light of the former.[14]

Mainly through the influence of Friedrich Schlegel, but with Humboldt playing a significant supporting role, both the close analysis of the grammars of particular languages, such as Sanskrit, and comparative grammar developed rapidly into major fields of scientific achievement in nineteenth-century Germany. For example, August Wilhelm Schlegel became Germany's first professor of Sanskrit. And prominent early practitioners of comparative grammar included Bopp (1791–1867), in his work on the Indo-European languages; Jakob Grimm (1785–1863), in his work on the Germanic languages; and August Wilhelm Schlegel, in his work on the Romance languages.

## 3. Hermeneutics

As a linguist, classicist, literary theorist, and translator, Humboldt was much occupied with questions of interpretation throughout his career.

One of his most striking theoretical positions on this subject—in which he evidently followed Schleiermacher—[15] is that all understanding includes a residue of misunderstanding, and is therefore never more than approximate.

However, Humboldt's most important contribution to the theory of interpretation rather concerns the bearing of interpretation on the human sciences, especially history. This contribution is mainly found in his essay *On the Task of the Historian* (1821). There he develops the following positions. (1) He conceives the task of the historian as above all one of discovering what actually happened (rather than explaining it). (2) He rejects apriorist approaches to history, such as those of Kant and Hegel. (3) He instead advocates an empirically based approach to it. (4) More specifically, he conceives the historian's main task as one of *understanding* the *ideas* at work in history (rather than discovering causal laws that govern history). (5) He conceives such understanding as requiring the interpretation of people's particular (linguistic) expressions as parts of larger wholes, and therefore advocates the sort of shuttle-cock alternation between parts and wholes in interpretation that Herder and Schleiermacher had already seen as the key to accomplishing that.

These positions all have deep roots in Herder and Schleiermacher. For example, positions (1)–(5) all reflect features of Herder's approach to history. And positions (4) and (5) in addition reflect principles from Schleiermacher's hermeneutics.

Humboldt's positions in the essay would later be taken over and developed further by such important historians and historiographers as Ranke, Droysen, and Dilthey. The essay was especially important as a source of this later tradition's sharp distinction between *understanding* [*Verstehen*], as the characteristic method of history and the other human sciences, and *explanation* [*Erklären*], i.e. explanation in terms of causal laws, as the characteristic method of the natural sciences.

## 4. Translation-Theory

Humboldt was both a practicing translator and a theorist of translation. Indeed, his very first publication, in 1787, consisted of a set of translations (from Xenophon and Plato). And his early essay *Concerning the Study of Antiquity, and of Greek Antiquity in Particular* (1793) already contained theoretical reflections on translation.

In that essay he distinguished between several different goals that translations may serve, and between different characters that translations need to have in order to serve those goals; and he argued that, while in its more mundane forms translation should be lax, in its higher forms it should strive for both semantic and musical fidelity.[16]

During his 1803–8 stay in Rome he translated a number of Pindar's *Pythian* and *Olympian Odes*, Aeschylus' *Agamemnon*, and various other works (strikingly difficult material). When he eventually published his translation of the *Agamemnon* in 1816 he included an introduction in which he laid out his theory of translation in some detail. Eduard Fraenkel, the brilliant twentieth-century scholar of the *Agamemnon*, has described "the translation and even more so the introduction" as "a great monument of the deeper understanding of Greek poetry and art."

The main lines of the mature theory of translation that Humboldt presents in the introduction are as follows: (1) Translation faces the challenge of coping with aesthetic and especially conceptual divergence (except in connection with merely physical vocabulary). (In *On the Bhagavad-Gita* [1825] Humboldt adds that this entails that translation can only ever be an approximation.) (2) But translation remains indispensable, both because it provides access to works for people who lack the original language and because it enriches the target language. (3) One key to achieving optimal translation lies in exploiting the mutability of each language; in fact, any language can be made to express any thought. (In *On the Bhagavad-Gita* [1825] Humboldt adds that this requires translating one-word-for-one-word wherever possible.) (4) Another key to achieving optimal translation lies in the possibility of imitating the music of the foreign language (in particular its meter). This is important because such music expresses an author's sentiments with more immediacy and nuance than can be achieved by words alone, and is indeed fundamental to the intellectual, and even the moral-political, standpoint of the author and his nation. The ancient Greeks were especially, indeed uniquely, subtle in their use of rhythm. The poet Klopstock and the translator-poet Voss have already shown the way for translators in this area by successfully imitating Greek meters in German. (5) Overall, a translation should contain a touch of the foreign, but should avoid outright strangeness. It should not be willfully obscure, but nor should it make clear and easy what was already obscure in the original.[17] (6) The competing notion that the translator should furnish what the author would have written had he written in the target language is illegitimate, since no author could have written what he wrote in another language. (7) Attempts at the optimal sort of translation that Humboldt recommends can serve as stepping stones to even better attempts. (8) There is also an advantage to having multiple translations of a given work, since this provides readers with multiple images of the work.

This theory for the most part reproduces the theory of translation that Herder had already adumbrated in the *Fragments on Recent German Literature*

(1767–8) and that Schleiermacher had developed more systematically in *On the Different Methods of Translation* (1813) (just three years before Humboldt published his introduction, note).[18] Although Humboldt does not actually name Schleiermacher, his debt to the latter's essay seems clear from the chronology and from the striking similarity of the positions involved.[19] This similarity extends even to such fine points of detail as the alleged exemption of vocabulary for physical objects from the problem of conceptual divergence.[20] (As has already been mentioned, Humboldt is also indebted to Schleiermacher in the closely related area of hermeneutics.[21])

## 5. Anthropology

Humboldt played an important role in the birth of the modern discipline of cultural or social anthropology.

His essay *Plan of a Comparative Anthropology* from around 1795–7 (I suspect the later date) is of some significance in this connection. For it champions a project that had been sketched by Herder in the 10th Collection of his *Letters for the Advancement of Humanity* (1793–7) (and other places) of developing, in a spirit of cosmopolitan respect for the Other, a comprehensive, empirically grounded investigation of the various peoples of the world in their cultural distinctiveness.[22] However, the role of this particular essay of Humboldt's in the birth of modern cultural anthropology was not great. For the term "Anthropology [*Anthropologie*]" in its title is to some extent a false friend (in modern German, cultural anthropology is not *Anthropologie* but *Ethnologie*); the essay is only in part concerned with topics relevant to cultural anthropology; and it was not published until 1903, by which time it seems to have attracted little attention.

Instead, Humboldt's main contributions to the birth of modern cultural anthropology took three other forms (again all deeply rooted in his Herderian inheritance):

(1) His role in establishing the understanding/explanation distinction and in identifying understanding as the primary task of the human sciences was of seminal importance not only for the historians and historiographers Ranke, Droysen, and Dilthey, but also, and largely through them, for the founders of modern cultural anthropology. A central case in point here is Franz Boas, the father of American anthropology. As George Stocking and Matti Bunzl have shown, the distinction in question already underlies Boas's early article *The Study of Geography* (1887), and the conception that understanding rather than explanation is the primary task of anthropology became increasingly pronounced as Boas's career proceeded. Similarly, the founder of British anthropology (as a

discipline grounded in intensive fieldwork), Bronislaw Malinowski, strongly emphasized understanding over explanation, especially in his anthropological practice.

(2) Humboldt was also a seminal influence on the emergence of the discipline of *Völkerpsychologie*—a discipline founded by Lazarus and Steinthal, and then developed by Wilhelm Wundt. Both the discipline's basic project of exploring different peoples' collective psychologies in their distinctiveness from each other and its emphasis on the investigation of languages as the primary means for achieving that were largely inspired by Humboldt. The discipline of *Völkerpsychologie* went on to play a fundamental role in the birth of modern cultural anthropology—strongly influencing both the founder of American anthropology, Boas, and the founder of British anthropology, Malinowski (who had studied with Wundt in Leipzig, and had even begun writing a dissertation on *Völkerpsychologie*).

(3) Humboldt's work in linguistics also provided direct inspiration to the founders of modern cultural anthropology, who praise and imitate it in connection with the linguistic side of their own anthropological work. In particular, both Boas's seminal investigations of the languages of the native Americans and Malinowski's seminal investigations of the language of the Trobriand islanders (in *Coral Gardens and their Magic*) are avowedly continuous with Humboldt's linguistic work.[23]

## 6. Aesthetics

Humboldt's main work in aesthetics is his *Aesthetic Essays I: On Goethe's "Hermann and Dorothea"* from 1799 (as previously mentioned, he also published an essay in French at the same period which discusses some of the same topics). In part this work is a detailed interpretation of a particular poem by Goethe, his modern epic *Hermann and Dorothea*. But in part it is also a broader exploration of issues in aesthetics.

The work is in some ways rather conservative and old-fashioned, especially when compared with the pathbreaking work that the Schlegels were doing at this period. For one thing, it assumes that epic poetry enjoys a high status as a modern genre, and by contrast speaks rather disparagingly of the novel—this at a time when epic poetry was actually in its death throes as a genre and the novel in ascent, and moreover the Schlegels were beginning to provide a theoretical recognition of, and rationale for, that fact. For another thing, in continuity with the previous generation of German theorists of literature (for example, Lessing and Herder), Humboldt uncritically accepts Aristotle's theory of the nature of ancient tragedy as a genre (for example, Aristotle's thesis that tragedy's function is to arouse pity and fear, and thereby to purge/purify those emotions)—this at a time when the Schlegels were beginning to call Aristotle's theory into question with great cogency, a process which would continue subsequently with Nietzsche's *The Birth of Tragedy* and with twentieth-century scholarship.

However, Humboldt's work also contains a number of more original and interesting ideas. First and foremost, it develops a new and distinctive theory of the very nature of artistic production (a theory much more in the spirit of Humboldt's German Romantic contemporaries than his views on epic poetry, the novel, and tragedy).[24] A long tradition, reaching back at least as far as Plato and Aristotle, had identified the function of art as an imitation of nature, and had conceived the artist's faculty of imagination as serving to reproduce (while perhaps also recombining) what the artist had previously found in his sensory experience of nature (this was still the basic picture in Humboldt's important French predecessor Condillac, for example).[25] Humboldt breaks sharply with that tradition. For him, the imagination is a faculty that *destroys* pre-existing ways of experiencing the world and instead creates *new* ones. And the function of art is not to imitate reality but instead to transcend it in a process of such imaginative creativity: the poet's art "consists in his ability to render the imagination creative."[26] In this respect, Humboldt's aesthetics is part of the Romantic revolution.[27]

Second, but less importantly, Humboldt also develops a mildly interesting general theory of literary genres. One component of the theory is an insistence (very much in the spirit of Herder) that any evaluation of a work of literary art must be undertaken strictly in terms of the standards set by its own genre. Another component is a systematic attempt to define each genre, and to do so mainly in terms of a specific *mood* that distinguishes it.[28] Here Humboldt's primary model is evidently Aristotle's association of tragedy with pity and fear. Humboldt's main concern in his own work is to extend such an account to cover the case of epic poetry. In that connection, he identifies the relevant mood as, roughly, one of lively, sensuous, objective observation (or more elaborately: lively sensuous activity, enthralled interest, disinterested composure, and a comprehensive view). How promising such an approach to genre may be remains questionable.

Beyond literature, Humboldt's interest in art was rather limited. This is largely due to the fact that unlike some of his Romantic contemporaries (for example, Friedrich Schlegel), he tends to deny that music and visual art express meaning.[29] Such a position limits the value of his aesthetic theory.

One final point worth noting in connection with his aesthetics is that, in addition to developing the distinctive theory of the imaginative creation of works of literary art described above, he also sometimes models his ethical ideal of *Bildung*, or individual self-cultivation, on such artistic creation.[30]

## 7. Political Philosophy

Early in his career, in 1791, Humboldt wrote his most important work on political philosophy: *Ideas towards an Attempt to Fix the Limits of the State's Operation*.[31] This work is a passionate plea for liberalism and for a correspondingly minimal state (though its last chapter does also accord the state a positive function). In particular, the work champions the value and importance of individuality, and criticizes state control of education and religion for the constraint that it imposes on the free development of individuality. Both the work's principle of individuality and its advocacy of a minimal state echo Herder.

Humboldt's work was not published until 1851. As a result, its influence within Germany was slight. However, it eventually had a much stronger impact in Britain, where it influenced John Stuart Mill and Matthew Arnold among others.

Concerning Mill: Humboldt's work appeared in an English translation in 1854. Mill began writing *On Liberty* in 1854, publishing it in 1859. Both in *On Liberty* itself and in his *Autobiography* (1873) Mill pays warm tribute to Humboldt's work and to its influence on his own. In *On Liberty* he especially acknowledges his debt to Humboldt's central principle of *individuality*. However, the impact of Humboldt's work on his own clearly also went well beyond the principle of individuality itself. The following account of Humboldt's work will incorporate some parenthetical remarks about this broader impact on Mill.

Humboldt argues that the flourishing of individuality requires freedom of action: "that on which the whole greatness of a human being in the end rests, for which the individual human being must strive eternally, and which he who wants to affect human beings may never lose sight of, is individuality [*Eigentümlichkeit*] of force and culture," and "this individuality is effected through freedom of action."[32] (Mill in *On Liberty* likewise appeals to the principle of individuality in order to justify maximal freedom of action.)

Humboldt also argues that "every effort of the state is to be rejected to interfere in the private affairs of the citizens anywhere where they do not have immediate relation to the injury of the rights of the one person through the other,"[33] and that "to punish actions which bear solely on the agent or happen with the consent of the person they affect is forbidden by just the same principles which do not even permit them to be limited; and therefore, not only may none of the so-called crimes of the flesh (except rape), whether they annoy or not, attempted suicide, etc. be punished, but even the murder of another person with his consent would have to remain unpunished were it not that in this last case the too easy possibility of a dangerous misuse made a punishing law necessary."[34] In the roughly contemporary essay *On Improving Morals by Means of State Institutions* (1792) Humboldt in particular argues that the state must not try to inculcate morality, pointing out that doing so is not only self-defeating but also tends to stifle the sensuous forces that create everything remarkable.[35] (Similarly: Mill in *On Liberty* famously articulates what he calls the "one very simple principle" which it is "the object of this essay...to assert," namely "that the sole end for which mankind are warranted, individually or collectively, in interfering with the liberty of action of any of their number, is self-protection. That the only purpose for which power can be rightfully exercised over any member of a civilized community, against his will, is to prevent harm to others. His own good, either physical or moral, is not a sufficient warrant." Mill disallows treating mere annoyance to others—in contrast to actual harm—as a ground for interference: "There are many who consider as an injury to themselves any conduct which they have a distaste for, and resent it as an outrage to their feelings... But there is no parity between the feeling of a person for his own opinion, and the feeling of another who is offended at his holding it." And Mill includes consensual acts between more than one person in the protected sphere: this sphere is one "comprehending all that portion of a person's life and conduct which affects only himself, or if it also affects others, only with their free, voluntary, and undeceived consent and participation.")

Humboldt also in his work champions freedom of thought and expression, developing several arguments in its support. First, under Herder's influence, he argues for freedom of thought and expression on the grounds that it is required in order for there to be the sort of competition between opposing views that produces the discovery and refinement of truth. He writes that part of the "harm of limiting freedom of thought" concerns "the results of inquiry," "incompleteness or incorrectness in our scientific cognition."[36] Again like Herder before him, he recognizes that ancient Athens constitutes powerful empirical evidence for such a dependence of intellectual advances on freedom of thought and expression, since this was a society that was both strongly committed to such freedom and the source of extraordinary intellectual advances.[37] (Mill would later repeat this first argument for freedom of thought and expression in *On Liberty*, but would fail to exploit Herder and Humboldt's compelling example of ancient Athens.)

Second, again in continuity with Herder, Humboldt argues that realization of the ideal of individuality requires not only freedom of action but also freedom of thought and expression. Specifically, he argues that free inquiry is vital for

producing "self-activity," "autonomy" in thought and action,[38] and that individ-
ualities require a free reciprocal self-revelation to, and influencing of, each other
for their development.[39] (This second line of argument again reappears in Mill's
*On Liberty*, albeit less prominently than the first.)

Third, again in continuity with Herder, Humboldt argues that freedom of
thought (and expression) is required for the sort of autonomy in decision-making
that is a precondition of genuine moral virtue (or for that matter, vice); so that,
because genuine moral virtue is of immense positive value, freedom of thought
(and expression) is so as well. Thus, as we just saw, in the work from 1791 he argues
that free inquiry is essential for producing "self-activity" and "autonomy" in
thought and action. And in *On Religion* (1789) he had already argued more elaborately that freedom of thought (and expression) is vital for generating reflection,
self-consistency, and deep grounding in the principles that guide our actions, as
well as for self-activity as opposed to reliance on foreign authority; that in these
ways it is essential for moral character; and that, since people's very raison d'être
lies in the development of moral character, freedom of thought (and expression)
is therefore of vital importance as well.[40] (Mill in *On Liberty* articulates an argument along similar lines in the course of paying tribute to Humboldt.)

Two further aspects of Humboldt's liberalism, found mainly in other works,
deserve mention as well. One of these is his commitment to the rights of Jews.
In an official memorandum from 1809, *On the Plan for a New Constitution for the
Jews*, he argues forcefully for immediate and full emancipation of the Jews in
Prussia (i.e. for according them exactly the same legal rights as Christians). In
the course of doing so, he condemns racial thinking in general as misguided,
arguing that one should instead focus on the qualities of individuals; and he
condemns widespread prejudices against Jews in particular as empirically base-
less and pernicious.

Another additional aspect of his liberalism is a certain feminism. In two early
essays which he published in 1795—*On the Difference between the Sexes and Its
Influence on the Organic Nature* and *On Masculine and Feminine Form*—he argues
that the highest form of human cultivation can only be achieved by combining
the qualities of the male and the female, and that ideal physical beauty likewise
requires a balance of the characteristic features of both sexes. Elsewhere he
champions a relationship of equality and openness between man and wife.[41]
This sort of feminism was also developed in one form or another by several of
the Romantics, especially Friedrich Schlegel and Schleiermacher.

Nor was Humboldt's broad liberalism merely theoretical or ephemeral. On
the contrary, he lived by his liberal principles throughout his life. He was by no
means a perfect human being (for example, the biographical record includes a
few casual anti-semitic remarks, and he had recurrent impulses to dominate

women, on which he sometimes acted by having relations with prostitutes and in other ways). But what is more striking is the earnestness and persistence with which he tried to live up to his liberal principles. One example of this is his championing of a liberal constitution for the German federation at the Congress of Vienna in 1814–15, and then again for Prussia in 1819—in the latter case, despite encountering strong opposition, and with the eventual result that he was dismissed by the king. Another example is his forceful attempt in 1810 to secure for the University of Berlin an independent financial base that would free it from state interference, an attempt that he made despite incurring much opposition and eventually being forced to resign as a result. Another example is the fact that—after finding himself in the ironic and uncomfortable position of being responsible for government censorship in 1808—he wrote an official memorandum on freedom of the press in 1816 in which he argued for abolishing government censorship, and for instead placing regulation of the press in the hands of the law courts. Another example is his strong (albeit unsuccessful) championing of Jewish rights in Prussia in the official memorandum *On the Plan for a New Constitution for the Jews* from 1809, as well as his strong (and more successful) championing of Jewish rights as Prussia's representative at the negotiations leading up to and including the Congress of Vienna. Another example is his liberal, egalitarian, open, and caring relationship with his wife (as reflected in their correspondence, for instance).

Turning from domestic politics to international politics, another important component of Humboldt's political philosophy, again continuous with Herder's, is a strong commitment to cosmopolitanism—i.e. to the moral dignity of, and the need to respect, all humankind in all its variety. Humboldt already articulates this ideal in fragmentary writings from 1795–7. He also often expresses it in his linguistic works (e.g. *On the Diversity of Human Language Structure* [1827–9] and *On the Languages of the South Sea Islands* [1828]). It is also reflected in the very scope of his fascination with languages, which extends far beyond his native Germany and Europe to include, and indeed especially focus on, the native languages of America, the Far East, and the Pacific region.

One particularly noteworthy aspect of his cosmopolitanism, again continuous with Herder, is his strong opposition to the notion that there are deep racial differences between human beings.[42] In his view, such racial differences as occur only involve superficial physical traits, such as skin color, so that they are quite unlike the differences between animal species, which include distinct psychological and behavioral traits; and human beings should therefore above all be considered as individuals (albeit linguistically-culturally shaped ones).[43] Accordingly, he is highly critical of racism, especially as it occurs in the slave-trade and in anti-semitism.[44]

Admittedly, his cosmopolitanism stands in tension with other features of his thought. In particular, his ranking of languages, which places inflected Indo-European languages at the top, but the isolating language of China and the agglutinative languages of America lower down, involves a certain Eurocentrism, as does his frequent praise of ancient Greek language and culture as the most perfect of all. Nonetheless, his cosmopolitanism is deeply sincere.[45]

One final noteworthy point in the area of political philosophy concerns Humboldt's attitude towards his own political activity, and in particular towards its occasional failures. Already quite early in his career he encountered in classical sources, and himself adopted, a principle that the most important thing is to act in certain ways, rather than to attain the purpose of one's action.[46] Moreover, one of the things that most attracted him to the Indian poem *Bhagavad-Gita* in the 1820s was a similar principle that he found there. His commitment to this principle throws considerable light on his idealistic, dogged, but also fatalistic attitude towards his own political activity.

Such an attitude might appear chillingly self-centered—and a similar impression can arise in connection with Humboldt's commitment to individual *Bildung*, or self-cultivation.[47] Accordingly, several commentators have gone as far as to accuse Humboldt of narcissism (e.g. Kaehler and Henningsen). However, in both connections closer inspection of his position tends to allay such concerns. For it is also an important part of his principle concerning political activity that by acting politically in an appropriate, even if unsuccessful, way one sets a good example for other people to follow (his own version of the principle is in this respect closer to the classical versions of it that he encountered first—for example, the version implied by Herodotus's account of the conduct of the Spartans at Thermopylae—than to the version in the *Bhagavad-Gita*). Similarly, his commitment to individual *Bildung* is as much a concern about other people's *Bildung* as about his own, and he conceives his own *Bildung* as a way of setting others a good example to follow.[48]

## 8. Philosophy of Education

Humboldt not only theorized about education, but also put his theories into practice when he found himself appointed to the section of Prussia's interior ministry responsible for education in 1808.

Already in *Ideas towards an Attempt to Fix the Limits of the State's Operation* (1791) he takes a hostile stance towards *state* education. And in an essay published shortly afterwards, *On Public Education by the State* (1792), he elaborates on that negative stance, arguing that education by the state is inimical both to freedom and to diversity. Accordingly, when he wrote an official memorandum concerning the founding of the University of Berlin in 1809, one of his central proposals was to establish the financial independence of the university from the crown by means of a land grant.

The reform of the educational system that he began in 1808 was thoroughgoing, affecting all levels of education. At the primary school level he was sympathetic with the gradualist and liberal educational methods of the Swiss educator Pestalozzi. At the secondary school level, he reformed the *Gymnasium* in such a way as to put greater emphasis on classical languages and literatures. This did not exclude other subjects, but it did tend to marginalize both religion and natural science. The rationale for this reform lay partly in his conception of the fundamental role that language plays in relation to thought together with his belief in the superiority of the classical languages (see on this *Essay on the Languages of the New World* [1812]), and partly in his broader ideal of *Bildung*, or self-cultivation, which motivated turning to the classical world as an outstanding ethical model (see on this *Concerning the Study of Antiquity, and of Greek Antiquity in Particular* [1793] and *History of the Fall and Demise of the Greek Free States* [1807–8]). His reforms also pursued the ideal of *Bildung* at the university level. Accordingly, he rejected the sort of vocational and utilitarian conception of university-level education that predominated in France. Instead, his positive model of the university comprised three central components: (1) A commitment to the freedom of the university—including not only the sort of financial freedom from the state that has already been mentioned, but also freedom in the modes of activity and interaction open to faculty and students. (2) A commitment to an endless search for new knowledge, rather than merely a propagation of already-acquired knowledge, as the central function of the university. (We tend to take this ideal for granted today, but that is largely because of Humboldt's massive influence. The ideal was in fact grounded in some rather distinctive features both of the German culture of his day—for example, Lessing's famous preference for a search for truth over its possession, and the Romantics' conception that the human condition in regard to knowledge is one of "endless approximation [*unendliche Annäherung*]"—and of his own personal style of academic work, as exemplified by his self-consciously endless research on languages for instance.) (3) A commitment to combining research with teaching within the same institution—a model which Humboldt cogently argues not only produces the best teaching but is also more productive for research than the alternative of the purely research-oriented academy.

Humboldt's educational theory and reforms exercised enormous influence on the future course of German education and, especially at the university level, of Western education generally. Their influence has in the main been extremely beneficial. But they have also had certain negative consequences—for instance, a tendency to elitism due to the retention of education in private hands;[49] and a tendency to accord insufficient weight to the natural sciences.

## 9. Philosophy of Religion

Humboldt was not a very religious person. Indeed, compared to most of his contemporaries he had relatively little sympathy with or interest in religion per se. He had much more interest in religion's relation to the state, though.

Ironically, Humboldt's first publication was concerned with religion: *Socrates and Plato on the Deity, Providence, and Immortality* (1787). This work mainly consists of translations from Plato and Xenophon. But it also conveys Humboldt's own position on religion at this early period: a standard Enlightenment sympathy with natural religion based on common sense and reason, combined with a hostility towards both fanaticism and skepticism.

With time Humboldt's own views on religion became more skeptical, however. His most systematic discussion of the subject occurs in *On Religion* (1789). There he holds that the propositions of religion cannot be demonstrated (for example, he was entirely skeptical of Moses Mendelssohn's supposed proof of God's existence), and that they are instead purely matters of faith, and "entirely subjective."[50] He also argues that morality is quite separable from religion.[51] Somewhat later, in a letter to Brinkmann from October 22, 1803 he rejects such religious propositions as the existence of God and human immortality in an even more decided way.[52]

The mature Humboldt was not *entirely* without religion, though. He was certainly not a Christian. But, like his friend Goethe, he had considerable sympathy with paganism. This can already be seen from *Latium and Hellas* (1806), for example.[53] Some verses that he wrote in about 1815 are also revealing:

> Ich bin ein armer heidnischer Mann,
> Der die Kirchen nicht leiden kann;
> Ich leb' in der alten vergangenen Zeit,
> Drum wähle ich mir die Einsamkeit.
> [I am a poor heathen man,
> Who churches cannot stand;
> I live in ancient times long gone,
> Hence I opt to be alone.][54]

Similarly, in *On the Task of the Historian* (1821), while he avoids using conventional religious terms such as "God," he does nonetheless posit a vaguely conceived "governance of the world [*Weltregierung*]."

Concerning religion and the state, Humboldt already in *On Religion* argues forcefully that the state must not seek to impose religion on its citizens. This liberalism, which he subsequently repeats in *Ideas towards an Attempt to Fix the Limits of the State's Operation* (1791), is perhaps his most emphatic and important principle in connection with religion. His advocacy of complete emancipation of the Jews is one significant aspect of it.

# Notes

1. For a helpful corrective, see M.L. Manchester, *The Philosophical Foundations of Humboldt's Linguistic Doctrines* (Amsterdam and Philadelphia: John Benjamins, 1985), esp. ch. 1.

2. Concerning the influence of Herder's *Treatise* on the essay, cf. H. Gipper and P. Schmitter, *Sprachwissenschaft und Sprachphilosophie im Zeitalter der Romantik* (Tübingen: Gunter Narr, 1985), p. 62, and the secondary literature cited there (especially that by Lauchert, Sapir, and Menze); also, H. Gipper, *Wilhelm von Humboldts Bedeutung für Theorie und Praxis moderner Sprachforschung* (Münster: Nodus, 1992), pp. 77 ff., 108–9.

3. Cf. R. Haym, *Wilhelm von Humboldt. Lebensbild und Charakteristik* (Berlin: Gaertner, 1856), pp. 493 ff.

4. W. von Humboldt, *On Language: On the Diversity of Human Language-Structure and its Influence on the Mental Development of Mankind* (Cambridge: Cambridge University Press, 1988), pp. 83–4: "Even for [external physical objects] the word is not the equivalent of the object that hovers before the sense, but rather the conception thereof through language-production at the moment of finding the word. This is a notable source of the multiplicity of expressions for the same objects; and if in Sanskrit, for example, the *elephant* is now called the twice-drinking one, now the two-toothed one, and now the one equipped with a single hand, as many different concepts are thereby designated, though always the same object is meant." This doctrine strikingly anticipates, and may well have influenced, Frege's sense/referent distinction, and his position that reference to particulars is mediated by senses which take the form of definite descriptions.

5. Humboldt even borrows some of his verbal formulations of this doctrine from Herder. For example, Herder had written in his *Treatise* that "language turns out to be a natural organ of thought"; likewise, Humboldt writes in the Kawi-introduction that "language is the forming organ of thought."

6. For example, he writes in the preface to his translation of Aeschylus' *Agamemnon*: "A word is so little a sign for a concept that the concept

cannot arise, let alone be held fast, without the word" (*Wilhelm von Humboldts Gesammelte Schriften* [henceforth WHGS], ed. A. Leitzmann et al. [Berlin: B. Behr, 1903–], 8:129).

7. As Herder puts it in the *Ideas*: "The finest essay on the history and the diverse character of the human understanding and heart...would be a *philosophical comparison of languages*: for a people's understanding and character is imprinted in each of them" (G6:353).

8. For a detailed discussion of Humboldt's conception of languages as "organisms," see R.L. Brown, *Wilhelm von Humboldt's Conception of Linguistic Relativity* (The Hague/Paris: Mouton, 1967), ch. 3. It is important to note that for Humboldt the application to language of the concept of an "organism"—as of other biological concepts (e.g. relationship and descent)—is self-consciously metaphorical.

9. For details, see Essay 4.

10. For further discussion, see Essay 4.

11. See e.g. Gipper and Schmitter, *Sprachwissenschaft und Sprachphilosophie*, pp. 90–1.

12. See e.g. ibid., pp. 86 ff.

13. Cf. Humboldt's frequent counterintuitive-sounding claim that a language can only emerge *all at once*.

14. For an early expression of this sort of picture of language, see WHGS 3:296: "One does not reach the actual essence of language by any dissection, however complete it might be. It is like a breath that surrounds the whole, but, too fine, loses its form for the eye in the individual element, just as the mist of the mountains only has shape from a distance but when one enters it swirls shapelessly."

15. Schleiermacher and Humboldt both lived in Berlin and knew each other well. See Gipper and Schmitter, *Sprachwissenschaft und Sprachphilosophie*, pp. 96–7.

16. WHGS 1:280.

17. It is noteworthy in this connection that Humboldt's own translations—for example, his translations from the *Bhagavad-Gita*—are often quite radically foreignizing.

18. Concerning the Herder–Schleiermacher theory, see *After Herder*, Essays 4 and 12.

19. As I mentioned in a previous note, Humboldt and Schleiermacher both lived in Berlin and knew each other well.

20. This point of agreement is especially striking because it seems to contradict Humboldt's earlier position in *Latium and Hellas* (1806) that there are

differences in meaning between the words *hippos, equus,* and *Pferd* (WHGS 3:170).

21. Noting these clear debts to Schleiermacher in Humboldt's hermeneutics and translation theory answers a question about intellectual influence between the two men posed but left open by Gipper and Schmitter at *Sprachwissenschaft und Sprachphilosophie,* pp. 96–7.

22. For a later expression of a similar vision by Humboldt, see his 1812 prospectus for a work on the Basque people and language (WHGS 3:288 ff.), which puts more emphasis than the *Plan* on the central role of language in such an investigation.

23. For more on Humboldt's role in the founding of modern cultural anthropology, see *After Herder,* Essay 6.

24. Concerning the Romantics' version of the theory, see E. Fiesel, *Die Sprachphilosophie der Deutschen Romantik,* pp. 9 ff.; E. Behler, *German Romantic Literary Theory,* pp. 202–3, 302–3; also, M.H. Abrams, *The Mirror and the Lamp* (New York: Oxford University Press, 1953).

25. For a detailed discussion of this tradition, see Abrams, *The Mirror and the Lamp.*

26. As K. Müller-Vollmer argues in *Poesie und Einbildungskraft: Zur Dichtungstheorie Wilhelm von Humboldts* (Stuttgart: Metzler, 1967), Humboldt's theory has Fichtean roots (his Paris notebooks from 1798 show that he was an enthusiast for Fichte's views at this period).

27. In a later re-statement of the theory Humboldt adds another characteristically Romantic theme: directedness towards the Infinite. See WHGS 5:335–7.

28. There had already been precedents for such a theory in Sir William Jones and J.G. Sulzer. See Abrams, *The Mirror and the Lamp,* pp. 87–9.

29. See e.g. *On Language,* pp. 159–61.

30. See e.g. *History of the Fall and Demise of the Greek Free States* (1807–8), at WHGS 3:198.

31. For further discussion, see *After Herder,* Essay 7.

32. WHGS 1:107.

33. Ibid., p. 111.

34. Ibid., p. 207.

35. Cf. ibid., pp. 57 ff.

36. Ibid., p. 160.

37. Already in *On Religion* (1789) he had written, somewhat hyperbolically, that the ancients had enjoyed "unlimited freedom of thought, boundless tolerance" (WHGS 1:51).

38. WHGS 1:160.

39. Ibid., pp. 122–3, 128. A similar argument would later be developed more elaborately by Schleiermacher in *Toward a Theory of Sociable Conduct* (1799).

40. WHGS 1:73–6.

41. See e.g. WHGS 3:159–60.

42. *Pace* Hans Aarsleff's characterization of him as a racist in his linguistic theories.

43. See esp. *On the Diversity of Human Language Structure*, at WHGS 6:196–203; and Humboldt's writings against anti-semitism, in particular *On the Plan for a New Constitution for the Jews*.

44. See again the two texts cited in the preceding note.

45. It is perhaps also worth mentioning that, like Herder, Humboldt even extends his sphere of moral concern beyond human beings to include animals. See WHGS 1:14 n.

46. See e.g. *Latium and Hellas* (1806), at WHGS 3:154.

47. For an early statement of this commitment, see WHGS 1:69, where Humboldt presents individual *Bildung* as the highest purpose of the state and legislation.

48. See e.g. *Concerning the Study of Antiquity, and of Greek Antiquity in Particular* (1793), at WHGS 1:281; cf. 284.

49. Elitist tendencies also occur at certain other points in Humboldt's thought, for example in his championing of the rights of—often oppressive—local aristocracies in connection with constitutional questions.

50. WHGS 1:64–6, 68.

51. Ibid., pp. 67 ff., 70, 73.

52. *Wilhelm von Humboldts Briefe an Karl Gustav Brinkmann*, ed. A. Leitzmann (Leipzig: Karl W. Hiersemann, 1939), pp. 155–7.

53. WHGS 3:151–7.

54. WHGS 9:90.

# 4

# Herder, Schlegel, Humboldt, and the Birth of Modern Linguistics

In this essay I would like to try to sketch an account of the origins of the modern science of linguistics. All three of the thinkers mentioned in the title—Herder, Friedrich Schlegel, and Wilhelm von Humboldt—played important roles in the birth of the new discipline. However, it was Herder who laid the foundations, and after him it was Friedrich Schlegel who played the most pivotal role, namely in his *On the Language and Wisdom of the Indians* (1808). By contrast, Wilhelm von Humboldt's contributions, while significant, were less fundamental. And they were also to some extent counterbalanced by more dubious positions that he adopted.

This essay will begin with a historical overview. It will then focus on the main positive contributions made by Schlegel and subsequently refined by Humboldt. Finally, it will consider two further lines of argument due to Schlegel and especially Humboldt which are of more questionable value.

## I

Let me begin by sketching, perforce a little dogmatically, the main steps in the early development of the new discipline, as I see them.

Herder laid the discipline's foundations with the following four principles:

(1) Thought is essentially dependent on and bounded by language—that is, one can only think if one has a language, and one can only think what one can express linguistically.

(2) Meanings or concepts consist (not in the sorts of items, in principle autonomous of language, with which much of the philosophical tradition has equated them—for example, things referred to, Platonic forms, or the mental "ideas" favored by the British Empiricists and others, but instead) in word-usages.

(3) Mankind exhibits profound differences in modes of thought, concepts, and language, especially between different historical periods and cultures.[1]

(4) Because of principles (1) and (2), investigating the differences in the characters of people's languages can, and should, serve as a primary and reliable means for discovering the differences in their modes of thought and concepts.[2]

In *On the Language and Wisdom of the Indians* (1808) Friedrich Schlegel essentially took over this set of positions. He is vague about his commitment to doctrines (1) and (2) in the work itself. But it is clear from both earlier and later works. For example, already in 1798–9 he writes that "every spirit has its word, the two are inseparable";[3] in the Cologne lectures on philosophy from 1804–6 he intimately associates reason with language (in Herder's manner),[4] and states that "each concept must be a word";[5] and in the Cologne lectures on German language and literature from 1807 he opens by saying that language is fundamental to all human activities because "one cannot think without words."[6] Likewise in the *Lectures on the History of Literature* (delivered in 1812, published in 1815), he says:

What is there more completely characteristic of man or of greater importance to him than language? Reason alone excepted, and even she must perforce employ the vehicle of language . . . Reason and language, thought and word, are . . . essentially one.[7]

Concerning his commitment to doctrine (3), he had already written in the *Philosophy of Philology* (1797), for example, of "the immeasurable difference . . . , the quite distinctive nature of antiquity."[8] And doctrine (4) is the implicit foundation of his procedure in *On the Language and Wisdom of the Indians* of undertaking an investigation of the Sanskrit language in the first part of the work as a prelude to then exploring Indian thought and conceptualization in subsequent parts. Indeed, doctrine (4) constituted the most important motive for the new science of linguistics: the science was supposed to provide a reliable window on people's varying modes of thought and conceptualization.[9]

However, in *On the Language and Wisdom of the Indians* Schlegel also built on this inherited Herderian foundation in some original ways. The following are his main additions:

(a) Whereas Herder, like much of the Enlightenment before him, had usually given the impression that languages were merely aggregates of particular words/concepts, Schlegel develops a more holistic conception of languages which sees such particular items as only possible in the context of a larger linguistic whole—a conception he expresses by characterizing languages as "organisms" or "systems." (Strictly speaking, he restricts this conception to what he calls "organic," i.e. inflected, languages, though.)

(b) He identifies as the most fundamental unifying principle of such linguistic "organisms" their *grammar*.

(c) The early Herder of the *Treatise on the Origin of Language* (1772) had implied at one point that grammar was inessential to language in its more original and natural forms, being merely a product of the late theoretical oversophistication of grammarians,[10] and at another point (somewhat inconsistently) that grammar was basically the same across all languages (with the exception of Chinese).[11] In contrast, the later Herder of the *Ideas for the Philosophy of History of Humanity* (1784–91) had argued that languages differ dramatically in their grammatical structures: in addition to exhibiting rich variety in *other* ways, "in the structure [*Bau*] of language, in the relation, the ordering, and the agreement of the parts with each other, it is almost immeasurable."[12] Rejecting the early Herder's position but accepting this position of the later Herder, Schlegel argues that grammars differ deeply in their character from one language to another, and thereby constitute deep differences in particular words/concepts as well (which may also differ for more superficial reasons).[13]

(d) Schlegel consequently identifies "comparative grammar" (an expression and concept that he virtually introduces for the first time in *On the Language and Wisdom of the Indians*)[14] as the primary task of an empirical investigation of languages.

(e) Besides the fundamental motive already mentioned above of providing a reliable window on different modes of thought and concepts, another important motive behind this project of comparative grammar which Schlegel emphasizes lies in his conviction that it promises to shed more light on the genealogical relations between languages than merely lexical comparisons can do.[15]

(f) Schlegel himself begins the process of actually comparing different grammars in an empirically careful way. In doing so, he introduces the following broad typology: a contrast between, on the one hand, "organic," or highly inflected, languages, of which Sanskrit is his main example, and on the other hand, "mechanical," or uninflected, languages, of which Chinese is his main example.[16] He also demonstrates the genealogical relations between the various Sanskritic (or as we would now call them, Indo-European) languages with greater cogency and accuracy than had ever been achieved before.[17]

(g) In addition, he draws from this comparison of grammars certain normative conclusions concerning the relative merits of different languages as instruments of thought—in particular, arguing for the superiority of highly inflected languages such as Sanskrit and its relatives over uninflected languages such as Chinese. His main case for the superiority of the former over the latter lies in a claim that inflected languages have a privileged connection with "awareness

[*Besonnenheit*]," or rationality. This whole aspect of his position is much more dubious than the preceding ones, not only factually but also ethically. However, it should at least be noted that he is himself innocent of ethnocentric motives here (his own ethical orientation is instead decidedly cosmopolitan; indeed, one of the main purposes of his book is to show that Europe and Asia are "one large family," as he actually puts it), and that he takes considerable pains to try to forestall any inference from his normative ranking of languages to an invidious ranking of peoples.

Friedrich Schlegel's *On the Language and Wisdom of the Indians* (1808) quickly inspired a whole wave of important work based on the same general principles. This wave centrally included Bopp's *On the Conjugation System of the Sanskrit Language in Comparison with That of the Greek, Latin, Persian, and Germanic Languages* (1816), which focused on the Indo-European languages and their grammars;[18] Friedrich's brother August Wilhelm Schlegel's Sanskrit studies, and *Observations on Provençal Language and Literature* (1818), which focused on the Romance languages and their grammars; and Jakob Grimm's *German Grammar* (1819), which focused on the Germanic languages and their grammars. Friedrich Schlegel's principles also soon inspired the general linguistics of Wilhelm von Humboldt, which the latter developed mainly in a series of public addresses and unpublished manuscripts that he wrote during the 1820s and in his crowning work *On the Diversity of Human Language-Structure and its Influence on the Mental Development of Mankind* (1836).[19]

## II

As a contributor to general linguistics (in contradistinction to specialized empirical work in linguistics) Humboldt was the most important of these successors.

Humboldt essentially took over not only Herder's doctrines (1)–(4) but also Schlegel's doctrines (a)–(g). In the works of Humboldt's just mentioned he is clearly committed to versions of Herder's doctrines (1)–(4) (indeed, his commitment to them is even clearer than Schlegel's).[20] Moreover, he takes over all of Schlegel's doctrines (a)–(g), albeit with modifications: He takes over doctrine (a)—but generalizes it to cover all languages (not only "organic" languages). He also takes over doctrine (b). He also takes over doctrine (c)—though his commitment to it stands in uneasy tension with a continued commitment to the older conception of a *universal* grammar. He also takes over doctrines (d) and (e). He also takes over doctrine (f)—but elaborates on it, in particular by contrasting the category of inflective languages, not merely with a single category of "mechanical" languages, but with the two categories of "agglutinative" languages (exemplified by some of the Native American languages) and "isolating" languages (such as Chinese).[21] Finally, he also takes over doctrine (g) in all of its essential parts.[22]

Humboldt's borrowings from Herder and Schlegel arose through several channels. These included: (i) direct acquaintance with Herder's work; (ii) direct acquaintance with Schlegel's *On the Language and Wisdom of the Indians* (and thereby indirect acquaintance with Herder's ideas as well); and (iii) direct acquaintance with relevant work by August Wilhelm Schlegel, Bopp, and Grimm (and thereby indirect acquaintance with both Friedrich Schlegel's and Herder's ideas as well).

Concerning (i), Humboldt met and corresponded with Herder, and was familiar with a broad range of Herder's publications.[23] In particular, Humboldt's student notes show that he already knew Herder's *Treatise on the Origin of Language* in the 1780s.[24] Indeed, Humboldt's first essay concerning language, *On Thinking and Speaking* (1795–6),[25] clearly echoes Herder's *Treatise*—for example, in advancing a doctrine that our awareness of objects as distinct from ourselves and our desires is coeval with our development of language.[26] Moreover, Humboldt's mature theory of language echoes a plethora of further Herderian doctrines (in addition to the one just mentioned and doctrines (1)–(4)).[27]

Concerning (ii), Humboldt explicitly discusses Schlegel's *On the Language and Wisdom of the Indians* with warm approval (albeit also some criticism). For example, he does so in *On the Grammatical Structure of Languages* (1827–9).[28]

Concerning (iii), Humboldt explicitly discusses the works of August Wilhelm Schlegel, Bopp, and Grimm with warm approval as well (albeit again mixed with some criticism). For example, he does so at many points in the Kawi-introduction.

By contrast, there is little reason to suppose that Condillac or the Ideologues exercised a strong positive influence on Humboldt's core positions—as Hans Aarsleff has proposed, citing Humboldt's stay in Paris during the late 1790s and early 1800s.[29]

## III

The development from Herder to Schlegel to Humboldt that has just been sketched represented dramatic intellectual progress in many respects, but in other respects was of more equivocal value, or even regressive. Let us take a closer look at it, beginning with the positive side of the story, the dramatic progress.

Schlegel's positions (a)–(f) (that is, all of them except (g)) had a seminal, enduring, and invaluable impact on the development of linguistics. His most important insight here was that—contrary to Herder's early position in the *Treatise* according to which languages are merely aggregates of individual words/concepts, and grammar is either inessential or else basically invariant across languages (a position which in Schlegel's view is only true of "mechanical" languages at best), but conformably with Herder's late position in the *Ideas* that languages vary greatly in their grammatical structures—languages are of their very nature systems, in particular systems constituted by grammars, and these systems moreover differ profoundly from case to case, especially in virtue of having very different grammars.

This insight produced a certain deepening of Herder's standard picture that thought and concepts essentially depend on language, and consequently vary as the latter varies, and that it is therefore possible and desirable to access the former in their variety in a reliable way by means of a close examination of the latter in *their* variety. In Herder's initial version of that picture, for example at the time of the *Fragments* and the *Treatise*, it essentially applied just at the level of *individual lexical* items. By contrast, for the Herder of the *Ideas*, then for Schlegel following his lead, and for the tradition of linguistics that they together founded, while it does apply at that level, (i) that level itself already involves complex systematic interrelationships between particular words/concepts which are internal to the identities of each concept, differ deeply from language to language, and therefore need to be identified as part of the examination of languages that is to disclose the varying nature of thought and concepts.[30] Moreover, and perhaps even more importantly, (ii) the picture also applies at the deeper level of *grammar*, where the sharp differences that occur between languages also constitute further dimensions of difference at the lexical level.[31]

Humboldt played an important role by continuing and further developing this whole new position. Concerning principle (i), he generalized Schlegel's account of languages as "systems" or "organisms" to cover *all* languages, and therefore extended principle (i) to include all languages without exception. In addition, he provided much more explicit and sophisticated demonstrations of the sorts of systematic interrelationships in question, and of their distinctiveness to particular languages, than Schlegel had yet achieved. This can be seen by comparing Schlegel's very rudimentary attempts at such demonstrations in *On the Language and Wisdom of the Indians* with Humboldt's much more developed attempts in his essays on the *Bhagavad-Gita*, for instance.[32]

Concerning principle (ii), Humboldt introduced a whole series of refinements (or at least, arguable refinements). The first of these again consisted in an extension of Schlegel's relevant points to *all* languages. Schlegel had essentially

confined his points concerning grammar to "organic," or inflected, languages—
seeing "mechanical," or uninflected, languages as instead approximating to the
model of language as a mere aggregate of words/concepts that had been
espoused by more traditional theories. In contrast, Humboldt came to hold that
the points in question applied without exception, since even languages which
initially seemed to work in the latter, merely aggregative way, such as Chinese,
in fact had a form of grammar governing all their parts (in this particular case,
a form of grammar heavily dependent on word-order and context).

Humboldt's second refinement concerned the *rationale* for holding that
grammar is just as essential to language as individual words/concepts, and also
that it is internal to the character of the latter. Schlegel had not provided much
of an argument here at all. By contrast, Humboldt does. His case turns on a
principle that had already been articulated by, and that he probably borrowed
from, Kant: that it is the *sentence* rather than the word that constitutes the fundamental unit of language, since this is the smallest unit that can perform a
linguistic task.[33] According to Humboldt, a sentence cannot be formed simply
by aggregating words/concepts; they also have to be *related together* in a certain
way by the language-user.[34] And it is grammar that constitutes the form of such
relating.[35] According to Humboldt, this not only makes a grammar just as essential to a language as its lexical component, but it also makes the grammar internal to the lexical component, so that variations in the former will ipso facto
constitute variations in the latter.[36] That is not a trivial inference; for it would
not be logically inconsistent to hold that concepts require grammar in order to
serve their function in sentences, and that grammars vary, but that such variations do not affect the character of the concepts involved. However, the inference does seem plausible on empirical grounds—that is, it does seem empirically
plausible to say that differences in grammar between languages normally produce corresponding differences in the concepts of the languages (at least subtle
ones). Compare, for example, languages whose grammars require gender mark-
ings for nouns with languages whose grammars do not.[37]

Humboldt's third refinement concerns Schlegel's typology of languages/gram-
matical principles. In *On the Language and Wisdom of the Indians* (1808) Schlegel
had basically just set up the twofold distinction already mentioned: "organic," or
inflective, vs. "mechanical," or non-inflective. His brother August Wilhelm, in
*Observations on Provençal Language and Literature* (1818), developed that twofold
distinction into a threefold distinction: inflective vs. affixive (or agglutinative) vs.
grammarless. (August Wilhelm's specific examples included: Sanskrit vs. certain
Native American languages and Basque vs. Chinese, respectively.) Humboldt
essentially took over this threefold distinction. However, in doing so his role was
not merely passive. For one thing, he had himself contributed to distinguishing

the new middle category through his own early work on Basque (a point which August Wilhelm himself makes explicitly in the book just mentioned).[38] For another thing, Humboldt reconceives August Wilhelm's third category as "isolating" rather than truly grammarless. For yet another thing, Humboldt makes the theoretically important move of coming to regard the three types in question as primarily types of *linguistic mechanism* rather than types of whole languages— types of linguistic mechanism which can only be used to distinguish between whole languages in a secondary and approximate way, namely according to the extent to which particular languages tend to rely more on one of these types of linguistic mechanism than on the others.[39] It may well be that this threefold scheme requires still further elaboration, but if so, it seems likely that the required elaboration will build on it rather than abandoning it altogether.[40]

Humboldt's fourth refinement lies in the much greater empirical breadth and precision with which he investigated and characterized different languages in this spirit. Schlegel's empirical knowledge of languages was impressive for its day, but it did not compare with Humboldt's. Humboldt was eventually able to draw on a knowledge of over two hundred different languages from around the world, many of which he knew thoroughly, as well as on a rich body of empirical analysis of language that had been done in the intervening period by August Wilhelm Schlegel, Bopp, Grimm, and others.

Humboldt's fifth arguable refinement concerns a principle that had already been implied by Friedrich Schlegel: that the grammatical structure of a person's language virtually *determines* the general character of his thought and concepts.[41] Humboldt focuses much more on this question than Schlegel had done, and he complicates Schlegel's position concerning it. Sometimes Humboldt himself tends to advocate such a determinism—albeit while emphasizing that it only concerns the *general character* of thought and concepts, leaving the individual much freedom within that framework.[42] More often, though, he tends to speak against the idea that there is any strong form of determinism here—in particular, insisting that the converse influence, namely of thought on language, is possible and occurs as well;[43] that one can acquire new modes of thought and conceptualization by acquiring new languages;[44] and that any language can be made to express any thought.[45] A similar equivocation reappears later in the writings of Boas and Sapir, who were both heavily influenced by Humboldt.[46] It can be argued that Humboldt performed an important service by focusing on this difficult issue and complicating it in the ways just mentioned.

Humboldt's sixth arguable refinement lies in a famous thesis he advances to the effect that different languages, especially in virtue of differences in their grammars, constitute different "worldviews [*Weltansichten*]."[47] His claim here is in part just that the (lexical and) grammatical differences between languages constitute cognitive differences, differences in the thoughts, concepts, etc. which people entertain (i.e. a claim we have already considered). But it is also in part that such (lexical and) grammatical differences and the cognitive differences they constitute produce differences in *perception* (the perceptual word *-ansicht* now functioning in a more literal sense than in the former case).[48]

This whole position, originally invented by the later Herder and Schlegel and then developed further by Humboldt, led to some of the most important work in twentieth-century linguistics. Principle (i) (the principle of semantic holism at the lexical level configured differently across different languages) formed the basis for the theory of the "semantic field" that was developed early in the twentieth century by Trier and Weisgerber (in explicit continuity with Humboldt).[49]

Principle (ii) formed the core of what has come to be known as the "Sapir-Whorf hypothesis"—i.e. roughly, the hypothesis that the different characters of different languages produce different types of thought/conceptualization (which can be explored by investigating the former). For what is distinctive about this hypothesis is the double picture of linguistic variation not only at the lexical level but also at the *grammatical* level producing different types of thought/conceptualization.[50] For example, one of Whorf's most interesting illustrations of the hypothesis concerns the fact that the "tense" structure of Hopi verbs turns out to be strikingly different from that of Indo-European languages, in that the "future tense" in Hopi is in fact used indiscriminately both for events which we would ourselves classify as future events relative to the speaker and for events which we would instead classify as involving something like the imperceptible in its striving towards manifestation, regardless of their temporal location relative to the speaker.[51] The "Sapir-Whorf hypothesis" emerged in the linguistic work of Boas, Sapir, and Whorf,[52] all of which stands in a direct line of descent from Humboldt (and thereby also Schlegel and ultimately Herder).[53]

Both the theory of the "semantic field" and the "Sapir-Whorf hypothesis" remain controversial today. However, it seems likely that both are correct in some form.[54]

## IV

The preceding section identified some ways in which the transition from Herder to Schlegel to Humboldt represented important progress. However, in other ways the transition was of more equivocal value or even regressive. In this and the following section I would like to discuss two such ways. Let us begin with a case in which the transition was of equivocal value.

Herder had not really been interested in *ranking* languages.[55] In particular, he had not been interested in doing so on the basis of differences in their grammars.[56] Indeed, his normal position concerning cultures generally (including their linguistic foundations in particular) had been hostile to any ranking—largely on the grounds that a ranking would require overlooking the facts that different cultures achieve similar goals by different means, and especially that different cultures have different goals.[57]

In sharp contrast, Schlegel, and then following him Humboldt, drew from their comparative investigation of the grammars of languages some strongly differential normative conclusions concerning the relative merits of languages as instruments of thought (see (g) above). In particular, they both argued for the superiority of highly inflected languages, such as Sanskrit and its relatives, over uninflected languages, such as Chinese. Indeed, as I mentioned, along with the two motives of providing a window on the thought and conceptualization of other peoples and discovering the genealogical relationships between languages, this normative project constituted a third main motive behind their enterprise of comparative grammar.

Schlegel and Humboldt's normative project already encountered sharp criticism, on both factual and ethical grounds, during their lifetime, especially from two of Humboldt's correspondents in America: Pickering and Duponceau.[58] And the Boas-Sapir-Whorf tradition in American linguistics subsequently continued this rebellion against it.[59]

In the specific form that Schlegel and Humboldt had given it, their normative ranking of languages does indeed seem objectionable, on both factual and ethical grounds. Let us consider some of its factual weaknesses first, then some of its ethical ones.

Concerning the facts: Schlegel's case for the superiority of inflected languages such as Sanskrit over uninflected languages such as Chinese mainly consists in a combination of sheer wonderment at the supposed marvel of developed inflection, together with a claim that inflected languages have a privileged connection with "awareness," or rationality, which uninflected languages lack. However, this is all very dubious. Concerning the supposed marvel of developed inflection, why should one not rather see Chinese's great versatility in using more minimal, uninflected materials as an equal or even greater marvel?[60] And the claim of a special connection between inflection and "awareness," or rationality, seems groundless.

Humboldt's case for a differential ranking is considerably more sophisticated, but still quite dubious. It is interesting to note in this connection that in some of his earlier work, such as the *Essay on the Languages of the New World* (1812), he himself seems to have been more inclined to take a Herderian position: languages are indeed deeply and fascinatingly different, but not better or worse than each other.[61] Why did he turn away from this position towards sharing Schlegel's conception of a sharply differential ranking?

Sometimes Humboldt's case is that whereas inflected languages such as Sanskrit establish just the right sort of relationship between concept and grammar, namely a co-manifestation of both in the morphology of a word, with the concept dominating in the stem while the grammar plays a perceptibly distinct role in the inflecting prefix, suffix, or stem-modification, "isolating" languages such as Chinese fail to manifest grammar in the morphology of words at all, and at an opposite extreme agglutinative languages allow grammar to fuse with and dominate concept in the morphology of a word/sentence.[62] However, even if one were to grant the descriptive part of this case, it is difficult to see why the middle course assigned to inflected languages here should be regarded as a "Goldilocks" formula, rather than simply as one of three equally viable ways of proceeding. For example, as Humboldt himself virtually concedes at points in his *Letter to Monsieur Abel-Rémusat* (1826), it seems attractive to say that inflected languages like Sanskrit simply accomplish by means of inflection a very similar set of tasks to those that an isolating language like Chinese accomplishes just as well by such different means as fixed word-order and a heavier reliance on context.

Sometimes Humboldt's case is that marking grammatical relations in the morphology of words, as inflected languages do, is superior to failing to do so, in the manner of Chinese for example, because it facilitates the flight of thought, making more elaborate sentences and thoughts possible.[63] However, this line of argument is rather plausibly contradicted by Humboldt's generally very positive assessment of Chinese language and thought;[64] as well as by his observation that the diminution of inflection in the course of the development of the Indo-European languages (compare Sanskrit with modern English, for example) has *facilitated* thought, thereby contributing to modern Europe's outstanding intellectual achievements.[65]

Sometimes Humboldt's case instead consists in assuming that some particular explicit feature of Indo-European grammar is implicitly universal, and then faulting a non-Indo-European language for not realizing it explicitly (for example, the expression of relations by means of inflection, a clear morphological or syntactic distinction between verb and noun, a sharp distinction between word and sentence, or even the placing of the verb between the subject and the object).[66] However, his assumption of the implicit universality of the feature in question is in most cases quite implausible.

Sometimes his case instead turns on criticizing certain distinctive features of non–Indo–European grammars (and semantics) as dysfunctional. However, his criticisms tend to show insufficient sensitivity to the possibility, and indeed likelihood, that the distinctive mode of life, or social context, within which the features in question occur might in fact make them functional. For example, in *On the Dual Form* (1827) he implicitly criticizes languages in which the third-person singular pronoun always specifies posture or distance from the speaker. But this criticism invites the response that such an economical inclusion of the sort of information in question within the pronoun might be very useful in a society that lives by hunting or warfare, i.e. activities which put a premium on quick communication of this sort of information. Again, in the Kawi-introduction he criticizes Chinese for extending the word "son" to compound kinship words which connote juniority irrespective of direct descent or gender.[67] But this criticism invites the reply that, given certain social structures and practices, such an extension might very well serve a positive social function, for instance that of promoting a certain form of social solidarity.

In short, while Humboldt tries hard to make a case for his differential ranking of languages according to their grammars, his arguments are unconvincing.

Besides thus being factually dubious, the sort of ranking of languages that Schlegel and Humboldt both propose is also ethically dubious, in that it can easily encourage (and eventually did encourage) an invidious ranking of peoples themselves. Neither Schlegel nor Humboldt was himself guilty of ethnocentric or xenophobic motives, at least not at a conscious level. On the contrary, Schlegel was committed to a cosmopolitan respect for the Other throughout his career; indeed, part of his purpose in *On the Language and Wisdom of the Indians* was to show that Europe and Asia are "one large family" (as he actually puts it), whose literatures should be treated as a single whole. Similarly, Humboldt was committed to cosmopolitanism throughout his career. Indeed, his very project of investigating languages from all over the world reflects that cosmopolitanism, and he often expresses his cosmopolitan values explicitly in the course of his linguistic works (e.g. in *On the Diversity of Human Language Structure* [1827–9] and *On the Languages of the South Sea Islands* [1828]). Moreover, both Schlegel and Humboldt took considerable pains to try to forestall the inference from their ranking of languages to an invidious ranking of peoples. Among the specific points that Humboldt makes in this connection are the following: having a language at all is a great achievement; languages only differ in the *degree* to which they fall short of the inflective ideal; even if one people's *language* is inferior to another's, this deficit may be counterbalanced or outweighed by its *other* intellectual virtues; and every language can be made to express any thought.[68]

Still, the Schlegel-Humboldt ranking of languages easily lends itself to invidious and pernicious ideological uses. And it could even be argued that at an unconscious level Schlegel and Humboldt were to some degree complicit in this.

To this extent the sort of rejection of the Schlegel-Humboldt project of ranking languages that characterizes the American tradition in linguistics and anthropology seems justified. On the other hand, the general idea that different languages may be differentially effective as vehicles for thought is by no means an intrinsically foolish one. And I want to suggest that it would be a mistake to dismiss it hastily with a dogmatic neo-Herderian insistence that all languages are just equally good, as the Boas-Sapir-Whorf tradition rather tended to do.[69]

What, then, can be salvaged from the Schlegel-Humboldt notion of a ranking of languages as vehicles of thought? As we have seen, in the specific form they gave it, it largely rested on dubious aesthetic preferences and metaphysical conceptions concerning language (Schlegel), together with oversight of the possibility that similar goals might be achieved equally well by different linguistic means, disregard of the possibility that the goals served by languages may themselves differ, and dubious assumptions concerning implicit linguistic universals (Humboldt). However, it seems likely that certain sorts of differential rankings of languages that avoid these pitfalls may still be warranted. Indeed, on reflection, this seems obviously true at the lexical-semantic level. For example, a "primitive" society which develops technological aspirations similar to those of more "advanced" societies will certainly need to add some technical terms/concepts to its existing linguistic resources which the latter societies already have. But the point may well also apply at the grammatical level. For example, A.H. Bloom has argued with some plausibility that grammatical peculiarities of Chinese make it more difficult for Chinese speakers to entertain counterfactual thoughts than it is for speakers of Indo-European languages, thereby inhibiting certain forms of scientific thought.[70]

This position promises to steer between the Scylla of the dubious Schlegel-Humboldt position and the Charybdis of a dogmatic neo-Herderian egalitarianism: It promises to be more factually realistic than either. It also promises to avoid the pernicious ethical consequences of the Schlegel-Humboldt position, and to be more consonant with their cosmopolitan ideals. This is so for two main reasons. First (*pace* the Schlegel-Humboldt position), the sorts of lexical and grammatical superiorities/inferiorities that are in question here are local ones within a language, rather than global ones affecting a whole language; consequently, language X might be lexically or grammatically inferior to language Y in one area, but equal or superior to language Y in another area (or other areas). Second (*pace* Schlegel, but in continuity with a principle of Humboldt's), there is nothing in such a position to prevent a language that is currently inferior in some lexical or grammatical respect from developing or adding lexical/grammatical forms in the future in order to make up the deficit in question.


# V

Let us now turn to what is arguably the most striking example of outright regress in the transition from Herder to Schlegel to Humboldt. The person guilty of this regress is Humboldt.

It is probably in general true to say that modern scholarship has tended to exaggerate Humboldt's importance for the science of linguistics at the expense of Herder and Friedrich Schlegel. For one thing, as we have seen, after Herder had laid the foundations, it was Schlegel who first developed the pivotal ideas of the new discipline; Humboldt's role was not to invent but only to refine. For another thing, during the nineteenth century, when the science of linguistics was being developed, Humboldt's contribution was largely a backwater. The central tradition of the discipline instead ran directly from Herder and Friedrich Schlegel to Bopp, August Wilhelm Schlegel, and Grimm (all of whose seminal publications in linguistics preceded Humboldt's, which only appeared in the 1820s and 1830s), and thence without any detour via Humboldt to the most important work done in linguistics later in the century, for example by Schleicher.[71] It was really only in the twentieth century that Humboldt came to enjoy great influence and prestige in linguistics—with Boas, Sapir, and Whorf; the neo-Humboldtian "semantic field" theorists Trier and Weisgerber; Saussure; Bloomfield; and most recently Chomsky.[72]

But there is also another respect in which modern scholarship has tended to exaggerate Humboldt's importance for linguistics at the expense of Herder and Friedrich Schlegel. This concerns Humboldt's most striking departure from their position: the fact that he not only continues, and indeed develops, the thesis already adumbrated by Herder in the *Ideas* and then elaborated by Schlegel in *On the Language and Wisdom of the Indians* that there are deep grammatical differences between languages, but also, in sharp tension with doing so, retains a form of the seventeenth-century doctrine that there is a *universal* grammar innate to, and shared by, all human beings.

In *Cartesian Linguistics* and other works Noam Chomsky has emphasized this aspect of Humboldt's position, warmly endorsed it, and closely identified it with his own theory of an innate universal "generative grammar."[73]

Most of the secondary literature on this subject in German has been deeply hostile to Chomsky's account. But the bulk of the criticism that has been

offered has focused on disputing Chomsky's *interpretation* of Humboldt's position.[74] Now, there are certainly many points of detail in Chomsky's interpretation that can be faulted—for example, his implausible identification of
Humboldt's conception of a language's "inner form" with the generative grammatical rules posited by his own linguistics.[75] However, Chomsky's fundamental
interpretive claim that, like himself, Humboldt is committed to the existence,
not only of particular grammars, but also of a universal grammar innate to all
human beings is beyond serious question.[76] The main problem with Chomsky's
account is not an *interpretive* one. Rather, it lies in his *approval* of this side of
Humboldt's position. For the theory of an innate universal grammar, whether
in its original seventeenth-century version, Humboldt's version, or Chomsky's
own version, is in fact highly dubious.[77]

Seventeenth-century theorists of an innate universal grammar had generally
relied on a naive assumption that certain features of their own languages, or of
Indo-European languages a bit more broadly, which were in fact rather distinctive constituted such an innate universal grammar.[78] Humboldt often criticizes
this sort of false projection of a locally familiar grammatical pattern onto all
languages.[79] Accordingly, his own version of the doctrine of an innate universal
grammar is intended to avoid this sort of naive parochialism. Whether it fares
much better in the end seems very doubtful, however.

Let us, then, consider his own version of the doctrine. It may be worth
beginning here by discussing two of its features which are likely to look like
fatal flaws at first sight but which are probably in fact not. First, his very combination of an emphasis on the deeply different characters of grammars with
this insistence on a universally shared grammar is likely to seem flatly inconsistent. However, it is really not. Seventeenth-century theorists had already distinguished between universal grammar and particular grammars, and had assigned
*certain* features of languages to the former category but *other* features to the
latter category. Humboldt basically just takes over that perfectly consistent
position.[80]

Second, Humboldt's methodology might seem inconsistent as well, because
he sometimes advocates an empirical approach to determining the nature of
universal grammar,[81] but at other times an apriorist approach.[82] However, here
too the inconsistency is only apparent rather than real. For his considered position is in fact the perfectly consistent one that it should be possible *both* to
derive the relevant grammatical features a priori *and* to confirm empirically
that they are present in all languages.

In order to see the *real* problems in Humboldt's own version of the doctrine,
one therefore needs to go beyond such rather general features of his position
to consider its more specific features. His own version of the doctrine

fundamentally consists in an attempt to derive a certain set of grammatical principles a priori from *logic* (in particular, from logic as conceived by Kant).[83] His clearest and fullest statement of such a project occurs in *On the Grammatical Structure of Languages* (1827–9).[84] There he basically argues as follows (proceeding from the more fundamental to the less): Relation requires the *verb*, and since language is essentially addressed to another person, also the *pronoun*.[85] Moreover, the specific (Kantian) categories of relation yield the main grammatical cases: the category of causality yields the *nominative*, the *accusative*, and the *instrumental*; the category of substance and accident yields the *genitive*; and the category of reciprocity (which Humboldt calls "double relation") yields the *dative*. The aforementioned grammatical principles can all be derived from logic more or less directly, without the mediation of any extra concepts. By contrast, other grammatical features do require such mediation: The *ablative, locative*, and *narrative* cases require the mediation of such extra concepts as place (for the locative) and narration (for the narrative). Likewise, the *subjunctive* and *optative* moods require the mediation of extra concepts—the former the mediation of the concept of dependent positing (in contrast to the independent positing of the indicative mood), the latter the mediation of the concept of inclination.

However, this is all quite problematic on reflection. Concerning, first, the a priori derivation just sketched itself: It is left quite unclear why relation needs to take the form of a verb. For example, it seems possible to imagine primitive forms of language in which whole sentences occur without the involvement of any verb at all (think, for instance, of Wittgenstein's builders with their "Slab!" etc.—[86] i.e. sentences/words that are non-verbal, or at least pre-verbal).[87] Moreover, that language is *essentially* addressed to another person seems questionable, and would in any case not show that the (second-person) pronoun was fundamental to language, for we address many linguistic acts to other people without using a (second-person) pronoun. Moreover, the correlation of the various grammatical cases with the three Kantian categories of relation looks arbitrary. Why should the nominative and accusative cases be correlated with causality, given that they are not only used in sentences such as "Tom kills John" but also in sentences such as "Tom sees John"? Why should the genitive case be correlated with substance and accident, given that it just as often connotes causal relations (for example, of parent to offspring, or of author to book), relations of ownership, etc.? Why should the dative case be correlated with reciprocity, given that it usually connotes an asymmetric relation of some sort? And so on.

Furthermore, concerning Humboldt's intention that this a priori deduction should be confirmed by an empirical survey of languages: What about sentences of Latin or Arabic that lack any verb (i.e. sentences concerning which people are sometimes tempted, but no doubt naively, to say that some form of the verb "to be" is tacitly implied)? And what about a language like Chinese in which the whole case system is absent? And so on.

Humboldt does indeed have a general strategy for dealing with such embarrassing empirical evidence: concede that the grammatical feature in question is not explicitly expressed, but insist that it is nonetheless added "in thought" by users of the language.[88] However, this strategy is itself highly problematic. If the "thought" in question is supposed to be *conscious* thought, then the strategy lays itself open to refutation by the testimony of native informants. If, on the other hand, it is supposed to be *unconscious* thought, then, unless we are offered some independent way of empirically verifying such claims, the original goal of finding independent empirical confirmation for the thesis of universal grammar has in effect been abandoned.

In short, Humboldt's a priori deduction of a universal grammar is unconvincing, and the empirical confirmation of it that he seeks lacking.

Nor is there any good reason to suppose that after the failure of its seventeenth-century and Humboldtian incarnations, the doctrine of an innate universal grammar has now at last enjoyed "third time lucky" with Chomsky. Chomsky holds that there exists a set of grammatical rules which are innately known by all human beings, but which then undergo differential specification in the empirically learned particular grammatical rules of particular languages. Unlike Humboldt's, Chomsky's fundamental argument for this doctrine is empirical in nature (though apriorist relative to a certain important body of evidence that one might have expected him to consider—concerning which more anon): Human beings acquire a creative, infinite mastery of uses of language's finite means which far outstrips their limited exposure to empirical evidence during the language-learning process, and which is indeed in certain cases entirely unsupported by such evidence (for example, in the cases of the structure-dependent nature of English Yes/No questions, and of the modes of "binding" of pronouns to their antecedents). The only hypothesis that can plausibly explain this feat is innate knowledge of a universal grammar that is not derived from, but merely activated by, exposure to empirical evidence. That is the argument.

However, there are a number of serious problems with this argument. These include the following:

(1) It rests on a false assimilation of knowing *how* to knowing *that*. Mastery of a language and of its grammar is at its most fundamental level an example of knowing how to do something rather than of knowing that something is the case (though a grammarian may indeed go on to acquire knowledge *that* concerning the competence in question, and this fact—together with the

closely related fact that we commonly use the word "grammar" in two quite different senses—seems to have encouraged Chomsky's confusion here).[89] This point is important because it quite takes the wind out of the sails of Chomsky's core argument. That can be seen from the evident absurdity of the following analogous argument: "When a human being learns how to ride a bicycle, he acquires a creative, infinite mastery of uses of the bicycle on the basis of exposure to very limited empirical experience (so that he can now maneuver successfully in a potential infinity of new ways—on new sorts of bikes, in new sorts of environments, confronting new sorts of obstacles, etc.). The only hypothesis that can plausibly explain this feat is that he has an innate knowledge of a set of rules for bicycle riding which is not derived from, but merely activated by, his limited experience." The explanandum here does, no doubt, require, or at least invite, an explanans. However, it seems absurd to suppose that this should take the form of referring to *knowledge that a set of rules applies* (it seems far more likely that it should take the form of referring to a neurophysiological mechanism, for example). The same is true of the language-mastery case.[90] Moreover, this point is reinforced by the fact that the explanans which Chomsky champions implies the existence of a *knowledge that such-and-such rules apply* which is not only innate but also *pre-linguistic*—a prima facie absurdity.[91]

(2) Despite assertions to the contrary by Chomsky,[92] there is not even a single documented case of a language-learner acquiring competence in following a grammatical principle without having had prior exposure to corresponding empirical examples (this is true even of the structure-dependent nature of English Yes/No questions, and the modes of "binding" of pronouns to their antecedents).[93] Moreover, Chomsky's claims of the insufficiency of the empirical examples that *are* available to language-learners for acquiring the creative, infinite mastery that they do acquire without a dependence on innate knowledge lose all plausibility when one abandons Chomsky's naive picture of what empirical learning would have to be like for a more sophisticated and realistic picture—that is, when one abandons his picture of it as plain induction for a picture more along the lines of hypothesis-generation and -testing.[94] Nor, it should be noted, need the denial of Chomsky's thesis that human beings have an innate knowledge of a universal grammar involve an implausible denial that they have *any* innate abilities specially relevant to language learning—for example, perceptual and articulating abilities (ones relevant to the discrimination and production of phonemes), and refined pattern-recognition abilities (ones relevant to the discernment of grammatical patterns in linguistic data).[95]

(3) Finally, it is a rather shocking fact that in developing his doctrine of an innate *universal* grammar Chomsky only pays serious attention to English, and

to a lesser extent a handful of other modern European languages (mainly French and German), but not to the myriad additional languages, and indeed whole language-families, found in the world.[96] This approach contrasts strikingly and unfavorably with Humboldt's two-sided approach in developing his own version of such a doctrine—an approach which, as we saw, involved not only providing an a priori argument for it but also *confirming it by a broad empirical survey of languages*. Indeed, Chomsky's approach seems quite perverse on reflection, especially given the avowedly empirical nature of his fundamental argument. For, even if that highly abstract empirical argument were a plausible one (which, as we have seen, it is not), it would still be startlingly bad scientific practice simply to ignore a whole further body of empirical evidence that is of such obvious relevance to the truth/falsehood of the doctrine of an innate universal grammar as the characters of all the particular languages actually known to exist.[97]

This is not, though, to concede that if it did turn out that there were certain grammatical features which all known human languages shared, that would be *sufficient* to show that the doctrine of an innate universal grammar was true. By no means. It does not seem especially unlikely that there are such generally shared features. For example, even Sapir holds that "no language wholly fails to distinguish noun and verb, though in particular cases the nature of the distinction may be an elusive one."[98] But the fact of certain generally shared features (if it is a fact) is not nearly enough to establish that there is an innate universal grammar (it is only a necessary condition for doing so, not a sufficient condition). That is because there are quite a number of alternative explanations which might apply instead. For example, it might be that certain features, perhaps including certain grammatical features, are strictly universal across languages because they are implied by the very meaning of the term "language" (a plausible *non*-grammatical candidate would be "meaning-bearing"; languages are meaning-bearing by definition, as it were). Or it might be that all human languages share certain grammatical features because they all ultimately share a common origin buried somewhere in the mists of pre-history.[99] Or it might be that certain grammatical features belong to all human languages because of contingently shared features of the environment, human life, etc. which give rise to them.[100] And so on.

In sum, at least to judge from its three main incarnations in the seventeenth-century theorists, Humboldt, and Chomsky, the doctrine of an innate universal grammar looks like a serious mistake. Therefore, in the predominantly progressive transition from Herder to Schlegel to Humboldt, Humboldt's revival of this doctrine represented a retrograde step.

## VI

To conclude, the upshot of the account just sketched is roughly as follows. The tradition of Herder, Schlegel, and Humboldt established the modern discipline of linguistics. After Herder had laid the discipline's foundations, it was Schlegel who made the most pivotal moves, with Humboldt contributing some significant refinements. However, running alongside this main current of progress there were also some more equivocal and even regressive countercurrents—including Schlegel and Humboldt's conception of a ranking of languages as vehicles of thought according to the character of their grammars, and especially Humboldt's notion of an innate universal grammar.

In addition, Herder and Schlegel deserve somewhat more of the credit for the original development of the discipline than they usually receive, and Humboldt somewhat less.[101] For not only were Herder and Schlegel the innovators of the main positive moves that occurred, whereas Humboldt's positive contribution rather took the form of refinements; but it is also the case that their influence on the development of the discipline during the nineteenth century was greater than his; and moreover, that he was more heavily implicated than they were in the negative countercurrents involved, especially in the unfortunate resurrection of the antiquated notion of an innate universal grammar.

## Notes

1. Concerning Herder's commitment to doctrines (1)–(3), see *After Herder*, Essays 1–4.
2. For an early example of Herder's commitment to this sort of position, see his recommendation in the *Fragments* (1767–8) that one should explore the changing nature of people's moral views and concepts by carefully examining the changes that have occurred in their use of moral vocabulary (G1:322). For a later and more general statement of such a position, see for instance the following passage from the *Ideas* (1784–91): "The finest essay on the history and the diverse character of the human understanding and heart... would be a *philosophical comparison of languages*: for a people's understanding and character is imprinted in each of them" (G6:353).
3. KFSA 18:289.
4. *Friedrich Schlegels philosophische Vorlesungen aus den Jahren 1804 bis 1806*, 2:28–9, 223.

5. Ibid., 2:83 (though contrast 1:60).

6. KFSA 15/2:3.

7. F. Schlegel, *Lectures on the History of Literature*, pp. 6–7.

8. F. Schlegel, *Philosophy of Philology*, in "Friedrich Schlegels 'Philosophie der Philologie' mit einer Einleitung herausgegeben von Josef Körner," p. 16. Cf. p. 54: "absolute difference."

9. As E. Fiesel points out—*Die Sprachphilosophie der Deutschen Romantik*, pp. 215–24—this sort of rationale for the new discipline, though predominant in Herder, Schlegel, and Humboldt, tended to recede from nineteenth-century forms of the discipline after Humboldt (arguably to the discipline's great detriment).

10. G1:762.

11. G1:803.

12. G6:353.

13. Schlegel's emphasis on the striking differences between languages includes not only deep grammatical differences and more superficial verbal/conceptual differences but also such intermediate differences as, for instance, the fact that the Manchou language relies much more heavily on onomatopoeia than other languages (KFSA 8:167).

14. Strictly speaking, the expression had already been used by his brother August Wilhelm in a review article from 1803.

15. Schlegel had some forerunners in this idea. See on this H. Gipper and P. Schmitter, *Sprachwissenschaft und Sprachphilosophie im Zeitalter der Romantik*, pp. 22–6.

16. In connection with the latter type, Schlegel not only emphasizes Chinese but also cites both Alexander von Humboldt's collection of Native American grammars and Wilhelm von Humboldt's ongoing work on the Basque language (KFSA 8:153–5).

17. In doing this, he especially builds on, and credits, the work of Sir William Jones. Cf. Gipper and Schmitter, *Sprachwissenschaft und Sprachphilosophie*, pp. 47–8.

18. Bopp's work closely follows Schlegel's *On the Language and Wisdom of the Indians* not only in its contents but also in its form (for example, like the latter concluding with a set of translations).

19. Concerning this subsequent history, cf. J. Trabant, *Apeliotes oder der Sinn der Sprache. Wilhelm von Humboldts Sprachbild* (Berlin: Akademie Verlag, 1986), p. 163; Gipper and Schmitter, *Sprachwissenschaft und Sprachphilosophie* (as well as other works by Gipper); H. Nüsse's introduction to KFSA, vol. 8; and Fiesel, *Die Sprachphilosophie der Deutschen Romantik*, pp. 110 ff.

20. There are a few complications here that should be noted, however. Humboldt's version of doctrine (1) is not very consistent, ranging all the way from a claim of outright identity between thought and language, through a claim of their strict interdependence, to a claim of their mere interaction (of a sort allowing thought a measure of independence from language). The same is true of his commitment to doctrine (2). He sometimes commits himself to it fairly explicitly, for example in the following remark from the preface to his translation of Aeschylus' *Agamemnon*: "A word is so little a sign for a concept that the concept cannot arise, let alone be held fast, without the word" (WHGS 8:129). But at other times he adopts a more conventional dualistic picture of the relation between concept and word. (Concerning this equivocation, cf. H. Gipper, *Wilhelm von Humboldts Bedeutung für Theorie und Praxis moderner Sprachforschung*, pp. 19–21, 88–93.) It should also be noted that Humboldt develops various novel rationales for these doctrines, some of which are rather weak (for example, the one in the Kawi-introduction at WHGS 7:55).

21. Some of the secondary literature would also add a fourth category here: "incorporative" languages. However, as Trabant argues convincingly (*Apeliotes*, pp. 181 ff.), for Humboldt "agglutinative" and "incorporative" seem to be essentially alternative ways of describing a single linguistic process or type (the former term viewing it from the perspective of the word, the latter rather from that of the sentence).

22. Besides taking over Schlegel's three main motives for comparative grammar—providing a window on other modes of thought and conceptualization (Herder's doctrine (4)); determining the genealogical relations between languages (Schlegel's doctrine (e)); and making possible a normative ranking of languages as vehicles for thought (Schlegel's doctrine (g))—Humboldt sometimes also adds a fourth: comparative grammar contributes to a better knowledge of one's *own* language (see e.g. *Essay on the Languages of the New World*, at WHGS 3:340–1), or indeed of *any* particular language (see e.g. W. von Humboldt, *Essays on Language* [Frankfurt am Main: Peter Lang, 1997], p. 8).

23. One of the richest sources of evidence for this is Humboldt's correspondence with Schiller (*Der Briefwechsel zwischen Friedrich Schiller und Wilhelm von Humboldt* [Berlin: Aufbau, 1962], vols. 1 and 2).

24. See WHGS 7/2:372. Cf. Gipper and Schmitter, *Sprachwissenschaft und Sprachphilosophie*, p. 62.

25. This traditional dating of the essay has sometimes been disputed, but the reasons for questioning it do not seem strong.

26. Concerning the essay's echoing of Herder's *Treatise*, cf. Gipper and Schmitter, *Sprachwissenschaft und Sprachphilosophie*, p. 62, as well as the secondary literature cited there (especially that by Lauchert, Sapir, and Menze); and Gipper, *Wilhelm von Humboldts Bedeutung*, pp. 77 ff., 108–9.

Humboldt in his essay recasts the basically Herderian doctrine mentioned here in somewhat more Kantian-Fichtean terms. This is in keeping with a more general philosophical sympathy with Kant and Fichte that he shows during the 1790s (e.g. in his Paris notebooks). It may well be significant that the period to which the essay evidently belongs, 1795–6, had just seen the publication not only of Fichte's *Wissenschaftslehre* but also of an essay by Fichte on the origin of language, *Von der Sprachfähigkeit und dem Ursprunge der Sprache* (1795).

27. A few examples culled from the Kawi-introduction and other works: Herder's account of the origin of language in terms of its interdependence and coevalness with "awareness [*Besonnenheit*]"; Herder's doctrine that language, and hence also mental life more generally, and indeed the very self, is fundamentally social in nature; Herder's doctrine that linguistic reference to features of the world is never direct but is always mediated through concepts; Herder's conception that language fundamentally consists of heard sounds; Herder's conception that language is essential to man; Herder's conception that verbs are the most fundamental part of language; and even Herder's doctrine that human language and rationality are intimately dependent on human beings' upright posture.

28. WHGS 6:418.

29. H. Aarsleff, "Guillaume de Humboldt et la pensée linguistique des idéologues," in *La Grammaire générale. Des modistes aux ideologues*, ed. A. Joly and J. Stéfanini (Lille: Presses Universitaires de Lille III, 1977); also W. von Humboldt, *On Language*, editor's introduction.

For a broad and cogent reply to Aarsleff's thesis, see H. Gipper, "Schwierigkeiten beim Schreiben der Wahrheit," in his *Wilhelm von Humboldts Bedeutung* (reproduced as "2. Exkurs" in Gipper and Schmitter, *Sprachwissenschaft und Sprachphilosophie*); also, W. Oesterreicher, "Wem gehört Humboldt?" in *Logos Semantikos: Studia Linguistica in Honorem Eugenio Coseriu 1921–1981* (Berlin and New York: de Gruyter, 1981).

Concerning doctrines (1) and (2) in particular, note that the content of Humboldt's *On Thinking and Speaking* and its plausible traditional dating to 1795–6 show Humboldt already adopting these doctrines *before* the relevant Paris period, and on the basis of his acquaintance with *Herder*, not the French. So, while he did indeed encounter a weak form of the doctrines in Condillac (see esp. WHGS 14:449), it seems unlikely that Condillac was their main source for him. That is especially true given that his comments on Condillac and the Ideologues in his Paris notebooks (including the passage at 14:449) are predominantly, indeed almost entirely, *negative* in spirit.

In addition, it is worth noting that even the weak form of doctrines (1) and (2) that Humboldt found in Condillac ultimately had a German source, namely Herder's German predecessor Wolff, whom Condillac explicitly (albeit grudgingly) credits for them in *An Essay on the Origin of Human Knowledge*. (See on this *After Herder*, Essay 2.)

There is, however, one possible exception to the general rule that Condillac was relatively unimportant as a positive influence on Humboldt, which will be noted later in this essay.

30. This particular insight belongs less to Herder and Schlegel than to the tradition they founded. It is not yet explicitly developed by Herder even in the *Ideas*. Schlegel implies it more clearly in *On the Language and Wisdom of the Indians* with his conception of languages as "systems," "organisms," etc., but still does not develop it explicitly. Subsequently, his brother August Wilhelm and Humboldt develop it more explicitly, especially in their discussions of Sanskrit terminology. Schlegel's sometime friend Schleiermacher is explicit about it as well, for example in *On the Different Methods of Translation* (1813).

31. Herder already implies this insight in the *Ideas*, and Schlegel develops it explicitly in *On the Language and Wisdom of the Indians*. Like the former insight, this insight from Schlegel's work already finds a strong echo in Schleiermacher's *On the Different Methods of Translation* (1813) (despite Schleiermacher's officially cold reception of the work).

32. See e.g. Humboldt's discussion of the Sanskrit concept *yôga* at WHGS 5:221 ff.

33. See e.g. the Kawi-introduction, at *On Language*, pp. 128 ff.

34. See e.g. WHGS 7:109; 6/2:337. For a similar view, cf. E. Sapir, *Language: An Introduction to the Study of Speech* (San Diego, New York, London: Harcourt Brace Jovanovich, 1921), p. 93.

35. See e.g. WHGS 6/2:337. Cf. M.L. Manchester, *The Philosophical Foundations of Humboldt's Linguistic Doctrines*, pp. 60 ff.

This is the one significant point at which Aarsleff's thesis that Condillac exercised a deep influence on Humboldt's linguistic theory has some plausibility. See in this connection Humboldt's report on Condillac in his Paris notebooks of 1798: in Condillac's *An Essay on the Origin of Human Knowledge* "it turns out that all our higher abilities rest on the *connection of ideas*, which is therefore the highest principle of all cognition, and this connection depends on *signs* which we apply to it"; Condillac and the French metaphysicians "place inordinate weight on the linking of concepts with signs and consequently universal grammar seems to them such an essential part of metaphysics" (WHGS 14:445, 449).

36. See e.g. *On the National Character of Languages*, at WHGS 4:420: "words and syntax simultaneously form and determine concepts."

37. Cf. J. A. Lucy, *Language Diversity and Thought: A Reformulation of the Linguistic Relativity Hypothesis* (Cambridge: Cambridge University Press, 1996). Lucy points out that the position that grammatical variations produce corresponding semantic variations later underlies the work of Sapir and Whorf (pp. 81–2), and he also supports it himself.

38. August Wilhelm also explicitly credits Humboldt's brother Alexander for having played a similar role, namely through his investigations of the native American languages. Alexander indeed seems to have been the first person to use the term "agglutinative" in print.

39. Cf. Trabant, *Apeliotes*, pp. 181 ff. It would therefore be unproblematic for Humboldt to classify Chinese as an isolating language despite the fact that Chinese also involves a certain amount of agglutination, for example.

40. See, for example, Sapir's more complicated scheme in *Language: An Introduction to the Study of Speech*, ch. 6, which does indeed build on Humboldt's scheme rather than abandoning it altogether. Concerning other more complicated schemes due to Finck and Lohmann, see Gipper, *Wilhelm von Humboldts Bedeutung*, pp. 49–51.

41. See esp. *On the Language and Wisdom of the Indians*, at KFSA 8:313–15. I say "virtually" because Schlegel explicitly allows that this determining may be overcome by "genius."

42. See e.g. the Kawi-introduction, at *On Language*, pp. 62–4. R. L. Brown, *Wilhelm von Humboldt's Conception of Linguistic Relativity* emphasizes this side of Humboldt's position (but also notes, correctly, that there are contrary strands in Humboldt's work).

43. See *On Language*, pp. 33, 46–7, 62–4; *Letter to Monsieur Abel-Rémusat, on the Nature of Grammatical Forms in General, and on the Genius of the Chinese Language in Particular* (1826), at WHGS 5:290. Cf. Schlegel's similar point about "genius," mentioned in the note before last.

44. This was one of Humboldt's own motives in acquiring new languages.

45. Note, though, that Humboldt's considered version of this insistence that any language can be made to express any thought qualifies it in certain important ways: *to some extent* and *due to the flexibility, i.e. modifiability, of language* (see *Essays on Language*, p. 11), and also *taking into account the use of metaphors and circumlocutions* (see *On Language*, p. 33).

46. See Lucy, *Language Diversity and Thought*, ch. 1. George Stocking has discussed this equivocation in Boas as well, especially in his essay "The Boas Plan for the Study of American Indian Languages."

47. See e.g. WHGS 4:27.

48. For an interesting discussion of both the lexical and the grammatical versions of this sort of thesis, which tends to support them against some well-known attacks, see Lucy, *Language Diversity and Thought*, ch. 5 (together with Lucy's accompanying empirical case study).

> Humboldt sometimes in addition implies the still more radical position that the constitutive role of language extends beyond thoughts, concepts, and perceptions, to include also their *objects*. There is therefore much truth in the interpretation of his position developed by Heintel, Scharf, and several other German-language commentators according to which he is offering a linguistic extension of the Kantian transcendental project of identifying the conditions of the possibility of experience, including the objects of experience. Since this more radical extension of his position is philosophically problematic, however, I shall leave it to one side here.

49. See Gipper and Schmitter, *Sprachwissenschaft und Sprachphilosophie*, pp. 120 ff.

50. Cf. ibid., pp. 85–6. Also, Lucy, *Language Diversity and Thought*.

51. See B.L. Whorf, "An American Indian Model of the Universe," in his *Language, Thought, and Reality* (Cambridge, Mass.: MIT Press, 1982). Cf. Lucy, *Language Diversity and Thought*, ch. 2, which discusses other examples from Whorf.

52. For an account of this, see Lucy, *Language Diversity and Thought*, chs. 1 and 2.

53. Cf. Brown, *Wilhelm von Humboldt's Conception of Linguistic Relativity*, pp. 12–16; Gipper and Schmitter, *Sprachwissenschaft und Sprachphilosophie*, p. 85. Boas, who was German by birth and education, was deeply steeped in the works of Humboldt and the Humboldtian tradition (he also explicitly discusses Herder on occasion). Sapir, besides receiving that knowledge from Boas, himself knew Humboldt's writings directly (as well as Herder's). For example, he published a substantial early essay in 1907 on Herder's *Treatise on the Origin of Language* in which he discusses both Herder and Humboldt: E. Sapir, "Herder's 'Ursprung der Sprache,'" *Modern Philology*, 5/1 (1907). It is less clear whether Whorf had direct knowledge of Humboldt's ideas, but that he at least had indirect knowledge of them through Sapir is certain.

54. For a sympathetic discussion of the theory of the "semantic field," see the works by Gipper already cited. For a sympathetic discussion of the "Sapir-

Whorf hypothesis," see Lucy, *Language Diversity and Thought* (together with its companion empirical case study).

55. Herder does sometimes seem to favor earlier and more primitive forms of language, namely for their sensuousness, musicality, lack of grammatical constraint, etc., over later and more developed forms of language, which he sees as more abstract, less musical, more grammatically constrained, etc. But to a large extent his motive here is to *counterbalance the pretensions of the latter to superiority* rather than to conclude that the former really are superior. Also, he does sometimes evaluate *phases* of a language's history negatively, for example the French-dominated German of his own day. However, that is not a negative judgment on the language per se, but rather on a decadent form of it.

56. In the *Treatise* he had taken two positions concerning grammar, neither of which really involved this. As I mentioned in the preceding note, he suggests at points that earlier and more primitive languages are better than modern and more developed languages because the former are still unconstrained by grammar; however, this should probably not be read as his final evaluation, but rather merely as a phase in a counterbalancing strategy. At other points in the same work he implies (somewhat inconsistently) that grammar is basically invariant across all languages (except for Chinese)—which would actively preclude any ranking of languages on the basis of grammar. In the *Ideas*, where he introduces the thesis that there are deep grammatical differences between languages, he still does not make this thesis the basis for a ranking of languages.

57. As we shall see below, both of these points are highly relevant to the case of language, though whether they rule out differential rankings between languages altogether is less clear.

58. Cf. Aarsleff's editorial introduction to Humboldt, *On Language*, pp. lxi ff.

59. See e.g. E. Sapir, "Language," in his *Selected Writings in Language, Culture, and Personality* (Berkeley and Los Angeles: University of California Press, 1985), p. 20.

60. Cf. Sapir, *Language: An Introduction to the Study of Speech*, p. 97: "An intelligent and sensitive Chinaman, accustomed as he is to cut to the very bone of linguistic form, might well say of the Latin sentence, 'How pedantically imaginative!'".

61. WHGS 3:337 (though contrast p. 340). Cf. later the *Letter to Monsieur Abel-Rémusat*, at WHGS 5:282 (though, again, contrast pp. 292–3).

62. See e.g. *On Language*, pp. 106–7, 145.

63. See e.g. the *Letter to Monsieur Abel-Rémusat*, at WHGS 5:254 ff.

64. See ibid., and *On Language*, p. 230.

65. *On Language*, pp. 205 ff.

66. Concerning the last example, Humboldt's rather naive view that the natural order of the sentence is subject–verb–object (cf. ibid., pp. 250–6) was perhaps encouraged by the accidental fact that this happens to be the usual word order not only in Indo-European languages but also in Chinese.

67. *On Language*, pp. 265–6.

68. See e.g. ibid., pp. 216–19.

69. See e.g. Sapir, "Language," p. 20. Also, Whorf, *Language, Thought, and Reality*, p. 263: "In their linguistic systems, though these systems differ widely, yet in the order, harmony, and beauty of the systems, and in their respective subtleties and penetrating analysis of reality, all men are equal."

70. For a balanced discussion of Bloom's argument and of the responses that it has provoked, see Lucy, *Language Diversity and Thought*, ch. 6.

71. An exception to the rule is Steinthal, who was indeed strongly influenced by Humboldt.

72. Cf. Trabant, *Apeliotes*, pp. 164 ff.

73. N. Chomsky, *Cartesian Linguistics* (New York and London: Harper and Row, 1966).

74. See esp. E. Coseriu, "Semantik, innere Sprachform und Tiefenstruktur," *Folia Linguistica*, 4 (1970); H.-W. Scharf, *Das Verfahren der Sprache: Humboldt gegen Chomsky* (Paderborn: Schöningh, 1994).

75. See N. Chomsky, *Current Issues in Linguistic Theory* (The Hague/Paris: Mouton, 1964), p. 17.

76. Astonishingly, Coseriu and Scharf both quite overlook this fact. Nor is Brown's less extreme position that Humboldt started out with such views but then eventually more or less abandoned them correct (*Wilhelm von Humboldt's Conception of Linguistic Relativity*, pp. 95 ff.). Brown himself cites much evidence to the contrary from rather late works, and this can easily be further enriched from such texts as *Grundzüge des allgemeinen Sprachtypus* (1824–6) and *Von dem grammatischen Baue der Sprachen* (1827–9). Indeed, virtually all of Humboldt's linguistic writings contain at least some sort of commitment to an innate universal grammar, including his final testament, the Kawi-introduction (see *On Language*, pp. 54, 215).

On the other hand, in fairness to these commentators, it is true that the amount of space that Humboldt devotes to continuing and developing the Herder-Schlegel message of deep linguistic diversity is vastly greater than the amount he devotes to this contrary(-looking) theme of an innate universal grammar. For example, one can read through almost the entirety of such substantial works as the *Letter to Monsieur Abel-Rémusat* and *On the Diversity of Human Language Structure* without encountering this theme. And Humboldt himself already comments revealingly on this asymmetry in his interests in a letter to Brinkmann from 1803: "The inner, mysteriously wonderful connection between all languages, but above all the lofty pleasure of entering with each new language a new system of thought and feeling, attract me infinitely" (*Wilhelm von Humboldts Briefe an Karl Gustav Brinkmann*, p. 157). As will become clear in what follows, I consider this asymmetry of interest a point in Humboldt's favor.

77. Cf. Gipper, "Individuelle und universelle Züge der Sprachen in der Sicht Wilhelm von Humboldts," in his *Wilhelm von Humboldts Bedeutung*. Among the German secondary literature, Gipper's comes closest to the position I take here.

78. For some examples, see Chomsky, *Cartesian Linguistics*, pp. 31–51.

79. See e.g. *Letter to Monsieur Abel-Rémusat*, at WHGS 5:297.

80. Cf. Chomsky, *Cartesian Linguistics*, pp. 52–4.

81. See e.g. *Essay on the Languages of the New World*, at WHGS 3:325–6; *Grundzüge des allgemeinen Sprachtypus*, at WHGS 5:449–50.

82. See e.g. *Essay on the Languages of the New World*, at WHGS 3:339; *Grundzüge des allgemeinen Sprachtypus*, at WHGS 5:373 ff., 451–3; *Von dem grammatischen Baue der Sprachen*, at WHGS 6:345–8.

83. At least generically, this project was continuous with that of A.F. Bernhardi in works which he published near the beginning of the nineteenth century.

84. WHGS 6:345–8. Cf. *Grundzüge des allgemeinen Sprachtypus*, at WHGS 5:451–3.

85. Cf. *Essays on Language*, pp. 151–3.

86. L. Wittgenstein, *Philosophical Investigations* (1953; 2nd rev. ed. Oxford: Blackwell, 1958), par. 2.

87. As Sapir notes in his essay on Herder's *Treatise*, where Herder had advanced a thesis of the primacy of the verb in language similar to Humboldt's in connection with his famous example of the origin of language in an isolated focus on the bleating of a sheep, language would not in such circumstances as these yet have the differentiation of functions for words that would warrant characterizing the sentence/word in question as either a verb or a noun ("Herder's 'Ursprung der Sprache,'" p. 123).

88. See e.g. *Von dem grammatischen Baue der Sprachen*, at WHGS 6:389–91; *Grundzüge des allgemeinen Sprachtypus*, at WHGS 5:471; *On Language*, p. 185.

89. Chomsky initially made this error quite unreflectively—see e.g. *Current Issues in Linguistic Theory*, pp. 9–10; *Aspects of the Theory of Syntax* (Cambridge, Mass.: MIT Press, 1965), pp. 25–7. He did eventually come to recognize and address a version of the problem just raised—at *Reflections on Language* (Glasgow: Fontana/Collins, 1976), pp. 164–6—but his manner of doing so, rather than dispelling, reinforces the impression of his confusion about it.

90. It might be objected here that the two cases are not analogous because in the linguistic case the mastery in question involves a potentially infinite set of *normative* assessments about what *should* be said, so that in this case an explanation in terms of knowledge that rules apply is superior to one in terms of, say, neurophysiology. However, this is not a good objection. For in fact the mastery of bike-riding involves a potentially infinite set of *normative* assessments about what *should* be done as well ("I should swerve in order to avoid the rock," etc.).

91. Cf. Scharf, *Das Verfahren der Sprache*, pp. 43, 67–8. Chomsky is explicitly committed to the claim that thought and knowledge can be non-linguistic, so he would not himself be too worried by this additional criticism. However, that commitment just looks like a further implausibility in his position. Moreover, even if non-linguistic knowledge were possible, could it include contents as abstract and complicated as those of Chomskyan generative grammar?

92. e.g. N. Chomsky, *Language and Mind* (New York: Harcourt Brace Jovanovich, 1972), pp. 11–12: "The normal use of language is innovative, in the sense that much of what we say in the course of normal language use is entirely new, not a repetition of anything that we have heard before and not even similar in pattern... to sentences or discourse that we have heard in the past."

93. Cf. L.J. Cohen, "Some Applications of Inductive Logic to the Theory of Language," *American Philosophical Quarterly*, 7/4 (1970), p. 306 n. 14; M. Tomasello, *Constructing a Language* (Cambridge, Mass.: Harvard University Press, 2003), pp. 288–9.

94. Cf. Cohen, "Some Applications of Inductive Logic to the Theory of Language," and Tomasello, *Constructing a Language*.

95. Cf. Tomasello, *Constructing a Language*, p. 284.

96. Chomsky does also possess some knowledge of Hebrew, but he does not bring this to bear in his mature work in linguistics.

97. In view of these severe weaknesses in Chomsky's theory, one is led to wonder why it has nevertheless enjoyed the popularity that it has (in the

U.S.A.). There are no doubt many reasons for this—including Chomsky's own energy, ingenuity, and force of personality; and the eternal seductions of scientism (as opposed to, rather than identical with, science; a real scientist would never be as uninterested in a whole body of obviously relevant empirical evidence as we have just seen Chomsky to be; even Ptolemy at least got as far as inventing epicycles, he did not simply ignore the observable course of the planets). But another, and especially interesting, part of the explanation lies in the area of political ideology. Doctrines of universal grammar (like other universalistic doctrines, for example concerning concepts or moral values) are Janus-faced in their political relevance: they can be motivated by and/or serve cosmopolitan, egalitarian impulses; or they can be motivated by and/or serve ethnocentric, inegalitarian impulses, namely insofar as it is found that other peoples do not in fact clearly instantiate the putatively universal structure involved, so that they have to be seen as instantiating it only very imperfectly instead (in particular, less perfectly than ourselves). In the seventeenth-century universal grammarians, Humboldt, and Chomsky, the conscious political motivation is of the former, enlightened sort. However, one only needs to remember the case of Humboldt, and his ranking of different languages as better or worse in light of their different degrees of realization of the supposed universal grammar in question, with European languages faring well in the ranking, while native American and Chinese languages fare ill, in order to see that the contrary, ethnocentric and inegalitarian, motive can co-reside in such a theorist at a less conscious level and/or be a powerful force that moves his society to embrace and encourage his theory. Chomsky's case seems to me similar: his own conscious political motives are clearly, indeed stridently, cosmopolitan and egalitarian. However, when it comes to explaining the strangely widespread enthusiasm for his theory in the U.S.A., it seems likely that it is rather the contrary, invidious motive that is playing the bigger causal role. In this particular case, there is also a further political motive to consider, one that may be less invidious, but is equally indifferent to truth: The U.S.A. is very distinctive as a country in that it combines people from many different cultural backgrounds into a single nation, and therefore faces the constant danger of unusually strong centrifugal forces. This puts a premium on ideologies that play down intellectual and moral differences and instead play up similarities. In this respect too, a theory like Chomsky's exactly fills the ideological bill.

98. Sapir, *Language: An Introduction to the Study of Speech*, p. 119.

99. For a discussion of some intriguing empirical evidence that tends to support such a possibility, see S.J. Gould, "Grimm's Greatest Tale," in his *Bully for Brontosaurus* (New York: Norton, 1992).
100. Humboldt's essay *On the Dual* provides an explanation of this sort for one, not indeed universal, but at least broadly shared, grammatical feature of languages, namely the dual form.
101. *Pace* e.g. Gipper, "Wilhelm von Humboldt als Begründer moderner Sprachforschung," esp. pp. 37–9.

# PART III
# Hegel

# 5

# Hegel on Language

Georg Wilhelm Friedrich Hegel (1770–1831) is the most famous philosopher treated at length in this book. He is well known as the author of an elaborate and influential form of idealism. However, he was also deeply interested in questions concerning language throughout his career. This essay will attempt to give a brief introduction to Hegel and his philosophy as a whole, but then mainly an overview of his philosophy of language. This will be done under the following headings:

1. Intellectual Life
2. Hegel's System
3. Hegel's Philosophy of Language
4. The Early Hegel on Language
5. The Jena Hegel on Language
6. The Hegel of 1807–27 on Language
7. The Hegel of 1827–31 on Language
8. Hegel's Deviations from Herder on Language
9. Concluding Overview

## 1. Intellectual Life

Since Hegel and his philosophy will already be familiar to most readers, and several good accounts of them are already available,[1] I shall be concise on these subjects here. Georg Wilhelm Friedrich Hegel (1770–1831) was born in Stuttgart, the son of a civil servant in the service of the Duke of Württemberg. His family was Lutheran.

After attending the local *Gymnasium*, he entered the theological seminary in Tübingen in 1788. The seminary was also attended by Hölderlin and Schelling, with whom he became friends and intellectual allies, in particular sharing with them an enthusiasm for a form of metaphysico-religious monism, the ancient Greeks, and the ideals of the French Revolution.

After finishing his theological studies, he became a private tutor in Bern in 1793, then in Frankfurt in 1796 (this time with Hölderlin's help). During the Bern and Frankfurt periods he wrote extensively on religion and ethics (many of these writings were eventually published in the twentieth century by Herman Nohl under the collective title *Hegels theologische Jugendschriften* [1907]).

In 1799 his father died, leaving him a modest legacy that allowed him to stop tutoring. In 1800 he went to the University of Jena, the leading university of the time, where Schelling (though five years his junior) had just become professor of philosophy following Fichte's departure in 1799 as a result of accusations of atheism. This initiated a period of close collaboration between Hegel and Schelling. After completing a doctoral dissertation on the planets, and with Schelling's help winning appointment as an unsalaried lecturer (*Privatdozent*), Hegel in 1801 published his first book, *The Difference between the Fichtean and Schellingian Systems of Philosophy*. He also co-founded and -published with Schelling the *Critical Journal of Philosophy*, a journal devoted to propagating Schelling's philosophy of identity in which Hegel authored several important articles. During his time in Jena he also wrote extensive manuscripts, in which he began to develop his own philosophical system. Intellectual and personal tensions soon emerged between Schelling and Hegel, however, and in 1803 Schelling left for a position in Würzburg. In 1805 Hegel became associate professor in Jena. In 1806, on the eve of Napoleon's confrontation with, and defeat of, the Prussians at the Battle of Jena (an episode which Hegel warmly welcomed), Hegel finished his first major work, the *Phenomenology of Spirit* (which appeared in 1807; a second, partly revised edition followed in 1832).

After a short stint as editor of a pro-Napoleonic newspaper in Bamberg, Hegel served from 1808 until 1816 as headmaster of a school in Nuremberg, where he continued to develop his philosophical system in the course of lecturing to his pupils, and eventually published his *Science of Logic* (1812–16; second, revised edition 1832). During this period he also married Marie von Tucher, who was twenty-two years his junior. The marriage was a happy one and produced two sons.

From 1816 until 1818 Hegel served as professor of philosophy at the University of Heidelberg, publishing there the first edition of the only complete statement of his philosophical system, the *Encyclopedia of the Philosophical Sciences in Outline* (1817; two further editions, both substantially revised, followed in 1827 and 1830).

In 1818 he was called to serve as professor of philosophy at the recently founded University of Berlin. This was where he first became really famous. While in Berlin he published the *Philosophy of Right* (1821), the two new editions of the *Encyclopedia* (1827 and 1830), and, beginning in 1827, articles for a new journal that he co-edited, the *Yearbooks for Scientific Criticism*. These articles include two that are especially significant for his philosophy of language: a review of work by Wilhelm von Humboldt concerning the episode of the Indian poem *Mahabharata* known as the *Bhagavad-Gita* (1827), and a review of Hamann's collected works (1828).

Hegel died in Berlin in 1831 during a cholera epidemic, possibly from the disease. In the years immediately following his death versions of his famous Berlin lecture series on the Philosophy of World History, Aesthetics, the Philosophy of Religion, and the History of Philosophy were published for the first time as part of his collected works.

## 2. Hegel's System

Hegel's philosophical system achieved something like its final form in about 1806 (at least in his head), thereafter undergoing only relatively modest changes.

Though considered by many people (including myself) to be Hegel's greatest work, the *Phenomenology of Spirit* (1807) was conceived by *him* merely as a sort of introduction to the system. However, he conceived it as an introduction of a very unusual and ambitious sort, in that he intended it, not only to show the ordinary consciousness the inadequacy of its present standpoint and the necessity of ascending to the standpoint of the system, but also to justify the system in the face of skeptical challenges, and indeed to constitute the concepts and the truth of the system for the first time.[2]

After publishing the *Phenomenology of Spirit*, Hegel gradually published the system itself—beginning with the *Science of Logic* (first edition 1812–16), and then completing the task with the *Encyclopedia* (1817), which contains a more concise version of the Logic followed by a Philosophy of Nature and a Philosophy of Spirit/Mind [*Geist*]. Finally, the *Philosophy of Right* (1821) and Hegel's Berlin lecture series on the Philosophy of World History, Aesthetics, the Philosophy of Religion, and the History of Philosophy then elaborated on the highest levels of the system.

As has already been mentioned, the system comprises Logic, Philosophy of Nature, and Philosophy of Spirit (in that order). It posits Absolute Spirit (i.e. Hegel's version of God) as a single principle that encompasses and explains everything. Accordingly, each of the system's three parts is intended to capture an essential aspect of Absolute Spirit's constitution or self-realization: The Logic expounds Absolute Spirit as a self-developing conceptual hierarchy which pervades and explains all natural and spiritual phenomena, but expounds it in abstraction from these phenomena—or as Hegel puts it, in the form of "God as he is in his eternal essence before the creation of nature and a finite spirit."[3] The Philosophy of Nature then expounds the realization of the same self-developing conceptual hierarchy in natural phenomena. Accordingly, nature is there interpreted as a self-developing hierarchy that mirrors the self-developing conceptual hierarchy of the Logic—merely mechanical phenomena occurring at its lower end, while organic ones, beginning with plants and then proceeding to animals, are located at its higher end. The Philosophy of Spirit then continues expounding the realization of the Logic's self-developing conceptual hierarchy, but this time at the higher level of spiritual, or mental, phenomena (which begin with human beings). Accordingly, here too the phenomena in question are interpreted as a self-developing hierarchy corresponding to the self-developing conceptual hierarchy of the Logic—specifically, as a hierarchy that ascends from general mental characteristics of individual human beings to the social and political institutions of the state and their historical development, and finally to art, religion, and philosophy, which are interpreted as a sequence of increasingly adequate expressions of the truth about Absolute Spirit, and hence as its return to itself and achievement of an essential knowledge of its own nature.

Among other things, this whole system is a sort of defense or rational re-working of the Christian conception of God. In particular, its three parts constitute an attempt to make sense of the Christian conception of a God who is three in one—the Logic depicting God as he is in Himself; the Philosophy of Nature, God the Son; and the Philosophy of Spirit, God the Holy Spirit.[4]

## 3. Hegel's Philosophy of Language

With this brief sketch of Hegel's life and philosophy before us, we can now turn to consider, more specifically, his philosophy of *language*. For although there is no discrete section of his system called "Philosophy of Language" (as there *is* a discrete Philosophy of Spirit/Mind, for example),[5] his philosophy as a whole is pervasively and deeply concerned with language,[6] and advances a set of striking, thoughtful, sophisticated views about it.

The central thesis of this essay is that Hegel's views about language should be seen as appropriating, elaborating, and revising *Herder's*.[7] In order to perceive this situation, it is helpful to realize at the outset that throughout his career Hegel's philosophy owed a *broad* range of debts to Herder. Hegel did not himself clearly acknowledge this—partly due to a certain habitual stinginess in crediting contemporaries (e.g. Hölderlin and Schelling); partly due to the fact that Herder had damaged his own public reputation by publishing an angry and irresponsible attack on Kant in the *Metacritique on the Critique of Pure Reason* (1799),[8] as well as by falling out with Goethe, Schiller, and others in varying degrees; and partly due to Hegel's sense that Herder, while his positions might be correct, had failed to give them a properly scientific, systematic form.[9] Nonetheless, a number of commentators have identified such debts to Herder convincingly.[10] And I have myself elsewhere made a case for the existence of such debts.[11] To summarize the general picture that emerges from this research briefly: Not only were Hegel's early theological writings strongly influenced by Herder (as Dilthey, Schwarz, Haering, and Harris have shown), but in addition, many central features of Hegel's mature system were so as well. These include Hegel's neo-Spinozistic monism (which can largely be traced back to Herder's *God: Some Conversations* [1787]);[12] Hegel's very concept of *Geist* (which is heavily indebted to several of Herder's works, including *On the Cognition and Sensation of the Human Soul* [1778]);[13] and Hegel's conception of history as a progressive realization of Reason (which is heavily indebted to Herder's *Ideas for the Philosophy of History of Humanity* [1784–91]).[14] Indeed, Hegel implicitly acknowledges that he is indebted to Herder for several of his own mature positions (including his neo-Spinozistic monism and his concept of *Geist*) in a neglected and much misunderstood section of the *Phenomenology of Spirit* of 1807 which turns out to be entirely concerned with Herder's standpoint: "The Spiritual Animalkingdom [*Das geistige Tierreich*]."[15]

It should therefore come as no great surprise that Hegel's views about language owe a large debt to Herder as well (after all, if Herder is known for anything it is his philosophy of language). To be more precise, Herder's influence on Hegel's views about language occurred in three main phases, separated by two phases of relapse towards contrary, more conventional positions. Let me briefly summarize these phases.

The *first* phase of Herder's influence on Hegel's views about language already occurred very early in Hegel's career, as early as the late 1780s. At this time Hegel in particular took over from Herder a conception of the primacy of hearing over vision and hence of the spoken over the written word; a principle that thoughts or concepts are essentially dependent on and bounded by language; and a principle that linguistic-conceptual resources vary markedly between different historical periods and different cultures. (The earliness of this Herderian influence on Hegel's views about language should not be too surprising on reflection given Herder's well-established broader influence on Hegel's early theological writings.)

That phase of influence was then followed by a short phase of partial relapse which lasted from about 1796 until about 1800. During this phase Hegel in the poem *Eleusis* (1796) and *The Spirit of Christianity and its Fate* (1798–1800) temporarily abandoned Herder's fundamental principle that thought is essentially dependent on and bounded by language in favor of the age-old idea (already found in Plato, for example) that certain thoughts are ineffable.

The *second*, and most important, phase of Herder's influence occurred during the period 1803–7, a period that began with Hegel's *First Philosophy of Spirit* (1803–4) and culminated in his *Phenomenology of Spirit* (1807). As we shall see, Hegel during this period took over a broad range of positions from Herder's philosophy of language. (This should again not be too surprising on reflection, since the period in question was immediately preceded by a flurry of heightened interest on Hegel's part in other aspects of Herder's thought. This interest can be seen in two works of Hegel's whose projects are heavily influenced by Herder, namely *The Spirit of Christianity and its Fate* [1798–1800] and *The German Constitution* [1799–1802], in Hegel's respectful discussion of Herder in *Faith and Knowledge* [1802], and in the fact that Hegel wrote a review of Herder's *God: Some Conversations* in 1802.[16])

This second phase of influence was then followed by a long phase of relapse which lasted from about 1807 until about 1827, as Hegel developed and published versions of the philosophical system to which the *Phenomenology of Spirit* had been intended to serve as the introduction. This relapse consisted partly just in a sharply diminished interest in language. But it also consisted partly in Hegel's temporary renunciation of certain Herderian principles which he had previously espoused. Specifically: Already in a subordinate strand of the chapter of the *Phenomenology of Spirit* on "Religion," but then especially in the *Aesthetics* lectures, Hegel again lapses from Herder's principle that thought is essentially dependent on and bounded by language (albeit in a manner that is different from the relapse in 1796–1800). Already in the unpublished Nuremberg *Encyclopedia* (1808 onwards), and then especially in the published versions of the *Encyclopedia* (1817 onwards), the Philosophy of Spirit contains a short account of language which abandons Herder's conception that meaning consists in word-usage in favor of a more conventional dualistic picture of the relation between words and meanings. And already in later parts of the *Phenomenology of Spirit* such as the "Religion" chapter, but then especially in the late lecture series on art, religion, and philosophy, Hegel tends to renounce Herder's insistence that there are sharp linguistic-intellectual differences between historical periods and cultures, and that one should therefore resist the temptation to interpret others' outlooks in ways that assimilate them to one's own, in favor of positing a large measure of linguistic-intellectual commonality across periods and cultures, at least in the areas of art, religion, and philosophy, and so deeming assimilative interpretation appropriate in these areas.

Finally, in a *third* and last phase of Herder's influence, the period 1827–31 saw Hegel return to a strong interest in language and to Herder-inspired views about language, as he published two long and respectful review articles on the work of a pair of thinkers who were profoundly concerned with language and deeply influenced by Herder—Wilhelm von Humboldt (1827) and Hamann (1828)— and as he in the second and third editions of the *Encyclopedia* (1827/1830), the 1830 cycle of the *Lectures on the Philosophy of World History*, and the preface to the second edition of the *Science of Logic* (1832) himself greatly increased his focus on language. This re-orientation brought with it a significant return to Herderian positions concerning language. In particular, Hegel returned to Herder's princi- ple that thought is essentially dependent on and bounded by language (especially in the 1827 and 1830 editions of the *Encyclopedia*), and he also largely returned to Herder's principles of linguistic-intellectual diversity across historical periods and cultures and of the corresponding need to avoid assimilative interpretation (especially in the 1828 review of Humboldt).

In what follows, I would like to develop this chronological account in more detail. In the course of doing so, I shall pay especially close attention to the most important phase of Herder's influence on Hegel's views about language, the period 1803–7.


## 4. The Early Hegel on Language

There already exists a fairly broad consensus in the relevant secondary literature that the very *early* Hegel was strongly influenced in his views about language by Herder. In particular, it has been widely argued that Hegel's reflections on language in his early *Materials towards a Philosophy of Subjective Spirit* (a text that dates from the Tübingen or Bern periods)[17] exhibit such an influence.[18] This seems very plausible. In particular, the following two features of Hegel's posi- tion in the text can plausibly be traced back to Herder: the implication that language has its origins in the natural sounds of objects, only subsequently becoming extended in its application to non-sounding objects via sensuous analogies (Herder had argued for such a view in his *Treatise on the Origin of Language* [1772]);[19] and the broader assumption of a primacy of hearing over vision (Herder had also argued for this in his *Treatise*).[20]

But it also seems clear to me that Herder's impact on the very early Hegel's views about language reaches well beyond that particular text. For example, when Hegel in another very early fragment (from 1788) argues that the Greeks had certain modes of expression, or words, which we lack, and therefore had certain concepts which we inevitably lack,[21] both his assumption that concept-possession essentially depends on a mastery of corresponding words and his picture of the disparateness of the verbal-conceptual resources possessed by different languages clearly echo Herder.[22]

So much for the earliest phase of Herder's influence on Hegel's philosophy of language. There followed, however, a short phase towards the end of Hegel's work on the early theological writings, roughly the period 1796–1800, during which he tended to lapse from such Herderian principles temporarily, especially by coming to suppose that certain thoughts (in particular, thoughts of a religious nature) are *ineffable*. This temporary lapse is visible in Hegel's poem *Eleusis* (1796) and in *The Spirit of Christianity and its Fate* (1798–1800).[23] It is probably no accident that Hegel was in close contact with Hölderlin at this time, for Hölderlin was similarly committed to the idea that there are deep ineffable truths (for example, in his novel *Hyperion*).

## 5. The Jena Hegel on Language

By far the most interesting phase of Hegel's philosophy of language, though, belongs to the period that stretches from about 1803–4, when he wrote his *First Philosophy of Spirit*, until about 1807, when he published the *Phenomenology of Spirit*. The secondary literature has been much less unanimous on the question of whether or not Herder exercised a strong influence on Hegel's philosophy of language during *this* period. For instance, the best book on Hegel's philosophy of language, Bodammer's *Hegels Deutung der Sprache*, seems skeptical that he did.[24] However, it seems clear to me that he *did*, and indeed that Hegel's philosophy of language during this period was basically Herderian through and through (excepting only some rather modest modifications). Let me therefore now identify some of the main continuities involved. The following twelve seem to me especially striking and important.

(1) Herder had advanced the distinctive thesis that thought is essentially dependent on and bounded by language—i.e. that one can only think if one has a language, and one can only think what one can express linguistically. Hegel already implies the same thesis in his *First Philosophy of Spirit* of 1803–4. For example, he writes there: "Language/speech [*Sprache*] only exists as the language/speech of a people, *and Understanding and Reason, likewise*"; language/speech is "the becoming of Understanding and Reason."[25] The same thesis then goes on to play a very central role in the *Phenomenology of Spirit* as well. For example, it underpins Hegel's implicit assumption in the work's opening "Sense-

certainty" section that the fact that all linguistic (including gestural) expression turns out to be, not a *meinen*, but instead *allgemein* shows that Sense-certainty's conception of its own thought/cognition as a *meinen* is untenable.[26] It reappears more explicitly in the work's "Physiognomy and Phrenology" section as follows:

> Although it is commonly said that reasonable men pay attention not to the word but to the thing itself, yet this does not give us permission to describe a thing in terms inappropriate to it. For this is at once incompetence and deceit, to fancy and to pretend that one merely has not the right *word*, and to hide from oneself that really one has failed to get hold of the thing itself, i.e. the concept. If one had the concept, then one would also have the right word.[27]

The thesis also guides Hegel's discussion in the section of the "Religion" chapter titled "The Artificer," where it constitutes Hegel's implicit reason for being inclined (albeit a little equivocally, and rather contrary to his later position in the *Aesthetics*) to deny that the non-linguistic architecture and sculpture of the ancient Egyptians can really express thoughts/meanings.[28] By contrast—in yet another reflection of the thesis—Hegel implies that with the language-using Sphinx, which he discusses towards the end of "The Artificer," and then with the linguistic art of the Greeks, which he discusses in "The Religion of Art," thought/meaning *does* emerge.[29] Indeed, even in the *Encyclopedia* of 1827 and 1830 Hegel still retains a version of the thesis. Thus in both editions he writes at paragraph 462, "It is in names that we *think*," and then elaborates in a corresponding addition [*Zusatz*] that "we . . . only have determinate, genuine thoughts when we give them the form of objectivity, . . . i.e. the form of externality . . . Only the *articulated sound*, the *word*, is such an inward external thing. To want to think without words . . . is therefore clearly an absurdity."[30] Lest any residual doubt remain that Herder was the original source of this thesis in Hegel, note also that in the course of expressing it Hegel sometimes characterizes language as the "organ" of thought, or of the inner,[31] and expresses approval of the ambiguity of the Greek word *logos* as between "speech" and "reason"[32]—both things that Herder had already distinctively done in his *Treatise on the Origin of Language* and *On the Cognition and Sensation of the Human Soul*.[33]

(2) Herder had also advanced the distinctive thesis that meanings or concepts are—not, as much of the philosophical tradition had held, items in principle independent of language, such as referents, Platonic forms, subjective mental "ideas" in the manner of the British Empiricists, or whatnot, but instead—*word-usages*. In the *Phenomenology of Spirit* Hegel implicitly adopts the same position. Thus, concerning its negative side, much of the work is implicitly devoted to criticizing and rejecting theories which equate meanings with referents (see the

"Sense-certainty" section), Platonic forms and the like (see the implied criticisms of Plato's theory of forms in the section "Force and the Understanding," and of the similar Stoic theory of the *lekton* in the "Stoicism" section), or subjective mental "ideas" (see the section "Physiognomy and Phrenology"). And concerning the position's positive side, the work instead implicitly equates meanings or concepts with word-usages. Thus, as we have already noted, Hegel writes in the "Physiognomy and Phrenology" section that "if one had the concept, then one would also have the right word." And one of the work's most central and distinctive tasks presupposes the equation in question as well: the task of modifying the existing usages of German words in order to constitute the new concepts required for the articulation of Hegel's own philosophical system.[34]

(3) Herder—in *On the Cognition and Sensation of the Human Soul*, for example—had argued that all concepts are dependent on corresponding sensations, but that where the sensations of human beings are concerned a converse dependence holds as well. Similarly, in the *First Philosophy of Spirit* Hegel implies that all our concepts are based on sensation;[35] and conversely, he argues that even such human sensations as that of blueness are implicitly conceptually articulated.[36] Likewise, later, in the *Encyclopedia* (1827 and 1830), paragraph 8 he writes:

There is an old phrase often wrongly attributed to Aristotle, and supposed to express the general tenor of his philosophy, *Nihil est in intellectu quod non fuerit in sensu*: there is nothing in thought which has not been in sense and experience. If speculative philosophy refused to admit this maxim, it can only have done so from a misunderstanding. It will, however, on the converse side no less assert: *Nihil est in sensu quod non fuerit in intellectu*.[37]

(4) Herder had argued in the *Treatise on the Origin of Language* that indeed not only all thoughts, concepts, and human sensations, but all human mental contents *whatever* are of their very nature implicitly articulated by concepts/language. Similarly, Hegel implies such a position in his *First Philosophy of Spirit* when he represents language as fundamental to all spiritual phenomena; and again in the *Phenomenology of Spirit* when he characterizes language as the "real existence [*Dasein*]" of the self and of Spirit.[38] Indeed, even much later, in the second edition of the *Science of Logic* from 1832 (as well as other late texts), he still holds that all human mental contents are in essential part implicitly constituted by conceptual thought, and hence by language:

Nowadays we cannot be too often reminded that it is *thinking* which distinguishes man from beasts. Into all that becomes for man something inward, a representation, at all, into all that he makes his own, language has penetrated.[39]

(5) Herder had also—at first equivocally in the *Treatise on the Origin of Language* (1772), but then unambiguously in *On the Cognition and Sensation of the Human Soul* (1778)—advanced the doctrine that language is fundamentally *social*. The same doctrine plays a central role in Hegel's Jena writings. Thus, already in the *First Philosophy of Spirit* Hegel writes:

Language only exists as the language of a people, and Understanding and Reason, likewise…Language is something universal [*ein Allgemeines*]…something resounding in the same way in the consciousness of all; every speaking consciousness immediately comes to be another in it. In respect of its content too, language for the first time comes to be true language, to express what each person means [*meint*], in a people.[40]

The same doctrine is central to the *Phenomenology of Spirit* as well. For example, this is a large part of the force of the "Sense-certainty" section's message that language cannot express what one *meint* (i.e. thanks to a typical Hegelian pun: *means* solely *by oneself*) but only *das Allgemeine* (i.e. thanks again to a typical Hegelian pun: a *general concept* that is *common to all people*). And as I have attempted to show in detail elsewhere, the work as a whole also undertakes to *prove* this doctrine by offering a systematic critique of *individualistic* conceptions of meaning which shows each of them to be untenable.[41] This doctrine also inflects the work's conception of its previously mentioned task of constructing new concepts by modifying existing word-usages in a certain way: because concepts are fundamentally social in nature, this needs to be done *collectively* by a linguistic community.[42]

(6) Herder had argued—especially in the *Treatise on the Origin of Language* and *On the Cognition and Sensation of the Human Soul*—that because the self is essentially a thinker (and a locus of other mental processes which essentially involve thought), and thought essentially depends on language, *the self essentially depends on language*. Similarly, as we saw in the preceding paragraph, Hegel already in the *First Philosophy of Spirit* holds that the individual consciousness essentially depends on language. And in the *Phenomenology of Spirit* he in effect repeats the same position by saying that language is the "real existence [*Dasein*]" of the self.[43]

(7) Herder had moreover argued—again especially in the *Treatise on the Origin of Language* and *On the Cognition and Sensation of the Human Soul*—that because the self is essentially a thinker (and a locus of other mental processes that essentially involve thought), and thought is essentially linguistic, but language is fundamentally dependent on society, *the self fundamentally depends on society*:

The human being is…a creature of the herd, of society…No individual human being exists for himself, he is inserted into the whole of the species, he is only one for the continuing series…The instruction of the single soul is the parental language's circle of ideas.[44]

Hegel repeats this doctrine in his Jena writings. Thus, as we recently saw, he writes in the *First Philosophy of Spirit*:

Language only exists as the language of a people, and Understanding and Reason, likewise...Language is something universal [*ein Allgemeines*]...something resounding in the same way in the consciousness of all; every speaking consciousness immediately comes to be another in it.

Likewise, he writes in the *Phenomenology of Spirit*:

The power of speech [*Die Kraft des Sprechens*]...is the real existence [*Dasein*] of the pure self as self; in it, self-consciousness's autonomous individuality comes into existence as such, so that it exists for others. Otherwise, the "I"...is non-existent, is not there [*ist nicht da*]...Speech/language [*Sprache*]...contains [the "I"] in its purity, it alone expresses the "I," the "I" itself. This real existence of the "I" is, qua real existence, an objectivity which has in it the true nature of the "I." The "I" is this particular "I"—but equally the universal "I"...The "I" that expresses itself is heard [*vernommen*]; it is an infectious bondedness [*Ansteckung*] in which it has immediately passed into unity with those for whom it is a real existence, and is a universal self-consciousness.[45]

(8) Herder had also argued that whole peoples, and even God, essentially depend on language as the required medium for their essential thinking.[46] Similarly, Hegel in the *First Philosophy of Spirit* represents language as the most fundamental activity of a people;[47] in the "Spirit" chapter of the *Phenomenology of Spirit* likewise characterizes language as the "real existence [*Dasein*]" of Spirit (i.e. of national Spirits);[48] and later in the 1830 cycle of the *Lectures on the Philosophy of World History* continues to imply the same view when he argues that language is a precondition of history.[49] Moreover, Hegel also conceives God (or Absolute Spirit) as essentially linguistic.[50]

(9) Herder had argued—especially in *Ideas for the Philosophy of History of Humanity* and *Metacritique on the Critique of Pure Reason*—that language never makes immediate contact with particulars but instead always works through universal concepts. Hegel continues the same position in the "Sense-certainty" section of the *Phenomenology of Spirit*, where he argues that even such words as "this," "now," "here," and "I," which might at first sight seem to make immediate contact with particulars, in fact always express the universal [*das Allgemeine*].[51]

(10) Herder—in the *Treatise on the Origin of Language* and the *Ideas for the Philosophy of History of Humanity*, for example—had argued that the sense of hearing is superior to vision, and that accordingly spoken language is not only prior but also superior to written language. Hegel already in his early *Materials towards a Philosophy of Subjective Spirit* implies the same position—and that alphabetical writing (which reflects the spoken word) is therefore superior to hieroglyphic writing (which fails to do so).[52] And he continues to hold these

views ever henceforth, including during the period 1803–7. Thus, he again accords priority and superiority to the spoken word in his *First Philosophy of Spirit* (as can be seen from passages already quoted above). He also does so in the *Phenomenology of Spirit*, where, for example, he writes (in a passage that has likewise already been quoted) that it is the "power of speech [*Kraft des Sprechens*]" that is the real existence of the self, and that the self that expresses itself is "heard [*vernommen*]."[53] And he preserves the same views in later writings as well—where, for instance, one still finds him holding that alphabetical writing (i.e. writing that reflects speech) is therefore superior to hieroglyphic writing (i.e. writing that fails to reflect speech).[54]

(11) Herder—for example, in the *Fragments on Recent German Literature* (1767–8) and *This Too a Philosophy of History for the Formation of Humanity* (1774)—had held that people's linguistic-conceptual resources and beliefs differ sharply from historical period to historical period, and from culture to culture. Similarly, Hegel often adopts the same position. We have already seen one example of this from his very early writings. But his writings from the period 1803–7 also contain striking examples. For instance, the *Phenomenology of Spirit* espouses such a position in developing its history of sharply different "shapes of consciousness" (and of spirit and religion) (which in particular pays close attention to the distinctive *linguistic* characters of the different "shapes" that occur).[55] In the same vein, Hegel writes shortly afterwards in his address *On Classical Studies* from 1809 that "the young mind must be led into a remote and foreign world. Now, the screen best suited to perform this task of estrangement for the sake of education is the world and language of the ancients."[56] Such a position also sometimes recurs in Hegel's later writings, for example in his 1827 review of Humboldt.

(12) Because of the phenomenon of difference just described, Herder—again in *This Too a Philosophy of History for the Formation of Humanity*, for example—had insisted on the importance in interpretation of resisting the temptation to impose one's own conceptual and epistemic position on texts (and on non-linguistic forms of expression such as visual art) from other periods and cultures which in fact express concepts and beliefs different from one's own. Hegel often adopts the same position. For instance, in the introduction to the *Phenomenology of Spirit* he writes concerning the work's investigation of the history of shapes of consciousness:

We do not need to import criteria, or to make use of our own bright ideas and thoughts during the course of the inquiry; it is precisely when we leave these aside that we succeed in contemplating the matter in hand as it is *in and for itself.*[57]

Such a position sometimes recurs in Hegel's later work as well, for example in his 1827 review of Humboldt.[58]

These, then, are twelve distinctive positions from Herder's philosophy of language which Hegel basically takes over to form the core of his own philosophy of language during the period 1803–7.

## 6. The Hegel of 1807–27 on Language

As I have already shown in relation to several of the Herderian positions discussed in the previous section, Hegel's espousal of Herder's positions concerning language during the period 1803–7 retained a profound influence on much of his later thought. Nonetheless, the period between the publication of the *Phenomenology of Spirit* in 1807 and about 1827 largely represented a lapse from such positions.

In part this lapse simply took the form of a diminished interest in language, which instead of being the pervasive and fundamental topic that it had been for Hegel during the period 1803–7, now came to play a much less pervasive and shallower role in his thought, mainly indeed being relegated to a rather short and inconspicuous section of the *Encyclopedia* (in the 1827 and 1830 editions, paragraphs 458–64).

But the lapse also involved Hegel actually rejecting a number of the Herderian positions discussed above. For example, contrary to position (1), Hegel already in a quiet counterstrand of the section of the *Phenomenology of Spirit* called "The Artificer," and then much more emphatically in the *Aesthetics* lectures from the 1820s, adopts the position that not all thought need be linguistically expressible by the thinker, that some thought may instead have a foundation in a non-linguistic expressive medium, such as architecture (as in the case of the ancient Egyptians) or sculpture (as in the case of the ancient Greeks).[59]

Similarly, contrary to position (2), Hegel already in the unpublished Nuremberg *Encyclopedia* (1808 and onwards), paragraphs 155–8 develops,[60] and in the last published editions of the *Encyclopedia* (1827 and 1830), paragraphs 458–64 still retains, a sharply dualistic theory of the (linguistic) sign [*Zeichen*] according to which it is the external expression of an inner meaning—[61] a theory very much in the spirit of just the sort of Enlightenment dualism concerning language and meaning that position (2) had been targeted against.

Finally, contrary to positions (11) and (12), Hegel already in the later parts of the *Phenomenology of Spirit*, such as the "Religion" chapter, and then especially in his late lecture series on art, religion, and philosophy tends to move to the position that at least in those three areas of culture the appearance of a deep diversity of outlook turns out to be merely superficial, masking a common attempt to express the monistic standpoint of his own philosophy, and that accordingly at least in those three areas a form of interpretation that assimilates past expressions to his own monistic standpoint is appropriate.

## 7. The Hegel of 1827–31 on Language

That lapse was not Hegel's final word, however. For there was also a third phase of strong Herderian influence on his views about language. This occurred during the period from about 1827 until his death in 1831. (This important final phase of Hegel's philosophy of language has hardly been noticed by the secondary literature at all.)

This phase found some of its earliest manifestations in, and was perhaps occasioned by, Hegel's composition in 1827–8 of two detailed, respectful reviews of works by a pair of thinkers who had themselves been profoundly influenced by Herder's philosophy of language: Wilhelm von Humboldt, whose work on the *Bhagavad-Gita* episode in the Sanskrit poem *Mahabharata* Hegel discussed in a long review in 1827,[62] and Hamann, whose collected works Hegel reviewed at length in 1828.[63] Both of these reviews are heavily concerned with issues about language (in the former case pervasively; in the latter case, in the form of a respectful discussion of Hamann's *Metacritique* from 1784).[64]

Hegel's new interest in the views concerning language held by people who had been deeply influenced by Herder, and his renewed interest in the topic of language itself, continued in the editions of the *Encyclopedia* from 1827 and 1830, where in particular he added material endorsing Humboldt's observation that languages usually become less rather than more grammatically elaborate as civilization progresses (citing Humboldt by name in the 1830 edition).[65] And they also continued in the introduction to the 1830 cycle of the *Lectures on the Philosophy of World History*, where Hegel explicitly mentioned Friedrich Schlegel's *On the Language and Wisdom of the Indians* (1808),[66] and then enthused about the revolutionary recognition of the relatedness of the Indo-European languages that it had inaugurated.[67]

Hegel's renewed conviction in the fundamental importance of language, and his renewed sympathy with Herderian views about it, also manifested themselves during this period in some more systematic ways. For example, the 1827 and 1830 editions of the *Encyclopedia* added much new material on language, saliently including the insistence at paragraph 462, "It is in names that we *think*,"[68] and the connected *Zusatz* material from which I quoted earlier. And the preface to the second edition of the *Science of Logic* from 1832 strikingly emphasized that language plays a fundamental role in all human mental life, and in particular that it does so in Hegel's own Logic.

This final phase of Hegel's thought represents a rather stunning reversion to some of the Herderian positions that he had already espoused in 1803–7, but had lapsed from in the intervening period. In particular, paragraph 462 of the *Encyclopedia* (1827 and 1830), in such statements as the one just quoted above and the related *Zusatz* material, and the preface to the second edition of the *Science of Logic* revert to positions (1) and (2), the positions that thought is essentially dependent on and bounded by language and that meaning consists in word-usage.[69] And Hegel's review of Humboldt also tends to revert to positions (11) and (12), namely in its remarks on the sharp differences that exist between the ancient Indians' outlook and that of modern Europeans, and in its corresponding insistence on avoiding an assimilation of the former to the latter in interpretation.[70]

## 8. Hegel's Deviations from Herder on Language

So far this essay has mainly been concerned to show that Hegel has a philosophy of language, to make a case that it is deeply indebted to Herder's, and to distinguish three periods in which the latter exercised an influence on it, including the especially important period 1803–7.

Although I have largely abstracted from this fact so far, even during the period 1803–7, when Hegel's philosophy of language was most profoundly influenced by Herder, his appropriation of Herder's positions involved some quite significant modifications and elaborations of them. Moreover, as we have seen, during the next period of Hegel's career, 1807–27, he turned to deeper revisions and indeed rejections of them. It seems to me that the modifications and elaborations from the period 1803–7, which mainly occur in the *Phenomenology of Spirit*, are for the most part very imaginative and interesting, and in some cases genuinely insightful, though often philosophically questionable in the end. But it seems to me that the more radical shift away from Herder's positions that Hegel took during the period 1807–27 was in general both less imaginative (largely consisting just in a reversion to more traditional philosophical positions, such as meaning/word dualism) and more decidedly retrograde.[71] That is why, despite the fact that this period was in some ways the core of Hegel's career as a philosopher, I have characterized its positions on language as merely a "lapse" from Herderian positions. Finally, Hegel's return to Herderian positions towards the end of his life, during the period 1827–31, strikes me as by contrast for the most part his attainment of a sort of final wisdom. In what follows I would like to say something about the various modifications, elaborations, revisions, and rejections that were involved in these shifts, in order to try to lend more plausibility to this overall picture. In doing so, I shall organize the discussion in terms of my previous list of Hegel's twelve basic debts to Herder's philosophy of language during the period 1803–7.

Consider first position (1), the thesis that thought is essentially dependent on and bounded by language. This is certainly Hegel's official position in the *Phenomenology of Spirit* from 1807. However, as I mentioned in passing, even there, the section of the "Religion" chapter called "The Artificer," which treats Egyptian architecture and sculpture, while it does for the most part try to stay faithful to that position, also, inconsistently, contains hints that such arts already expressed thoughts which the Egyptians were not yet able to articulate linguistically. For example, Hegel writes there that Spirit "does not yet know the content of this activity [i.e. its own] within itself, but in its work, which is a thing"; the work "includes within it an inner meaning."[72] Later, in the *Aesthetics* lectures from 1823–9, Hegel, in continuity with those hints, revises the position in question more emphatically and unambiguously, now coming to hold as his official position that under certain circumstances people *can* have thoughts which they are not yet able to express linguistically, but only in some other expressive medium, such as architecture (as in the case of the ancient Egyptians) or sculpture (as in the case of the ancient Greeks).[73]

Indeed, at points in the *Aesthetics* lectures Hegel's departure from position (1) seems to be even more extreme than that. The new position just described would still be compatible with a large measure of continuity with position (1), in that Hegel might at least still be retaining his original idea—contradicting the Enlightenment's standard sharp dualism concerning the relation of thought to its expression—that thought essentially depends on and is bounded by a material-perceptible mode of expression (the revision merely lying in the fact that he now broadens such modes to include in addition to language also other symbolic media). However, at points in the *Aesthetics* lectures he actually seems to argue that ancient "symbolic" architecture (such as that of the Egyptians) was characterized by a *discrepancy* between its expressive form and its semantic content—[74] which would imply that he is at least abandoning the claim of an essential *bounding* of thought by its material-perceptible mode of expression. Even this would still leave a modest residue of continuity with position (1). For one thing, the claim of an essential *dependence* of thought on a material-perceptible mode of expression would still be retained. For another thing, Hegel does not go as far as to deny that the thoughts that are sustained by non-linguistic modes of expression, such as ancient architecture, can *ever* be linguistically expressed by *anyone*. On the contrary, he holds that they always eventually can, and indeed that their eventual linguistic expression will always be more adequate than their original non-linguistic expression.[75] Nonetheless, Hegel's new position seems pretty far removed from his original Herderian position (1).[76]

Hegel's new position certainly represents an interesting alternative to that earlier one. But is it really a philosophical improvement on it? In "Hegel and Some (Near-)Contemporaries: Narrow or Broad Expressivism?"[77] I have argued that it is *not*, that it is in the end philosophically inferior to the earlier position.

If that is right, then Hegel's evident tendency to revert to position (1) at the very end of his life, especially in paragraph 462 of the *Encyclopedia* of 1827 and 1830 and in the preface to the 1832 edition of the *Science of Logic*, arguably shows his attainment of a sort of final wisdom.

Consider next position (2)—the denial that meanings/concepts are items independent of language, such as referents, Platonic forms, subjective mental "ideas" in the manner of the British Empiricists, and so on, and the equation of them instead with word-usages. The *Phenomenology of Spirit* not only espouses this position, but also elaborates on it in at least two significant ways: First, the work makes a more ambitious attempt to *prove* it than any yet to be found in Herder. This proof essentially takes the following form. First of all, the proof systematically runs through all of the alternative theories about meanings/concepts that history has thrown up, such as the theory that meaning is an immediate referent (in the section "Sense-certainty"), the Platonic theory of forms (in the section "Force and the Understanding"), the Stoics' variant of that theory, namely their account of the *lekton* (in the "Stoicism" section), and the Empiricists' theory of subjective mental "ideas" (in the section "Physiognomy and Phrenology"), showing in each case that these theories are untenable—in particular, because inconsistent with the decisive role that linguistic behavioral criteria play in our everyday ascriptions to people of an understanding of meanings/concepts. The proof then on that basis infers to an equation of meanings/concepts with word-usages instead, as the only viable alternative theory (recall here Hegel's observation in the "Physiognomy and Phrenology" section: "If one had the concept, then one would also have the right word").

Second, as I mentioned previously, the *Phenomenology of Spirit* also founds on the basis of this position (now treated as an assumption) a certain very distinctive and elaborate project. Already in a famous letter to Voss from 1805, and in some roughly contemporaneous fragments preserved by his biographer Rosenkranz, Hegel had committed himself to a project of making philosophy speak German (rather than, say, a Latin-based terminology). However, he also believes that the concepts that are currently available in German are inadequate for the expression of his own philosophical standpoint.[78] One main reason for this is that they invariably imply dualisms, which are incompatible with the monism of his own philosophical standpoint.[79] On the assumption that concepts consist in word-usages, this problem leads to the following solution: *modify* the existing word-usages of the relevant German vocabulary in order to make it express new, adequate concepts.[80] This is a central task of the *Phenomenology of Spirit* (which, incidentally, helps to explain the work's distinctive sort of obscurity: the fact that it uses familiar vocabulary but in unfamiliar ways).[81]

Both of these elaborations of position (2) within the *Phenomenology of Spirit* are sophisticated and interesting. The first of them, Hegel's development of an ambitious argument for position (2), seems of genuine value. The second of them is also intriguing, at least in its generic form, though in the more specific form that it receives from Hegel it rests on some large philosophical claims which may or may not be well-founded in the end (for example, claims concerning the inadequacy of our everyday concepts due to their inherent dualism).

However, as we have noted, Hegel not only elaborated on position (2) in these ways, but also in some of his later works went on to revise, and even reject, it. In particular, paragraphs 155–8 of the Nuremberg *Encyclopedia* (1808 onwards) already develop, and paragraphs 458–64 of the last two editions of the published *Encyclopedia* (1827 and 1830) still retain, a sharply dualistic theory of the (linguistic) sign as the external expression of an inner meaning, a theory which is much more in the spirit of a conventional Enlightenment dualism than in the spirit of Herder's position (2), and which seems incompatible with the latter. Jacques Derrida has correctly identified and plausibly criticized this sharply dualistic theory from the *Encyclopedia* in his well-known article, "The Pit and the Pyramid: Introduction to Hegel's Semiology."[82] But Derrida overlooks the fact that Hegel had earlier espoused the anti-dualistic and more philosophically attractive position (2). Here again, then, Hegel after publishing the *Phenomenology of Spirit* deviated from his Herderian heritage, and the deviation was a retrograde step.

If this is right, then Hegel's tendency to revert to position (2) at the very end of his life, both in a newer strand of the *Encyclopedia* of 1827 and 1830 (especially paragraph 462) and in the preface to the 1832 edition of the *Science of Logic* (a tendency that Derrida again overlooks), shows his attainment of a sort of final wisdom in this area too.

Consider next position (3)—the thesis that concepts depend on corresponding sensations, and in the case of human beings also conversely. After the period 1803–7 Hegel generally stayed faithful to the latter dependence (i.e. of human sensations on concepts). He sometimes stayed faithful to the former dependence (i.e. of concepts on sensations) as well—for example, in the passage that I already quoted from *Encyclopedia* (1827 and 1830), paragraph 8. However, in other places he seems rather to have renounced it. Here are some prima facie examples: (a) At *Encyclopedia* (1827 and 1830), paragraph 462 he insists that it is possible to think using only words, without intuitions or images. (b) His mature conception both of the progress that occurs within art in the transition from symbolic art (architecture) to classical art (sculpture) to romantic art (painting, then music, and finally poetry), and of the progress that occurs in the broader transition from art to religion to philosophy (especially, Logic), qua expressions of the Absolute, is largely cast in terms of increasing degrees of *abstraction* from the sensuous. (c) He explicitly describes the concepts of his Logic as "a priori" or "pure" (thus echoing Kant's sharp distinction between such concepts and empirical ones), and accordingly in several passages of the Logic seems explicitly to deny that they have any sensuous content.[83]

Evidence (a) and (b) might perhaps be squared with position (3) in roughly the following ways. Concerning (a), Hegel's point at *Encyclopedia*, paragraph 462 seems to be, not so much that thinking can dispense with a sensuous basis *altogether*, but rather that it can occur without a sensuous basis being *concurrently* active in the form of intuitions or images. Thus it is noteworthy that the particular example that he uses there in order to illustrate his point is thinking of a *lion*—i.e. a concept which clearly still seems to be grounded in sensation in *some* way. And concerning (b), his conception that there is an increase in abstraction from the sensuous as one ascends from less to more adequate forms of cognition of the Absolute within art and in the transition from art to religion to philosophy (in particular, the Logic) would not, strictly speaking, preclude even the highest forms of such cognition retaining *some* degree of essential anchorage in the sensuous. However, evidence (c) *does* seem to imply a departure from position (3).

What, then, is Hegel's considered position here? I would suggest that, rather than simply returning to Kant's sharp distinction between "a priori" and empirical concepts and hence abandoning the Herderian position (3) altogether, Hegel modifies position (3) in an interesting way and thereby charts a sort of via media. In Herder, the thesis that all concepts essentially depend on corresponding sensations might be seen as fusing together a claim about their necessary *source* with a claim about their necessary cognitive *content* (albeit while conceding that sensations are sometimes involved in their cognitive content only in a metaphorical way). Hegel in effect separates those two claims, retaining the claim that all concepts necessarily have a sensuous source, but rejecting the claim that they necessarily have a sensuous cognitive content (even a metaphorical one). In particular, according to Hegel the concepts of the Logic do not. Thus, in an interesting passage in the *Aesthetics* he argues that all languages involve a process whereby "a word which originally signifies something sensuous is carried over into the spiritual sphere," as for example in the case of the word *begreifen* (to grasp, to comprehend), or *Begriff* (grasp, concept), but that:

Gradually the metaphorical element in the use of such a word disappears, and by custom the word changes from a metaphorical to a literal expression... If, for example, we are to take *begreifen* in a spiritual sense, then it does not occur to us at all to think of a perceptible grasping by the hand.[84]

Accordingly, in the *Science of Logic* he writes concerning the relation between the "representations" that words express in common life and the concepts that they express in his Logic:

Philosophy has the right to choose from the language of common life, which is made for the world of representations, such expressions as seem to come close to the determinations of the concept. It cannot for that reason be a question of proving for a word chosen from the language of common life that the same concept is connected with it in common life, for common life has no concepts, but only representations. It must therefore suffice if representation in connection with those of its expressions that get used for philosophical determinations has some approximate inkling of the latter's distinctions; just as in connection with those expressions it may be the case that one recognizes in them the shadings of representation which more closely relate to the corresponding concepts.[85]

This Hegelian variation on Herder's position (3) is a subtle and interesting one.

Position (4), the thesis that all human mental contents are at least in an implicit way conceptually-linguistically articulated, does not undergo any *explicit* revision during the period 1807–27. However, Hegel's retreat from positions (1) and (2) during that period does seem to *imply* a revision of it, namely by calling into question whether language need be involved here. To the extent that my negative assessment of that retreat from positions (1) and (2) was correct, this implied revision of position (4) was similarly retrograde. So here again, Hegel's later explicit recommitment to position (4) in the preface of the 1832 edition of the *Science of Logic* represents his achievement of a final wisdom.

Consider next position (5)—the thesis that language is fundamentally social. Hegel's version of this position in the *Phenomenology of Spirit* already involves three significant modifications of Herder's version. First, whereas Herder had in effect only claimed that language is *causally* dependent on society, Hegel makes the stronger claim that it is *essentially* so. Second, unlike Herder, Hegel tries to provide an ambitious *demonstration* of such an essential dependence. This demonstration consists in an attempt to survey all of the possible *individualistic* models of linguistic meaning/conceptualization that the history of thought has generated—for example, Sense-certainty's model of meaning as an immediate, private *meinen*; Force and the Understanding's Platonic model of meaning as mental contact with a Platonic form; Stoicism's similar model of meaning as mental contact with a *lekton*; and Physiognomy and Phrenology's empiricist model of meaning as an individual's mental "idea"—and to show that each of these models proves to be untenable on closer inspection, in order thereby to warrant an inference to the alternative account that linguistic meaning/conceptualization instead consists in participation in a socially shared pattern of word-usage.[86] Third, Hegel also builds on the foundation of this position a more specific conception of his (already discussed) project of establishing by means of the *Phenomenology of Spirit* new usages of familiar German words in order thereby to constitute the new concepts that are required for the articulation of his own philosophy: given that meanings/concepts are essentially constituted by *socially shared* word-usages, it is necessary that the new usages in question become broadly *shared* by his contemporaries, and achieving this is therefore an essential part of his conception of the project.[87]

These three Hegelian innovations are all sophisticated and interesting. The stronger form of the sociality thesis that Hegel espouses would be endorsed by many recent philosophers as well—for example, the later Wittgenstein, John McDowell, and Robert Brandom. Moreover, the elaborate argument that Hegel provides in its support makes his position in a way *superior* to theirs. For they tend to underestimate the counterintuitiveness of the thesis of linguistic meaning's essential sociality. Consider, for example, the intuitively compelling objection expressed by the following rhetorical question: If there had been only one man in the whole history of the world, a sort of cosmic Robinson Crusoe created, say, by a chance confluence of atoms or whatnot, and he had developed a practice of keeping count of his goats and other animals by using different marks for each species and a set of strokes for their numbers on his cave wall, would not those signs have had meanings? Accordingly, the philosophers just mentioned tend to leave the thesis without any real justification.[88] By contrast, Hegel *recognizes* that the thesis is profoundly counterintuitive, and accordingly *does* try to provide a compelling justification for it.

Nonetheless, I strongly suspect that both his strong form of the thesis and the ambitious justification that is designed to establish it fail in the end. This is because there is an individualistic theory of meaning available—indeed, one already known to Hegel—which seems well able to withstand criticism. This is Herder's theory that a person's understanding of a meaning consists in his possession of a real "force" that manifests itself in a certain characteristic pattern of (linguistic) behavior. (By *real* here I mean: not *reducible* to that pattern of behavior, but including an underlying source of it.) Or as one might perhaps more naturally put Herder's thought today: a real *disposition* to a certain characteristic pattern of (linguistic) behavior.[89] I therefore suspect that in the end Hegel's stronger form of the sociality thesis is mistaken. Herder's original, weaker form of the thesis, which only claims that linguistic meaning is *causally* dependent on society, seems more likely to be true.

Concerning position (6), the thesis that the self is essentially dependent on language, although Hegel nowhere explicitly retracts this thesis to my knowledge, his temporary retraction of position (1) during the period 1807–27 implies a retraction of this thesis as well. However, if I am correct in judging that his retraction of position (1) during that period was a philosophical mistake, then this implied retraction of position (6) was a mistake as well. On the other hand, his recommitment to position (1), and consequently also to position (6), in the last years of his life—especially, in *Encyclopedia*, paragraph 462 (for position (1)), and in the preface to the 1832 edition of the *Science of Logic* (for position (6))—again constitutes his attainment of a sort of final wisdom here.

Consider next position (7)—the argument that since the self is essentially a thinker, and thought essentially depends on language, and language fundamentally depends on society, the self fundamentally depends on society. Hegel's version of this position in the *Phenomenology of Spirit* is already slightly different from Herder's because of the difference in the strengths of their versions of position (5), the thesis of the fundamental sociality of language: Whereas Herder in effect only claims that the self is causally dependent on society (since for him, although the links between the self and thought and between thought and language are essential ones, that between language and society is not), Hegel is committed to the stronger claim that the self is *essentially* dependent on society. This is once again a sophisticated and interesting variation on Herder's original position. However, for the reasons already mentioned in connection with position (5), it again seems to me likely that Herder's original position is philosophically superior to Hegel's variation on it in the end.

In addition, Hegel's implicit retraction of position (6) during the period 1807–27 (as discussed above) implies a retraction of position (7) as well (or at least a need to reformulate it in terms, not of language specifically, but of a broader range of expressive media). However, for the same reason as I gave in connection with position (6), such a retraction (or reformulation) of position (7) seems misconceived on reflection. By contrast, Hegel's implied return to a version of position (7) during the last few years of his life would again be the attainment of a sort of final wisdom here.

Concerning position (8), the thesis that society and even God are essentially linguistic, similar points apply to those that applied to position (6): Hegel's temporary retraction of position (1) during the period 1807–27 implies a retraction of position (8) as well. But since the former retraction seems dubious in the end, so does the latter. By contrast, here again his restoration of position (1), and by implication also position (8), during the last few years of his life looks like a return to a better position.

Consider next position (9)—the insistence that language never makes direct contact with particulars but instead always works via general concepts. When developing this position in the *Ideas for the Philosophy of History of Humanity* and elsewhere, Herder primarily had in mind the difficult-looking case of proper names, concerning which his suggestion was that even these implicitly work by means of general concepts (as Frege, Russell, and others would later argue as well). Hegel's main contribution here, it seems to me, was to isolate and deal with another difficult-looking case: that of indexical expressions such as "this," "now," "here," and "I," which might well still seem to be capable of a direct reference to particulars even if proper names are not. In the "Sense-certainty" section of the *Phenomenology of Spirit* he argues that in fact these too essentially involve general concepts, or "universals." His argument is complex, but one of its most compelling strands is that in the absence of implicitly assumed general concepts (e.g. for "this," the general concept "physical object" or "color") such indexical expressions would be unable to achieve definite reference at all.[90]

Concerning position (10), the thesis that hearing is superior to vision, and that spoken language is therefore not only prior but also superior to written language: As we saw, Hegel's views on this subject remained continuous with Herder's, and virtually unchanged, throughout his career. It is not clear that this is a virtue, however. For position (10) includes several ideas, not all of which are equally valid. Insofar as it merely holds that where human beings are concerned spoken language is chronologically prior to and the basis of written language, it is on very strong ground. But insofar as it implies that *all* language, or even all *possible* language, is based on spoken language, it seems very dubious. Indeed, I would suggest that such a view is one of the more persistent and serious errors in the tradition of theorizing about language to which Herder and Hegel both belong.[91] Likewise, the implication that spoken language is inevitably *superior* to written language due to a superiority of hearing over vision seems very dubious.

Finally, consider positions (11) and (12)—the insistence that there are deep linguistic-intellectual differences and a corresponding frequent need to avoid falsely assimilative interpretations. As we saw, although Hegel initially showed a certain tendency to follow Herder in espousing these principles during the period 1803–7 or so, during the period 1807–27 or so he became more inclined to *contradict* them, especially in connection with the subject-matter of art, religion, and philosophy (God, or the Absolute).

Moreover, even within each period Hegel appears to be rather inconsistent. For example, already in the *Phenomenology of Spirit*, whereas earlier parts of the book do indeed tend to espouse positions (11) and (12)—the introduction championing non-assimilative interpretation, and the "Unhappy Consciousness" section accordingly representing Christianity as an outlook that does not, like Hegel's own, recognize God's identity with mankind, but instead sharply separates them—later parts of the book rather tend to contradict positions (11) and (12)—a passage from the "Religion" chapter which Gadamer in *Truth and Method* singles out for approval *advocating* assimilative interpretation,[92] and the same chapter accordingly now interpreting Christianity as an outlook that *does*, like Hegel's own, recognize God's identity with mankind. Similarly, whereas Hegel's later lecture series from the 1820s on art, religion, and philosophy tend to continue positions of the latter sort, his 1827 review of Humboldt rather tends to champion positions (11) and (12) again.

Hegel may not be guilty of any real inconsistency here in the end. In particular, it may be that the two sharply contrasting stances that he adopts at different points within the *Phenomenology of Spirit* correspond to significantly different contexts of interpretation which require different sorts of interpretation and correspondingly different criteria of meaning-identity, constitutive of somewhat different concepts of meaning—so that the two stances avoid really contradicting each other.[93] And in his 1827 review of Humboldt, which strikingly revives the Herderian themes of sharp linguistic-intellectual difference and the need for non-assimilative interpretation, but also implies that at least people's most general categories are shared by all languages and should therefore be interpreted in an assimilative manner, Hegel actually proposes a way of reconciling those two stances: roughly, by distinguishing between the superficial thoughts that another people expresses explicitly, or with self-transparency, and the deeper thoughts that it thereby expresses only implicitly, or unclearly.[94]

The more serious problem in this area is probably that—problems of inconsistency aside—Hegel's move towards a stance that downplays linguistic-intellectual difference and advocates assimilative interpretation seems a retrograde step in itself. Thus, in other work I have argued that downplaying linguistic-intellectual difference is a philosophical error.[95] And in "Hegel and Hermeneutics" and "Hermeneutics,"[96] I have made a case against the arguments that Hegel and others have offered in support of assimilative interpretation.

## 9. Concluding Overview

Aside from briefly introducing Hegel and his philosophy in a general way, this article has mainly been concerned to show the following things: The philosophy of language plays a central role within Hegel's broader philosophy. He developed his core positions concerning language under the strong influence of, and in substantial agreement with, Herder. This influence was especially marked during the years 1803–7, which culminated in the publication of the *Phenomenology of Spirit* (1807), but it also made itself felt during two other periods, one at the very beginning and the other at the very end of Hegel's career. Hegel did, however, also elaborate, modify, revise, and even reject several of Herder's positions, to some extent already in the *Phenomenology of Spirit*, but then especially during the period 1807–27. Whereas in the *Phenomenology of Spirit* such modifications tended to be philosophically imaginative and interesting, and indeed in certain cases genuinely insightful, during the period 1807–27 they rather tended to be unimaginative and philosophically retrograde. Finally, the very last years of Hegel's career, 1827–31, saw him make a strong and salutary return towards Herderian positions.[97]

## Notes

1. T. Pinkard, *Hegel: A Biography* (Cambridge: Cambridge University Press, 2000) is a good intellectual biography. C. Taylor, *Hegel* (Cambridge: Cambridge University Press, 1975) and M. Inwood, *Hegel* (London: Routledge and Kegan Paul, 1983) are both excellent general accounts of the content of Hegel's philosophy.
2. See my *Hegel's Idea of a Phenomenology of Spirit*.
3. G.W.F. Hegel, *Science of Logic* (New York: Humanities Press, 1976), p. 50. (I have often modified the translations cited in this essay or substituted my own without giving specific notice.)
4. See e.g. G.W.F. Hegel, *Lectures on the Philosophy of World History: Introduction* (Cambridge: Cambridge University Press, 1980), p. 51.
5. The closest thing to this would be Hegel's discussion of signs and language at *Encyclopedia of the philosophical Sciences in Outline* (1830) = G.W.F. Hegel, *Werke* (Frankfurt am Main: Surhkamp, 1970), vols. 8–10, pars. 458–64. However, as we shall see, this turns out not to be his most interesting statement on the subject.
6. Cf. the status of "dialectic" within Hegel's system: it too lacks any discrete section in the system but nonetheless plays a pervasive and deep role.
7. Cf. H. Freyer, "Sprache und Kultur," *Die Erziehung* (1928), esp. pp. 66–9. Freyer takes a similar view, but unfortunately provides few details.
8. Hegel criticizes Herder for this in his review of Hamann's works from 1828.
9. This is Hegel's attitude towards Herder in *Faith and Knowledge* (1802).

10. See esp. W. Dilthey, *Die Jugendgeschichte Hegels*, in his *Gesammelte Schriften* [henceforth DGS] (Stuttgart: B.G. Teubner and Göttingen: Vandenhoeck and Ruprecht, 1914–), vol. 4; J. Schwarz, *Hegels philosophische Entwicklung* (Frankfurt am Main: Klostermann, 1938); T. Haering, *Hegel: sein Wollen und sein Werk* (Leipzig/Berlin: B.G. Teubner, 1929–38), vols. 1 and 2; H.S. Harris, *Hegel's Development: Toward the Sunlight 1770–1801* (Oxford: Oxford University Press, 1972); C. Taylor, *Hegel*, and "Hegel's Philosophy of Mind," in his *Human Agency and Language: Philosophical Papers I* (Cambridge: Cambridge University Press, 1996).

11. See my *Hegel's Idea of a Phenomenology of Spirit*; "Das geistige Tierreich," in *Hegels Phänomenologie des Geistes*, ed. K. Vieweg and W. Welsch (Frankfurt am Main: Suhrkamp, 2008); and "Ursprung und Wesen des Hegelschen Geistbegriffs" (*Hegel-Jahrbuch*, autumn 2010).

12. See my "Das geistige Tierreich."

13. See my "Ursprung und Wesen des Hegelschen Geistbegriffs."

14. See *After Herder*, Essay 1.

15. See my *Hegel's Idea of a Phenomenology of Spirit*, pp. 332–48 and "Das geistige Tierreich."

16. For some further details, see my "Das geistige Tierreich." The review just mentioned was not published and is unfortunately now lost.

17. J. Hoffmeister, ed., *Dokumente zu Hegels Entwicklung* (Stuttgart: Frommann, 1936), pp. 210 ff.

18. See esp. J. Hoffmeister, "Hegels erster Entwurf einer Philosophie des subjektiven Geistes," *Logos*, 20 (1931), p. 150; T. Bodammer, *Hegels Deutung der Sprache* (Hamburg: Felix Meiner, 1969), pp. 267 n. 43, 272 n. 34; also D.J. Cook, *Language in the Philosophy of Hegel* (The Hague/Paris: Mouton, 1973), pp. 25–8.

19. Cf. Hoffmeister and Bodammer, as cited in the preceding note.

20. Cf. Cook, as cited in the note before last.

21. *Dokumente zu Hegels Entwicklung*, p. 170: the ancient Greeks "in general saw things in different relations, and expressed these connections of things to each other in their language, and hence had concepts which we can [not] have because we lack the words for doing so ... In this respect language is also for us a quite limited collection of particular concepts, in accordance with which we model everything that we see or notice. An essential advantage that the learning of foreign languages allows is indeed the enrichment of our concepts effected in this way, especially when the culture of the peoples who spoke this language was different from our own." Cf. p. 50.

22. Notice that the year in which this fragment was written, 1788, lies roughly in the middle of Herder's serial publication of his *Ideas for the Philosophy of*

*History of Humanity* (1784–91), in which both of the positions just mentioned are prominent. Even Hegel's reference in the fragment to *the ancient
Greeks seeing things in distinctive ways* (see preceding note) echoes Herder,
who had used the very same example (e.g. at *Fragments*, G1:559).

23. Concerning this anomalous phase, cf. Bodammer, *Hegels Deutung der
Sprache*, pp. 216–17. By contrast, Cook overlooks it.

24. See e.g. Bodammer, *Hegels Deutung der Sprache*, p. 133.

25. G.W.F. Hegel, *Jenaer Systementwürfe I* (Hamburg: Felix Meiner, 1986),
p. 226. My emphasis.

26. Cf. my *Hegel's Idea of a Phenomenology of Spirit*, p. 96; also, J. Simon, *Das
Problem der Sprache bei Hegel* (Stuttgart: Kohlhammer, 1966), pp. 21 ff. (As
Simon points out, this situation poses a prima facie problem for the work's
epistemological project, though, in that the thesis in question seems to be
functioning as a sort of *presupposition*.) The exact meaning of the *meinen* vs.
*allgemein* distinction will be explained later. For the moment it does not
matter.

27. G.W.F. Hegel, *Phenomenology of Spirit* (Oxford: Oxford University Press,
1977), p. 198.

28. See e.g. ibid., p. 423: "But the work still lacks the shape and outer reality
in which the self exists as self; it still does not in its own self proclaim that
it includes within it an inner meaning, it lacks language/speech [*Sprache*],
the element in which the meaning filling it is itself present. Therefore the
work, even when it is wholly purged of the animal element and wears
only the shape of self-consciousness, is still the soundless shape which
needs the rays of the rising sun in order to have sound which, generated
by light, is even then merely noise and not language/speech, and reveals
only an outer, not the inner, self."

29. See esp. ibid., pp. 424, 429–30.

30. Hegel, *Encyclopedia* (1830), par. 462. Cf. pars. 459–64.

31. *Phenomenology of Spirit*: "The speaking mouth, the working hand...are
the realizing and completing organs [*Organe*] which have the inner as
such in themselves" (p. 187); "the organ [*Organ*] of language/speech
[*Sprache*]" (p. 189).

32. G.W.F. Hegel, *Jenaer Realphilosophie* (1805–6) (Hamburg: Felix Meiner,
1969), p. 183: "*Logos* [is] reason,...and speech." Cf. G.W.F. Hegel, *Lectures
on the History of Philosophy* (Atlantic Highlands, NJ: Humanities Press,
1974), 3:204: "*Logos* is more definite than word, and there is a delightful
double significance in the Greek expression indicating as it does both
reason and speech."

33. Besides helping to demonstrate a debt to Herder, Hegel's approving remarks about the ambiguity of the word *logos* also afford one way of seeing that for Hegel his fundamental philosophical discipline of *Logic* is essentially linguistic. This can also be seen in various other ways—for example, from the Logic of the *Encyclopedia* (1830), par. 24, Zusatz 2; the preface to the second edition of the *Science of Logic*; and Hegel's statement at *Science of Logic*, p. 825 that "Logic exhibits the self-movement of the absolute Idea only as the original *word*, which is an outwardizing/utterance [*Äußerung*]."

34. For more on this task, see my *Hegel's Idea of a Phenomenology of Spirit*, ch. 4. Hegel already anticipates this task in a lecture from 1803–5 reported by K. Rosenkranz, *Hegels Leben* (repr. Darmstadt: Wissenschaftliche Buchgesellschaft, 1977), p. 184. There Hegel champions such an approach as superior to the alternative approach of using foreign terminology for philosophical concepts which our language cannot yet express, while also noting that it requires us to overcome habits of linguistic conformism: "We are not used to doing violence to language and forming *new forms from old words*."

35. *First Philosophy of Spirit*, in *Jenaer Systementwürfe I*, p. 197: "Consciousness . . . as concept has immediately raised itself out of *sensation*." Cf. *Phenomenology of Spirit*, p. 19.

36. *Jenaer Systementwürfe I*, pp. 202–3.

37. *Encyclopedia* (1830), par. 8.

38. *Phenomenology of Spirit*, pp. 308–9, 395, 405.

39. *Science of Logic*, p. 31. Cf. *Encyclopedia* (1830), pars. 2, 8, 24 (Zusatz 1), and 459.

40. *Jenaer Systementwürfe I*, p. 226.

41. See my *Hegel's Idea of a Phenomenology of Spirit*, ch. 4.

42. For more details, see ibid.

43. *Phenomenology of Spirit*, pp. 308–9. (The relevant passage is quoted in my next paragraph.)

44. *Treatise on the Origin of Language*, in *Herder: Philosophical Writings* (Cambridge: Cambridge University Press, 2002), pp. 139–41. Cf. *On the Cognition and Sensation of the Human Soul*, ibid., pp. 211–12.

45. *Phenomenology of Spirit*, pp. 308–9. Cf. pp. 395, 397, 430.

46. The former position (about peoples) is pervasive in Herder's writings. Herder commits himself to the latter position (about God) only in his later works (see *After Herder*, Essay 3).

47. *Jenaer Systementwürfe I*, pp. 226–7.

48. *Phenomenology of Spirit*, pp. 395, 405.

49. *Lectures on the Philosophy of World History: Introduction*, pp. 131–8. Cf. Bodammer, *Hegels Deutung der Sprache*, p. 142; Simon, *Das Problem der Sprache bei Hegel*, p. 143.

50. This is implied by his conception of God as fundamentally *Logic*, for instance (see e.g. *Science of Logic*, pp. 824–5). Cf. Bodammer, *Hegels Deutung der Sprache*, pp. 213–14; Simon, *Das Problem der Sprache bei Hegel*, pp. 148–50.

51. Cf. *Encyclopedia* (1830), par. 20.

52. *Dokumente zu Hegels Entwicklung*, p. 211.

53. Accordingly, Hegel sometimes implies that there is a deeply significant etymological connection between this verb *vernehmen* and the noun *Vernunft*, reason.

54. See e.g. *Encyclopedia* (1830), par. 459. Note that in retaining this position, Hegel was opposing a tradition of Romantic thought that accorded hieroglyphics priority and superiority over other forms of language (concerning this tradition, see Fiesel, *Die Sprachphilosophie der Deutschen Romantik*, pp. 175–80). Concerning the whole theme of (10), cf. Cook, *Language in the Philosophy of Hegel*, pp. 25–8, 122, 135; Bodammer, *Hegels Deutung der Sprache*, pp. 88, 92–5; Simon, *Das Problem der Sprache bei Hegel*, pp. 69 ff.

55. Sections in which the linguistic character of a "shape" is especially emphasized include "Sense-certainty," "Physiognomy and Phrenology," "Culture," "Conscience," "The Artificer," and "Religion in the Form of Art." Cf. Cook, *Language in the Philosophy of Hegel*, who notes this close attention to language, and traces some of its details. Also, A. Koyré, "Note sur la langue et la terminologie hégéliennes," *Revue philosophique de la France et de l'Étranger*, 112 (1931), pp. 416 ff. As Simon argues convincingly in *Das Problem der Sprache bei Hegel*, though, there is also an implicit reference to language in many other sections of the work (e.g. "Force and the Understanding").

56. G.W.F. Hegel, *Early Theological Writings* (Philadelphia: University of Pennsylvania Press, 1981), p. 328.

57. *Phenomenology of Spirit*, p. 54.

58. See Hegel, *Werke*, 11:132–3, 139–40, 141–2, 148–9, 189–90, 203. In this case Hegel is especially concerned to insist that it is a mistake to assimilate ancient Indian ethical conceptions to our own, as some interpreters have been inclined to do.

59. See e.g. already *Phenomenology of Spirit*, pp. 422–3: Spirit "does not yet know the content of this activity [i.e. its own] within itself, but in its work,

which is a thing"; the work "includes within it an inner meaning." Concerning this position in the *Aesthetics* lectures, see Essay 6.

60. Hegel, *Werke*, 4:51–2.

61. Concerning this theory's application to *linguistic* signs specifically, see esp. par. 461.

62. Hegel, *Werke*, 11:131 ff.

63. Ibid., pp. 275 ff.

64. The discussion occurs at ibid., pp. 326 ff. Incidentally, this discussion might prompt someone to suggest that it was actually *Hamann* rather than Herder who played the key role in forming Hegel's philosophy of language (especially given that Hegel compares Herder's *Metacritique* unfavorably with Hamann's in the course of it). However, such a suggestion seems to me implausible. For one thing, whereas Hegel's engagement with a broad range of Herder's thought can be documented from the earliest periods of his career, his interest in Hamann hardly seems to antedate this late review. For another thing, although Hegel mentions in the review that Hamann's *Metacritique* had already been published by 1800, he gives no indication that he was himself either then or later influenced by Hamann.

65. *Encyclopedia* (1830), par. 459.

66. Hegel, *Lectures on the Philosophy of World History: Introduction*, p. 132.

67. Ibid., p. 135: "A great historical discovery, like the discovery of a new world, has been made in the last twenty [years] or upwards in connection with the Sanskrit language and its affinities with the languages of Europe..." (Hegel does not explicitly mention Schlegel's work again in this specific connection, but the fact that he had done so just a few pages earlier and the phrase "the last twenty [years] or upwards" put the allusion to it beyond any doubt. Hegel's reluctance to praise Schlegel more explicitly is largely explained by the simple fact that he disliked him.)

68. This sentence had not appeared in the first edition of 1817.

69. Concerning the point that this is a reversion, note that it would be very difficult to reconcile these late commitments to positions (1) and (2) with Hegel's intervening deviation from position (1) in his *Aesthetics* lectures or his intervening deviation from position (2) in older strands of the *Encyclopedia*.

70. See *Werke*, 11:132–3, 139–40, 141–2, 148–9, 189–90, 203. Hegel in particular insists that ancient Indian ethical conceptions are sharply different from our own, and that it is therefore a mistake to assimilate them to our own, as some interpreters have been inclined to do.

71. Cf. Cook's similar assessment of the relative value of Hegel's views about language in these two periods at *Language in the Philosophy of Hegel*, p. 175. Accordingly, authors such as Derrida and Derbolav who have focused almost exclusively on Hegel's philosophy of language as it is found during the later of the two periods (especially as it occurs in the *Encyclopedia*) have discussed it at its worst.

72. *Phenomenology of Spirit*, pp. 422–3.

73. Bodammer and Cook both overlook this change in Hegel's position. See e.g. Bodammer, *Hegels Deutung der Sprache*, p. 220.

74. See *Hegel's Aesthetics* (Oxford: Clarendon Press, 1998), pp. 76–7, 300 ff., 421, 433.

75. To put it another way: While language has now ceased to be *constitutively* fundamental for Hegel, it is still *teleologically* fundamental, in that Hegel now conceives both the ascent from less to more adequate forms of art (e.g. from architecture to poetry) and the broader ascent from art to religion to philosophy as ascents from less adequate *non*-linguistic modes of expression to more adequate *linguistic* ones.

76. I put the additional point made in this paragraph tentatively because I think that despite first appearances Hegel may possibly in the end have a way of reconciling his remarks about symbolic art with a strict expressivism. See on this Essay 6.

77. Essay 6.

78. See e.g. *Science of Logic*, p. 708: "Philosophy has the right to choose from the language of common life, which is made for the world of representations, such expressions as seem to come close to the determinations of the concept. It cannot for that reason be a question of proving for a word chosen from the language of common life that the same concept is connected with it in common life, for common life has no concepts, but only representations... It must therefore suffice if representation in connection with those of its expressions that get used for philosophical determinations has some approximate inkling of the latter's distinctions."

79. See e.g. *Phenomenology of Spirit*, p. 23: "To talk of the *unity* of subject and object, of finite and infinite, of being and thought, etc. is inept, since subject and object, etc. signify what they are *outside* of their unity."

80. As Hegel already puts this in a lecture from 1803–5 from which I quoted in a previous note (no. 34): "doing violence to language and forming *new forms from old words*."

81. For more on this project, see my *Hegel's Idea of a Phenomenology of Spirit*, chs. 2 and 4; also, Cook, *Language in the Philosophy of Hegel*, pp. 166–74. For a very helpful account of the details of Hegel's distinctive philosophical

HEGEL ON LANGUAGE  175

use of language, see M. Inwood, *A Hegel Dictionary* (Oxford: Blackwell, 1992).

82. In J. Derrida, *Margins of Philosophy* (Chicago: University of Chicago Press, 1982), esp. pp. 82–4.

83. See e.g. *Encyclopedia* (1830), pars. 3, 12, 19, 24.

84. *Hegel's Aesthetics*, p. 404.

85. *Science of Logic*, p. 708.

86. For a more detailed account of this argument, see my *Hegel's Idea of a Phenomenology of Spirit*, ch. 4. The presence of such an argument in the text has previously been overlooked by commentators. For instance, Bodammer in *Hegels Deutung der Sprache* gives the impression that Hegel's commitment to the sociality of meanings/concepts rests on little more than a bad pun on two quite different senses of the expression *das Allgemeine*: *universal* concept, i.e. concept that applies in common to a whole multiplicity of instances, and concept *shared by all users* (see e.g. p. 94). Hegel does indeed exploit that pun, but he also *justifies it with this argument*; it does not substitute for an argument.

87. For some more details, see my *Hegel's Idea of a Phenomenology of Spirit*, ch. 4.

88. Wittgenstein may be an exception here. Certainly, S.A. Kripke's justly famous reading of Wittgenstein's rule-following argument in *Wittgenstein on Rules and Private Language* (Cambridge, Mass.: Harvard University Press, 1982) attributes to him a highly sophisticated justification. However, as Kripke himself makes clear, he is not in his book offering straightforward exegesis of Wittgenstein's views, but is rather amalgamating them with his own philosophical reactions to them. And it is somewhat doubtful to what extent Wittgenstein himself had such a sophisticated argument in mind. On the other hand, Kripke himself clearly *does* in his book constitute an exception to the pattern described here, which brings his position there very close to Hegel's. This is why I have discussed them in tandem in *Hegel's Idea of a Phenomenology of Spirit*, ch. 4.

89. For a defense of Herder's general conception of mental conditions as real "forces," see my "Ursprung und Wesen des Hegelschen Geistbegriffs." For a defense of the conception of understanding a meaning as a matter of being in a real disposition, see my *Wittgenstein on the Arbitrariness of Grammar*, ch. 4.

90. For a fuller discussion of Hegel's argument, see my *Hegel's Idea of a Phenomenology of Spirit*, pp. 211–12.

91. For more on this, see *After Herder*, Essay 3 and in the present volume Essay 6.

92. *Phenomenology of Spirit*, pp. 455–6. See on this Essay 7.

93. For a fuller articulation of this suggestion, see my *Hegel's Idea of a Phenomenology of Spirit*, pp. 416–19.

94. *Werke*, 11:184, 203–4. A further line of reconciliation implied by the text rather concerns subject-matter: the Herderian position applies to ethics, whereas the anti-Herderian position applies to logical categories.

95. See my "On the Very Idea of Denying the Existence of Radically Different Conceptual Schemes"; and "A Wittgensteinian Anti-Platonism," *The Harvard Review of Philosophy*, 16 (2009).

96. Essays 7 and 9.

97. This essay by no means gives an *exhaustive* treatment of Hegel's views about language. It may therefore be worth briefly listing some further interesting topics that have been more or less omitted: (a) the role of learning foreign languages in developing the self-alienation that is required for culture [*Bildung*], as discussed by Hegel in his 1809 address *On Classical Studies* (see Cook, *Language in the Philosophy of Hegel*, p. 20; also A. Berman, *L'Épreuve de l'étranger* [Paris: Gallimard, 1984]); (b) the theory of the "speculative proposition" that Hegel develops in the preface to the *Phenomenology of Spirit* (see Cook, *Language in the Philosophy of Hegel*, p. 142); (c) certain metaphysical aspects of Hegel's position concerning the superiority of speech over writing, including an alleged superiority of time over space (see the works by Bodammer, Cook, and Derrida already cited in this essay); (d) the ascent from non-linguistic to linguistic forms of art in Hegel's *Aesthetics* lectures; (e) the details of Hegel's project of teaching philosophy to speak German, including his avoidance of purism about this, and the sharp difference in spirit between this project and a superficially similar-looking Fichtean-Heideggerian German linguistic nationalism (see the works by Bodammer and Cook already cited); (f) Hegel's attitude concerning the significance of etymology for philosophy, in particular his selectiveness in this area, and his pragmatic, forward-looking, sometimes playful approach, which contrasts sharply with Heidegger's portentous retrospectivism (see the works by Bodammer and Cook already cited; also, Koyré, "Note sur la langue et la terminologie hégéliennes," pp. 427–8); (g) Hegel's linguistic holism. Concerning (g), Derrida at "The Pit and the Pyramid," p. 96 claims that Hegel only has a conception of language as consisting in isolated names, and in particular that he ignores the essential role of grammar in language. However, several features of Hegel's works suggest that he holds a quite contrary position. These include his discussion in the *First Philosophy of Spirit* of the essentially *relating* nature of language, and in particular the

linguistic relations of the word "blue" (*Jenaer Systementwürfe I*, pp. 202–3); his emphasis in the 1809 address *On Classical Studies* on the central role of *grammar*, with its logical-categorial significance, in the learning of foreign languages; similar reflections about grammar at *Encyclopedia* (1830), par. 459 and in the preface to the second edition of the *Science of Logic*; and also the self-developing categorial structure of his Logic itself.

# 6

# Hegel and Some (Near-) Contemporaries: Narrow or Broad Expressivism?

This essay is concerned with a rather specific question, but one that seems to me of central importance for both the philosophy of language and the philosophy of art. As is by now fairly well known, in the second half of the eighteenth century German philosophers, particularly Herder and Hamann, effected a sharp, and philosophically very plausible, break with a common Enlightenment assumption that meaning and thought are (at least in principle) separable from, and autonomous of, whatever material, perceptible expressions they may happen to receive, instead coming to regard such material, perceptible expressions as *essential* to meaning and thought. Following Charles Taylor, we might call this move one to "expressivism."[1] I do not intend to pursue here the fundamental question of whether expressivism is correct, though I am strongly inclined to believe that it is.[2] The question I want to focus on is rather: Assuming expressivism to be correct, what form should it take *exactly*? In particular, is the dependence of meaning and thought on external expressions strictly a dependence on *language* (in the usual sense of "language"),[3] or is it not perhaps rather a dependence on a broader range of expressive media, including, in addition to language (in the usual sense), also such non-linguistic arts as painting, sculpture, and music, so that a person might be able to entertain meanings and thoughts which he could not express in language but only in one of these other expressive media? Let me call the former position *narrow expressivism* and the latter *broad expressivism*.

A choice for either of these positions would in turn lead to some further interesting questions. For example, a choice for narrow expressivism would prompt the question whether, then, non-linguistic arts express no meanings or thoughts at all, or rather do so but in ways that are parasitic on language. And a choice for broad expressivism would prompt the question: Is, then, the transcendence of language by a person's meanings and thoughts that can occur merely a transcendence of *his* language, or can it also be a transcendence of language *tout court* (so that no amount of development in language could make the meanings and thoughts in question linguistically expressible)?

In raising the question of whether narrow or broad expressivism is correct, I mean to assume fairly everyday concepts of "meaning" and "thought"; I do not have unusual technical concepts in mind, and especially not ones that would guarantee a quick and easy answer to the question. In particular, "thought" in the relevant sense is neither an extremely general word for just any old mental process (as it became in Descartes's technical idiom) nor an extremely specific word for just one type of what we would usually call "thought," namely *linguistic philosophical* thought (as it became in Hegel's technical idiom). The former definition would quickly guarantee the falsehood of narrow expressivism (and probably indeed of expressivism itself); the latter definition would quickly guarantee its truth. One might tentatively define "thought" in the more everyday sense that I have in mind, à la Frege, as anything that can bear a truth-value (i.e. be true or false).[4]

# I

Let us begin with narrow expressivism. The prime representative of narrow expressivism in the period of German philosophy with which we are concerned was Herder, who already committed himself to a version of it as early as the mid-1760s. Herder developed it in the form of two closely related principles: (1) Meanings are to be equated—not with such items, independent of language, as referents, Platonic forms, or the mental "ideas" favored by the British Empiricists and others in the seventeenth and eighteenth centuries, but—with word-usages. (2) Thought is essentially dependent on and bounded by language. Thus, concerning the equation of meanings with word-usages, Herder already writes in *On Diligence in Several Learned Languages* (1764):

Whoever learns to express himself with exactness precisely thereby gathers for himself a treasure of determinate concepts. The first words that we mumble are the most important foundation stones of the understanding.[5]

And already in the *Fragments on Recent German Literature* (1767–8) he insists on the "adhesion of the thought to the word," or the "expression," states that in connection with the understanding of concepts "the question is not how an expression can be etymologically derived and analytically determined, but how it is *used*,"[6] and accordingly advocates that in order, for example, to understand the changing nature of people's moral concepts one must closely scrutinize their changing word-usages.[7] Again, concerning thought's essential dependence on and boundedness by language, Herder already writes in *On Diligence*, in the broader context from which I recently quoted:

What exactly is the connection between language and mode of thought? Whoever surveys the whole scope of a language surveys a field of thoughts and whoever learns to express himself with exactness precisely thereby gathers for himself a treasure of determinate concepts. The first words that we mumble are the most important foundation stones of the understanding, and our nursemaids are our first teachers of logic.[8]

And similarly, he already writes in the *Fragments* that language is

the form of cognition, not merely in which but also in accordance with which thoughts take shape, where in all parts of literature thought sticks [*klebt*] to expression, and forms itself in accordance with this... Language sets limits and contour for all human cognition.[9]

Herder also has some powerful philosophical arguments backing up these two principles, though I shall not go into these here.[10]

Narrow expressivism admits of cruder and subtler versions, however. It seems to me that Herder was initially inclined to adopt a rather naive and implausible version of it, but that he eventually developed a much more refined and attractive version. It may be not only exegetically but also philosophically instructive to consider in a little detail how his thinking on this subject developed.

The key work in this connection is his *Critical Forests* (1769, though the fourth and final part was not published until the middle of the nineteenth century). As we have just seen, by the time he wrote this work Herder was already firmly committed to narrow expressivism. However, his commitment to it there initially takes a naive and unsatisfactory form in relation to the potentially threatening question of what to say about the non-linguistic arts. For his way of saving narrow expressivism's claim that all meaning and thought are dependent on and bounded by language in the face of the phenomenon of the non-linguistic arts is to deny the non-linguistic arts any capacity to express meanings or thoughts *autonomously* of language by denying that they can express any meanings or thoughts *at all*. Thus he initially sets out in the work to argue that whereas words and poetry have a sense, a soul, a force, by contrast music is a mere succession of objects in time, and sculpture and painting are merely spatial;[11] that whereas poetry not only depends on the senses but also relates to the imagination, by contrast music, sculpture, and painting belong solely to the senses (namely, to hearing, feeling, and vision, respectively);[12] and that whereas poetry uses *voluntary, conventional* signs, by contrast music, sculpture, and painting employ only *natural* ones.[13]

Exacerbating this unsatisfactoriness into outright inconsistency, Herder from the start in the work also has a set of intuitions that are sharply at odds with this form of narrow expressivism, and even with narrow expressivism generally—intuitions which imply, far more plausibly, that non-linguistic art *can* express meaning and thought after all, and which even imply in a broad expressivist spirit that it can do so in ways that are neither achieved nor achievable by language. For example, in the first section of the work he intervenes in a quarrel that had arisen between Lessing and Winckelmann concerning the question which of the two is expressively superior, linguistic art (especially poetry), as Lessing thought, or visual art (especially sculpture), as Winckelmann thought, *in ways that tend to support Winckelmann's case for visual art*.[14] In particular, he argues against Lessing and for Winckelmann that sculpture can express not only the temporally transitory but also the eternal;[15] that painting is capable of representing not only objects but also actions;[16] that the *visual* aspects of a work of dramatic poetry such as Sophocles' *Philoctetes* are as important to its meaning as its *verbal* aspects;[17] and that moreover all genuine poetry is "a sort of painting [*eine Art Malerei*],"[18] so that, for example, even in its *verbal* aspects the *Philoctetes* is "a series of acting, poetic paintings."[19]

This unsatisfactory, and indeed inconsistent, position at the beginning of the *Critical Forests* evidently results mainly from a single oversight on Herder's part, namely a failure to see any way of reconciling two strong, and both very plausible, intuitions which he has and which do indeed stand in tension (though not in fact contradiction) with each other: on the one hand, his intuition that meaning and thought are essentially dependent on and bounded by language; and on the other hand, an intuition that non-linguistic arts do nevertheless express meanings and thoughts. Because of that failure, when in the grip of the former intuition, he feels compelled to deny the latter one; and when in the grip of the latter intuition, he treats this as equivalent to abandoning the former one. What he has not yet realized is that it is perfectly possible to maintain both of these intuitions consistently with each other, namely *by insisting that the meanings and thoughts expressed by non-linguistic arts must be derivative from and bounded by the artist's capacity for linguistic expression.*

However, by the time Herder wrote the later parts of the *Critical Forests* he had discovered this solution. Thus, in the third part, focusing on an especially clear and instructive example (that is, one which shows with unusual clarity both that non-linguistic art does sometimes express meanings and thoughts, and that the meanings and thoughts in question have a prior linguistic articulation or articulability), he observes that the pictorial representations on Greek coins are typically allegorical.[20] And by the time he composes the fourth part he is prepared to say the same about much painting as well, now writing, for example, of "the sense, the allegory, the story/history [*Geschichte*] which is put into the whole of a painting."[21] By 1778 at the latest he extends this account to sculpture as well. Thus, in the *Plastic* of 1778 he abandons the merely sensualistic conception of sculpture that had predominated in the *Critical Forests* and instead insists that sculpture is essentially expressive of, and so needs to be interpreted by, a *soul*.[22] But this no longer forces him into unfaithfulness to his principles to the effect that meaning and thought are essentially dependent on and bounded by language, for he now conceives the meanings and thoughts expressed by sculpture to have a linguistic source:

The sculptor stands in the dark of night and gropes towards the forms of gods. *The stories of the poets are before and in him.*[23]

Similarly, in relation to music, Herder in the early 1780s moves away from the merely sensualistic view of music that had predominated in the *Critical Forests* towards a view that allows music intellectual content, but he does so quite consistently with the principles that meaning and thought are essentially dependent on and bounded by language because he ties the content in question to a prior linguistic understanding: Whereas in *On the Effect of Poetic Art on the Ethics of Peoples in Ancient and Modern Times* from 1778 he was still only prepared to say that music was a dark expression of feelings,[24] in the *Theological Letters* of 1780-1 he praises the power of the instrumental side of contemporary church music to express ideas as well, describing it with Luther—in a way that is significant both because it implies the music's expression of a thought-content and because it implies that the content in question derives from a prior linguistic expression—as a "second theology" (i.e. second only to actual theology), and giving specific examples of how the instrumental aspects of a work like Handel's *Messiah* express Christian ideas whose expression was originally linguistic:

What a great work this *Messiah* is, a true Christian epic in sounds! When you right from the start discern the gentle *voice of consolation* and hear *mountain and valley even out* in the whole of nature at the arrival of the Messiah, until *the exaltedness, the exaltedness of the Lord, reveals* itself and *the whole world beholds Him together*...[25]

Similarly, Herder goes on in the *Letters for the Advancement of Humanity* (1793-7) to argue that modern instrumental music more generally (as it existed in his day of course!), with its special emphasis on harmony and melody, developed out of Christian hymns, which were by contrast partly verbal and less harmonic-melodic, and that by means of its harmony and melody it succeeds in expressing with special effectiveness a certain (quasi-Spinozistic) idea of the whole, including a harmonious whole of all peoples, which it took over from those hymns.[26]

There is also a further way in which Herder's considered position, the one at which he arrives by the end of the *Critical Forests*, implies that non-linguistic art involves meaning and thought, and hence language: The above points were concerned with the fact that, like linguistic arts such as poetry, non-linguistic arts such as painting, sculpture, and music are heavily involved in *expressing* meanings and thoughts. But by the time Herder writes the fourth part of the *Critical Forests* he also sees that meanings and thoughts, and hence language, are involved in non-linguistic arts in an even more fundamental way, namely as *presuppositions* of the very *perception* of such art (by the artist and his public). For in the fourth part of the *Critical Forests* Herder begins to argue—anticipating much twentieth-century work on perception generally (e.g. Hansen and Kuhn), and on the perception of non-linguistic art in particular (e.g. Panofsky and Gombrich)—that human perception generally, and human perception of non-linguistic artworks in particular, is of its nature laden with concepts, beliefs, and theory, and hence implicitly dependent on language.[27] Consequently, on Herder's considered view, non-linguistic art is really *doubly* dependent on meaning and thought, and hence on language: not only for the meanings and thoughts that it *expresses* but also for those that it *presupposes* in perception.[28]

In sum, the considered position at which Herder eventually arrives is a refined form of narrow expressivism. It insists that meaning and thought are essentially dependent on and bounded by language (in the usual sense of "language"). But it also allows the non-linguistic arts a power both to presuppose and to express meanings and thoughts. And it reconciles these two seemingly incompatible stances by holding that the power in question is one that the non-linguistic artist (or perhaps one ought really now to use scare-quotes there: "non-linguistic" artist) enjoys in virtue of, and in a manner bounded by, his linguistic capacity.[29]

This position has important implications both for Herder's philosophy of language and for his philosophy of art. Concerning his philosophy of language, it shows that his narrow expressivism can be plausibly reconciled with a forceful intuition which otherwise threatens to conflict with it, namely the intuition that much non-linguistic art expresses meanings and thoughts. Concerning his philosophy of art, it implies that the interpretation of non-linguistic artworks must be in important respects both analogous to the interpretation of linguistic expressions (namely, in ascribing meanings and thoughts) and dependent on it.

Subsequently, Friedrich Schlegel followed Herder in opting for refined narrow expressivism—a position which he applied with great skill to the interpretation of religious painting and cathedral architecture.[30]

## II

So much for narrow expressivism in both its naive and its refined forms. What about broad expressivism?

As far as I can see, the first representative of such a position was Hamann. In his *Metacritique on the Purism of Pure Reason* (1784) Hamann is *verbally* just as strongly committed as Herder to the two principles that constitute Herder's narrow expressivism—the principles that meaning is word-usage, and that thought is essentially dependent on and bounded by (Hamann even goes as far as to say: identical with) language. But Hamann nonetheless embraces broad expressivism. This might seem inconsistent, but in fact it is not, because, unlike Herder, Hamann understands the terms "language" and "word" as they occur in the two principles in unusually wide senses. For example, he explicitly includes as forms of the "language" on which he says thought depends not only language in the usual sense but also painting, drawing, and music.[31] (Herder and Hamann's verbal sharing of the two principles in question thus masks an important difference of philosophical position between the two men.)

A strikingly similar position to Hamann's is espoused a little later by Wackenroder and Tieck in *Outpourings of an Art-Loving Friar* (1797), which likewise represents painting and music as forms of "language" capable of expressing things that language in the narrower sense cannot.[32] (It seems highly likely that Wackenroder and Tieck are indebted to Hamann here.[33])

## III

However, the most important representative of broad expressivism in this tradition is Hegel.[34]

Hegel's commitment to expressivism in general is deep. For example, it reveals itself in a very general form in his Logic's principle that "essence must appear,"[35] and in a less general but more immediately relevant form in such statements as these: "As a man is outwardly, i.e. in his actions..., so is he inwardly,"[36] "The determinacy of the mind is...*manifestation*. The mind is not some determinacy or content whose expression or outwardness would only be a form distinct from it."[37]

The early Hegel of the *Phenomenology of Spirit* (1807) was basically still committed to a form of *narrow* expressivism (as Herder had been). For example, the argument of the opening "Sense-certainty" section implicitly assumes that meaning or believing anything requires an ability to express what one means or believes in language (or at least by the quasi-linguistic act of pointing).This can be seen from the fact that Hegel's critique of Sense-certainty's standpoint there consists in showing that the sort of cognition which Sense-certainty supposes itself to have would be *in principle inexpressible in language* (or by pointing). For *that* is only a telling criticism of Sense-certainty if such expressibility is in some way *essential* to cognition—which of course it is on an assumption that meaning and belief are necessarily expressible in language (or by pointing). Somewhat later in the book the "Physiognomy and Phrenology" section articulates the assumption in question more explicitly:

Although it is commonly said that reasonable men pay attention not to the word but to the thing itself,… this is at once incompetence and deceit, to fancy and to pretend that one merely has not the right *word*, and to hide from oneself that really one has failed to get hold of the thing itself, i.e. the concept. *If one had the concept, then one would also have the right word.*[38]

Finally, the same assumption also appears in the section of the "Religion" chapter called "The Artificer," where it constitutes Hegel's implicit reason for being inclined to deny that the non-linguistic architecture and sculpture of the ancient Egyptians can really express meanings or thoughts:

But the work still lacks the shape and outer reality in which the self exists as self; it still does not in its own self proclaim that it includes within it an inner meaning, it lacks language/speech [*Sprache*], the element in which the meaning filling it is itself present. Therefore the work, even when it is wholly purged of the animal element and wears only the shape of self-consciousness, is still the soundless shape which needs the rays of the rising sun in order to have sound which, generated by light, is even then merely noise and not language/speech, and reveals only an outer, not the inner, self.[39]

By contrast—in yet another reflection of the assumption in question—Hegel implies that with the language-using Sphinx, which he discusses towards the end of "The Artificer," and then with the linguistic art of the Greeks, which he discusses in "The Religion of Art," meaning and thought *do* emerge.[40]

However, there are already some hints in "The Artificer" of a contrary position: a form of *broad* expressivism that allows that architecture and sculpture of the sort in question there can in fact express meanings and thoughts despite being non-linguistic, simply in virtue of being a different sort of symbolism. For example, Hegel writes:"[Spirit] does not yet know the content of this activity [i.e. its own] within itself, but in its work, which is a thing"; the work "includes within it an inner meaning."[41] And it was this broad expressivism that subsequently became Hegel's considered position in the *Aesthetics* lectures of the 1820s.

Hegel's commitment to broad expressivism in the *Aesthetics* lectures can be seen in a general way from his subscription there to the following combination of views: On the one hand, he believes that all art, including non-linguistic art, has the function of expressing mind, meanings, concepts (including, more exalt-edly: *the* concept), and truth.[42] (He is more reluctant to say that it expresses *thought*.[43] However, that is merely because he uses the word "thought" in a technical sense that restricts it to linguistic philosophical thought. If one instead uses the word in our more everyday sense, in which it includes anything that can bear a truth-value, one will certainly want to say that he takes all art to have the function of expressing thought as well.) But on the other hand, he also takes it to be a criterion of art's having any real depth that what it expresses *not already be expressed or expressible in some other way*—[44] which in particular entails that in order to have any real depth non-linguistic art must express things which are not yet expressed or expressible linguistically. Thus it is easy to see in a general way that Hegel is committed to broad expressivism in the *Aesthetics* lectures.

However, Hegel's more detailed position on the question of narrow versus broad expressivism as he develops it in the *Aesthetics* lectures is curiously bifur-cated. As a preparation for illustrating this point, let me first give a brief sketch of the structure of Hegel's overall aesthetic theory. Hegel famously distinguishes between three main types of art: symbolic, classical, and Romantic. The central symbolic art is architecture; the central classical art, sculpture; Romantic art comprises three arts, ascending from painting, through music, to its culmination in poetry. With certain qualifications, this sequence is conceived by Hegel in historical terms: symbolic architectural art was mainly realized among the ancient Egyptians, then classical sculptural art among the ancient Greeks, and finally Romantic painting, music, and poetry in the Christian era. This sequence is not conceived by Hegel in straightforwardly progressive terms, however. Indeed, for him art in a sense already reached its culmination with the classical sculpture of the ancient Greeks, since this was their highest mode of expressing the Absolute (or God), after which Romantic art was only a second- or even third-rate expression of the Absolute for the culture to which it belonged, because inferior to higher expressions of the Absolute which were now avail-able in religion and (eventually) philosophy. For our present purposes, it is of course Hegel's account of the first four arts in this sequence—architecture, sculpture, painting, and music (insofar as it is instrumental)—which is of great-est interest, since these are non-linguistic arts (unlike voiced music and the final art in the sequence, poetry, which are of course linguistic).

Now I said that Hegel's detailed position in the *Aesthetics* lectures concerning the question of narrow versus broad expressivism is curiously bifurcated. It is so in the following way. On the one hand, Hegel is indeed a broad expressivist where ancient architecture and sculpture are concerned: He understands Egyptian (and certain other ancient forms of) architecture to be a symbolic expression (albeit an imperfect one) of the Absolute, and he emphasizes that this meaning or (in *our*, not Hegel's, sense of the word) thought which the architecture in question expressed was *not yet articulated or articulable in any other way*.[45] Similarly, he implies that Greek sculpture was the *highest* expression of the Absolute of which the Greeks were capable.[46] Accordingly, rather than seeing Greek sculpture as subject to interpretation in the light of Greek linguistic texts, as one might perhaps have expected, he instead takes the more surprising and striking converse view that Greek sculpture is an indispensable tool for fully interpreting such texts:

> In its poets and orators, historians and philosophers, Greece is not to be understood at its heart unless we bring with us as a key to our comprehension an insight into the ideals of sculpture and unless we consider from the point of view of their plasticity not only the heroic figures in epic and drama but also the actual statesmen and philosophers.[47]

In short, just as the general position I recently ascribed to him would lead one to expect, Hegel gives a broad expressivist account of Egyptian architecture and Greek sculpture.

But on the other hand, more surprisingly, and in sharp contrast, Hegel's treatment of the other two non-linguistic arts—painting and instrumental music—in the *Aesthetics* lectures is still in the spirit of *narrow* expressivism. To be more precise, Hegel is somewhat torn between naive and refined narrow expressivism in relation to these arts, but his considered position concerning them seems to be refined narrow expressivism. In other words, in his considered view, these two non-linguistic arts do express meanings and thoughts (at least in many cases), but the meanings and thoughts in question are parasitic on a prior linguistic articulation or articulability. This whole position can be seen from the text in two main ways: First, as I mentioned earlier, for Hegel, whereas architecture and sculpture are paradigmatically "symbolic" and "classical" arts respectively, painting and music (along with poetry) are paradigmatically "Romantic" arts. But according to Hegel "Romantic" arts are grounded in, and express, the outlook of the Christian religion, i.e. an outlook whose primary expression is *linguistic* (the Bible).[48] Second, Hegel's detailed interpretive comments on painting and instrumental music reinforce this moral that he understands whatever meanings and thoughts they express to have a prior linguistic articulation or articulability. To consider painting first, that is certainly true of his interpretations of Christian religious painting. For example, when he interprets Raphael's controversial painting the *Transfiguration* he does so in terms of ideas from the Bible, and indeed actually quotes from Matthew's Gospel what he takes to be the central biblical text expressed in the painting: "Where two or three are gathered in my name, there am I in the midst of them."[49] But the same sort of

thing is also true of Hegel's interpretation of the other main category of painting on which he focuses: Dutch genre painting. Occasionally he treats this in a
naive narrow expressivist spirit as *merely* imitative of the Dutch landscapes and
other aspects of daily life that it depicts. But in more considered remarks he
rather treats it in a refined narrow expressivist spirit, pointing out—very perceptively, I think—that it does not merely imitate in this way but also expresses
such thought-imbued sentiments as the Dutch's pride in their hard-won political autonomy, their hard-won religious autonomy (Protestantism), and a landscape that is largely their own creation.[50] Similarly: Hegel sometimes characterizes
instrumental music in a naive narrow expressivist way, as not expressing meanings or thoughts at all but only contentless subjectivity or feeling,[51] whatever
meanings or thoughts it may prompt being prompted only accidentally.[52] But
in more considered remarks he rather interprets instrumental music in a refined
narrow expressivist spirit, implying that it sometimes does, and moreover ought
to, intimate meanings and thoughts (albeit vaguely), and evidently understanding the meanings and thoughts in question to be ones that are already linguistically expressed or expressible rather than a monopoly of the instrumental music
in question.[53]

This bifurcation between broad and narrow expressivism in Hegel's treatment
of the four non-linguistic arts in the *Aesthetics* lectures already constitutes a deep
tension in his account. But, while it may reasonably strike one as strange and suspi-
cious, it does not yet in itself constitute an outright inconsistency. For claiming that
*some* non-linguistic arts express meanings and thoughts which are not yet expressible in other ways is consistent with claiming that *other* non-linguistic arts only
express meanings and thoughts which *are* already expressible in other ways.[54]

However, the later Hegel's intuitions in this area *are* in fact sufficiently torn
to involve outright inconsistency. For not *only* does he in this way combine a
normal commitment to broad expressivism motivated by his interpretation of
ancient architecture and sculpture with a (sometimes naive but in more considered versions refined) narrow expressivism in relation to painting and music,
but in addition he makes explicit commitments to a *global* narrow expressivism
which cannot be reconciled with his normal broad expressivism. Consider, for
example, the following passage from the *Encyclopedia* (1827 and 1830):

It is in names that we *think* . . . We . . . only have determinate, genuine thoughts when we
give them the form of objectivity, of being distinguished from our inwardness, i.e. the
form of externality, and indeed of such an externality as at the same time bears the
imprint of the greatest inwardness. Only the *articulated sound*, the *word*, is such an inward
external thing. To want to think without words, as Mesmer once tried to, is therefore
clearly an absurdity . . . The inexpressible is in truth only something dark, fermenting,
which only achieves clarity when it is able to attain verbal expression.[55]

In sum, the later Hegel's normal position is a form of broad expressivism. But his broad expressivism stands in tension with his treatment of certain areas of non-linguistic art in the spirit of (naive or in more considered passages refined) narrow expressivism. And that tension in his position is indeed exacerbated into an outright inconsistency by late statements of commitment to a global narrow expressivism.[56]

# IV

So far we have encountered within the eighteenth- and nineteenth-century German philosophical tradition three incompatible answers to the central philosophical question that I raised at the start of this essay (all of them sharing the fundamental assumption of expressivism): the naive and the refined forms of narrow expressivism which Herder successively developed, and the broad expressivism preferred by Hamann and Hegel.

We have also seen some evidence of what seems to me a striking and significant further fact: namely, that the tradition in question vacillated among these alternative positions not only *between* but also *within* its individual thinkers. For, as we saw, Herder in the *Critical Forests* not only makes a transition from naive narrow expressivism to refined narrow expressivism, but even at points seems inclined to adopt a form of broad expressivism (namely, in the series of remarks supporting Winckelmann's case for the expressive superiority of visual art over linguistic art). And as we also saw, Hegel is torn not only across periods but even within periods between narrow expressivism and broad expressivism, and concerning the former between naive and refined forms of narrow expressivism. However, it may be worth reinforcing this point by briefly considering a couple of further examples.

Schleiermacher is another good example of this sort of vacillation. His highly conflicted position in this area is perhaps clearest from his late lectures on aesthetics. In those lectures he at first sets out to develop a slightly modified version of the theory that Herder had initially developed in the *Critical Forests*, i.e. a theory which correlates the several non-linguistic arts with the different senses, as Herder's theory had done (merely revising Herder's correlation of sculpture with the sense of touch to include vision as well as touch). Like Herder's theory, Schleiermacher's is motivated by a commitment to narrow expressivism, a conviction in the fundamentalness of language (in the usual sense) to all meaning and thought, which it seeks to vindicate in a naive way: non-linguistic arts, such as sculpture and music, do not express meanings or thoughts autonomously of language because they do not express meanings or thoughts *at all*. For instance, Schleiermacher argues that music expresses, not representations or thoughts, but only physiologically based "life-conditions [*Lebenszustände*]." However, in the course of developing this naive narrow expressivist position Schleiermacher abruptly realizes that it is untenable. For in the middle of his discussion of sculpture he suddenly recalls Pausanias' account that the very earliest Greek sculptures were merely rough blocks whose function was to serve, precisely, as symbols of religious *ideas* (oops!).[57] Accordingly, at this point Schleiermacher changes tack: He now acknowledges that non-linguistic arts *do* (at least sometimes) express meanings and thoughts after all. And he goes on to vacillate between two new and mutually conflicting accounts of that fact: (1) The arts in question express meanings and thoughts in such a way that these are at least sometimes not (yet) linguistically articulable. (In particular, Schleiermacher implies that the early Greek sculpture just mentioned expressed religious ideas which only *later* got expressed linguistically.[58]) (2) The arts in question express meanings and thoughts in virtue of a pre-existing linguistic articulation or articulability of those meanings and thoughts in the artist.[59] In the end, then, having given up his initial—and evidently untenable—naive narrow expressivist position, Schleiermacher is left torn between these two more promising-looking positions, which, however, give contradictory answers to our central question: (1), a version of broad expressivism similar to Hamann's and Hegel's, and (2), a refined form of narrow expressivism similar to the one Herder had eventually arrived at.

Finally and more briefly, Dilthey is in a way torn as well. Until around 1900 he was evidently attracted to a form of narrow expressivism.[60] However, after about 1905—when he wrote his classic work on the early Hegel, *Die Jugendgeschichte Hegels*, and in the process, it seems, fell under the influence of the predominant broad expressivist strand in Hegel—he instead turned to broad expressivism.[61]

This pervasive vacillation not only between but even within the individual thinkers of the German tradition with which we are concerned is, I would suggest, symptomatic, not of their incompetence, but rather of the extreme difficulty of the philosophical choice between narrow expressivism (especially in its refined form) and broad expressivism.

# V

What *is* the correct choice here? Due to the extreme difficulty just mentioned, it would be rash to offer a confident or final answer here. However, I would at least like to *attempt* an answer.

One thing that *can*, I think, be said with some confidence in this area is that the naive form of narrow expressivism from which Herder and Schleiermacher both started out—the form of it which denies that non-linguistic arts express meanings or thoughts *at all*—is quite untenable. Indeed, only an excessively parochial focus on modern abstract art (e.g. Jackson Pollock) and modern music (e.g. Schönberg) could even tempt one to suppose otherwise for long. As we saw, Herder and Schleiermacher both come upon a *casus crucis* which shows the untenability of naive narrow expressivism clearly enough—for Herder Greek coins, for Schleiermacher Greek religious sculpture. But its untenability can also be shown by means of countless other examples—for instance, ancient Egyptian and Mesopotamian wall friezes depicting the events of specific wars and battles (or more recent equivalents such as the Bayeux tapestry); medieval and early modern religious paintings based on episodes from the Bible;[62] "program" music of the sort composed by Liszt and Smetana (such as the latter's cycle of symphonic poems *Ma Vlast*, with its expression of thoughts about specific features of Czech geography and history);[63] and so on. To deny that such non-linguistic art expresses meanings or thoughts at all would be pretty clearly absurd. Indeed, in many cases—for example, the ancient wall friezes recently mentioned—that is arguably its *primary* function. In order to be plausible, therefore, narrow expressivism must instead take the more refined form which Herder, Schlegel, and Schleiermacher eventually gave it.

# VI

But is refined narrow expressivism correct or is broad expressivism? This seems to me a far more difficult question to answer. What I want to suggest (albeit tentatively) is that refined narrow expressivism is the more correct of the two positions, but that there are certain important grains of truth in broad expressivism (grains of truth which help, I think, to explain the vacillations in the German tradition that I noted). Let me develop each of these points in turn.

In order to make plausible the first point (that refined narrow expressivism is the more correct of the two positions) I shall offer some criticisms first of Hegel's version of broad expressivism and then of a possible non-Hegelian version of it. In effect I shall argue for preferring refined narrow expressivism over broad expressivism by first criticizing Hegel's broad expressivist account of ancient architecture and sculpture but then supporting his refined narrow expressivist account of painting and instrumental music (against possible broad expressivist accounts of them).[64]

As we saw, Hegel's overall broad expressivism rests mainly on his broad expressivist intuitions about two cases: the architecture of the ancient Egyptians and the sculpture of the ancient Greeks. In sharp contrast, his intuitions about later painting and instrumental music are refined narrow expressivist ones. Now it should, I suggest, immediately arouse suspicion here that it is the older cases, for which his knowledge of relevant linguistic, textual, cultural, and biographical context is naturally thinner, which receive a broad expressivist treatment, whereas the more recent cases, for which his knowledge of such context is naturally richer, receive a refined narrow expressivist treatment. That is to say, it seems reasonable to suspect that whereas his refined narrow expressivist interpretation of the more recent material is evidentially well-grounded, his broad expressivist interpretation of the ancient material, his denial of a linguistic or textual basis to the meanings and thoughts it expresses, is merely a result of his relative ignorance of relevant evidence.

This general suspicion about Hegel's broad expressivist interpretation of the older material is, I think, borne out by closer scrutiny of his treatment. Consider first the case of Egyptian architecture. It does seem beyond serious doubt that such architecture expresses religious meanings and thoughts, as Hegel takes it to (though whether, as he also believes, the thoughts in question are true ones is of course quite another matter). But why should one believe the meanings or thoughts in question to be ones that were linguistically unexpressed and inexpressible by the Egyptians rather than linguistically expressed or expressible ones? Is Hegel's inclination to do so not simply an error resulting from the fact that in his day people did not yet have the means to identify the Egyptians' linguistic expressions of, or linguistic means for expressing, the meanings or thoughts in question because Egyptian hieroglyphics had not yet been properly deciphered, nor Egyptology yet established as a proper academic discipline? (Champollion first deciphered Egyptian hieroglyphics in the 1820s, the decade in which Hegel gave his *Aesthetics* lectures, but only published the full results in 1832 in his *Grammaire égyptienne* and *Dictionnaire égyptien*.[65] Academic Egyptology really only began after Richard Lepsius's expedition of 1842.) In other words, Hegel seems simply to have misinterpreted the fact that while the buildings in question clearly express religious meanings and thoughts *he happens not to know any Egyptian linguistic expressions of, or linguistic means for expressing, the meanings and thoughts in question due to his lack of relevant information* as a situation in which the buildings clearly express religious meanings and thoughts *which were not linguistically expressed or expressible by the Egyptians.*[66]

What about Greek sculpture? Prima facie at least, one would think that the salient point to note here would be Herder's point that Greek sculpture was deeply grounded in, and expressive of, ideas from Greek poetry and myth, i.e.

ideas which were already *linguistically* expressible and indeed expressed—so that the case of Greek sculpture conforms well with *refined narrow* expressivism.

Hegel's contrary, *broad* expressivist, interpretation of Greek sculpture rests on his judgment that it was the Greeks' *highest* expression of the Absolute, that it expressed something about the Absolute which no other area of Greek culture, and in particular no *linguistic* area, yet expressed or was able to express (at least, not as clearly). What was the something in question? Hegel's answer is not exactly obvious from his texts, but it seems to be roughly that Greek sculpture already expressed *God's identity with man* (not merely God's qualitative *similarity* with man, note; in Hegel's view, *that* had already been quite well expressed by other areas of Greek culture besides sculpture, for example poetry)[67]—and that in this way it anticipated Christianity's subsequent more explicit, linguistic expression of such an identity.[68] This is part of the force of his remark that Greek "sculp- ture...individualizes the character of the gods into an entirely specific human form and perfects the anthropomorphism of the classical Ideal,"[69] and of his frequent characterization of Greek sculpture as combining *universality* with *indi- viduality*, which in essential part means: divinity with humanity.

However, this Hegelian interpretation of Greek sculpture again looks quite dubious on closer inspection. There are two main problems with it (standing in mild tension with each other): First, it seems vulnerable to the objection that it involves an erroneous reading-in of a meaning or thought that was not yet intended by the Greek sculptors. After all, are not the Greeks' pervasive and clear expressions in their traditional literature of a sharp numerical distinction, or non-identity, between gods and men (coincident with the qualitative dis- tinction between divine immortality and human mortality) a reason for reject- ing this Hegelian interpretation of their sculpture? Did not, for example, Phidias make his statue of Zeus at Olympia—or even later, Chares his statue of Helios at Rhodes (the "Colossus of Rhodes")—as huge as he famously did in impor- tant part precisely in order to accord with such a traditional conception of a sharp distinction between gods and men?

Second, someone might, though, reasonably respond to such an objection on Hegel's behalf that the historical situation is not so clear-cut. In particular, someone might point to the general exaltation of the human in comparison with the divine that occurred in fifth-century Athenian democratic culture, taking a secular form in Protagoras, and a (still more relevant) religious form in Aeschylus (whose Prometheus has sometimes been interpreted as really man- kind itself, for example); and also to the Orphic-Pythagorean tradition that culminated in Plato's *Phaedo*, with its own very different way of effacing the division between the human and the divine (namely, by classifying the human soul as immortal and hence divine). Hegel may indeed himself have such evidence in mind—for he singles out as human embodiments of Greek sculpture's ideal both, on the one hand, fifth-century Athenian democratic leaders (e.g. Pericles, Thucydides, and Xenophon) and, on the other hand, Socrates and Plato.[70] However, such a response on Hegel's behalf, rather than helping him, actually leads to serious difficulties of its own. For one thing, it is by no means clear that this evidence can overturn the anti-Hegelian interpretation of the intended significance of sculpture based on traditional literature (perhaps the sculptors were more rooted in that than in this more avant-garde philosophy and literature). For another thing, and more importantly, such a response is self-defeating, because the two strands of Athenian culture to which it appeals were both *linguistic* ones that *pre-existed or at least co-existed with* the sculpture in question. In other words, ironically, the very existence of such evidence for the ideas in question turns out to be a problem for Hegel. For while his theory could in principle have withstood the *absence* of any independent evidence for such ideas, since, as we saw, it is part of his position that sculpture *leads* the rest of the culture in developing them, it cannot withstand the *presence* of *philosophical-literary* evidence for them, because the very linguistic nature of such evidence entails that in superficially seeming to support the theory (namely, by showing that the sculptors may at least have had the relevant ideas in mind) it in reality refutes it (namely, by showing its claim of the ideas' autonomy of language to be erroneous).[71]

In the end, therefore, Hegel's broad expressivist interpretation of Greek sculpture again looks implausible.

In sum, the main evidence on which Hegel bases his broad expressivism seems not to support it. His conviction that it does evidently results from a mistaken reading-*out* of linguistic meanings and thoughts where they were probably in fact present (especially in the case of Egyptian architecture) and from a mistaken reading-*in* of not-yet-linguistic meanings and thoughts where they were probably in fact either absent or else linguistic (especially in the case of Greek sculpture).[72] Hegel's broad expressivism concerning architecture and sculpture therefore seems implausible; refined narrow expressivism looks like the more plausible position in connection with these arts.

However, in order to complete the case in favor of refined narrow expressivism over broad expressivism, I would like now to speak in *support* of Hegel's (and Herder's) refined narrow expressivist way of explaining painting and instrumental music.

Although Hegel himself evidently feels otherwise, painting and especially instrumental music are unusually potent sources of a temptation to broad expressivism. For in contemplating these artforms, especially instrumental music, we surely do often receive a powerful sense that meanings and thoughts are being expressed which it is beyond the capacity of (existing or perhaps even any) language to capture. Accordingly, Wackenroder and Tieck had developed their broad expressivism mainly in connection with painting and instrumental music. And theories of these artforms—especially of instrumental music—which attribute to them some sort of ineffable meaning and thought abound. Here are two further examples: (1) The later Dilthey in his essay *Musical Understanding* treats instrumental music as a prime example of broad expressivism, arguing that while instrumental music often expresses merely linguistic thoughts, in its highest forms it also expresses non-linguistic ones, in particular ones about the nature of Life itself.[73] (2) Hanslick argues that music expresses strictly *musical* ideas,[74] and, following his lead, Stephen Bungay argues (in rejection of Hegel's approach to instrumental music) that it is just obvious that non-linguistic musical ideas and thoughts occur.[75]

Despite the admitted seductiveness of this broad expressivist intuition about painting and especially instrumental music, my suspicion is that Hegel and Herder are in the end right to judge that these artforms should be explained in a narrow expressivist way. I would therefore like now to make a few points in this spirit, focusing on the especially interesting case of instrumental music. (Corresponding points would apply to painting, and probably also to other non-linguistic arts.)

The sense that instrumental music conveys meanings and thoughts which it is beyond the power of (existing or even any) language to express can indeed be very strong, and I do not want to suggest that it should be dismissed lightly. Nonetheless, it seems to me likely that it is illusory in the end. (It may be salutary in this connection to remind oneself of the—presumable—illusion to which we often fall victim in waking from a dream that we have entertained meanings and thoughts in the dream that are linguistically inexpressible. In other words, we are not immune to illusions of the general sort in question here.)

Consider first Dilthey's attempt to vindicate that sense. Dilthey believes that instrumental music in its highest forms expresses some sort of metaphysical or quasi-religious thought (about "Life"). This is a common enough conviction, and it may very well be correct. But why should one take the thought involved to be linguistically inexpressible rather than—as Herder, Hegel, and Adorno all imply—linguistically expressible (and perhaps indeed derived from linguistically expressed metaphysics or religion)?[76] Certainly, the sort of thought that Dilthey refers to may be only quite *vaguely* expressible in language. But is there really any reason to suppose that the music expresses it any *less* vaguely?

Bungay's attempt to vindicate the sense in question is different. His claim is not that instrumental music expresses metaphysical or religious thoughts which transcend language, but rather that it expresses distinctively *musical* ideas and thoughts which transcend language. This claim strikes me as somewhat more plausible, but still in the end very questionable. It seems important to distinguish two sorts of cases here. First, there are cases in which a relevant person, say a composer, possesses a linguistic or notational means of expressing the putative musical ideas or thoughts in question. In such cases it *does* seem to me appropriate to speak of his having musical ideas and thoughts. But then, these are cases in which he can express them *linguistically*—even musical notation being plausibly considered a part of language. Second, there are certainly also cases in which a person develops putative musical ideas or thoughts *without* having any corresponding linguistic or notational means for expressing them (think, for example, of the once fairly common phenomenon of the skilled jazz or blues musician who does not read music and is verbally inarticulate to boot). However, is it really so clear that in such cases we should speak literally of the person's having musical *ideas and thoughts*—rather than say (an attractive alternative) of his creating and perceiving complex sound-patterns and -relationships? To my linguistic ear, at least, such a characterization would seem out of place if meant literally (though no doubt fine if only meant metaphorically).[77] In short, it seems to me that non-linguistic *musical* ideas and thoughts may well, again, be a will-o'-the-wisp.

However, to turn now from refutation to diagnosis, I suspect that there are also certain deeper sources feeding the delusive temptation to suppose that instrumental music expresses linguistically inexpressible meanings and thoughts. In particular, I want to suggest that this temptation arises from instrumental music's peculiar combination of a certain sort of inarticulateness with a certain sort of articulateness—namely, relative inarticulateness in the expression of meanings and thoughts and relative articulateness in the expression of nuances of feeling and emotion (in both cases, relative as compared to language).[78] This combination of features can easily give rise to illusions that instrumental music expresses linguistically inexpressible meanings and thoughts in at least two ways: First, instrumental music often expresses a composer's *linguistically expressible* meanings and thoughts but in ways which are vague, making it hard for a listener to pin them down with any precision (from the music). This genuine presence of definite linguistically expressible meanings and thoughts which, however, the listener finds himself unable to pin down linguistically with any precision easily becomes misconstrued by him as a presence of definite meanings and thoughts which cannot be linguistically expressed.[79] Second, music often expresses and communicates more precisely than could be achieved by language (alone) certain nuances of feeling and emotion—that is, certain psychological states which are other than meanings and thoughts but which can easily be mistaken for them (especially given that they do *involve* them,[80] and that other meanings and thoughts are expressed in the music as well).[81]

In sum, I suggest that when one thinks through the several possible forms and sources of the intuition that instrumental music expresses linguistically inexpressible meanings and thoughts in the above ways, the intuition in the end proves to be illusory.

As I implied earlier, analogous points hold for painting as well (and probably also for other non-linguistic arts). For painting too sometimes expresses (vague) metaphysical or (quasi-)religious thoughts; it too involves technical "ideas" and "thoughts" which are sometimes linguistically expressible by the artist and sometimes not (e.g. concerning perspective or color); and it too tends to combine relative inarticulateness in the expression of meanings and thoughts with relative articulateness in the expression of nuances of feeling and emotion (the former part of which point is perhaps obvious; concerning the latter part, think for example of Rembrandt's self-portraits).

## VII

However, as I said earlier, I think that there are nonetheless certain important grains of truth in broad expressivism. I have in mind two in particular. (My suspicion is that these may help to explain the persistent vacillations between narrow and broad expressivism which, as we saw, afflicted thinkers in the eighteenth- and nineteenth-century German tradition.)

The first grain of truth seems to me very difficult to capture correctly, but here is my tentative effort, articulated in four parts: (1) As was recently mentioned, non-linguistic art often succeeds in expressing fine nuances of affective feeling or emotion which language (alone) cannot. (2) Moreover (a point which Herder, Wackenroder, Tieck, and Hegel anticipate in their accounts of music, the Schlegels and Hegel extend to sculpture, and Collingwood more recently develops on an even broader front), in many cases it not only expresses but also in part *constitutes* them, in the sense that they would not exist without such expression.[82] (3) Furthermore (as Proust and Gombrich both imply), close analogues of these two points seem to hold true for perceptual sensations as well (for example, an impressionist painting may both express a certain sort of visual sensation more accurately than could be done by language alone and also partly constitute that sort of sensation).[83] (4) In consequence of such points (as Herder already implies), the expressibility and even the very existence of certain meanings and thoughts—most obviously, ones which actually refer to the affective feelings and perceptual sensations in question,[84] but also ones which depend on them in other ways in virtue of a broad dependence of meaning on affective feeling and perceptual sensation—[85] depend on non-linguistic art's expression of the relevant feelings and sensations; whatever linguistic expressions of the meanings and thoughts may occur are in a sense parasitic on non-linguistic art's expression of the relevant feelings and sensations.[86]

This dependence of the expressibility, and even the very existence, of certain feelings and sensations, and hence of certain meanings and thoughts, on the expressive power of the non-linguistic arts comes quite close to what the broad expressivist had in mind. However, I want to suggest (albeit still tentatively) that it nevertheless falls short of actually entailing broad expressivism, and remains consistent with narrow expressivism. This is for two main reasons. First (focusing on points (1)–(3)), the nuances of feeling and sensation which according to this view can only be expressed, and are moreover in part constituted, through non-linguistic art are not themselves meanings or thoughts (only possible foundations for such).[87] And second (focusing on point (4)), it is consistent with this view that language should still be both *necessary for* and *able to express* the meanings or thoughts which those nuances of feeling and sensation support; it is just that language can only constitute and express them insofar as it is aided by relevant non-linguistic art in a certain way.[88]

# VIII

A second grain of truth that I see in broad expressivism is as follows. It seems to me that refined narrow expressivism, as it was standardly conceived in the German tradition we have been considering, rests on a certain mistaken assumption, and that it therefore needs to make a concession in the direction of broad expressivism—though one which can, and I think should, take the form of a modification bringing it slightly closer to broad expressivism rather than an abandonment of it for the latter or even an adoption of a position mid-way between the two.

What is the mistaken assumption in question? The refined narrow expressivist in this tradition generally thinks of language in the usual sense as restricted to a very limited range of material-perceptual media, namely audible noises made with the mouth (speech) and visible but non-pictorial marks on paper, wax, stone, or some similar substance (writing) (in addition, strongly privileging the former over the latter). Herder in particular normally thinks of language in such a restrictive way—[89] and so too (largely under his influence) do other narrow expressivists, such as Schleiermacher,[90] and Wilhelm von Humboldt.[91] (The broad expressivist Hegel normally has such a conception of language in the usual sense as well.[92]) But now, how, a broad expressivist may well ask the narrow expressivist, could these two sorts of material-perceptual media, among the many others that are conceivable (and perhaps even actual), possibly possess the sort of privilege as fundamental vehicles of meaning and thought that the narrow expressivist is attributing to them? Would this not be inexplicable, a sort of miracle?[93] Indeed, is it not, on reflection, *clear* that other material-perceptual media at least could, and perhaps also do, serve as fundamental vehicles of meaning and thought as well—for example, the sort of highly conventional, "unrealistic" pictures that are used to express ideas in ancient Egyptian painting (pictures distinct from, but closely related in form and function to, hieroglyphics),[94] or—beyond the sphere of art—sign-language as used by the deaf,[95] gestures,[96] and perhaps even more exotic media such as some animals may actually use (e.g. touch and chemical emissions)?[97]

I think that the refined narrow expressivist simply has to concede this point. That might seem like a huge concession to broad expressivism. However, I would suggest that on the contrary the refined narrow expressivist both can and should make it in a way which allows him to insist that he is thereby only modestly revising his position rather than abandoning it for broad expressivism or even taking up a position mid-way between the two. This is for the following three reasons:

First, and perhaps most importantly, it seems plausible to say that such alternative material-perceptual media could only share with spoken and written language the function of serving as fundamental vehicles of meaning and thought to the extent that they took on the same sort of *highly rule-governed, conventional* character as spoken and written language have,[98] and thereby themselves became naturally describable as language in a sense of "language" which only barely, if at all, goes beyond the usual sense of the word.[99] The example of deaf sign-language illustrates this fact—both in the sense that such sign-language displays the same highly rule-governed, conventional character as spoken and written language, and in the sense that it shows how naturally and seamlessly we extend our usual concept of "language" to cover a materially-perceptually unusual case provided only that that character is present.[100]

Second, this criterion *excludes*, rather than including, many forms and aspects of non-linguistic art, and moreover the very ones that we tend to think of as most responsible for making it *art*, namely those that are not guided by rules or conventions but instead issue from a sort of spontaneity and innovation. In other words, not only will any so-called "non-linguistic" medium which can serve as a fundamental vehicle for meaning and thought to that same extent turn out in fact to be language in something very much like the usual sense of the word "language," but it will also to that same extent turn out *not* to be art in the usual sense of the word "art."[101]

Third (and somewhat less importantly), while it does indeed seem clear that alternative material-perceptual media such as those recently mentioned *could* serve as fundamental vehicles of meaning and thought independently of spoken and written language, it seems doubtful that they do so to any great extent *in practice*. For example, the meanings and thoughts which the ancient Egyptian artist expressed through his conventional pictures were presumably in fact ones which he was already able to articulate in spoken (and perhaps also written) language; the heavy dependence of deaf sign-language on pre-existing spoken and written language is obvious as well (albeit that the exact degree and nature of the dependence are controversial); gesture too typically functions alongside equivalent spoken or written language rather than instead of it (think, for example, of the circling index finger at the temple signifying "He's crazy"); and when one turns to animals' unusual material-perceptual media, even granting that these do sometimes sustain meanings and thoughts autonomously of spoken and written language (as, despite the controversial nature of the point, I think one probably should), the meanings and thoughts in question seem likely to be quite limited in nature.

For these three reasons, then, the concession that refined narrow expressivism needs to make to broad expressivism here can and probably should take the form of a fairly modest modification of it rather than an abandonment of it for broad expressivism or even the adoption of a position mid-way between the two.

## IX

To conclude, it seems to me that in the contest between narrow and broad forms of expressivism refined narrow expressivism proves to be more or less the correct position, but that in order to be *strictly* correct it needs to concede to broad expressivism, first, that language's expressiveness is in certain areas deeply dependent on that of the non-linguistic arts, and second, that *spoken and written* language is not the only possible fundamental vehicle for meaning and thought, but other forms of language, including some which at least border on art, could, and perhaps even to a certain extent actually do, serve as such fundamental vehicles as well.

If this is correct, then we may draw the following morals for the philosophy of language and the philosophy of art. First, concerning the philosophy of language: the philosophy of language can in good conscience continue to advance Herder's two narrow expressivist principles that meaning consists in word-usage and that thought is essentially dependent on and bounded by language (as long as it is borne in mind that the words and language in question may require extra-linguistic help and that they need not be restricted to *spoken and written* words and language).There is, after all, no need to make room for non-linguistic vehicles of meaning and thought, as broad expressivism implied.

Second, concerning the philosophy of art: much as Herder's considered position implied, even the interpretation of many so-called "non-linguistic" artworks both needs to be similar to the interpretation of language and linguistic texts (in likewise imputing meanings and thoughts) and depends on it; it will never be necessary to entertain the possibility that such artworks express meanings or thoughts which transcend the artist's language; and indeed, it will not usually even be necessary to entertain the possibility that they express ones which transcend his *spoken and written* language.

# Notes

1. See C. Taylor, *Hegel*, pp. 16 ff.; also, "The Importance of Herder," in *Isaiah Berlin: A Celebration*, ed. E. and A. Margalit (Chicago: University of Chicago Press, 1991). For the purposes of the present essay the term "expressivism" should be understood as innocent of the implication—suggested by its etymology, and evidently intended by Taylor—that what is expressed is something *more than* its material, perceptible manifestations. Some of the "expressivists" whom I will be discussing do in fact believe that (for example, Herder, for whom expressions are manifestations of an underlying "force"), but I would argue that at least one of them rather thinks of the content's material, perceptible manifestations as fully constituting it (namely, Hegel—see e.g. *Encyclopedia* [1830], par. 383: "The determinacy of the mind is . . . *manifestation*. The mind is not some determinacy or content whose expression or outwardness would be only a form distinct from it. So it does not reveal *something*, but its determinacy and content is this revelation itself"). For present purposes, therefore, "expressivism" simply connotes a content's essential dependence on material, perceptible manifestations, but leaves open the question of whether or not there is anything more to the former than the latter.
2. For some discussion of this question, see *After Herder*, Essay 2.
3. One of the morals that will emerge in the course of this essay is that the notion of "language in the usual sense of 'language'" is more problematic than it may initially seem. But let us for the moment employ it naively.
4. This definition admittedly captures only *part* of our everyday concept of "thought." In particular, it omits the everyday idea of "thinking *of* (something, someone)."

5. G1:27.

6. G1:421–3. Cf. *On the Spirit of Hebrew Poetry* (1782), G5:1007: "Let us seek the word's concept not from etymologies, which are always uncertain, but according to the clear use [*Gebrauch*] of the name in its various times."

7. G1:322 (Greek slightly amended): an interpreter must "trace the metamorphoses which in Greek the words *anêr, anthrôpos, agathos, kalos, philokalos, kalosk'agathos, kakos, epicheirêtês*, and in Latin *vir, homo, bonus* and *melior* and *optimus, honestus, pulcher* and *liberalis, strenuus* and such national words have undergone, which were the honor of their age, and changed with it."

8. G1:27.

9. G1:556–7; cf. 177, 394–7, 403–4, 407–10, 426, 558, 606–8 (though contrast 259, 404–6).

10. See *After Herder*, Essay 2.

11. *Critical Forests* (1), G2:193–4. Cf. R. Haym, *Herder nach seinem Leben und seinen Werken* (Berlin: Gaertner, 1880), 1:241–6.

12. *Critical Forests* (1), G2:214–15. Cf. Haym, *Herder*, 1:258–9.

13. *Critical Forests* (1), G2:192–3. Cf. Haym, *Herder*, 1:246. This little theory of the arts has sometimes been touted as Herder's main achievement in aesthetics—for example, by R.E. Norton in *Herder's Aesthetics and the European Enlightenment* (Ithaca: Cornell University Press, 1991). But as I have already implied, and will be going on to argue in more detail, it is a naive and untenable theory, and Herder's real achievement in aesthetics is other than and contrary to it.

14. Cf. Haym, *Herder*, 1:233 ff.

15. *Critical Forests* (1), G2:131–8. Cf. Haym, *Herder*, 1:240.

16. *Critical Forests* (1), G2:200–1.

17. Ibid., p. 95. Cf. Haym, *Herder*, 1:234.

18. *Critical Forests* (1), G2:195. Cf. Haym, *Herder*, 1:242.

19. *Critical Forests* (1), G2:107.

20. *Critical Forests* (3), S3:396–7, cf. 419–20. In my view, the commonly neglected and disparaged third part of the *Critical Forests* therefore takes a seminal step towards his considered and best theory.

21. *Critical Forests* (4), G2:313, cf. 380. This represents a change of mind from *Critical Forests* (3), where Herder had argued that the presence of an allegorical sense in coins *distinguished* them from paintings, which by contrast offered a picture simply *as picture* (S3:419–20).

22. G4:296–301, 319. Cf. Haym, *Herder*, 2:69–70.

23. G4:317 (emphasis added). Cf. the 1778 essay *On the Effect of Poetic Art on the Ethics of Peoples in Ancient and Modern Times*, G4:172: Phidias's

statue of Jupiter (i.e. Zeus) developed out of two Homeric verses. The *Ideas for the Philosophy of History of Humanity* (1784–91) repeats this solution in relation to sculpture. Thus, on the one hand, the *Ideas* is committed to the principles that meaning and thought are dependent on and bounded by language: "A people has no idea for which it has no word" (G6:347). But on the other hand, the work also accords sculpture a capacity to express meanings and thoughts, namely—preserving consistency with the principles just mentioned—meanings and thoughts which the sculptor has in virtue of a pre-existing linguistic capacity. For example, the work observes that Greek sculpture rests on Greek poetry (especially Homer) and on Greek hero-legends (G6:529–33). For an even later formulation of this solution, see *Homer a Favorite of Time* (1795), S18:428–9, where Herder gives a slightly fuller statement of his view that Greek sculpture (and painting) expresses Homeric thought.

24. G4:201.
25. G9/1:554–5.
26. G7:454.
27. G2:290, 296–7, 308, 324. Herder makes this point mainly in connection with *visual* perception.
28. For a similar recent position concerning (visual) non-linguistic art, see E. Panofsky, *Meaning in the Visual Arts* (Chicago: University of Chicago Press, 1982), pp. 28–31.
29. It is admittedly a somewhat puzzling fact that Herder's last major work on aesthetics, the *Calligone* (1800), fails to articulate this position clearly, but instead tends (though not consistently) to revert to the sort of sensualistic theory of the non-linguistic arts with which the *Critical Forests* had begun: music is basically concerned just with expressing feelings (S21:63–4, 70–1, 186–90), sculpture does not express concepts (S21:169–71, 343–4), etc. However, I do not take this to be a sign that the interpretation of Herder's considered position that I have given here is after all mistaken. Rather, I take it to be a sign of the inferiority of this late work of Herder's (an inferiority which is also manifested in other ways, as well as in other late works of his such as the *Metacritique*).
30. See Essay 2.
31. "The oldest language was music... The oldest writing was painting and drawing" (*Johann Georg Hamanns Sämtliche Werke*, ed. J. Nadler [Vienna: Verlag Herder, 1949], 3:286). Hamann indeed believes that, beyond such human expressive media, *the whole realm of nature* is an expressive "language," namely God's.

The notion that non-linguistic art is really a form of language has, of course, become something of a commonplace in our century (see e.g. Collingwood and Goodman).

32. See W.H. Wackenroder and L. Tieck, *Herzensergießungen eines kunstliebenden Klosterbruders*, esp. pp. 57–60, 101–2; cf. *Phantasien über die Kunst für Freunde der Kunst*, pp. 82–3, 99, 104–7, 111.

33. Besides the striking points of similarity just mentioned, some further indications of such a debt include their book's religious orientation and its additional depiction of nature as God's language (*Herzensergießungen*, pp. 57–9; cf. L. Tieck, *Franz Sternbalds Wanderungen*, pp. 890 ff.).

34. It is not entirely clear whether Hegel was influenced by Hamann, Wackenroder, or Tieck in this area. The most promising-looking source of enlightenment concerning Hamann, a late review that Hegel wrote of Hamann's collected works, *Über Hamanns Schriften* (1828), unfortunately provides few if any clues. Hegel clearly was influenced by Herder and Hamann's shared expressivism, but the influence seems to have come from Herder rather than from Hamann (see Essay 5), and the closer specification of it as broad expressivism may have been due more to Hegel's originality than to any borrowing. As for Wackenroder and Tieck (and thereby indirectly Hamann again), while it is not impossible that Hegel's broad expressivism owes something to them, it is a striking fact that the specific arts and the cultural context in connection with which Wackenroder and Tieck espoused broad expressivism, namely painting and music within Christian culture, are ones in connection with which, as we shall see in this essay, Hegel *rejects* it in favor of narrow expressivism (for him, the broad expressivist possibility is instead mainly realized in architecture and sculpture, and in ancient Egypt and Greece respectively).

35. *Encyclopedia* (1830), par. 131.

36. Ibid., par. 140.

37. Ibid., par. 383.

38. *Phenomenology of Spirit*, tr. Miller, p. 198; emphasis added. (I have sometimes modified Miller's translation without specific notice.)

39. Ibid., p. 423.

40. See esp. ibid., pp. 424, 429–30.

41. Ibid., pp. 422–3. Concerning this tension within the *Phenomenology of Spirit*, cf. S. Hahn, "Hegel on Saying and Showing," *The Journal of Value Inquiry*, 28/2 (1994).

42. See e.g. *Hegel's Aesthetics*, pp. 31–2, 91–2, 102–3, 173–4. In connection with the last item mentioned, truth, it is one of Hegel's most distinctive doctrines about art that, along with the higher media of religious *Vorstellung*

and philosophical thought, it constitutes one of the three main media through which human beings express the truth, the Absolute.

For this reason it seems to me misleading of Taylor to say that for Hegel art is not representational (*Hegel*, ch. 17). There is a *grain* of veracity in such a claim, namely that Hegel does not think of the truth that art expresses on the model of a correspondence between a representation and an independent fact (see e.g. *Encyclopedia*, par. 24, Zusatz 2). But that is not something that distinguishes art from any other way of expressing the truth in Hegel's view, for it applies just as much to *religion and philosophy* as to art. (To put the point another way: for Hegel art is as representational as any way of expressing the truth could *ever* be.) And what is most striking about Hegel's view of art is surely that, unlike many other theorists of art, for example Kant, he *does* consider art to be an expression of truth, and hence representational in this (perhaps not maximal, but nonetheless strong) sense.

43. See e.g. *Hegel's Aesthetics*, pp. 181, 311.

44. See e.g. ibid., pp. 39–40, 51, 282, 311. Hegel distinguishes as mere "comparative" symbolic artforms a class of artforms which fail this criterion because they do merely express something that is already expressed or expressible in some other way and which are in consequence merely superficial, including fable, parable, simile, metaphor, and allegory (ibid., pp. 380–1, 397, 400).

45. Ibid., p. 636. A puzzle arises in connection with this case, though—not just concerning whether Hegel is a *broad* expressivist rather than a narrow one, but rather concerning whether he is really a consistent expressivist *at all*. For he emphasizes that the architecture in question here expresses its content, the Absolute, only very imperfectly, that there is an externality and looseness of relation between the architectural expression and the content that it seeks to express (ibid., pp. 76–7, 300 ff., 421, 433). This would not pose a serious puzzle concerning his expressivism if he understood the architecture in question to be merely an inferior means of expressing that content alongside other, superior, expressive means, or if he understood the content only imperfectly expressed to be merely an object, rather than an *intentional* object. But neither of these things seems to be the case; he considers the architecture to be its producers' *highest* expression of the content in question, and he evidently thinks of the discrepancy as one with an *intentional* object rather than merely with an object. So the puzzle is a real one. It is possible that Hegel's position here is simply inconsistent with his normal commitment to expressivism, that he is simply nodding. On the other hand, it also seems possible that his implicit position is more subtle,

and escapes contradiction with his expressivism. How so? Here is a suggestion: In *Hegel's Idea of a Phenomenology of Spirit* I pointed out that at different places in the *Phenomenology* Hegel seems to ascribe inconsistent meanings to Christianity, in the "Unhappy Consciousness" section characterizing it as a religion which sharply *distinguishes* man and God, but in the "Religion" chapter as a religion which *identifies* them. And I suggested, in effect, that, rather than really being inconsistent here, Hegel is implicitly working with two different concepts of "meaning"—on the one hand, a fine-grained concept oriented to exact scrutiny of linguistic usage and historical context (call this "meaning$_1$"), and on the other hand, a coarse-grained concept oriented rather to recovering as much truth as possible from an interpreted expression, where truth is adjudicated from the interpreter's own standpoint, the employment of this second concept of meaning being warranted by the fact that, when considered in the former, fine-grained, way, all expressions, in Hegel's view, turn out to have been implicitly inconsistent (call this second concept "meaning$_2$"). (One might perhaps think of these as Herderian–Schleiermacherian and proto-Gadamerian concepts of meaning, respectively.) So Hegel's double interpretation of Christianity in the end avoids any real inconsistency because it in effect amounts to a claim that Christianity means$_1$ that man and God are distinct but means$_2$ that they are identical. Now my suggestion in connection with ancient architecture is that Hegel may be implicitly adopting a similar position— that what he has in mind here may be, not a discrepancy between *the* meaning of the architecture and a content that is mentally entertained though not expressible by the producers of the architecture (which really *would* be inconsistent with his official expressivism), but rather a discrepancy between what the architecture means$_1$ and what it means$_2$ (so that there is no question of any content that is mentally entertained though not expressed or expressible, and so no real conflict with expressivism).

46. See e.g. *Hegel's Aesthetics*, p. 438: "art in Greece has become the supreme expression of the Absolute" (sculpture being in Hegel's view the highest form of Greek art). Cf. p. 102.

47. Ibid., p. 719. Cf. pp. 1186–7, 1195.

48. See e.g. ibid., p. 526.

49. Ibid., p. 860.

50. See e.g. ibid., pp. 597–600. It is, I think, some measure of Hegel's perceptiveness here that even such a great modern art historian as Panofsky, who is normally anything but reluctant to find meanings and thoughts expressed in paintings, less plausibly denies them to the sort of painting in question here (*Meaning in the Visual Arts*, p. 32).

This is not necessarily to say that the nature of the expression of meanings and thoughts here is exactly the same as in more obvious cases. For example, it may be less conscious than in the case of, say, a religiously allegorical medieval painting.

51. See e.g. *Hegel's Aesthetics*, pp. 28, 626, 891–4.

52. Ibid., pp. 899–900.

53. Ibid., pp. 902, 932, 954. Passages such as these show that readings of Hegel's position on instrumental music which emphasize his conception of it as contentless—e.g. E. Hanslick, *On the Musically Beautiful* (Indianapolis: Hackett, 1986), pp. 77, 83, and P. Moos, *Moderne Musikästhetik in Deutschland* (Berlin: Hermann Seemann Nachfolger, 1902), pp. 18 ff.—tell only half of the story.

54. Nor does Hegel's view that the meanings and thoughts expressed by painting and instrumental music are parasitic on language lead to any inconsistency when one adds in his conception, mentioned earlier, that art must fulfill its expressive function in an original, non-parasitic way if it is to avoid inferiority. For Hegel thinks that painting and (especially) instrumental music *are* in a way inferior artforms. Indeed, the bifurcation identified here and this normative conception together constitute a large part of the explanation of his famous thesis of the "end of art" (as commentators have sometimes called it), i.e. his thesis that art in some sense loses its importance after the Greeks and their sculpture.

55. *Encyclopedia* (1830), par. 462 (including Zusatz). Someone might, I suppose, try to defend Hegel against my charge of inconsistency by arguing that he here means the words "think" and "thoughts" in his highly specific technical sense, so that his insistence that *this* requires words still leaves him room to allow that there might be thinking of a more generic sort without words (for example, in non-linguistic art). Such a defense would be implausible, however. For Hegel here implies that the absence of words leaves one, not merely without "thought" in some highly specific technical sense, but without very much at all: "only something dark, fermenting," so that Mesmer's attempt to think without words was "clearly an absurdity."

A somewhat more plausible attempt at a defense would be to suggest that Hegel's return to a global narrow expressivism in this passage postdates most of the *Aesthetics* lectures (1823–9) and so represents a change of mind rather than an inconsistency. I think there is something to this (see Essay 5). However, I would suggest that the alternative formulation "change of mind *and* inconsistency" may be more apt here, for Hegel nowhere points out, or otherwise shows signs of recognizing, the conflict between this late position and his slightly earlier one in the *Aesthetics* lectures, let alone resolves the conflict by abandoning the latter.

56. Let me conclude these remarks by adding one final point of less crucial importance for our present purposes. Hegel also takes a clear position on the *further* question that I noted broad expressivism would naturally lead to: Do the meanings and thoughts articulated in an original, non-parasitic way by non-linguistic artforms merely transcend the language of the *artist* or rather language *tout court*? Hegel gives the former answer, not the latter. This can be seen in two main ways: First, among the arts themselves, he considers poetry to be capable, in virtue of its use of language, of expressing everything that the other arts can express (and consequently to be in a sense the highest of the arts) (*Hegel's Aesthetics*, pp. 626–7, 702–3). Second, regarding the relation between art and other areas of culture, he believes that the meanings and thoughts concerning the Absolute which during earlier phases of history were only articulable by non-linguistic artforms such as architecture and sculpture eventually in later phases of history receive a superior linguistic formulation in religion and especially philosophy, in accordance with his conception of art, religion, and philosophy as an ascending hierarchy of areas of culture which are all concerned with expressing the same subject-matter (the Absolute) but in different and increasingly adequate ways.

57. Aesthetics lectures, in *Friedrich Schleiermacher's sämmtliche Werke* [henceforth FSSW] (Berlin: G. Reimer, 1835– ), 3/7:579–80.

58. FSSW 3/7:584–5. This suggests that on this broad expressivist side of his final position Schleiermacher, like Hegel, would answer the further question which broad expressivism prompts, Are the thoughts in question transcendent merely of the *artist's* language or rather of language *tout court?*, with the former answer rather than the latter.

59. FSSW 3/7:587–8 (Schleiermacher actually only says in virtue of "something universal," "a representation," but the dependence on language seems clearly implied).

60. See e.g. *The Development of Hermeneutics* (1900), in H.P. Rickman, ed., *Dilthey: Selected Writings* (Cambridge: Cambridge University Press, 1979), pp. 248–9. (Dilthey associates this position with predecessors such as Schleiermacher and Preller.)

61. See e.g. *Dilthey: Selected Writings*, pp. 218 ff., as well as Dilthey's discussion of music at DGS 7:220 ff. Unlike Hamann, who, as we saw, stretches the word "language" to include non-linguistic media, and even to some extent Hegel, who occasionally does the same (for example, at *Hegel's Aesthetics*, p. 636 he calls symbolic architecture a wordless "language"), the later

Dilthey speaks in terms of a broad class of "expressions." However, the *substance* of their positions is similar.

62. Panofsky, *Meaning in the Visual Arts* provides a rich illustration of the point from such cases. As Panofsky puts it, "In a work of [visual] art, 'form' cannot be divorced from 'content': the distribution of color and lines, light and shade, volumes and planes, however delightful as a visual spectacle, must be understood as carrying a more-than-visual meaning" (p. 168).

63. The idea of program music, with its incorporation of meanings and thoughts into music, has admittedly come under attack from various quarters—for example, from E. Hanslick, *On the Musically Beautiful*, pp. 35, 43, 74–5, 78–9; and more recently, R. Scruton, *The Aesthetics of Music* (Oxford: Oxford University Press, 1999), pp. 133–4. However, such attacks are not persuasive. Scruton develops his attack as follows: "The claim was made by Liszt, that music could be tied to a program, in such a way that it would be necessary to understand the program in order to understand the music. Such 'program music' must be heard as the unfolding of a poetic narrative...But was he right?" (ibid., p. 133). However, given the closeness of the connection between an author's intentions to express such and such in his work and what he actually expresses in it, and hence between the former and what must be grasped in order to understand it—even if, as should be conceded, this closeness falls short of making the failure of his intentions a sheer impossibility (cf. Wittgenstein, *Philosophical Investigations*, p. 18: "Can I say 'bububu' and mean 'If it doesn't rain I shall go for a walk'?")—there is surely something a bit paradoxical in the suggestion that a major composer like Liszt might simply be mistaken here. That is to say, one would surely need *very* strong reasons to justify overriding a major composer's own conception of what he is expressing in this way. What could these possibly be? Hanslick develops several which might potentially do the job, including the following: (1) an evaluative argument that implementing the model in question makes for inferior music, (2) an argument that it violates the purely musical nature of music, and (3) an argument that it *cannot* occur. However, it seems to me that argument (1) comes to grief when confronted with a magnificent work like *Ma Vlast*, and that argument (2) does so as well (unless reduced to a safe but irrelevant tautology). As for the more important argument (3), Hanslick's case seems to be that the very same music could equally well be associated with quite *different* meanings and thoughts. But this consideration surely has little force. For is not just the same true of much if not all *linguistic* expression (where we do not for this reason question whether expression

really occurs at all)? In short, program music seems to hold up well as an example against such attacks.

It is perhaps worth adding something here about the role of linguistically expressible meanings and thoughts in instrumental music more generally. Hanslick and others deny that instrumental music *ever* expresses linguistically expressible meanings or thoughts. However, such an extreme position seems very implausible. For example, as Scruton points out, religious music often expresses thoughts of God (*The Aesthetics of Music*, p. 167). By contrast, S. Bungay concedes that instrumental music *sometimes* expresses linguistically expressible meanings and thoughts, but considers it a disastrous mistake to suppose that it *always* does or should (*Beauty and Truth* [Oxford: Oxford University Press, 1984], p. 137). This is a more modest position, and accordingly seems more plausible. However, one may reasonably wonder whether even this position is not misleading. It at least seems to me that instrumental music has the function in question a good deal more commonly than Bungay implies. Bungay cites the opening of Beethoven's Fifth Symphony as his star counterexample, claiming that Beethoven did not think up its famous theme in order to express a fateful mood, and that it is a matter of indifference "whether or not [listeners] think it represents the march of Fate, or anything else." I am not convinced. It may be significant in this connection to recall that when asked about the meaning of his *Appassionata* Sonata Beethoven replied, "Just read Shakespeare's *The Tempest*" (Hanslick, *On the Musically Beautiful*, p. 37). *Pace* Bungay, it seems likely that in composing the opening of the Fifth Symphony Beethoven did in fact have thoughts of fate, human struggle (outer and inner), and so forth in mind and did in fact mean to express those thoughts. Consequently, it seems plausible to say that a listener who failed to entertain such thoughts would ipso facto have a deficient aesthetic response to the music. In order to persuade oneself that linguistically expressible meanings and thoughts are at least not irrelevant to the adequacy of an aesthetic response in this case one might usefully ask oneself the question, Could a listener have an adequate aesthetic response to this music if he habitually thought of, say, clowns and their antics when he heard it (i.e. had what one might—albeit tendentiously in this context—call "inappropriate" thoughts)? The answer seems to be pretty clearly No. I would suggest that the same answer applies if the question is instead, Could the listener's aesthetic response to this music be adequate if it included no linguistically expressible thoughts at all, or none of the ones that Beethoven had in mind? (For additional defense of the principle that instrumental music expresses linguistically expressible meanings and thoughts, cf. T.W. Adorno, *Aesthetic Theory* [Minneapolis: University of Minnesota Press, 1997], esp. the "Draft Introduction" on pp. 332–59.)

This issue is closely linked to another that has been much debated in the literature, namely whether or not certain *feelings* or *emotions* are expressed by instrumental music and therefore need to be captured by listeners in some way if they are to understand the music properly. A long tradition says Yes, but a significant one—including Hanslick, *On the Musically Beautiful*, and more recently D. Raffman, *Language, Music, and Mind* (Cambridge, Mass.: MIT Press, 1993), pp. 57–9—says No. Similar considerations to those just adduced concerning linguistically expressible meanings and thoughts seem to me to show that the correct answer here is Yes. For example (to focus first on the question of what composers *intend* to express), Beethoven described himself as being "incited by moods, which are translated...by me into tones that sound, and roar and storm about me until I have set them down in notes" (J.W.N. Sullivan, *Beethoven: His Spiritual Development* [New York: Vintage Books, 1960], p. 33), and he also said that music should "strike fire in the soul" (Hanslick, *On the Musically Beautiful*, p. 61). Moreover, if one conducts thought-experiments concerning emotions analogous to those that I recently proposed concerning meanings and thoughts—Would habitually having the "wrong" sort of emotional reaction to the opening of the Fifth Symphony, for example one of mirth, be compatible with having an adequate aesthetic response to it? Would a sheer absence of emotional reaction, or an absence of the sort of emotional reaction intended by the composer?—they seem to confirm that a certain sort of emotive response is indeed internal to musical understanding. One reason why this further question is closely linked to the previous question is that emotions require meanings and thoughts as intentional contents, so that allowing linguistically expressible meanings and thoughts a role in musical expression and understanding at least makes it easier to see—and may even be necessary for seeing—how emotions can have one.

To sum up the positive picture of much instrumental music that seems to emerge from such considerations one can hardly do better than quote a passage from its arch-opponent Hanslick which is deeply uncharacteristic of him, inconsistent with his usual position, and perhaps even a little internally inconsistent: "Thoughts and feelings run like blood in the arteries of the harmonious body of beautiful sounds. They are not that body...but they animate it" (*On the Musically Beautiful*, p. 82).

64. Of course, it should be possible to construct the philosophical argument without talking about Hegel at all. But my hope is that reference to him

will add to it by making it more interesting rather than subtract from it by making it intolerably ad hominem.

65. Champollion had indeed already produced preliminary publications in the 1820s, such as the *Letter to M. Dacier*, and one can see from a brief passage in Hegel's *Lectures on the Philosophy of History* (*Werke*, 12:247–8) that he had some sort of familiarity with them. But the point still stands.

66. Cf. Bungay, *Beauty and Truth*, p. 102. Bungay offers a similar diagnosis of Hegel's general inclination to see the Egyptians as intrinsically mysterious, but he does not bring the point to bear on the more specific issue with which I am concerned here, namely Hegel's broad expressivist interpretation of the Egyptians.

67. That traditional Greek poetry and myth had already expressed the gods' qualitative similarity with men (in contrast to the Judeo–Christian tradition, which instead emphasizes God's qualitative dissimilarity with men) was already a prominent theme in Hegel's so-called early theological writings.

68. See e.g. *Hegel's Aesthetics*, p. 435. Strictly speaking, Hegel's position here must, I think, be a little more complicated. It might be objected to the position I have just attributed to him that even if the Greeks had not yet linguistically *expressed* such an identity, still, such an identity was surely already linguistically *expressible* by them (after all, they had the linguistic concepts *theos, anthrôpos,* and *esti!*). Hegel's response to such an objection would, I suspect, be that, strictly speaking, what Greek sculpture expressed was not merely the identity of God and man but their "absolute identity" or "identity in difference," and that *this* is a concept which the Greeks did *not* yet possess in a linguistic form.

69. Ibid., p. 490.

70. Cf. Bungay, *Beauty and Truth*, p. 113. In connection with the second of the two traditions mentioned, notice that Hegel says of all these individuals that they "stand[] like immortal, deathless images of the gods, beyond the reach of death and temporality."

71. This problem is not, I think, significantly reduced if, following a suggestion I made in a recent note, one understands sculpture's message to be, for Hegel, more strictly the "identity in difference" of God and man. It could in fact quite plausibly be argued that the two strands of philosophical-literary culture in question here express some such conception (cf. Herodotus' use of expressions like "the Egyptian Zeus": is this the same god as the Greeks' or a different one?; in a way both). But then, once again, in thus superficially seeming to support Hegel's theory on the one

hand, they would to the same extent really be undermining it on the other.

72. A really hard-boiled Hegelian might, I suppose, respond to this sort of criticism that the nature of the Absolute and its necessary self-development has been independently proved by Hegel's Logic and that it is therefore legitimate for Hegel to impute corresponding non-linguistic meanings and thoughts to the historical art in question despite the absence of supporting evidence or even in the face of contrary evidence. However, such a response would not be very convincing. First, it seems quite unlikely that Hegel really proved any such thing in his Logic (though, of course, it would require a detailed examination of his Logic to show that he did not). Second, it is an important part of Hegel's own official methodology—on which he prides himself in comparison with Schelling, for example—that in applying the Logic to empirical evidence one must not, so to speak, *strong-arm* the latter (see e.g. the preface to the *Phenomenology of Spirit*, and the introduction to the *Encyclopedia*'s Philosophy of Nature).

73. DGS 7:220 ff.

74. Hanslick, *On the Musically Beautiful*, pp. 10, 28.

75. Bungay, *Beauty and Truth*, p. 137.

76. We have already encountered Herder's version of such a position on instrumental music. Concerning Hegel's implication that instrumental music sometimes expresses a metaphysical meaning—presumably, given his general refined narrow expressivist approach to instrumental music, a language-based one—see especially *Hegel's Aesthetics*, p. 932, where he notes that instrumental music sometimes develops dissonances and oppositions together with their resolution in harmony and melody, i.e. a self-developing structure like that of his Absolute. (For a helpful discussion of this aspect of Hegel's account of instrumental music, see H. Heimsoeth, "Hegels Philosophie der Musik," in *Hegel Studien*, 2 [1963], pp. 197–201. Herder had already given his own model of instrumental music's metaphysical significance this more specific structure in places—concerning which, cf. W. Wiora, "Herders Ideen zur Geschichte der Musik," in *Im Geiste Herders*, ed. E. Keyser [Kitzingen am Main: Holzner, 1953], pp. 109–10—and may therefore have influenced Hegel here.) Similarly, Adorno suggests that Beethoven's symphonies express an idea, shared with his age's Hegelian philosophy, of the resolution of oppositions in a harmonious totality (in contrast to the later string quartets, which rather express a denial of any such overarching resolution) (*Aesthetic Theory*, pp. 45, 107, 110, 116, 141, 185, 209, 222, 298, 307).

77. It is not necessary for my philosophical purposes to expect—no doubt implausibly—that everyone, or even most people, will share these linguistic intuitions about such cases. It would be enough if these are cases in which our collective linguistic intuitions are uncertain, torn. For, provided that is so, then the philosophical arguments which support narrow expressivist principles (concerning which, see *After Herder*, Essay 2), together with the plausibility of explaining away *other* apparent counterexamples to such principles (concerning which, see *After Herder*, Essay 3), can cumulatively create a justification for preferring the linguistic intuitions which I am championing here over contrary ones. A similar situation obtains in at least one other area where narrow expressivism confronts hard cases: that of the "intelligent" behavior of some non-language-using (or scarcely-language-using) animals. Of course, in neither of these areas (neither the musical nor the animal) need a decision to exclude the sort of performance in question from the sphere of *ideas and thoughts* strictly so called involve any denial of its deep kinship with the latter, or any implication of its superficiality in comparison with the latter. On the contrary, it may in a sense be ideas and thoughts that are the more superficial relatives here.

78. In suggesting that instrumental music expresses something about feeling or emotion that cannot be as accurately expressed by language (alone), I am in broad agreement with a long tradition that includes both composers and philosophers. For example, the composer Mendelssohn says that musical feeling is indescribable because it is too precise for words (see Sullivan, *Beethoven*, pp. 20–1; Scruton, *The Aesthetics of Music*, p. 165). The philosopher Herder holds a version of the position in question as well (see *After Herder*, Essay 3). And so too does the philosopher S. Langer in several works, including *Feeling and Form* (London: Routledge and Kegan Paul, 1953), *Problems of Art* (New York: Charles Scribner's Sons, 1957), and *Philosophy in a New Key* (Cambridge, Mass.: Harvard University Press, 1978) (though one might hesitate to subscribe to her more specific justification of it, à la Wittgenstein's *Tractatus*, in terms of a "logical form" shared between the feeling and the music).

The suggestion that instrumental music expresses feeling or emotion, and that it conveys the nuances thereof more precisely than language (alone) can do, requires some defense and qualification, however. For it is not always conceded that instrumental music expresses feeling or emotion at all, let alone that it does so more precisely than language (for example, Hanslick and Raffman both deny this). Perhaps the most serious objection to such a position is one that was first raised by Hanslick (*On the Musically Beautiful*, pp. 8–10): feelings and emotions of their very nature incorporate intentional objects, which seem beyond the reach of musical expression. Scruton (*The Aesthetics of Music*, pp. 165 ff.) has provided a very perceptive two-part response to this sort of objection, which we can take over and build on here. First, he points out that instrumental music often *does* in fact express intentional objects (e.g. religious music expresses the thought of God). Second, he notes that, despite the fact that emotions essentially include intentional objects, it is in an important sense possible to identify emotions without pinning down their intentional objects—that if, for instance, one comes upon an unknown woman weeping in a park, one may be able by observing her behavior to identify the character of her emotion without knowing the intentional object involved (e.g. whether she is weeping over the death of a parent, the thanklessness of a child, abandonment by a husband, or what not). I would add here, third, that in such cases it may also in a certain sense be possible to identify the emotion from observation of the person's behavior *more precisely* than could be achieved from a verbal description, that the person's complex behavior in its context may convey to one the quality of the emotion in a way that could not be matched by a mere verbal description either of the behavior and context or of the emotion itself (though only "in a certain sense," because of course in another sense, namely that of pinning down the intentional object, the identification is ex hypothesi *less* precise). This situation suggests that, similarly, nuances of emotion may in a certain sense be expressed more precisely by instrumental music than could be achieved by language (even though in another sense—that concerned with the identification of the intentional object—they can usually only be expressed less precisely).

79. A variant of this illusion can arise in connection with a composer's *musically technical* meanings and thoughts, which are capable of linguistic or notational expression by him. These will be precisely graspable by a listener who has technical expertise in music. However, a layman will again often sense their presence but find himself unable to pin them down linguistically with any precision, and so be encouraged to imagine that linguistically inexpressible meanings and thoughts are involved.

80. Concerning this point, see the note before last.

81. There may also be further sources of the delusive temptation to ascribe ineffable meanings and thoughts to music. For example, Raffman somewhat plausibly diagnoses such a temptation in terms of the existence of a sort of musical grammar, which leads to a false expectation of a musical semantics due to the conjunction of grammar with semantics in the linguistic case (*Language, Music, and Mind*, pp. 40–1).

82. Concerning Herder's version of this conception of the function of music, see Wiora, "Herders Ideen zur Geschichte der Musik," p. 118. Concerning Wackenroder and Tieck's, see *Phantasien über die Kunst, für Freunde der Kunst* (1799), p. 83. Concerning Hegel's, see A. Nowak, *Hegels Musikästhetik* (Regensburg: G. Bosse, 1971), pp. 62, 138, 146, 151–2, 184. For the Schlegels' and Hegel's extension of the point to (ancient) sculpture, see esp. A.W. Schlegel's lectures on art and literature, together with a passage from *Hegel's Aesthetics* quoted earlier (p. 719; cf. pp. 1186–7, 1195). For Collingwood's broader version of the same conception, see R.G. Collingwood, *The Principles of Art* (Oxford: Oxford University Press, 1969), esp. p. 274.

83. For Proust's suggestion of such a position, see esp. M. Proust, *À l'ombre des jeunes filles en fleurs*. For Gombrich's fuller development of such a position, see especially E.H. Gombrich, *Art and Illusion* (Princeton, NJ: Princeton University Press, 1972).

84. For example, someone might describe himself as having felt in an "*Eroica* mood" today (though hopefully with some irony!).

85. Concerning Herder's (and even Hegel's) commitment to an empiricist theory of meaning of a certain sort, see *After Herder*, Essays 2 and 4, and in the present volume Essay 5. Since the arrival of Fregean-Wittgensteinian anti-psychologism about meaning, such theories have fallen out of favor, but some such theory may nonetheless well be correct.

86. It is perhaps ultimately in this sense that one should understand Herder's point (mentioned earlier) that the visual aspects of a dramatic work like Sophocles' *Philoctetes* are as important to its meaning as its verbal aspects. A similar position lies behind a central thesis of Herder's in translation theory: Herder insists that the translator (especially of poetry) must aim to reproduce not only the meaning of a text but also its musical aspects, and he sees this not merely as a desideratum over and above the more fundamental one of reproducing the meaning exactly but rather (or also) as an essential requirement for achieving the latter, because he believes that it is often only the musical aspects of the text that reveal the exact nature of the feelings which are partly constitutive of the meanings expressed by the text. See e.g. G2:1159, where he implies that it is essential to preserve Shakespeare's rhymes in translation because of the semantically relevant nuances of feeling which only they convey exactly.

87. This point still holds true even if—as I think one should—one includes among the nuances of feeling and sensation expressed (or received) through non-linguistic art ones which are only imaginatively entertained rather than simply had. (For a sense of this distinction, contrast actually

feeling a certain sort of shame and merely imagining what it is like to feel it.) Cf. *After Herder*, Essay 4.

88. The narrow expressivist's concession of this sort of dependence of certain areas of linguistic meaning and thought on non-linguistic art might sound like a big one. However, it will seem less dramatic if it is kept in mind that linguistic meanings and thoughts are dependent on extra-linguistic items and circumstances in *many* ways (which is not, though, to deny that there is anything special about this case of dependence in particular; for one thing, it is a case of dependence on a certain sort of *expression*).

89. See e.g. *Ideas*, G6:347–55, where he attempts to account for what he takes to be the unique suitedness of speech as a vehicle for thought. This attempt stands in a longer historical tradition (concerning which see Nowak—who is evidently himself sympathetic to it—at *Hegels Musikästhetik*, pp. 42, 47, 89–90). As will become clear in a moment, my own view is that this is an attempt to explain something that is in fact false.

90. When discussing the language on which he says thought depends (or with which he even says thought is identical) Schleiermacher hardly ever even considers the possibility of forms of language other than speech and writing. (One notable exception: Schleiermacher's psychology lectures, at FSSW 3/4:46.)

91. See esp. W. von Humboldt, *On Language*, pp. 54–6, where he closely follows Herder's account in the *Ideas* concerning why speech is especially suitable as a vehicle of thought.

92. See Essay 5. Passages such as *Hegel's Aesthetics*, p. 636 where Hegel speaks of architecture as a wordless "language" are either metaphorical or anomalous.

93. Herder himself perceives this oddity in a way, though without realizing that it constitutes an objection which he needs to address: "How strange that a moved breath of air should be the sole, or at least the best, medium of our thoughts and sensations!" (G6:347).

94. Concerning these, see Gombrich, *Art and Illusion*, ch. 2 and pp. 123–4.

95. As I pointed out in *After Herder*, Essay 2, Abbt and Süßmilch had rightly allowed that such sign-language can support (rational) thought, whereas Herder implausibly tends to resist doing so (see esp. *Ideas*, G6:347). We can now see *why* Herder inclines to this implausible position, namely because of his excessively restrictive conception of the possible material-perceptual media of language.

96. Already before Herder and his tradition, E.B. de Condillac had plausibly emphasized that in certain cultures (Condillac mainly focuses on the ancient Greeks and Romans, though one could add other examples, for instance certain native American cultures) gesture takes on a far larger

burden of communication than it does in our own (*An Essay on the Origin of Human Knowledge* [1746] [Gainsville, Fla.: Scholars' Facsimiles and Reprints, 1971], pp. 199 ff.).

97. For an illuminating broad discussion of animals' diverse expressive media, and of the evidence that these provide for animals' possession of concepts and thoughts, see D.R. Griffin, *Animal Thinking* (Cambridge, Mass.: Harvard University Press, 1984), chs. 8–10; *Animal Minds* (Chicago: University of Chicago Press, 2001), esp. ch. 9; and "Windows on Animal Minds," *Consciousness and Cognition*, 4/2 (1995).

98. This is admittedly vague. It would, indeed, be no small or easy task to say exactly what sort of "highly rule-governed, conventional character" spoken and written language do have. But perhaps this question can be bracketed here.

99. It could be argued that there are already hints of this insight in Hamann's extension of the term "language" to cover all of the artistic expressive media which he considers capable of serving as fundamental vehicles of meaning and thought in addition to language more narrowly conceived (in particular, painting, drawing, and music). Likewise, it could be argued that there are already hints of it in Hegel's characterization of symbolic architecture as a "language" (*Hegel's Aesthetics*, p. 636), and in his implication that symbolic architecture's expressive capacity rests on its highly *conventional* character (ibid., p. 722—though he rather spoils the point by implying in this particular context that the architecture in question is not a fundamental vehicle for meaning or thought after all but only expresses a meaning or thought that pre-exists in people's minds in another form).

100. F. de Saussure, *Course in General Linguistics* (New York: McGraw-Hill, 1966), pp. 10–11 argues for a similarly liberal conception of the possible material-perceptual forms that language might take to the one I am advocating here.

101. Two test cases on which one might try out this point: the ancient Egyptian pictures recently mentioned, and the Greek musical modes in their rigid association with certain occasions and moods (concerning which, cf. Hanslick, *On the Musically Beautiful*, p. 63).

# 7

# Hegel and Hermeneutics

Hegel played a large role in the development of modern hermeneutics, or interpretation theory,[1] inheriting richly from its past (especially Herder) and bequeathing copiously to its future (especially Dilthey and Gadamer).

Certain of Hegel's contributions in this area concern what one might call the *scope and significance* of interpretation, and are, I think, of clear validity and importance. In this connection, he especially championed several ideas which were to some extent already in the air, but to which he lent new force and influence. Among these are the following.

First, he plausibly identified as expressions of mind and meaning, and hence as standing in need of interpretation, not only linguistic texts and discourse, but also non-linguistic art (especially architecture, sculpture, painting, and instrumental music);[2] a broad set of socio-political institutions and activities which he calls "objective mind";[3] and also individual actions.[4] Subsequent hermeneutics largely took over this broadening of focus. For example, Dilthey and Gadamer both likewise take for granted the meaningfulness, and hence interpretability, of non-linguistic art;[5] Dilthey adopts a version of Hegel's conception of "objective mind" (indeed, singling this out as one of Hegel's most important contributions);[6] and again like Hegel, Dilthey emphasizes that in addition to intentional expressions of mind and meaning (such as linguistic texts and discourse, art, and socio-political institutions), there are also unintentional ones, in particular people's actions, which consequently stand just as much in need of interpretation in order to be understood.[7]

Second, Hegel recognized that *history* is therefore a process that centrally involves expressions of mind and meaning, and that the historian consequently needs to deploy interpretation as his main tool in order to understand them in their variety.[8] Dilthey subsequently takes over this position. Accordingly, in *Die Jugendgeschichte Hegels* he praises Hegel as a "founder of the history of the innerness of the human spirit,"[9] and he himself makes mind and its expressions, in all their variety, the central subject-matter of history, therefore identifying (at first psychology but later on) hermeneutics, in the sense of theoretically informed interpretation, as the central method of the historian.[10]

Third, Hegel also recognized that the interpretation of historical Others is essential for a proper *self*-understanding.[11] One of his reasons for this is that it is only by comparing one's own outlook with the different outlooks of (historical) Others that one can become fully cognizant of its character.[12] Another of his reasons is that perceiving how one's own outlook has developed out of other outlooks which were its historical antecedents enables one to comprehend it more fully.[13] In one variant or another, this whole conception has remained central to historically-hermeneutically oriented philosophy since Hegel. For example, its latter part reappears in Nietzsche's project of a "genealogy of morals" and in Foucault's of an "archaeology of knowledge."[14]

I shall not pursue these important Hegelian contributions concerning the *scope and significance* of interpretation any further in this essay, however. Instead, I would like to consider his ideas about the *very nature of interpretation* itself. For he also had ideas in *this* area that have exercised a strong influence on the subsequent development of hermeneutics—though whether for good or ill in this case is a question that we will need to consider.

# I

Two positions that were central to pre-Hegelian hermeneutics—by which I mean mainly the hermeneutics of Herder, together with its substantial continuation by Hegel's contemporary Schleiermacher—[15] were the following:

(1) Interpretation of a linguistic text or discourse is a matter of recovering an author's original meaning—something that had the character it did independently of whatever history, and in particular whatever history of interpretation, may have taken place since. Because concepts, beliefs, and so forth vary from age to age, culture to culture, and even individual to individual within a single age and culture, in both subtle and not-so-subtle ways, this requires that the interpreter resist a constant temptation to assimilate the concepts, beliefs, and so on expressed by a text or discourse to his own (or to others with which he happens to be especially familiar). In particular, he should not assume that what is expressed will turn out to be true by his own lights. Instead, he normally needs to use a set of scrupulous interpretive methods in order to arrive at an accurate understanding (for example, careful scrutiny of the passages in which a particular word occurs for the purpose of discerning the rule governing its use and hence its meaning).[16]

(2) Meaning consists in word-usage, and accordingly, thought is essentially dependent on and bounded by (Schleiermacher would even say, albeit too strongly: identical with) language. Therefore, to the extent that apparently non-linguistic arts such as architecture, sculpture, painting, and instrumental

music express meanings and thoughts, they must in fact do so in virtue of a prior *linguistic* articulation or articulability of those meanings and thoughts by the artist—so that interpretation of the meanings and thoughts in question needs to proceed via interpretation of the artist's language.[17]

A prominent strand of Hegel's thought rejected these two positions, however, and by doing so exercised an enormous influence on the subsequent course of hermeneutics, especially in Dilthey and Gadamer.

Thus, as Gadamer points out, and takes as his own model, in *Truth and Method*, a prominent strand in Hegel rejects position (1) in favor of a form of interpretation which (like that championed by Gadamer himself) involves a significant measure of assimilation of what is interpreted to the interpreter's own viewpoint, including the interpreter's own concepts and beliefs.[18] For example, as Gadamer notes,[19] Hegel advocates such an alternative approach to interpretation when he writes in a rather poetical passage of the "Religion" chapter of the *Phenomenology of Spirit* (1807) that is concerned with the transition from polytheistic Greek and Roman culture to the more modern standpoint of monotheistic Christianity:

The works of the Muse now lack the power of the Spirit, for the Spirit has gained its certainty of itself from the crushing of gods and men. They have become what they are for us now—beautiful fruit already picked from the tree, which a friendly Fate has offered us, as a girl might set the fruit before us. It cannot give us the actual life in which they existed, not the tree that bore them, not the earth and the elements which constituted their substance, not the climate which gave them their peculiar character, nor the cycle of the changing seasons that governed the process of their growth. So Fate does not restore their world to us along with the works of antique Art, it gives not the spring and summer of the ethical life in which they blossomed and ripened, but only the veiled recollection of that actual world. Our active enjoyment of them is therefore not an act of divine worship through which our consciousness might come to its perfect truth and fulfillment; it is an external activity—the wiping-off of some drops of rain or specks of dust from these fruits, so to speak—one which erects an intricate scaffolding of the dead elements of their outward existence—the language, the historical circumstances, etc. in the place of the inner elements of the ethical life which environed, created, and inspired them. And all this we do, not in order to enter into their very life but only to possess an idea of them in our imagination. But, just as the girl who offers us the plucked fruits is more than the Nature which directly provides them—the Nature diversified into their conditions and elements, the tree, air, light, and so on—because she sums all this up in a higher mode, in the gleam of her self-conscious eye and in the gesture with which she offers them, so, too, the Spirit of the Fate that presents us with those works of art is more than the ethical life and the actual world of that nation, for it is the *inwardizing* in us of the Spirit which in them was still [only] *outwardly* manifested; it is the Spirit of the tragic Fate which gathers all those individual gods and attributes of the [divine] substance into one pantheon, into the Spirit that is itself conscious of itself as Spirit.[20]

Moreover, as I have argued elsewhere,[21] the "Religion" chapter of the *Phenomenology of Spirit* is also striking for actually *implementing* an approach to interpretation which assimilates the interpreted material to Hegel's own standpoint. For example, in sharp contrast to the preceding "Unhappy Consciousness" section of the work, which had interpreted Christianity in a scrupulously non-assimilating way as a position that *failed* to recognize what Hegel believes to be God's identity with mankind, the "Religion" chapter instead interprets Christianity as a position that *expressed* the insight that God and mankind are identical.

Nor is such an alternative approach to interpretation by any means confined to the later parts of the *Phenomenology of Spirit*: it is theoretically espoused, implemented, or both in many other texts of Hegel's as well, including some of his earliest and some of his latest. For example, already in *The Life of Jesus* from early 1795 we find Hegel assuming that the standpoint of Kantian moral philosophy is basically correct,[22] and interpreting the Jesus of the gospels as expressing that standpoint as well. Likewise, in his 1802 essay *On the Nature of Philosophical Critique* Hegel advocates interpreting past philosophy in such a way as to maximize the recovery from it of what is true by his own philosophical lights, and in other essays from the same period, such as *Faith and Knowledge*, he actually implements that interpretive approach. Finally, and most famously, Hegel's later lecture series on art, religion, and philosophy self-consciously employ such an approach as well.[23]

Somewhat similarly, especially in his mature *Aesthetics* lectures, Hegel rejects position (2), namely in favor of a position according to which, while meaning and thought do indeed essentially depend on the possession of some material-perceptible medium of expression or other, this need not be *language* but may in certain cases be a different expressive medium, such as architecture (as in the case of the ancient Egyptians) or sculpture (as in the case of the ancient Greeks).[24] (To be a little more specific, Hegel's move to this position takes the less radical of two possible forms: although he believes that in certain cases a person can, by using such alternative expressive media, express meanings and thoughts which *the person himself* cannot express linguistically, he does not believe that the person can thereby express meanings and thoughts which are inexpressible by language *tout court*.[25])

This move of Hegel's has again had a large impact on the subsequent development of hermeneutics, especially in Dilthey. Until around 1900 Dilthey was strongly attracted to position (2). For example, he favors that position in *The Development of Hermeneutics* (1900), where he associates it with such predecessors as Schleiermacher and Preller.[26] However, in 1905 he wrote his classic study of the early Hegel, *Die Jugendgeschichte Hegels*, and apparently in the course of doing so fell under the influence of the alternative Hegelian position just described. For he henceforth treated not merely language but a broader class of "expressions" as fundamental to meaning and thought.[27] For instance, he argues in his essay *Musical Understanding* that instrumental music, while it does indeed sometimes express linguistically articulable thoughts, in its highest forms also expresses thoughts which are *not* linguistically articulable (ones about "Life").[28] Similarly, Gadamer usually seems inclined to reject position (2), and to accept instead a version of Hegel's alternative position.[29]

In short, a prominent strand of Hegel's thought rejected positions (1) and (2), and thereby prepared the ground for the subsequent hermeneutic theories of Dilthey and Gadamer.

## II

But are these two Hegelian turns in hermeneutics progress? As a prelude to addressing that question, it is worth observing that Hegel himself actually seems quite torn about them, that much of the time he himself rather seems inclined to stay *faithful* to positions (1) and (2).

Thus, counterbalancing the passages from later parts of the *Phenomenology of Spirit* that seem to reject position (1), there are earlier parts of the same work which seem instead to *accept* it. For example, in a passage from the introduction which echoes Herder both in thought and terminology, Hegel writes concerning the work's investigation into the history of "shapes of consciousness":

We do not need to import standards [*Maßstäbe*], or to make use of our own bright ideas and thoughts during the course of the inquiry; it is precisely when we leave these aside that we succeed in contemplating the matter in hand as it is *in and for itself*.[30]

And as has already been mentioned, while the work's late "Religion" chapter interprets Christianity in an assimilative manner as an outlook that expresses the Hegelian insight of God's identity with mankind, the earlier "Unhappy Consciousness" section on the contrary interprets Christianity in the anti-assimilative spirit of position (1) as an outlook that *fails* to recognize God's identity with mankind.[31]

Likewise, the other writings of Hegel's from various periods which seem to reject position (1) are counterbalanced by writings from an equally wide range of periods which seem rather to accept it. For example, as early as 1788 we find Hegel arguing that the ancients, in particular the Greeks, had concepts different from ours, and that it is therefore one of the main advantages of learning their languages that we thereby enrich our conceptual resources.[32]

Again, in sharp contrast to *The Life of Jesus* from early 1795, the later parts of *The Positivity of the Christian Religion* from shortly thereafter are written very much in the spirit of position (1). For instance, they emphasize the sharp *differences* between ancient Judeo-Christian moral-religious thought and what Hegel takes to be the correct moral-religious outlook, and go to considerable interpretive pains to depict the former as it actually was. Again, the 1809 speech *On Classical Studies* emphasizes the importance of penetrating ancient Greek and Roman thought in its alienness from our own by means of a scrupulous study of the relevant languages and texts. Finally (and perhaps most strikingly), in a long and thoughtful review article from as late as 1827 on work by Wilhelm von Humboldt,[33] Hegel shows great respect for two close associates of the Herder-Schleiermacher tradition in hermeneutics, namely Humboldt himself and A.W. Schlegel; strongly praises Humboldt's approach, in the spirit of Herder and Schleiermacher, of scrupulously going back to the ancient Indians' original texts and language in order to discover their outlook in its "distinctiveness [*Eigentümlichkeit*]," and of refusing to go beyond the strict sense of the original;[34] and indeed himself hunts down and rejects a series of false assimilations of ancient Indian concepts and beliefs to modern European ones.[35]

Similarly, counterbalancing Hegel's prominent rejection of position (2) in his late *Aesthetics* lectures, there are several features of Hegel's works which rather seem to show him *espousing* position (2). For one thing, his earlier treatment of aesthetic matters in the *Phenomenology of Spirit* seems much more strongly *in favor* of position (2) than opposed to it. It is indeed possible to find in the short, cryptic statements about ancient architecture and sculpture near the start of the "Religion" chapter a few anticipations of his later position concerning these artforms (passages that represent them as artforms which, though non-linguistic, did at least in *some* way already express religious thoughts not yet expressed or expressible in any other way).[36] But the main thrust of the work is instead strongly supportive of position (2). Thus, to begin with some earlier parts of the work, Hegel's whole strategy of argument in the "Sense-certainty" section presupposes that meaning and thought essentially require articulability in language (or by the quasi-linguistic act of pointing).[37] And in the "Physiognomy and Phrenology" section he writes even more explicitly:

Although it is commonly said that reasonable men pay attention not to the word but to the thing itself,... this is at once incompetence and deceit, to fancy and to pretend that one merely has not the right *word*, and to hide from oneself that really one has failed to get hold of the thing itself, i.e. the concept. *If one had the concept, then one would also have the right word.*[38]

Accordingly, when we reach the treatment of ancient Egyptian architecture and sculpture in the "Religion" chapter, Hegel for the most part implies that because these artforms lacked language, they were *not* really meaningful:

On account of the merely *abstract* intelligibleness of the form, the significance of the work is not in the work itself, is not the spiritual self. Thus either the works receive Spirit into them only as an alien, departed spirit that has forsaken its living saturation with reality and, being itself dead, takes up its abode in this lifeless crystal [i.e. the pyramid]; or they have an external relation to Spirit as something which is itself there externally and not as Spirit—they are related to it as to the dawning light, which casts its significance on them [i.e. the sun/Amun Ra]...But the work still lacks the shape and outer reality in which the self exists as self; it still does not in its own self proclaim that it includes within it an inner meaning, it lacks speech, the element in which the meaning filling it is itself present. Therefore the work, even when it is wholly purged of the animal element and wears only the shape of self-consciousness, is still the soundless shape which needs the rays of the rising sun in order to have sound which, generated by light, is even then merely noise and not speech, and reveals only an outer, not the inner, self...The soul of the statue in human shape does not yet come forth from the inner being, is not yet speech, the outer existence that is in its own self inward.[39]

Nor is this tension merely one between the early Hegel and the late Hegel, for even the late Hegel is still at points strongly attracted to position (2). One symptom of this is the fact that within the *Aesthetics* lectures themselves, although (as I noted) he interprets certain non-linguistic arts, namely ancient architecture and sculpture, as counterexamples to position (2), he instead interprets other non-linguistic arts, namely Christian-era painting and instrumental music, as *conforming* to position (2): to the extent that they express meaning or thought at all, it has a prior linguistic articulation or articulability. To be a little more precise, Hegel sometimes in the *Aesthetics* lectures commits himself to the naive and untenable view that these two non-linguistic arts simply do not express meanings or thoughts at all; however, in more considered remarks he rather suggests that they do (at least in some cases), but that the meanings and thoughts in question are parasitic on a prior linguistic articulation or articulability. This whole position can be seen from the text in two main ways: First, for Hegel, whereas ancient architecture and sculpture are paradigmatically "symbolic" and "classical" arts respectively, Christian-era painting and music (along with poetry) are paradigmatically "Romantic" arts. But, according to Hegel, "Romantic" arts are grounded in, and express, the outlook of the Christian religion, i.e. an outlook whose primary expression is *linguistic* (the Bible).[40] Second, Hegel's specific interpretations of Christian-era painting and instrumental music reinforce the moral that he understands whatever meanings and thoughts they express to have a prior linguistic articulation or articulability. To take painting first, that is certainly true of his interpretations of Christian religious painting. For example, when he interprets Raphael's controversial painting the *Transfiguration* he does so in terms of ideas from the Bible, and indeed actually quotes from Matthew's Gospel what he takes to be the central biblical text expressed in the painting: "Where two or three are gathered in my name, there am I in the midst of them."[41] But the same is also true of his interpretations of the other main category of painting on which he focuses: Dutch genre painting. Occasionally he treats this rather naively as lacking meanings and thoughts altogether, as *merely* imitative of the Dutch landscapes and other aspects of life that it depicts. However, in more considered remarks he instead treats it as indeed expressing meanings and thoughts, but ones which had a prior linguistic articulation or articulability, pointing out—very perceptively, I think—that it is not in fact merely imitative, but also expresses such thought-imbued sentiments as the Dutch's pride in their hard-won political autonomy, their hard-won religious autonomy (Protestantism), and a landscape which was largely their own creation.[42] Similarly concerning instrumental music: Hegel sometimes rather naively characterizes this as not expressing meanings or thoughts at all but only contentless subjectivity or feeling,[43] whatever meanings or thoughts it may prompt being caused to occur only accidentally.[44] But in more considered remarks he instead implies that it sometimes does, and moreover ought to, convey meanings and thoughts (albeit vaguely), evidently understanding the meanings and thoughts in question to be ones which were already linguistically expressed or expressible by the composer rather than a monopoly of the instrumental music in question.[45]

Moreover, in an even clearer late expression of commitment to position (2), Hegel's *Encyclopedia* (1827 and 1830) repeats the claim of thought's essential dependence on and boundedness by language which we encountered in the *Phenomenology of Spirit*:

It is in names that we *think*... We... only have determinate, genuine thoughts when we give them the form of objectivity, of being distinguished from inwardness, i.e. the form of externality, and indeed of such an externality as at the same time bears the imprint of the greatest inwardness. Only *the articulated sound*, the *word*, is such an inward external thing. To want to think without words, as Mesmer once tried to, is therefore clearly an absurdity... The inexpressible is in truth only something dark, fermenting, which only achieves clarity when it is able to attain verbal expression.[46]

In short, a significant heretical side of Hegel both starts out and remains strongly inclined to stay *faithful* to positions (1) and (2).

# III

Now it may possibly be that Hegel in the end has ways of reconciling these apparent conflicts in his position (this is usually a Hegelian forte, related to his dialectical method's emphasis on the reconciliation of contradictions).

For example, concerning the apparent conflict between rejecting and espousing position (1), I have argued elsewhere that at least in the *Phenomenology of Spirit* this conflict is probably in the end more apparent than real—the result of a transition that occurs within the text between significantly different theoretical contexts requiring different approaches to interpretation and correspondingly different concepts of meaning.[47] And in his 1827 review of Humboldt, Hegel more explicitly articulates a somewhat similar strategy of reconciliation. To recast his thought there a bit in terms of a later distinction of Frege's, he in effect suggests that interpretation in conformity with position (1) is what is needed in order to specify people's *senses*, but that an assimilative sort of interpretation which violates position (1) is what is needed in order to specify their underlying *referents* (i.e. the features of reality that they are trying to express, however inadequately):

> Now to the extent that...objectless thinking is at the same time represented as essentially a relation to Brahma..., necessarily there is a determination of *this purely abstract thinking as Brahma himself,* a subjectivity that is identical with what is expressed as objective, so that this opposition disappears...It goes without saying that when the expressions "subjectivity" and "objectivity," let alone their unity, are used here, these inventions of the thinking reflection of modern times should not be attributed to the Indians, just as little as, when a thinking mythology shows what the *concept* of Zeus, Hera, Demeter, etc. is, that concept is thereby attributed to the Greeks as a reflective concept. One is no doubt right to say that they did not *have* this concept of Zeus. But this does not mean that such a concept, when it is correctly defined, was any less the content of their imaginative representation of Zeus. Ignorance of this distinction, whether a content only (ful)fills [*erfüllt*] the sensual or imaginative consciousness or the very same content is known by the reflecting consciousness as a thought and concept, has been the source of much misunderstanding and crude contradiction.[48]

Similarly, concerning the apparent conflict between rejecting and espousing position (2): One author who has noticed a version of this apparent conflict within the *Phenomenology of Spirit* has attempted to provide a systematic reconciliation for this case too.[49] And certainly, Hegel's asymmetrical treatment of different non-linguistic arts in the *Aesthetics* lectures, according to which ancient architecture and sculpture fail to conform to position (2) whereas later painting and instrumental music do conform to it, is neither inconsistent nor inadvertent.

It is not inconsistent, for to say that *some* non-linguistic arts express semantic content in an original way whereas *other* non-linguistic arts only do so in a way that is parasitic on language is not inconsistent. Nor is the asymmetry inadvertent. Indeed, far from being so, it plays an important systematic role for Hegel, constituting the foundation for his famous thesis of the end of art, i.e. his thesis that art loses much of its importance in the modern period.[50]

I shall not pursue these systematic questions any further here, however. Instead, I would like to consider the (prima facie) conflicts simply as such, and to say something towards their philosophical adjudication.

# IV

It seems to me very probable that positions (1) and (2) are in fact correct, and that the prominent strand in Hegel and (under his influence) subsequent hermeneutics which attacks them is misguided.

Consider to begin with position (1). It is not altogether easy to identify Hegel's reasons for rejecting this position in favor of interpreting viewpoints from the past in a way that assimilates them to his own concepts and principles, but I would suggest that the following three considerations all play important roles for him:

(a) One line of argument that seems prominent in *On the Nature of Philosophical Critique* and the *Phenomenology of Spirit* is essentially this: It turns out, Hegel believes, that when one interprets non-Hegelian views in the scrupulous manner of position (1), they all prove to be implicitly self-contradictory (indeed, at the very fundamental level of their basic concepts, or the general perspectives— the "shapes of consciousness"—within which they are articulated); that only Hegel's own standpoint is self-consistent; and that it alone is justified and true. Once this has been shown, further interpretation of non-Hegelian views in the manner of position (1) consequently seems rather pointless; it now seems more fruitful to interpret them in a charitable manner that strives to maximize the recovery of Hegel's own standpoint from them.[51]

(b) A second, closely related, line of argument is this: History, including in particular the history of expressions of meaning and thought in art, religion, and philosophy, can ultimately be seen to have been teleological in character, to have been aiming at the achievement of the standpoint of Hegelian philosophy in the modern world, a standpoint which (unlike those that preceded it) is at last self-consistent, justified, and true. This implicit teleology again warrants interpreting views from the past as attempts to express the standpoint of Hegelian philosophy.

(c) A further and very different line of argument is this: As I have explained in detail elsewhere,[52] Hegel holds the novel and radical position that mental states in general, including states of meaning in particular, are constituted by physical behavior, and that moreover they are so in an open-ended way such that as long as a person is still alive, and hence still able to engage in further behavior, he can continue to modify even his "past" mental states or states of meaning. (This is why in the *Phenomenology of Spirit* Hegel writes approvingly of "Solon, who thought he could only know [someone's particular individuality] from and after the course of the whole life,"[53] and why he makes the similar point about the supra-individual absolute mind that "of the Absolute it must be said that it is essentially a *result*, that only in the *end* is it what it truly is."[54]) Also, as I have again explained elsewhere,[55] Hegel holds the further position that meaning is essentially *social*, that it is of its very nature constituted by the linguistic behavior not merely of an individual but of a whole community or communal tradition. Now if one puts these two positions together, they seem to imply that as long as the relevant community or communal tradition continues to exist, even the meanings of a dead individual from the past are going to be subject to modification by it.[56] So I suggest that this is a further line of argument which inclines Hegel to reject position (1) in favor of his contrary proto-Gadamerian position concerning interpretation.

But how convincing are these arguments? A first point to note is that they seem to be inconsistent with each other. In particular, arguments (a) and (b) seem to imply that there *is* such a thing as the sort of original meaning that is aimed at by the interpretive method of position (1) (the problem being merely that it always turns out to be saying something self-contradictory, unjustified, and untrue; and something that is teleologically directed towards an ulterior message), whereas argument (c) seems to imply that there is *not*. However, since each of the arguments also faces independent problems, I shall not pursue this problem of their mutual inconsistency any further here.

None of the arguments seems to me compelling in the end. The plausibility of argument (a) ultimately depends on the plausibility of Hegel's attempts in his *Phenomenology of Spirit* and Logic to demonstrate that all non-Hegelian "shapes of consciousness" and all non-Hegelian basic concepts are implicitly self-contradictory. But surely, only the most hard-bitten and uncritical of Hegelians would want to claim that those attempts are successful. It seems very unlikely indeed that all non-Hegelian views (or for that matter, all non-*anything* views) are afflicted with implicit inconsistency.

Argument (b) fares no better. For it is surely in the end quite implausible to suppose that it is the case, let alone that Hegel has shown it to be the case, that the whole of human history, including in particular the whole history of culture, has been teleologically directed at the attainment of Hegelian philosophy in the modern world (or for that matter, at the attainment of any *other* modern viewpoint). Hegel's attempt to prove that it has rests on two main pillars: first, a demonstration of the standpoint of his mature Logic by means of the *Phenomenology of Spirit* and by the internal argument of the Logic itself; second, a demonstration in his later lecture series on art, religion, and philosophy that the viewpoints which have arisen in these several areas of culture over the course of past history can plausibly be interpreted as progressively more and more adequate expressions of that logical standpoint. But it would surely be very implausible to claim that either of these pillars stands up to critical scrutiny in the end.

Nor, I think, does argument (c) work—though since this is a more philosophically interesting argument, it may be worth considering in a little more detail than the others. A helpful way in which to see that and why argument (c) fails is to excavate one of the lines of thought that probably led Hegel to embrace his radical open-ended behaviorist conception of the mind and meaning in the first place. Hegel's predecessor Herder had—in continuity with a Rationalist tradition—held that mental states, including states of meaning, were "forces [*Kräfte*]," which he conceived in a realist manner as underlying conditions apt for producing certain patterns of behavior (not in an anti-realist manner as simply reducible to such patterns). However, Hegel in his early *Logic, Metaphysics, and Nature Philosophy* (1804–5) and then again more famously in the "Force and the Understanding" section of the *Phenomenology of Spirit* (1807) subjected such a realist conception of force to a critique which led him to reconceive force in anti-realist terms. Implicitly retaining Herder's generic conception of mental states, including states of meaning, as forces (as I suggest he in a sense did), but now reconceiving these forces in an anti-realist manner, left Hegel with his open-ended behaviorist theory.[57]

Now the important thing to note in this connection is that if Hegel's arguments against the realist conception of force can be satisfactorily answered (as I think they can, though I shall not attempt to show this here), then the Herderian position has plausible resources for undermining both Hegel's open-ended behaviorism and his social theory of meaning, and hence for undermining argument (c) in not just one but two ways.

First, and most obviously, Herder's position promises to undermine Hegel's open-ended behaviorism, namely by providing an attractive contrary theory that mental states, including states of meaning, are *underlying conditions* apt for producing patterns of behavior, conditions which moreover may very well occur *determinately at specific times within* an individual's life.

But second, Herder's position also promises to undermine Hegel's argument for his social theory of meaning. That argument, as Hegel develops it in the

*Phenomenology of Spirit*, takes the form of an attempt to show that none of the various ways in which one might try to validate our commonsense intuition that meaning is something that can in principle be purely individual, and that can be achieved determinately by an individual at a particular time within his life, is defensible.[58] Herder's conception of states of meaning as realist "forces" promises to undermine that argument by showing how meaning *could* be a purely individual achievement, and indeed one that occurred determinately at a particular time within an individual's life.[59]

Moreover, note that Herder's conception of mental states, and in particular states of meaning, as realist "forces" has several compelling intuitive advantages over Hegel's alternative conception of them. In particular, unlike Hegel's conception, Herder's can save, and make sense of, the following strong commonsense intuitions: that people are often in particular mental states which happen to receive no behavioral expression at all; that the fact of being in a mental state is constituted solely by something that occurs at the time to which we normally assign it (not in addition by future behavior); that a mental state is often a cause of the behavior that corresponds to it (not merely something constituted by that behavior); that there could at least in principle perfectly well be purely individual acts of meaning, for example if a sort of cosmic Robinson Crusoe, all alone in the universe, were to start keeping track of his goats by developing a system of chalk marks on his cave wall signifying the goats and their numbers (that any dependence of meaning on society is merely causal); and that what a person meant by a certain expression is a fact constituted solely by what occurred at the time to which we normally assign his having done so (not in addition by his own future behavior and that of a community or communal tradition to which he belongs).

In short, it seems likely that argument (c) breaks down at two key points, and moreover for reasons which one of the champions of position (1) in the previous hermeneutic tradition, namely Herder, had in essence already supplied.

However, it is also worth considering Gadamer's arguments for rejecting position (1), since these turn out to be significantly different from Hegel's. As far as I can see, Gadamer offers four main arguments, as follows.[60]

(a) Both in the case of linguistic and non-linguistic art and in the case of linguistic texts and discourse generally, interpretations change over time, and these changing interpretations are internal to the meaning of the art, text, or discourse in question, so that there is, after all, no such thing as an original meaning independent of these changing interpretations.[61]

(b) The original meaning of artistic or linguistic expressions from the past is always strictly speaking unknowable by us because of the essential role played in all understanding by a historically specific form of "pre-understanding" or "prejudice" from which one can never entirely escape.[62]

(c) The original meaning is something "dead," something no longer of any possible interest to us.[63]

(d) *All* knowledge is historically relative, so interpretive knowledge is so in particular.[64]

But how convincing is this case? A first point to note about it is that arguments (a)–(c) seem to be inconsistent with each other: argument (a) says that there is no such thing as an "original meaning," whereas arguments (b) and (c) say that there is (but that it is unknowable and "dead"); argument (b) says that it is unknowable, whereas argument (c) implies that it is knowable (but "dead," of no possible interest to us). However, Gadamer could possibly cope with this problem by recasting these three arguments in the consistent form: there is no such thing as an "original meaning"...; moreover, even if there were, we could not know it...; and furthermore, even if we could know it, it could be of no possible interest to us...[65] And as we shall see, the arguments face plenty of additional problems. So I shall not dwell on this problem of their mutual inconsistency any further here, but shall instead consider each of them separately.

Argument (a) seems implicitly incoherent. Take the case of texts, for example. To say that interpretations of a text change over time is presumably to say, roughly, that the author of the text meant such and such, that there then arose an interpretation A which meant something a bit different from that, that there then arose a further interpretation B which meant something a bit different again, and so on. In other words, the very notion of changing interpretations *presupposes* an original meaning (indeed, a whole *series* of original meanings, one belonging to the text, and then one belonging to each of its subsequent interpretations).[66] Furthermore, as far as I can see, Gadamer has no real argument to begin with for his surely very counterintuitive claim that subsequent (re)interpretations are internal to an author's meaning. In particular, the mere facts (both adduced by him in this connection) that (re)interpretations occur, and that authors often expect and even welcome this, by no means suffice to justify it.

Argument (b) runs into an epistemological problem: If one were always locked into a modifying pre-understanding, then how could one even know that the other perspectives being modified existed?[67] (In a formulation of his position which perhaps especially invites this sort of objection, Gadamer writes at one point that "the discovery of the historical horizon is always already a fusion of horizons."[68]) Moreover, as I have argued elsewhere, this sort of epistemological problem eventually leads to a conceptual one as well: a problem about whether in that case it would even make *sense* to speak of such perspectives.[69] Furthermore, Gadamer's assumption that pre-understanding is internal to understanding and that it is always historically specific in an insurmountable way seems very questionable to begin with. Anglophone philoso-phers will be likely to object to it that the notion that pre-understanding is internal to understanding violates an anti-psychologistic insight about meaning and understanding which we owe to Frege and Wittgenstein.[70] However, I believe that this anti-psychologism is in fact quite dubious.[71] So it is not on *this* ground that I would question Gadamer's assumption. Nor would I question his view that the forms of pre-understanding vary historically; that too seems very plausible. Instead, I would suggest that what is really wrong with his assumption is its implication that it is impossible to abstract from one's own pre-understanding and recapture the pre-understanding of a historical Other. Indeed, I would suggest that Herder's notorious conception that *Einfühlung* ("feeling one's way in") plays an essential role in the interpretation of texts from the past already quite properly pointed towards an ability which we possess to perform just this sort of imaginative feat, and towards the essential contribution that exercising this ability makes to our attainment of an exact understanding of past texts' original meanings.[72] It should also be noted here that even if it were true that an exact understanding of historical or cultural Others is always impossible—as Schleiermacher in fact normally held concerning *all* other peo-ple, though for a different reason from Gadamer's (namely, the alleged necessity of psychological individuality)—it would surely still be attractive to espouse position (1) as an *ideal* at which interpretation should *aim*—as Schleiermacher in effect did.

Argument (c) is perhaps the weakest part of Gadamer's case. Far from inevi-tably being "dead," or of no possible interest to us, the original meanings of texts and discourse from the past, and from contemporary Others, can be of *great* interest to us, and for *many* different reasons. One reason (which Herder and Dilthey had both already quite properly emphasized) is simply that the accurate discovery of such meanings satisfies our intellectual curiosity and enriches our experience. Another reason (again already important to Herder) is that it expresses and promotes respect and sympathy for Others. Another reason (again already important to Herder) is that it promises to acquaint us with con-cepts, beliefs, values, techniques, and so on which may help us to improve our own in various ways. Another reason (again already important to Herder, but also, as I mentioned earlier, to Hegel) is that it makes an essential contribution towards our *self*-understanding, both by enabling us to situate our own perspec-tive in a comparative context and by enabling us to understand how it arose out of antecedents. And no doubt there are many further good reasons as well.

Finally, argument (d) is not at all compelling either. One problem here lies in the well-known fact that the thesis of relativism seems to run into problems of self-contradiction in connection with the awkward question of whether, then, this thesis is *itself* of merely relative validity. Gadamer touches on this problem at various points, but his answers to it are naive and unconvincing: In one place he concedes that a self-contradiction arises, but responds that this merely shows the weakness of the sort of "reflection" that reveals this and objects to it![73] In another place he argues that the thesis of relativism is not "propositional" but merely something of which one has "consciousness," so that it and its own subject-matter are "not at all on the same logical level."[74] But surely, the alleged fact that what is involved here is merely a consciousness that relativism is true, rather than, say, an explicit assertion that it is true, would not diminish either the fact or the unacceptability of the self-contradiction one whit. Another problem with argument (d) is that, contrary to Gadamer's clear intention to claim that meaning's relativity to interpretations makes it distinctive vis-à-vis other subject-matters such as physical nature, and hence resistant to the sorts of methods that can legitimately be applied to them, in particular the "positivist," or objectivity-presupposing, methods of the natural sciences, this argument would leave meaning *no less (if also no more) objective than anything else.*

In short, it seems to me that neither Hegel nor Gadamer has provided us with any compelling argument at all against position (1).[75]

# V

Let us now turn to position (2). Since I have already discussed Hegel's stance towards this at some length in "Hegel and Some (Near-)Contemporaries: Narrow or Broad Expressivism?"[76] I shall be fairly concise here.

As I have mentioned, Hegel in his *Aesthetics* lectures treats ancient Egyptian architecture and ancient Greek sculpture as counterexamples to position (2)—as expressions of meanings and thoughts which were not yet expressible by the artists involved in any other way, and in particular not in a linguistic way. However, as has also been mentioned, Hegel in the very same lectures interprets other non-linguistic arts, in particular the painting and instrumental music of the Christian era, as *conforming* to position (2), as expressing whatever meanings and thoughts they express in a way that is parasitic on a prior linguistic articulation or articulability. Now it seems to me that the former side of this whole account is implausible, but that the latter side is plausible, so that, to this extent at least, position (2) looks like the correct position to adopt. Let me say something to justify each half of this assessment in turn.

Consider, to begin with, the side of Hegel's account that *conflicts* with position (2). To repeat: this side of his account appeals mainly to two cases, namely the architecture of the ancient Egyptians and the sculpture of the ancient

Greeks—whereas, in sharp contrast, his intuitions about later painting and instrumental music *conform* with position (2). Now it should, I think, immediately arouse one's suspicion here that it is the older materials, for which Hegel's knowledge of relevant linguistic, textual, cultural, and biographical context is naturally thinner, which receive the former treatment, whereas the more recent materials, for which his knowledge of such context is naturally richer, receive the latter treatment. That is to say, it seems reasonable to suspect that whereas his assessment of the more recent materials as conforming to position (2) is evidentially well-grounded, his assessment of the ancient materials as conflicting with position (2)—his denial of a linguistic or textual basis to the meanings and thoughts which they express—is merely a result of his relative ignorance of relevant evidence.

That general suspicion is, I think, borne out by closer scrutiny of his account. Consider, first, the case of ancient Egyptian architecture. It does seem beyond serious doubt that this expressed religious meanings and thoughts, as Hegel believes (though whether, as he also believes, the thoughts in question were *true* ones is of course quite another matter). But why should one suppose the meanings or thoughts in question to have been linguistically unexpressed and inexpressible by the Egyptians rather than linguistically expressed or expressible by them? Is Hegel's inclination to do so not simply an error resulting from the fact that in his day people did not yet have the means to identify the Egyptians' linguistic expressions of, or linguistic means for expressing, the meanings or thoughts in question because Egyptian hieroglyphics had not yet been properly deciphered, nor Egyptology yet established as a proper academic discipline?[77] In other words, Hegel seems simply to have misinterpreted the real situation that the buildings in question clearly express religious meanings and thoughts *for which, however, he happens not to know any Egyptian linguistic expressions, or linguistic means of expression, due to his lack of relevant information* as a situation in which the buildings clearly express religious meanings and thoughts *which were not linguistically expressed or expressible by the Egyptians.*[78]

What about Greek sculpture? Prima facie at least, one would surely think that the point to make here was one which Herder had already made forcefully and repeatedly, namely that Greek sculpture was deeply grounded in, and expressive of, ideas from Greek poetry and myth, i.e. ideas which were already *linguistically* expressible, and indeed expressed—so that the case of Greek sculpture conforms well with position (2).[79]

Hegel's contrary assessment of Greek sculpture rests on his judgment that it was the Greeks' *highest* expression of the Absolute, that it expressed something about the Absolute which no other area of Greek culture, and in particular no *linguistic* area of Greek culture, yet expressed or was able to express (at least, not as clearly). What was this something? Hegel's answer is not exactly obvious from his texts, but it seems to be that Greek sculpture already expressed *God's identity with mankind*,[80] and that in this way it already anticipated Christianity's subsequent more explicit, linguistic expression of such an identity.[81] For example, this is an important part of the force of his remark that Greek "sculpture...individualizes the character of the gods into an entirely specific human form and perfects the anthropomorphism of the classical Ideal,"[82] and of his frequent characterizations of Greek sculpture as combining *universality* with *individuality*—which in essential part means: divinity with humanity.

However, it seems to me that this Hegelian interpretation of Greek sculpture again turns out to be quite dubious on closer inspection. There are two main problems with it (standing in mild tension with each other). First, it seems vulnerable to an objection that it involves an erroneous reading-in of a meaning or thought that was not yet intended by the Greek sculptors. For the Greeks' pervasive and clear expressions in their traditional literature of a sharp numerical distinction, or non-identity, between gods and men (coincident with the qualitative distinction between divine immortality and human mortality) constitutes a good prima facie reason for rejecting this Hegelian interpretation of their sculpture. For example, did not Phidias make his statue of Zeus at Olympia as huge as he famously did in important part precisely in order to accord with such a traditional conception of a sharp distinction between gods and men?

Second, though, someone might reasonably respond to this objection on Hegel's behalf that the historical situation is not so clear-cut. In particular, such a person might point to the general exaltation of the human in comparison with the divine that already occurred in fifth-century Athenian democratic culture, taking a secular form in Protagoras, and a—for present purposes, even more relevant—religious form in Aeschylus (whose Prometheus has sometimes been interpreted as really mankind itself, for example), as well as to the Orphic and Pythagorean tradition which culminated in Plato's *Phaedo*, with its own very different way of effacing the division between the human and the divine (namely, by classifying the human soul as immortal and hence divine). Indeed, Hegel may well himself have such evidence in mind, for he singles out as human embodiments of Greek sculpture's ideal both fifth-century Athenian democratic leaders, on the one hand, and Socrates and Plato, on the other.[83] However, such a response on Hegel's behalf, rather than helping him, in the end only exacerbates his difficulties. For one thing, it is far from clear that this evidence can overturn the anti-Hegelian interpretation of the intended significance of Greek sculpture based on traditional literature (it may well be that the sculptors were intellectually rooted in that rather than in this more avant-garde literature and philosophy). For another thing, and more importantly, this response is self-defeating, because the two strands of Athenian culture to which it appeals were both *linguistic* ones which *pre-existed or co-existed with* the sculpture in question. In other words, ironically enough, the very existence of such evidence for the ideas in question poses a problem for Hegel; his theory could in principle have withstood the *absence* of any independent evidence for the occurrence of such ideas at the time (since it is part of his position that sculpture *leads* the rest of the culture in developing them), but it cannot withstand the *presence* of *literary-philosophical* evidence for them, for the very linguistic nature of such evidence entails that, in superficially seeming to support the theory (by showing that the sculptors may have had the relevant ideas in mind), it in truth rather refutes it (by showing its claim of the ideas' autonomy from language to be erroneous).[84]

In the end, therefore, as in the case of Egyptian architecture, Hegel's interpretation of Greek sculpture as conflicting with position (2) looks implausible.

In short, the main evidence on which Hegel bases his denial of position (2) seems not in fact to support that denial. His conviction that it does so results from his mistakenly reading-*out* linguistic meanings and thoughts where they were probably in fact present (especially in the case of Egyptian architecture) and from his mistakenly reading-*in* not-yet-linguistic meanings and thoughts where they were probably in fact either simply absent or else already linguistic (especially in the case of Greek sculpture).[85]

Concerning, next, Hegel's explanation of later painting and instrumental music in a way that *conforms* to position (2): As I hinted earlier, his considered observations about these arts in this spirit—namely, those in which he does ascribe to them meanings and thoughts, but meanings and thoughts which are linguistic in nature—are generally plausible and perceptive. Still, his refusal to see these arts as counterexamples to position (2) requires some further defense. For, although he himself evidently feels otherwise, painting and especially instrumental music are in fact unusually potent sources of a temptation to deny position (2).

Thus, in contemplating these arts, especially instrumental music, we surely do often receive a powerful sense that meanings and thoughts are being expressed which it is beyond the capacity of (existing or perhaps even any) language to capture. And accordingly, theories of these arts which attribute to them some sort of ineffable meaning and thought abound. Here are two examples: (a) As has already been mentioned, the later Dilthey in his essay *Musical Understanding* treats instrumental music as a prime example of the falsehood of position (2). Specifically, he argues that while instrumental music does indeed often merely express *linguistic* thoughts, in its highest forms it also expresses *non*-linguistic ones, in particular ones about the nature of "Life" itself.[86] (b) Hanslick argues that music expresses strictly *musical* ideas.[87] And, following his lead, Bungay argues—in explicit rejection of Hegel's approach to instrumental music—that it is just obvious that non-linguistic musical ideas and thoughts occur.[88]

Despite the admitted seductiveness of such intuitions about painting and especially instrumental music, I strongly suspect that Hegel is in the end right to judge that these arts should be explained in conformity with principle (2). Let me therefore make some points in support of such an assessment, focusing on the especially interesting case of instrumental music. (Corresponding points would apply to painting, and no doubt also to other non-linguistic arts.)

The intuition that instrumental music conveys meanings and thoughts which it is beyond the power of (existing or perhaps even any) language to express can indeed seem very compelling, and I do not want to suggest that it should be dismissed lightly. Nevertheless, it seems to me probable that it is illusory. (It may be salutary in this connection to remind oneself of the—presumable—illusion to which we often fall victim in waking from a dream that we have entertained meanings and thoughts in the dream that are linguistically inexpressible.)

Consider, first, Dilthey's attempt to vindicate that intuition. Dilthey believes that instrumental music in its higher forms expresses some sort of metaphysical or quasi-religious thought (about "Life").[89] This is a common enough conviction, and indeed it may very well be correct. But why should one take the sort of thought in question to be linguistically inexpressible rather than—as Herder and Hegel had both already implied—linguistically expressible (and perhaps, moreover, actually derived from linguistically expressed metaphysics or religion)?[90] Admittedly, the sort of thought to which Dilthey refers here may only be rather *vaguely* expressible in language. But is there really any reason to suppose that the music expresses it any *less* vaguely?

Bungay's attempt to vindicate the intuition in question is different. His claim is not that instrumental music expresses metaphysical or (quasi-)religious thoughts that transcend language, but rather that it expresses distinctively *musical* ideas and thoughts which do so. This claim strikes me as somewhat more plausible, but still in the end quite dubious. It seems important to distinguish between two sorts of cases here. First, there are cases in which the relevant person, say a composer, possesses a linguistic or notational means of expressing the putative musical ideas or thoughts in question. In such cases it *does* seem to me appropriate to speak of his having musical ideas and thoughts. But then, these are also cases in which he can express them *linguistically* (even musical notation being plausibly considered a part of language). Second, there are also cases in which a person develops putative musical ideas or thoughts *without* having any corresponding linguistic or notational means for expressing them (think, for

example, of the once common phenomenon of the skilled jazz or blues musician who does not read music and is verbally inarticulate to boot). But is it
really so clear that in such cases one should speak literally of the person's having
musical *ideas and thoughts*—rather than, say (an appealing alternative), of his
creating and perceiving complex sound-patterns and -relationships? To my linguistic ear, at least, such a characterization would sound out of place if meant
literally (though no doubt alright if only meant metaphorically). In short, it
seems that non-linguistic *musical* ideas and thoughts may well, once again, be a
will-o'-the-wisp.

However, to turn briefly from refutation to diagnosis, I suspect that there
are also some deeper sources feeding the delusive temptation to suppose that
instrumental music expresses linguistically inexpressible meanings and
thoughts. In particular, I would suggest that this temptation arises from instrumental music's peculiar combination of a certain sort of inarticulateness with
a certain sort of articulateness—namely, a relative inarticulateness in expressing meanings and thoughts and a relative articulateness in expressing nuances
of feeling and emotion (in both cases, relative as compared to language).[91]
This combination of features can easily give rise to illusions that instrumental
music expresses linguistically inexpressible meanings and thoughts in at least
two distinct ways: First, instrumental music often expresses a composer's *linguistically expressible* meanings and thoughts but in ways that are vague, making
it hard for a listener to pin down the meanings and thoughts in question with
any precision from the music. This genuine presence of definite linguistically
expressible meanings and thoughts which, however, the listener finds himself
unable to pin down linguistically with any precision easily gets misconstrued
by him as a presence of definite meanings and thoughts which cannot be
linguistically expressed.[92] Second, instrumental music often expresses and
communicates more precisely than could be achieved by language (alone)
certain nuances of feeling and emotion—that is, certain psychological states
which are other than meanings and thoughts but which can easily be mistaken for them (especially given that they do *involve* them,[93] and that other
meanings and thoughts are expressed in the music as well).[94]

In short, I suggest that when one thinks through the several possible forms,
and the likely deeper sources, of the tempting intuition that instrumental music
expresses linguistically inexpressible meanings and thoughts, the intuition in the
end proves to be illusory.

As I implied earlier, analogous points hold for painting as well (and no doubt
also for other non-linguistic arts). For painting too sometimes expresses (vague)
metaphysical or (quasi-)religious thoughts; it too involves technical "ideas" and
"thoughts" which are sometimes linguistically expressible by the artist and

sometimes not (for example, ones concerning perspective or color); and it too tends to combine a relative inarticulateness in the expression of meanings and thoughts with a relative articulateness in the expression of nuances of feeling and emotion (the former part of which point is perhaps obvious; concerning the latter part, think for example of the fine nuances of feeling and emotion expressed by Rembrandt's self-portraits).

In sum, on closer inspection, whereas Hegel's interpretation of ancient architecture and sculpture as counterexamples to position (2) seems implausible, his interpretation of subsequent painting and instrumental music as conforming with position (2) seems plausible. To this extent at least, position (2) in the end looks like the correct position to adopt.[95]

## VI

In conclusion, then, I would suggest that Hegel deserves high praise for having championed several valid and important principles concerning the *scope and significance* of interpretation, but that his contributions concerning the *very nature of interpretation* itself were much more ambiguous. In this connection, he was responsible for two dramatic and influential turns that occurred in the development of hermeneutics, but he was himself ambivalent about them, and they both arguably prove to have been mistakes on reflection (albeit important and interesting ones). Where the very nature of interpretation itself is concerned, therefore, it seems attractive in the end to propose the slogan: Back to the Herder-Schleiermacher tradition, and to the heretical strands in Hegel himself that remained faithful to it!

## Notes

1. Throughout this essay I shall be using the word "hermeneutics" in this traditional sense. In particular, it will not be used as a name for Heideggerian–Gadamerian philosophy.
2. See *Hegel's Aesthetics*. Much of the hermeneutic tradition before and even contemporaneous with Hegel tended to deny this: in particular, one side of Herder, who in the earlier parts of his *Critical Forests* had treated such art as merely sensuous rather than meaningful; Kant, with his famous theory of the non-conceptual nature of beauty; and one side of Schleiermacher, who, despite his project of developing hermeneutics into

a universal discipline, generally excluded non-linguistic art, instead treating it in a central strand of his lectures on aesthetics as merely sensuous rather than meaningful (just as Herder had done). On the other hand, Herder's mature position, which he began to develop in the later parts of the *Critical Forests*, Hamann's *Metacritique*, Tieck and Wackenroder's work, Friedrich Schlegel's work, and a later strand in Schleiermacher's lectures on aesthetics *did* accord meaning to non-linguistic art. So Hegel's position here was by no means without precedent.

3. See esp. *Encyclopedia* (1830), pars. 483–552.
4. See esp. *Lectures on the Philosophy of World History: Introduction*, pp. 81–5.
5. Some relevant material from Dilthey and Gadamer will be cited later in this essay.
6. See esp. W. Dilthey, *The Formation of the Historical World in the Human Sciences* (Princeton, NJ: Princeton University Press, 2002), pp. 170 ff.
7. See esp. ibid., p. 226. Concerning some later incarnations of this idea in Gadamer and in the anthropologist Clifford Geertz, cf. G.B. Madison, "Hermeneutics' Claim to Universality," in *The Philosophy of Hans-Georg Gadamer*, ed. L.E. Hahn (Chicago: Open Court, 1997), p. 353.
8. This position was not entirely without precedent. Voltaire and Herder had both argued for shifting the historian's focus away from traditional political-military history towards the history of culture, and hence for according interpretation a more central role in the discipline of history.
9. DGS 4:157.
10. See e.g. Dilthey, *The Formation of the Historical World*, esp. p. 299.
11. This insight was not without precedent. It had roots especially in Herder and his "genetic method."
12. See esp. Hegel's 1809 speech *On Classical Studies*, in *Early Theological Writings*, pp. 327–8. For some helpful discussion of this idea, and of its centrality to Hegel's conception of culture [*Bildung*], see H.-G. Gadamer, *Truth and Method* (New York: Continuum, 2002), pp. 12 ff.; and A. Berman, *L'Épreuve de l'étranger*, ch. 3.
13. This idea is especially prominent in Hegel's *Phenomenology of Spirit*. For a fuller discussion of both ideas as they appear in that work, see my *Hegel's Idea of a Phenomenology of Spirit*, pp. 430–46.
14. See my "Genealogy and Morality."
15. I am here presupposing a somewhat unorthodox picture of Herder as the leader in the development of hermeneutics in this period, for which I have argued elsewhere. See esp. *After Herder*, Essays 1, 2, and 4, and in the present volume Essay 9.

16. It should be mentioned that although this is a fairly conventional picture of what interpretation is like for Herder and Schleiermacher, it has been subjected to certain challenges since Gadamer's ascription of such a picture to them, and attack upon it. In particular, Irmscher has attempted to retrieve a contrary, proto-Gadamerian picture of interpretation from some of Herder's texts (see H.D. Irmscher, "Grundzüge der Hermeneutik Herders," in *Bückeburger Gespräche über J.G. Herder 1971* [Bückeburg: Grimme, 1973]), and Frank has attempted to do something similar for Schleiermacher (see M. Frank, *Das individuelle Allgemeine: Textstrukturierung und -interpretation nach Schleiermacher* [Frankfurt am Main: Suhrkamp, 1985], esp. the later parts of the book). These attempts seem to me problematic exegetically. But perhaps more importantly, their potential interest derives mainly from an assumption of the validity of Gadamer's own position which, as will become clear in the course of this essay, seems to me ill-grounded.

17. This is the position at which Herder eventually arrived in his maturest and best reflections on the subject, which begin in the later parts of the *Critical Forests*. It is also a position to which Schleiermacher was strongly attracted in his final reflections on the subject in his aesthetics lectures. For a more detailed account of Herder's and Schleiermacher's developing positions in this area, see *After Herder*, Essays 3 and 11, and in the present volume Essay 6.

18. Gadamer, *Truth and Method*, pp. 165–9. For Gadamer Hegel is thus an important forerunner and inspiration of such central hermeneutic principles of his own as that the interpreter must effect a "fusion of horizons" (pp. 306 ff.), accept (some measure of) his own distinctive "prejudices" (pp. 277 ff.), and in particular assume that the interpreted text or discourse is true by his own lights (pp. 292, 297, 303–5).

   Gadamer also perceives some significant differences between his own position and Hegel's, however. For a helpful discussion of these, see P. Redding, *Hegel's Hermeneutics* (Cornell: Cornell University Press, 1996), esp. pp. 48–9.

19. *Truth and Method*, pp. 167–8.

20. *Phenomenology of Spirit*, pp. 455–6.

21. See my *Hegel's Idea of a Phenomenology of Spirit*, pp. 417–18.

22. Hegel would of course soon afterwards abandon this assumption.

23. A few representative methodological statements from the *Lectures on the Philosophy of Religion*: "These definite religions... are included in ours as essential... moments, which cannot miss having in them absolute truth. Therefore in them we have to do not with what is foreign to us, but with

what is our own...The thought of incarnation, for example, pervades every religion"; in interpreting the definite religions we must "recognize the meaning, the truth...; in short get to know what is *rational* in them...We must do them this justice, for what is human, rational in them, is *our own*, too, although it exists in our higher consciousness as a moment only...We look at these definite religions in accordance with the Concept [i.e. the principle of Hegel's own philosophy]" (G.W.F. Hegel, *On Art, Religion, Philosophy*, ed. J.G. Gray [New York: Harper Torchbooks, 1970], pp. 198–200). Similar remarks could be quoted from Hegel's lectures on art and philosophy.

An interesting and revealing variation on this theme is found in a set of remarks at *Hegel's Aesthetics*, pp. 264 ff. concerning anachronism in the representation of past modes of thought, institutions, equipment, etc. in works of art: Hegel champions a moderate anachronism, particularly in preference to a pedantic exactness.

24. See Essay 6.

25. See ibid.

26. See W. Dilthey, *The Development of Hermeneutics*, in *Dilthey's Selected Writings*, esp. pp. 248–9.

27. See e.g. *The Formation of the Historical World*, pp. 168, 173, 230–1.

28. See ibid., p. 245. Dilthey's position here is not a straightforward borrowing of Hegel's, however. For one thing, unlike Hegel, Dilthey seems attracted to the more radical version of the alternative position in question (that according to which the content expressed by a non-linguistic medium is sometimes inexpressible by language *tout court*). For another thing, as we shall see in this essay, Hegel did not himself consider *instrumental music* a counterexample to principle (2).

29. See esp. H.-G. Gadamer, *Truth and Method*, pp. 398–402; *Gesammelte Werke* (Tübingen: J.C.B. Mohr, 1993), 8:4–5. Like much of the German tradition before him, however (see Essay 6), Gadamer vacillates on this question horribly. For instance, in some passages he seems on the contrary to *favor* position (2) (see e.g. *Truth and Method*, pp. 80–1, 398, 476), and his central thesis of the linguistic nature of all understanding (see e.g. ibid., p. 389) seems to commit him to doing so as well. Moreover, while the passages cited at the beginning of this note seem to support Hegel's own moderate version of the alternative position, other passages in Gadamer seem instead to support the more radical version, namely that non-linguistic art can sometimes express meanings and thoughts which are not linguistically expressible *at all* (see e.g. ibid., pp. xxii–xxiii; *Gesammelte Werke*, 8:388).

30. *Phenomenology of Spirit*, p. 54. Cf. Redding, *Hegel's Hermeneutics*, pp. 81–2. Concerning the echoes of Herder in this passage, see my *Hegel's Idea of a Phenomenology of Spirit*, p. 414.

31. See my *Hegel's Idea of a Phenomenology of Spirit*, pp. 417–18.

32. *Dokumente zu Hegels Entwicklung*, pp. 50, 170.

33. *Rezension der Schrift "Über die unter dem Namen Bhagavad-Gita bekannte Episode des Mahabharata. Von Wilhelm von Humboldt,"* in G.W.F. Hegel, *Werke*, vol. 11.

34. Ibid., pp. 132–3.

35. Ibid., pp. 141, 184, 203, etc. There is another side of Hegel's article which qualifies this whole strong identification with the pre-existing hermeneutic tradition, however: a thesis to the effect that there is nonetheless *something* which all human minds share in common, namely our most general concepts (ibid., pp. 149, 184, 203).

36. See on this Essays 5 and 6.

37. See Essay 6 and my *Hegel's Idea of a Phenomenology of Spirit*, p. 96.

38. *Phenomenology of Spirit*, p. 198; emphasis added.

39. Ibid., pp. 421–3; cf. pp. 423–4, 429–32. My suspicion is that Hegel's shift from basically accepting position (2) in the *Phenomenology of Spirit* of 1807 to basically rejecting it in the *Aesthetics* lectures from the 1820s was strongly influenced by his encounter with Creuzer's theory of symbolism during the intervening Heidelberg period. Cf. Gadamer, *Gesammelte Werke*, 4:402–3.

40. See e.g. *Hegel's Aesthetics*, p. 526.

41. Ibid., p. 860.

42. See e.g. ibid., pp. 597–600. It is a measure of Hegel's perceptiveness here that even such a great modern art historian as Panofsky, who is normally anything but reluctant to find meanings and thoughts expressed in paintings, less plausibly denies them to this sort of painting (Panofsky, *Meaning in the Visual Arts*, p. 32).

43. See e.g. *Hegel's Aesthetics*, pp. 28, 626, 891–4.

44. Ibid., pp. 899–900.

45. Ibid., pp. 902, 932, 954. Passages such as these show that orthodox readings of Hegel's position on instrumental music which emphasize his conception of it as contentless—e.g. E. Hanslick, *On the Musically Beautiful*, pp. 77, 83; and P. Moos, *Moderne Musikästhetik in Deutschland*, pp. 18 ff.—tell only half of the story.

46. *Encyclopedia* (1830), par. 462 (including Zusatz). As I implied in an earlier note, Hegel's vacillation concerning position (2) is shared by much eighteenth- and nineteenth-century German hermeneutic thought, and persists in Gadamer. For more on this subject, see Essay 6.

47. See my *Hegel's Idea of a Phenomenology of Spirit*, pp. 418–19. I shall say a little more about this in the next section (see there Hegel's argument (a)).

48. *Rezension der Schrift "Über die unter dem Namen Bhagavad-Gita bekannte Episode des Mahabharata. Von Wilhelm von Humboldt,"* p. 184. (Of course, for Hegel the referents in question here are themselves concepts.)

49. S. Hahn, "Hegel on Saying and Showing."

50. For a little more on this topic, see Essay 6.

51. Cf. my *Hegel's Idea of a Phenomenology of Spirit*, pp. 418–19. This is the transition within the *Phenomenology of Spirit* between different theoretical contexts requiring different strategies of interpretation, and correspondingly different concepts of meaning, that I referred to in the previous section.

52. *Hegel's Idea of a Phenomenology of Spirit*, pp. 93–102; "Ursprung und Wesen des Hegelschen Geistbegriffs."

53. *Phenomenology of Spirit*, pp. 188–9.

54. Ibid., p. 11.

55. *Hegel's Idea of a Phenomenology of Spirit*, pp. 205 ff.

56. Hegel hints at such a position in passages such as the following from the *Phenomenology of Spirit*: "Speech and work are outer expressions in which the individual no longer keeps and possesses himself within himself, but lets the inner get completely outside of him, leaving it to the mercy of something other than himself... In speech and action the inner turns itself into something else, putting itself at the mercy of the element of change, which twists the spoken word and the accomplished act into meaning something else than they are in and for themselves, as actions of this particular individual" (p. 187); "A conscious that opens up a subject-matter soon learns that others hurry along like flies to freshly poured-out milk, and want to busy themselves with it... Consciousness... learns what the nature of the 'matter in hand' really is... Its nature [is] such that its being is the action of the single individual and of all individuals and whose action is immediately for others, or is a 'matter in hand' and is such only as the action of each and everyone" (pp. 251–2).

57. For a more detailed treatment of this subject, see my *Hegel's Idea of a Phenomenology of Spirit*, ch. 2 and esp. p. 338 n. 109. See also my "Ursprung und Wesen des Hegelschen Geistbegriffs."

58. For a detailed account of this argument, see my *Hegel's Idea of a Phenomenology of Spirit*, pp. 207 ff.

59. For a fuller statement of what is essentially the same philosophical point, see my *Wittgenstein on the Arbitrariness of Grammar*, ch. 4, where I invoke a realist conception of *dispositions* similar to Herder's realist conception

of forces in order to defeat (Kripke and) Wittgenstein's more famous analogue of Hegel's argument (the "rule-following argument").

60. I do not really consider to be arguments, and therefore shall not here treat as such, a large family of Gadamerian exhortations that we should assimilate interpretation, in the sense of achieving *understanding* of a text, discourse, etc., to various other sorts of activities from which, prima facie at least, it is in fact crucially different—in particular, the *explication* or *application* of a text, discourse, etc.; the *translation* of a text, discourse, etc. into another language; conversation aimed at achieving agreement; legal "interpretation"; and the re-presentation of a work of (theatrical or musical) art. These Gadamerian exhortations seem to me little more than invitations to a nest of serious confusions—invitations which should be firmly declined.

61. See e.g. *Truth and Method*, pp. 339–40, 388. Note that this position is far more radical than, and indeed inconsistent with, the more attractive position, with which it could easily be confused, that successive interpretations undertaken from different historical vantage points often succeed in illuminating more and more aspects of the original meaning of a piece of art, text, or discourse.

62. See e.g. ibid., pp. 246 ff., 293, 301–2, 265–307; *Gesammelte Werke*, 2:475, 8:377.

63. See e.g. *Truth and Method*, p. 167; *Gesammelte Werke*, 8:377. Gadamer sometimes in this connection alludes to Nietzsche's famous argument along similar lines (see e.g. *Truth and Method*, p. 304; *Gesammelte Werke*, 4:326, 8:377).

64. See e.g. *Truth and Method*, pp. 199–200, 230 ff. It should be noted that Anglophone interpreters of Gadamer have tended misleadingly to deny or downplay this relativistic aspect of his position (see, for example, several of the articles in *The Cambridge Companion to Gadamer*, ed. R.J. Dostal [Cambridge: Cambridge University Press, 2002]).

65. Cf. Gorgias's treatise *Concerning Nature or What is Not*: there is nothing; even if there were, one could not know about it; and even if one could know about it, one could not communicate that knowledge to anyone else.

66. Gadamer's strange suggestion at one point that the interpreter's contribution always gets reabsorbed into the meaning and so vanishes (*Truth and Method*, p. 473) seems to be a symptom of this incoherence in his position. What he is really trying to say here is that there both is and is not a reinterpretation involved, but he masks this contradiction from himself and his readers by casting it in the more picturesque and less transparently

self-contradictory metaphorical form of a process of precipitation followed by reabsorption.

67. This brief statement of the objection is meant to be suggestive rather than
probative. For a fuller statement of this sort of objection against a relevantly similar position of Wittgenstein's, see my *Wittgenstein on the
Arbitrariness of Grammar*, esp. pp. 168–72.

68. *Gesammelte Werke*, 2:475.

69. See my *Wittgenstein on the Arbitrariness of Grammar*, esp. pp. 169–83. The
argument is complicated (in particular, it does not take the quick and crude
form of an appeal to verificationism), so I shall not go into it here.

70. Gadamer would no doubt reject the characterization of his theory of
pre-understanding as "psychologistic," on the ground that pre-
understanding is instead a feature of an ontologically deeper Husserlian
"life-world" or Heideggerian *Dasein*, or whatnot. Indeed, at one point
he himself expresses sympathy with a form of anti-psychologism, namely
Husserl's (*Gesammelte Werke*, 2:197). However, it could plausibly be
argued that the sort of anti-psychologism which we owe to Frege and
Wittgenstein conflicts not only with seeing run-of-the-mill psychological processes (such as having sensations or images) as internal to meaning
and understanding, but also with seeing Gadamerian pre-understanding
as internal to them.

71. See *After Herder*, Essays 2 and 4.

72. For more on this subject, see *After Herder*, Essay 4.

73. *Truth and Method*, p. 344.

74. Ibid., p. 448.

75. Despite fairly widespread assumptions to the contrary. See e.g. recently
R.B. Pippin, "Gadamer's Hegel," in *The Cambridge Companion to Gadamer*,
p. 236.

76. Essay 6.

77. Champollion first deciphered Egyptian hieroglyphics in the 1820s, the
very decade in which Hegel was delivering his *Aesthetics* lectures, but
really only published the results in 1832 in his *Grammaire égyptienne* and
*Dictionnaire égyptien*. Academic Egyptology really only began after Richard
Lepsius' expedition of 1842.

78. Cf. S. Bungay, *Beauty and Truth*, p. 102. Bungay offers a similar diagnosis of
Hegel's general inclination to see the Egyptians as intrinsically mysterious,
but does not bring this general point to bear on the more specific issue
with which I am concerned here.

79. Concerning Herder's statements of this point, see *After Herder*, Essay 3 and
in the present volume Essay 6.

80. Not merely God's qualitative *similarity* with mankind, note. In Hegel's view, *that* had already been well expressed by other areas of Greek culture besides sculpture, for example by poetry. Thus in his early theological writings he had emphasized that traditional Greek poetry and myth had already expressed the gods' qualitative similarity with men (in contrast to the subsequent Judeo-Christian tradition, which instead stressed God's qualitative dissimilarity to men).

81. See e.g. *Hegel's Aesthetics*, p. 435. Strictly speaking, Hegel's position must, I think, be a little more complicated than this. It could be objected to the position that I have just attributed to him that even if the Greeks had not yet linguistically *expressed* such an identity, it was surely at least already linguistically *expressible* by them (after all, they had the linguistic concepts *theos, anthrôpos*, and *esti*!). Hegel's response to such an objection would, I think, be that, strictly speaking, what Greek sculpture expressed was not merely the identity of God and mankind but their "absolute identity," or their "identity in difference," and that *this* is a concept which the Greeks did *not* yet possess in a linguistic form.

82. Ibid., p. 490.

83. Cf. Bungay, *Beauty and Truth*, p. 113. Concerning the second of the two traditions just mentioned, note that Hegel says of all these individuals that they "stand[ ] like immortal, deathless images of the gods, beyond the reach of death and temporality."

84. This problem is not, I think, significantly reduced if, following a suggestion made in a recent note, one understands Greek sculpture's message to be for Hegel more strictly the "identity in difference" of God and mankind. As it happens, the two strands of literary-philosophical culture in question here could fairly plausibly be interpreted as expressing some such conception, but in that case, once again, in thus superficially seeming to support Hegel's theory, they would in fact be undermining it.

85. A really hardboiled Hegelian might be tempted to respond to this sort of criticism that the nature of the Absolute and of its necessary self-development has been independently proved by Hegel's Logic and that it is therefore legitimate for Hegel to impute corresponding non-linguistic meanings and thoughts to the historical art in question despite the absence of supporting evidence or even in the face of contrary evidence. However, such a response would not be very convincing. First, it seems quite unlikely that Hegel really proved any such thing in his Logic (though it would of course require a detailed examination of his Logic to show that he did not). Second, it is an important part of Hegel's own official methodology—on which he prides himself in comparison with Schelling, for example—that in apply-

ing the Logic to empirical evidence one must not, so to speak, *strongarm* the evidence (see, for example, the preface to the *Phenomenology of Spirit*, and the introduction to the *Encyclopedia*'s Philosophy of Nature).

86. See *The Formation of the Historical World in the Human Sciences*, p. 245.

87. Hanslick, *On the Musically Beautiful*, pp. 10, 28.

88. Bungay, *Beauty and Truth*, p. 137.

89. The characterization of "Life" as a metaphysical or quasi-religious principle is mine rather than Dilthey's.

90. Concerning the mature Herder's commitment to this sort of position on instrumental music's expression of metaphysical or religious thoughts, see *After Herder*, Essay 3 and in the present volume Essay 6. Concerning Hegel's commitment to such a position, note the following: (a) Hegel's conception that instrumental music sometimes expresses metaphysical thoughts is especially clear at *Hegel's Aesthetics*, p. 932, where he notes that it sometimes develops dissonances and oppositions and their resolution in harmony and melody, i.e. a self-developing structure analogous to that of his Absolute. (For a helpful discussion of this aspect of Hegel's account of music, see H. Heimsoeth, "Hegels Philosophie der Musik," pp. 197–201.) (b) Given his general account of the nature of instrumental music, and especially his conception of it as a "Romantic" art founded on Christianity's message, such metaphysical thoughts must presumably in his view ultimately be language-based.

91. In suggesting that instrumental music expresses something about feeling or emotion which cannot be as accurately expressed by language (alone), I am in broad agreement with a long tradition which includes both composers and philosophers (for example, the composer Mendelssohn and the philosophers Herder and Suzanne Langer). Still, this suggestion requires some defense and qualification. For it is by no means always conceded that instrumental music expresses feeling or emotion at all, let alone that it does so more precisely than language. For example, Hanslick famously denies this. Perhaps the most serious objection to such a view is one that was first raised by Hanslick himself: feelings and emotions of their very nature incorporate intentional objects, which seem beyond the reach of musical expression (*On the Musically Beautiful*, pp. 8–10). Roger Scruton has provided a perceptive two-part response to this sort of objection which we can take over and build on here (*The Aesthetics of Music*, pp. 165 ff.). First, he points out that instrumental music actually often *does* express intentional objects (for example, religious music expresses the thought of God). Second, he notes that, despite the fact that emotions essentially include intentional objects, it is in an impor-

tant sense possible to identify emotions without pinning down their intentional objects—that if, for instance, one comes upon an unknown woman weeping in a park, one may be able by observing her behavior to identify the character of her emotion without knowing the intentional object involved (for example, whether she is weeping over the death of a parent, the thanklessness of a child, abandonment by a husband, or whatnot). I would add, third, that in such cases it may also in a certain sense be possible by observing the person's behavior to identify the emotion *more precisely* than could be achieved from a verbal description, that the person's complex behavior in its context may convey to one the quality of the emotion in a way that could not be accomplished by a mere verbal description either of the behavior and its context or of the emotion itself (though only "in a certain sense," because of course in another sense, namely that of pinning down the intentional object, the identification is ex hypothesi *less* precise). This situation suggests that, similarly, nuances of emotion may in a certain sense be expressed more precisely by instrumental music than could be achieved by language (alone) (even though, once again, in another sense—namely, that concerned with the identification of the intentional object—they can usually only be expressed less precisely).

92. A variant of this illusion can arise in connection with a composer's *technical* meanings and thoughts, which (as previously discussed) are capable of linguistic or notational expression by him. These will be precisely graspable by a listener who has technical expertise in music. However, a layman will again often sense their presence but find himself unable to pin them down linguistically with any precision, and so be encouraged to imagine that linguistically inexpressible meanings and thoughts are involved.

93. Concerning this, see the note before last.

94. There may well also be further sources of the delusive temptation to ascribe ineffable meanings and thoughts to instrumental music. For example, Diana Raffman somewhat plausibly diagnoses such a temptation in terms of the existence of a sort of musical grammar, which leads to a false expectation of a musical semantics due to the conjunction of grammar with semantics in the linguistic case (D. Raffman, *Language, Music, and Mind*, pp. 40–1).

95. See Essay 6 for two important qualifications of this assessment—which do not, though, overturn it.

# PART IV
# And Beyond

# 8

# Philosophy of Language in the Nineteenth Century

This essay focuses on nineteenth-century philosophy of language, conceived broadly in chronology but somewhat more narrowly in theme (for the most part, developments that occurred in such closely related fields as formal logic have been bracketed out).

Nineteenth-century philosophy of language emerged from the background of a revolution in thinking about the subject that had taken place in eighteenth-century Germany, overturning standard Enlightenment preconceptions. Herder (1744–1803) and to a lesser extent Hamann (1730–1788) were the main protagonists of this revolution.[1] Among the revolutionary principles they championed the following are most important:

(1) Thought is essentially dependent on and bounded by language—i.e. one can only think if one has a language, and one can only think what one can express linguistically. (Let us call this the *thought-language principle*.)

(2) Meanings or concepts consist, not in the sorts of items, in principle independent of language, with which much of the philosophical tradition has equated them—for example, referents, Platonic forms, or the mental "ideas" favored by the British Empiricists and others—but in word-usages. (Let us call this the *meaning-word principle*.)

(3) Meanings or concepts are of their very nature based in (perceptual and affective) sensations—though this grounding can involve metaphorical extensions; and in the case of human beings a converse dependence (i.e. of sensations on concepts) holds as well. (Let us call this the *meaning-sensation principle*.)

(4) Reference to particulars is never direct but is always mediated by general concepts, or "universals." (Let us call this the *principle of indirect reference*.)

(5) Mankind exhibits deep linguistic and conceptual-intellectual diversity, especially between different historical periods and cultures, but even to some extent between individuals living within a single period and culture. (Let us call this the *diversity principle*.)

(6) Language—and hence also thought, human mental life more generally, and indeed the very self—is fundamentally social in nature. (Let us call this the *language-sociality principle*.)

(7) Metaphysical philosophy is largely the product of confusions about language—in particular, disregard of principles (1), (2), and (3). (Let us call this the *principle of metaphysics as linguistic confusion*.)

(8) Due to point (5), interpretation of other people is often a very difficult task; and due to point (2), a large part of the solution to it consists in carefully discerning interpretees' word-usages, in light of empirical observation of the ways in which they have actually used words. (Let us call this the *principle of interpretive difficulty and discerning word-usage*.)

(9) Again due to (5), translation from one language into another is also often a very difficult task; and again due to (2), a large part of the solution to it consists in "bending" pre-existing word-usages from the target language over the course of the translation in order thereby to approximate the relevant word-usages and hence meanings in the source language. (Let us call this the *principle of translation difficulty and bending word-usage*.)

These seminal principles developed by the Herder-Hamann tradition would all go on to enjoy a vibrant afterlife in nineteenth-century philosophy of language.

## 1. Hegel

Many German philosophers from the early nineteenth century were very interested in language.[2] Few more so than Hegel (1770–1831).

Hegel adopted many of the principles listed above—though he also modified and developed them in significant ways. The period 1803–7, culminating in his *Phenomenology of Spirit* (1807), was especially important in this connection (the rest of his career less so).[3]

Concerning the *Phenomenology*: As can already be seen from the work's opening "Sense-certainty" section, Hegel is strongly inclined to accept the *thought-language principle*. However, early parts of the "Religion" chapter show that he is somewhat torn about it, since he is also tempted to broaden the range of symbolic media that can serve as vehicles for thought to include, besides language, non-linguistic arts such as architecture and sculpture. And this revised version of the principle later became his standard position in the *Aesthetics* lectures.

In the *Phenomenology* he also accepts a version of the *meaning-word principle*, developing in its support over the course of the book a systematic critique of alternative conceptions of meaning, such as those that equate meanings with referents ("Sense-certainty"), Platonic forms ("Force and the Understanding"), or mental "ideas" ("Physiognomy"). In addition, one of the central tasks of the work presupposes that principle, namely the task of modifying the everyday usages of words in systematic ways in order to enable them to constitute new, superior concepts. (This task largely explains the distinctive obscurity of the work.)

Hegel also accepts a version of the *meaning-sensation principle*. Thus he says later in the *Encyclopedia* that the pseudo-Aristotelian tag "There is nothing in the intellect that was not in the senses" is correct, provided only that the converse is admitted as well.

He also accepts the *principle of indirect reference*, in particular arguing in the "Sense-certainty" section that even the most promising-looking candidates for direct reference to particulars, indexical words such as "This," "Now," "Here," and "I," implicitly presuppose general concepts, or "universals."

He also accepts a version of the *diversity principle*. Thus the central project of the book is the exploration of the various different "shapes of consciousness" that have arisen over the course of history. However, here again the book is torn, for its later chapters also imply that there are some deep continuities in thought across times and places, namely in the domains of art, religion, and philosophy. And this contrary position also predominates in Hegel's later lecture series on those three domains.

Finally, the book also embraces the *language-sociality principle*, indeed developing over its course an argument that is designed to prove a particularly strong version of this principle that linguistic meaning (and hence also thought, human mental life generally, and the very self) is fundamentally social. The general strategy of the argument is to consider every possible individualistic account of meaning in turn and refute it, thereby motivating the conclusion that meaning is instead social in nature. In addition, Hegel presupposes this principle in the more specific way in which he conceives the work's task (already mentioned) of constructing new usages of words in order to constitute new, superior concepts: the task is, more specifically, to make these new usages broadly accepted by society.[4]

## 2. Interpretation- and Translation-Theory: Schleiermacher and Friedrich Schlegel

Some of the most important philosophical work done on language in the nineteenth century concerned the theory of interpretation ("hermeneutics") and the theory of translation. Schleiermacher (1768–1834) and Friedrich

Schlegel (1772–1829) were the main figures here. Their ideas on these subjects began to take shape in the late 1790s, when they were living together in Berlin. Many of the ideas are shared, and it is often unclear which of the two men was the original source. But since Schleiermacher's surviving treatments are more systematic and detailed than Schlegel's, we should mainly focus on the former here.

Schleiermacher's theories of interpretation and translation both rest on versions of the Herder-Hamann *thought-language, meaning-word*, and *diversity principles*. The *diversity principle* poses a profound challenge to both interpretation and translation, and the theories' main task is to cope with this challenge.

To this stock of inherited principles Schleiermacher adds a more *holistic* conception of meaning than was yet held by Herder or Hamann. At least three aspects of his semantic holism can be distinguished: (i) He espouses a doctrine of "the unity of the word-sphere." In effect, this says that the various distinguishable senses which a single word typically bears, and which are normally distinguished by a good dictionary entry (e.g. the different senses of "impression" in "He made an impression in the clay," "My impression is that he is reluctant," and "He made a big impression at the party"), always form a larger semantic unity to which they each essentially belong (so that any loss, addition, or alteration among them entails a change in each of them). (ii) He holds that any particular concept is partly defined by its relations to a "system of concepts." In this connection, he especially emphasizes a concept's relations as a species-concept to superordinate genus-concepts, relations as a genus-concept to subordinate species-concepts, and relations of contrast to coordinate concepts falling under the same genus-concepts. However, other types of conceptual relationships would be included here as well (e.g. those between "to work," "a work," and "a worker"). (iii) He holds that the distinctive nature of a language's *grammatical* system (e.g. its system of declensions) is partly constitutive of the character of the concepts expressed by the language. Schleiermacher perceives that this threefold semantic holism exacerbates the challenge to interpretation and translation already posed by the *diversity principle*.[5]

Schleiermacher lectured on hermeneutics frequently between 1805 and 1833. The following are some of his main principles:

(a) Hermeneutics is strictly the art of *understanding* verbal communication—as *contrasted*, not equated, with explicating, applying, or translating it.

(b) Hermeneutics should be a *universal* discipline—i.e. one that applies equally to both sacred and secular texts, to all subject-matters, to oral as well as written language, to modern texts as well as ancient, to works in one's own language as well as works in foreign languages, and so forth.

(c) In particular, the interpretation of sacred texts such as the Bible falls within it—this must not rely on *special* principles, such as divine inspiration (of either the author or the interpreter).

(d) Interpretation is in one way an easier task than is sometimes realized, in that an author's thoughts and meanings at least cannot transcend his linguistic competence (as, for example, Plato supposed). (This is an application of the *thought-language* and *meaning-word principles*.) But in another way interpretation is a much more difficult task than is usually realized: contrary to a common misconception that "understanding occurs as a matter of course," "misunderstanding occurs as a matter of course, and so understanding must be willed and sought at every point." (This is a consequence of the *diversity principle*: the principle that deep linguistic and conceptual-intellectual diversity occurs.)

How, then, is it to be accomplished?

(e) Before interpretation proper can even begin, the interpreter must acquire a good knowledge of the text's historical context.[6]

(f) Interpretation always has two sides: one "linguistic," the other "psychological." Linguistic interpretation's basic task (which rests on the *meaning-word principle*) is to infer from the particular known uses of a word to the rule governing them, i.e. to its usage, and thus to its meaning. Psychological interpretation instead focuses on the author's individual psychology. Linguistic interpretation is mainly concerned with what is shared in a language; psychological interpretation with what is distinctive to a particular author.

(g) Why must the interpreter complement linguistic interpretation with psychological in this way? Schleiermacher implies several reasons. First, a need to do so arises from the *diversity principle*, as it concerns individuals: the linguistic and conceptual-intellectual distinctiveness of individuals. This leads to the problem for linguistic interpretation that the actual uses of words that are available to serve as evidence from which to infer an author's exact usages or meanings are generally few in number and poor in contextual variety—a problem which the appeal to the author's psychology is supposed to help solve by providing additional clues. Second, an appeal to the author's psychology is required in order to resolve ambiguities in linguistic meaning that arise in particular contexts. Third, in order fully to understand a linguistic act one needs to grasp not only its linguistic meaning but also what more recent authors have called its "illocutionary" force or intention.

(h) Interpretation also requires two different methods: a "comparative" method (i.e. a method of plain induction) and a "divinatory" method (i.e. a method of tentative, fallible hypothesis based on but also going well beyond available empirical evidence).[7] Schleiermacher sees the former method as predominating on the linguistic side of interpretation (where it takes the interpreter from the particular uses of a word to the rule for use governing them all), the latter on the psychological side.

(i) Ideal interpretation is of its nature a holistic activity.[8] In particular, any given part of a text needs to be interpreted in light of the whole text to which it belongs, and both need to be interpreted in light of the whole language in which they are written, their historical context, a broader pre-existing genre, the author's whole corpus, and the author's overall psychology. This holism introduces a pervasive circularity into interpretation, for, ultimately, interpreting such broader items in its turn depends on interpreting parts of texts. This circularity might seem vicious. However, Schleiermacher denies that it is. Why? His solution is not that all of these tasks can be accomplished simultaneously—for that would be beyond human capacities. Instead, it turns on the (very plausible) thought that understanding is not an all-or-nothing matter but instead something that comes in *degrees*, so that it is possible to make progress towards full understanding in a gradual way. For example, concerning the relation between a part of a text and the whole text to which it belongs, he recommends that one first read through and interpret each of the parts of the text in turn as best one can in order thereby to arrive at an approximate overall interpretation of the text, and that one then apply this approximate overall interpretation in order to refine one's initial interpretations of the parts, which in turn gives one an improved overall interpretation, which can then be re-applied towards further refinement of the interpretations of the parts, and so on indefinitely.

Up to this point, Schleiermacher's theory is almost identical to Herder's, mainly just drawing together and systematizing ideas that were already scattered throughout a number of Herder's works. This continuity extends well beyond the *thought-language, meaning-word*, and *diversity principles*. For example, the theory also owes to Herder its two central moves (often wrongly thought to have been original with Schleiermacher) of complementing "linguistic" with "psychological" interpretation, and of identifying "divination" as the predominant method of the latter.[9] And both the theory's emphasis on the need for holism and its methodological solution for achieving it come from Herder as well.[10]

Schleiermacher's theory also contains some additional ideas which depart more sharply from Herder's, however. But it seems to me that it is precisely here that it tends to become most problematic. For example, whereas Herder's version of the *thought-language principle* restricts itself to the claim that thought is essentially dependent on and bounded by linguistic competence, Schleiermacher turns this into a principle of the outright *identity* of thought with language, or with inner language. But such a strong version of the principle is philosophically untenable—vulnerable to counterexamples in which thought occurs without any corresponding (inner) language use, and vice versa. Again, Schleiermacher adds to Herder's *meaning-word principle* a thesis that concepts are empirical schemata (à la Kant): rules for the production of sensory images. But this too is problematic. In particular, Kant's theory of schematism had implied a sharp dualism between concepts or meanings (conceived as something purely psychological) and word-usages, so that Schleiermacher's introduction of it here seems to imply the same, and hence to conflict with the *meaning-word principle*. Again, whereas for Herder the *diversity principle* is only an empirically established rule of thumb, Schleiermacher attempts to give an *a priori proof* that linguistic and conceptual-intellectual diversity occurs, even at the individual level, *universally*—a proof that is not only very dubious in itself (both in its a priori status and in its specific details), but also has the highly counterintuitive consequence (often explicitly asserted by Schleiermacher) that, strictly speaking, no one *ever* fully understands another person. Again, unlike Herder, Schleiermacher specifies psychological interpretation more closely as a process of identifying, and tracing the necessary development of, a single "seminal decision [*Keimentschluß*]" in the author that is the source of his work and unfolds itself as the work in a necessary fashion. But this too seems an unhelpful move. For how many works are actually composed, and hence properly interpretable, in such a way? Again, whereas Herder includes among the evidence relevant to psychological interpretation not only an author's linguistic behavior but also his non-linguistic behavior, Schleiermacher normally insists on a restriction to the former. But this seems misguided (e.g. the Marquis de Sade's recorded *acts* of cruelty are surely no less relevant to establishing the sadistic side of his psychology than his cruel *statements*). Again, whereas Herder rightly emphasizes that the correct identification of *genre* plays an essential role in interpretation, and that this is often extremely difficult due to variations in genres that occur across historical periods, cultures, individuals, and sometimes even between different works by the same individual, Schleiermacher pays little attention to this. Again, unlike Herder, who normally regards interpretation and natural science as similar activities, Schleiermacher sees the central role that "divination," or hypothesis, plays in interpretation as a ground for sharply *distinguishing* interpretation from natural science, and hence for classifying it as an art rather than a science, whereas he should arguably have seen it as a ground for judging them *similar* (a mistake that was caused by his false assumption that natural science works by plain induction rather than by hypothesis). And so forth.[11]

Friedrich Schlegel's hermeneutics, though less systematic and detailed than Schleiermacher's, is in certain ways superior to it, and more of an advance. It is found scattered throughout a number of Schlegel's works, including the

*Philosophy of Philology* (1797) and the *Athenaeum Fragments* (1798–1800). It resembles Schleiermacher's hermeneutics to a considerable extent. But it also includes the following five valuable features which are more or less missing from the latter: (i) Schlegel properly restores genre to a central place in the theory of interpretation, and largely continues Herder's insights about it. (ii) Schlegel recognizes that (superior) texts often express *unconscious* meanings: "Every excellent work...aims at more than it knows" (*On Goethe's Meister* [1798]). This is a very important point.[12] (iii) Schlegel emphasizes that works often express important meanings, not explicitly in their parts, but implicitly through the way in which the parts are put together to form a whole. This is again a very important point. (iv) In the essay *On Incomprehensibility* (1800) and elsewhere, Schlegel emphasizes that works typically contain confusions, and that it is essential for an interpreter to identify and explain these. As he already puts it in 1797:"It is not enough that one understand the actual sense of a confused work better than the author understood it. One must also oneself be able to know, *characterize*, and even *construe* the confusion even down to its very principles."This is another very important point. (v) Schlegel attributes meaning to the non-linguistic arts (e.g. music, sculpture, painting, and architecture), and develops a set of sophisticated principles for interpreting them.[13]

Schleiermacher's pupil Boeckh (1785–1867), an eminent classical philologist, later gave Schleiermacher's hermeneutics a re-statement that was even more systematic and detailed than Schleiermacher's own in lectures which were eventually published under the title *Encyclopedia and Methodology of the Philological Sciences* (1877). In the course of doing so he laudably restored genre to the central place that it had had in the hermeneutics of Herder and Schlegel. The combined influence of Schleiermacher's and Boeckh's treatments secured for this whole tradition of hermeneutics something like the status of the official interpretive methodology of nineteenth-century biblical and classical scholarship. The extraordinary quality of that scholarship constitutes eloquent testimony to its value.

Turning now to the theory of translation, Schleiermacher's whole position concerning translation again rests on the Herder-Hamann *thought-language, meaning-word*, and *diversity principles*, together with his own holism about meaning, which exacerbates the challenge to translation posed by the *diversity principle*.

Schleiermacher was himself a masterful translator, whose translations of Plato into German are still widely used and admired today, two centuries after they were done. His views about translation therefore come with a certain prima facie authority. He explains his theory of translation mainly in the classic essay *On the Different Methods of Translation* (1813). The following are his most important points:

(a) Translation proper (as opposed to mere imitation) is an extremely difficult task. For it faces a number of serious challenges which admit of partial, but
only partial, solution. The primary task of translation is to reproduce the original meaning accurately, and as will become clear in a moment, this is itself a
huge challenge. But there are also some further tasks which add to the difficulty.
For example, at least in the case of poetry it is necessary to reproduce not only
semantic but also musical features of the original, such as meter and rhyme.
Indeed, this is not only an aesthetic desideratum over and above translation's
primary task of reproducing meaning, but also an essential *part* of the latter,
since, for one thing, in poetry musical features serve as essential vehicles for the
precise expression of affective sensations and hence of meanings (a point that
rests on the *meaning-sensation principle*). Also, besides reproducing meaning a
translation should convey where an author was being conceptually conventional and where, by contrast, conceptually original—a task that can be accomplished to a certain extent by using older vocabulary from the target language
in the former cases and newer vocabulary from the target language in the latter
cases. In addition to being intrinsically difficult, both of these secondary tasks
will often stand in deep tension with the primary task of finding the closest
semantic fit—for example, it will often turn out that the target-word which
would best reproduce a rhyme or best reflect a concept's vintage is not the one
closest in meaning to the source-word.

(b) The central challenge for translation, though, lies in translation's primary
task of reproducing meaning accurately, and arises from the fact that translation
typically faces a conceptual gulf between the source language and the target
language (as the latter already exists). (This is an application of the *diversity
principle*.)

(c) Schleiermacher in particular notes the following complication that arises
here (which one might dub *the paradox of paraphrase*): if, faced with the task of
translating an alien concept, a translator attempts to reproduce its *intension* by
reproducing its *extension* through an elaborate paraphrase in his own language,
he will generally find that, as he gets closer to the original extension, he under-
mines the original intension in *other* ways.[14]

How, therefore, should translation proceed? The following points constitute
the core of Schleiermacher's answer:

(d) Because of such challenges the translator needs to have hermeneutic
expertise and to be an "artist" if he is to cope with the task of translation at all
adequately.

(e) The conceptual gulf that poses the central challenge here might in principle be tackled in one of two ways: either by bringing the author's linguistic-
conceptual world closer to that of the reader of the translation or by bringing

the reader's closer to the author's. The former approach had been advocated by Luther in his *Letter on Translation* (1530) and had been practiced by him in his translation of the Bible (he called it *Verdeutschung*, "Germanizing"). However, Schleiermacher finds it unacceptable, because it distorts the author's meaning. He therefore champions the alternative approach of bringing the reader towards the linguistic-conceptual world of the author as the only acceptable approach.

But how can that possibly be accomplished?

(f) The key, according to Schleiermacher, lies in the *plasticity* of language. Thanks to this plasticity, even if the usages of words, and hence the concepts, expressed by the target language *as it already exists* are incommensurable with the author's, the translator can "bend the language of the translation as far as possible towards that of the original in order to communicate as far as possible an impression of the system of concepts developed in it." (This solution presupposes the *meaning-word principle*.)[15]

(g) This approach requires translating a particular word from the source language in a uniform way throughout the translation rather than switching between two or more different ways of translating it in different contexts.

(h) It also inevitably results in translations which are less easy to read than those that can be achieved by the competing approach (*Verdeutschung*).[16] However, this is an acceptable price to pay given that the only alternative is a failure to convey the author's meaning at all accurately. Moreover, the offending oddities have a positive value, in that they constantly remind the reader of the conceptual unfamiliarity of the material being translated and of the "bending" approach being employed.

(i) In order to work effectively this approach needs to be applied consistently to large amounts of material, so that the reader both becomes generally accustomed to it and acquires enough examples of a particular word's unfamiliar use in enough different contexts to enable him to infer the unfamiliar rule for use that is involved.

(j) Even this optimal approach has severe limitations, however. In particular, it will often be impossible to reproduce the *holistic* aspects of meaning—the several related usages of a given word, the system of related words/concepts, and the distinctive grammar of the language. And because these holistic features are internal to a word's meaning, that will entail a shortfall in the communication of its meaning by the translation. For this reason—together with such additional reasons as those mentioned in (a)—even this optimal sort of translation is bound to remain imperfect, only a poor second best to reading the originals.

(k) It is still justified and important, however. This is true not only for the obvious reason that people who cannot read the original languages still need translations, but also for the less obvious reason that this optimal sort of translation through its "bending" approach enriches the conceptual resources of the target language, and through its approach of reproducing musical features, e.g. ancient meters, enriches the musical resources of the target language.[17]

(l) Nor—Schleiermacher adds in answer to a worry that Herder had expressed—need it be feared that this enrichment will deprive the target language of its authentic character. For in cases where a real conflict with that character occurs, the enrichments involved will soon wither from the language.

As in the case of Schleiermacher's theory of interpretation, not only the *thought-language, meaning-word,* and *diversity principles,* but indeed *most* of these principles about translation come from Herder (especially from the *Fragments on Recent German Literature* [1767–8]). In particular, Schleiermacher's emphasis on the importance of reproducing the musical features of an original (poetic) text, and on doing so not only for aesthetic reasons but also in order to convey its meaning accurately, as well as his central strategy of "bending" the target language in order to cope with the problem of conceptual incommensurability, both do so.

However, whereas Schleiermacher's theory of interpretation tended to worsen Herder's, his theory of translation tends to refine Herder's in some modest but significant ways. Among the positions listed above, examples of this occur in (a), where the ideal of making clear in translation at which points an author is being conceptually conventional and at which points conceptually original, and the strategy for achieving it, are novel; (c), where the paradox of paraphrase is original; (h), where the point that the discomfort that the "bending" approach causes readers actually serves positive functions is novel; (i), where the point that this approach needs to be implemented on a large scale is novel; (j), where the point that semantic holism inevitably limits the success of such translations is novel; and (l), which plausibly contradicts Herder.[18]

## 3. Philosophy of Language and the Birth of Linguistics: Friedrich Schlegel and Wilhelm von Humboldt

Modern linguistics was founded in the nineteenth century by two philosophers who were both deeply steeped in the Herder-Hamann tradition: Friedrich Schlegel, whose main work in this connection is *On the Language and Wisdom of the Indians* (1808), which largely focuses on Sanskrit and its literature; and Wilhelm von Humboldt (1767–1835), whose main work in this connection is the famous introduction to his massive study of the Kawi language, published separately under the title *On the Diversity of Human Language-Structure and its Influence on the Mental Development of Mankind* (1836).

Schlegel's and Humboldt's general theories of language contain *many* borrowings from the Herder-Hamann tradition.[19] But most importantly, they founded modern linguistics on principles taken over from that tradition—especially the *thought-language* and *diversity* principles, together with the resulting insight (already explicitly formulated by Herder in his *Ideas for the Philosophy of History of Humanity* [1784–91]) that an empirical investigation into languages in their diversity promises to provide a reliable window onto the diversity of modes of thought. This constituted their primary rationale for the new discipline of linguistics.

Building on that inherited theoretical foundation, they also develop the following more original positions:

(a) Contrary to an impression which Herder and Hamann had generally still given that languages are merely aggregates of particular words/concepts, they espouse a more holistic conception of languages according to which such particular items are only possible in the context of a larger linguistic whole—a conception they often express by characterizing languages as "organisms," "webs," or "systems."

(b) They identify *grammar* as the most fundamental unifying principle of such linguistic "organisms."

(c) In contrast to the early Herder—who in the *Treatise on the Origin of Language* (1772) had held that grammars are basically the same across all languages (except for Chinese)—but in continuity with the late Herder—who in the *Ideas for the Philosophy of History of Humanity* (1784–91) had instead come to posit deep differences between the grammatical structures of languages—they both see grammars as differing profoundly from one language to another, and as thereby also constituting significant differences in particular words/concepts (which may differ for more superficial reasons as well).[20] (However, it should be noted that in Humboldt this position still stands in uneasy tension with the older and more dubious—albeit, since Chomsky, recently again fashionable— idea of an implicit universal grammar.)

(d) They consequently identify "comparative grammar" (an expression that was first brought into currency by Schlegel's *On the Language and Wisdom of the Indians*) as the main task of the empirical investigation of languages.

(e) Besides the motive already explained of providing a reliable window on the diversity of thought, there is also another important motive behind comparative grammar which they emphasize: comparative grammar promises to shed more light on the genealogical relations between languages than merely lexical comparisons can do.

(f) They begin the process of actually comparing different grammars in an empirically careful way. In doing so, they develop a taxonomy of different types of grammars. Schlegel first draws a sharp contrast between, on the one hand, "organic," or highly inflected, languages, of which Sanskrit is his prime example; and on the other hand, "mechanical," or uninflected, languages, of which Chinese is his main example. His brother August Wilhelm Schlegel (1767–1845) and Humboldt then elaborate this taxonomy, adding a category of "agglutinative" or "incorporative" languages.

So far these steps taken by Schlegel and Humboldt constitute clear progress. But there is also a more dubious part of their position:

(g) They also draw from their comparison of different grammars certain strong normative conclusions about the relative merits of different languages as instruments of thought. In particular, they argue for the superiority of highly inflected languages such as Sanskrit and its relatives over uninflected languages such as Chinese. (This constitutes yet a third motive behind their project.)—This is a more dubious part of their position, both factually and morally. Concerning facts, their arguments for the superiority of one language-type over another are unconvincing. Schlegel's case consists in little more than wonderment at the supposed marvel of developed inflection, together with an implausible claim that it is necessary for human "awareness," or rationality. Humboldt's case often consists in assuming, implausibly, that some explicit feature of Indo-European grammar is implicitly universal, and then faulting a non-Indo-European language for not realizing it explicitly.[21] At other times it consists in faulting distinctive features of non-Indo-European grammars as dysfunctional, in ways which overlook the possibility that the distinctive mode of life or social context within which they occur might in fact make them functional.[22] Concerning morality, this part of their position is also morally suspect, in that it tends to encourage—and later did encourage—an invidious ranking of peoples. On the other hand, one should be hesitant to visit the sins of the sons on the fathers here (so to speak). Unlike their Nazi heirs, Schlegel and Humboldt were basically innocent of ethnocentric, xenophobic motives. Indeed, a large part of the purpose of Schlegel's book was to show that Europe and Asia are "one large family" (as he actually puts it) whose literatures should be treated as a single whole; and Humboldt often reveals similar cosmopolitan motives in his linguistic work.[23] Moreover, both men take considerable theoretical pains to try to forestall the inference of an invidious ranking of peoples from their normative conclusions about languages.[24]

Under the influence of Schlegel and Humboldt both the close analysis of individual languages, such as Sanskrit, and comparative grammar quickly developed into major fields of scientific inquiry in the nineteenth century. One early practitioner of the former was August Wilhelm Schlegel, who, under his younger brother's influence, became Germany's first real expert in Sanskrit. Prominent early practitioners of comparative grammar were Bopp (1791–1867), in his work on the Indo-European languages generally; Jakob Grimm (1785–1863), in his work on the Germanic languages in particular; and August Wilhelm Schlegel again, in his work on the Romance languages.[25]

## 4. From a Linguistic Critique of Philosophy to a Philosophical Critique of Language: Gruppe, Nietzsche, and Mauthner

The remainder of this essay will turn to some thinkers whose relations to the Herder-Hamann tradition are more ambiguous.

Three thinkers who share a broadly naturalistic, empirical, philological, and skeptical bent took over from the Herder-Hamann tradition the *principle of metaphysics as linguistic confusion*: Gruppe, Nietzsche, and Mauthner.[26]

In their own versions of that principle, Herder and Hamann had largely focused on attacking Kant. They had done so on three main grounds: first, for failing to recognize the essential dependence of thought and concepts on language (the *thought-language* and *meaning-word principles*), and consequently also the historicity and sociality of thought and concepts (the *diversity* and *language-sociality principles*); second, for violating, both in his theory and in his linguistic practice, the principle that all linguistic meanings must be based in sensations (the *meaning-sensation principle*); and third, for hypostatizing what are really just collections of activities, on the basis of a misleading grammatical analogy (e.g. "Reason").

The nowadays largely forgotten O.F. Gruppe (1804–1876) undertook in a series of works to extend this sort of critique to other "speculative," or metaphysical, philosophers as well. One of his first and main targets was Hegel, whom he criticized in this manner in his first work, *Antaeus: A Correspondence about Speculative Philosophy in its Conflict with Science and Language* (1831). His critique of Hegel is to a large extent misdirected because of Hegel's *own* deep commitment to the Herder-Hamann principles in question (as described above), which Gruppe overlooks.[27] However, some of his other extensions of this sort of critique are more plausible.

In developing his linguistic critique of metaphysical philosophy, Gruppe, like the Herder-Hamann tradition before him, assumes that language is an essential foundation for any thought, and contrasts metaphysical philosophers' errors in relation to language with what he takes to be language's sound condition in everyday use. The two remaining members of the group we are considering, Nietzsche and Mauthner, broke with him and the tradition in both these respects, (re-)introducing the idea of a *non*-linguistic form of thought or insight, and complementing the linguistic critique of metaphysical philosophy with a broader critique of language in general.

Nietzsche (1844–1900) is the most original member of this group. He takes over many ideas from the Herder-Hamann tradition, but also transforms them radically. He too offers a linguistic critique of metaphysical philosophy broadly in the spirit of the *principle of metaphysics as linguistic confusion*. Thus according to him the central error of metaphysical philosophers lies in positing imaginary entities over and above sensations—e.g. substances, selves, and God—and this is something they are seduced into doing by the distinctive grammar of Indo-European languages, in particular their *subject*-predicate structure (for this diagnosis, see e.g. *Beyond Good and Evil* [1886], par. 20).

However, Nietzsche also departs from his predecessors by representing even ordinary language and thought as subject to similar illusions. For one thing, according to him the illusory reifications just mentioned (substances, selves, God, etc.), and their source in subject-predicate grammar, are not confined to philosophers but afflict everyday (Indo-European) language and thought as well. For another thing, and even more fundamentally, according to him *all* language—and consequently, since he accepts a *version* of the *thought-language principle*, all thought too *in a way*—is distorting. Thus in his early lectures on rhetoric (1872–3) and the essay *On Truth and Lies in a Nonmoral Sense* (1873) he argues—in a radical transformation of the *meaning-sensation principle*—that *all* language-use is merely metaphorical and hence distorts its basis in sensations. His case for this has several parts. First, he adduces a fairly impressive array of empirical evidence for the widespread presence of metaphors in languages, e.g. the gendering of nouns. Second, he argues that our attempts to capture the reality of our sensations in language and thought inevitably involve not just one but two steps of creative transformation of it: initially that from the given sensory stimulus to a sensory image, and then that from the sensory image to the quite different medium of language and thought.[28] Third, he argues that any application of general concepts to sensory experience both distortingly abstracts from aspects of the latter (see in the essay just cited the *Schlange/schlingen* example) and distortingly assimilates to one another cases of sensory experience which are in reality unique in character (see in the same essay the example of the leaf). (This third argument implicitly assumes, in the spirit of the

Herder-Hamann *principle of indirect reference*, that the use of general concepts is fundamental to all descriptive language.)

These arguments implicitly rest on an assumption which is sharply at odds with the Herder-Hamann tradition's own version of the *thought-language principle*: namely, that we have a form of *non-linguistic insight into reality*, and specifically into what Nietzsche in later work calls "the formless unformulable world of the chaos of sensations" (*The Will to Power* [1883–8], par. 569). This assumption becomes explicit at around the period of the early texts discussed above in *The Birth of Tragedy* (1872), where Nietzsche posits a non-linguistic, musical form of insight into the primal Dionysiac chaos of reality. The fact that he is implicitly making this assumption in the texts discussed above explains why he is unconcerned there about such obvious potential objections to his arguments as the following (which have been leveled against them by some commentators): Is it not incoherent to purport to state or think how things really are as a basis for an argument whose conclusion is that *no* statement or thought can capture how things really are? And is that conclusion not indeed also *self*-defeating? Nietzsche's solution to these puzzles lies in the fact that the statements and corresponding thoughts in question are in both cases ultimately meant to be no more than poor surrogates for what is at bottom a non-linguistic insight.

However, in making this implicit assumption Nietzsche does not simply disregard or dismiss the Herder-Hamann tradition. Instead, he makes a large concession to it: he accepts a *version* of the *thought-language principle* (as well as a *version* of the *language-sociality principle*, the principle of the sociality of language and thought)—but a version restricted to *conscious* thought, which he considers to be merely superficial (see especially *The Gay Science* [1882], par. 354).

The philosophical plausibility of Nietzsche's case thus largely turns on the plausibility of this radical modification of the Herder-Hamann *thought-language principle*, this exemption of a putative form of non-linguistic insight from its scope.

In sum, Nietzsche's overall position in this area is heavily indebted to the Herder-Hamann tradition, but also transforms it almost beyond recognition—in particular, leaving us with the radically different picture that, not only metaphysics, but language and conscious thought in general are pervasively distorting, and that they stand in contrast to a deeper non-linguistic insight into reality.

A final member of this group of thinkers is F. Mauthner (1849–1923), whose most important works in this connection are *Contributions to a Critique of Language* (1902) and *Dictionary of Philosophy* (1910). Mauthner is heavily influenced by Nietzsche. Like Nietzsche, he develops a linguistic critique of metaphysical philosophy (as well as of related fields, e.g. theology and political theory) in which he rejects such concepts as the self and God as mere reifications superimposed on the chaos of sensations. Again like Nietzsche, he complements that critique with a broader critique of *all* language—in particular, arguing, as Nietzsche had done, that over and above the sorts of reifications just mentioned, all language involves a metaphorical distortion of sensations. And yet again like Nietzsche, he develops this argument on the basis of an assumption of a deeper non-linguistic insight into the chaos of sensations.

However, *unlike* Nietzsche (at least after *The Birth of Tragedy* [1872]), Mauthner conceives this deeper non-linguistic insight and its subject-matter in exalted religious terms—writing in this connection of a "godless mysticism." And again unlike Nietzsche, he not only assumes such an insight in his argument but also makes the ultimate goal of his critique of language the overcoming (or as he puts it, "suicide") of language and the attainment of this insight in its purity.

Mauthner is a much better philosopher than some of the secondary literature on him would lead one to suspect. Nonetheless, his ideas are largely derivative rather than original. His main importance arguably lies in his influence on the greatest twentieth-century philosopher of language, Wittgenstein (1889–1951). Wittgenstein already read Mauthner's *Contributions* before writing the *Tractatus* (1921) (he mentions Mauthner there, albeit somewhat critically), and the strong influence of the former work on the latter is obvious. For example, they share the conceptions that (philosophical) language is a "ladder" eventually to be kicked away, and that a non-linguistic mystical insight is of fundamental importance. This connection throws significant light on the *Tractatus*.[29] But it is perhaps even more important for another reason, namely that Mauthner seems to have functioned as a general conduit of ideas from the Herder-Hamann tradition to Wittgenstein. Anyone familiar with Wittgenstein's work, especially in his later period, cannot but be struck by the extraordinary measure of agreement between its central principles and the principles attributed to the Herder-Hamann tradition at the beginning of this essay—especially, the *thought-language, meaning-word, diversity, language-sociality*, and *metaphysics as linguistic confusion principles*. It would be implausible to suppose that this agreement is merely coincidental. And so one is moved to ask how Wittgenstein became acquainted with the Herder-Hamann tradition's principles. Mauthner is a large part of the answer to that question. He is himself explicitly committed to versions of most of the Herder-Hamann tradition's principles, including the five just mentioned. Moreover, his work contains copious explicit discussions of Herder, Hamann (whom he especially admires), and other people influenced by them.[30]

## 5. Theories of Meaning and Reference: J.S. Mill and Frege

Two further nineteenth-century philosophers whose relations to the Herder-Hamann tradition are again ambiguous made important contributions to the philosophy of language, and in particular to the analysis of meaning and reference: J.S. Mill (1806–73) and especially Frege (1848–1925). (As an arch-empiricist and an arch-rationalist respectively, the two are in many ways philosophical opponents.)

A good litmus-test for continuity with the Herder-Hamann tradition, and a reasonable criterion for being described as a "philosopher of language" in the strict sense, is adherence to the *thought-language* and *meaning-word principles*. Judged in these terms, Mill and Frege occupy equivocal positions.

Mill *is* committed to a version of the *thought-language principle*. Thus he begins his *System of Logic* (1843) with a chapter significantly titled "Of the Necessity of Commencing with an Analysis of Language" in which he argues that doing so is necessary because (a) "reasoning, or inference . . . is an operation which usually takes place by means of words, and in complicated cases can take place in no other way"; and especially (b) "a proposition . . . is formed by putting together two names . . ., is *discourse, in which something is affirmed or denied of something*." Mill does not commit himself to the *meaning-word principle*, the equation of meaning with word-usage, though his position could probably be married with such a principle without great difficulty.

Frege's position is even more equivocal. He too is committed to a version of the *thought-language principle*, but a very qualified one. As Dummett points out in "Was Frege a Philosopher of Language?" Frege between 1882 and 1924–5 repeatedly says that human beings can only think by means of language, and justifies his own focus on language in such terms.[31] However, Frege's version of this principle is heavily qualified: he explicitly emphasizes in 1924–5 that it applies only to *human beings*, and that he sees no impossibility in the existence of other creatures who think, or indeed even think the very same thoughts as human beings, *without* using language. Moreover, this qualification is a consequence of a positive theory of the nature of thoughts that is sharply contrary to the spirit of the *thought-language principle*, namely a form of Platonism (albeit one trimmed of some of the metaphysical bells and whistles of Plato's own Platonism). According to Frege's Platonism, thoughts are eternal objects quite independent of us, to which, in thinking, we merely come to stand in a certain cognitive relation. Frege is committed to such a theory from an early period, but articulates it most fully in his late essay *The Thought* (1918–19).[32] Concerning the *meaning-word principle, pace* Dummett (in the essay of his recently cited), Frege's position is completely inconsistent with it, since for him senses generally, like thoughts in particular (i.e. the senses of whole sentences), are eternal objects entirely independent of us.

In short, Mill and Frege are to some extent continuous with the Herder-Hamann tradition and can to some extent be described as "philosophers of language."[33] But the extent is not very great, especially in the case of Frege.[34]

Where Frege is concerned, the ambiguity of his relation to the Herder-Hamann tradition (including now its more direct heirs, such as Schleiermacher and Humboldt) also extends further. There are a few additional striking continuities—for example, in the classic essay *On Sense and Reference* (1892) Frege continues and develops the *principle of indirect reference*, the principle that linguistic reference to particulars is never direct but is always mediated by general concepts (a principle Humboldt had championed in the meantime). But Frege more commonly rejects the Herder-Hamann tradition in a sharp and deliberate way (albeit without naming names). For example, in *The Foundations of Arithmetic* (1884) and elsewhere he argues strongly against the sort of psychologism about concepts that is involved in the Herder-Hamann *meaning-sensation principle*, and against the Herder-Hamann tradition's related position that concepts emerge from human minds and history (he instead argues that it is only our *knowledge* of them that does so). Indeed, he evidently developed his own Platonism largely in deliberate opposition to these aspects of the Herder-Hamann tradition. Again, in his essay *On Concept and Object* (1892) he takes to task the Schleiermacher-Humboldt position that different individuals never use words with exactly the same meaning and that exact translations between languages are never possible, arguing that on the contrary in the relevant cases the *sense* or *thought* is often shared and communicated exactly, and it is only the psychological "coloring" that is discrepant. Thus his own important distinction between "sense" and mere "coloring" was developed in conscious opposition to the Schleiermacher-Humboldt position, and partly from a motive of avoiding it.[35] A further distinctive feature of Frege's position that sharply divides him from the Herder-Hamann tradition is a disparaging, or at best ambivalent, attitude towards ordinary language and a predominant ambition to develop an ideal logical language for scientific use, especially for realizing his "logicist" program of reducing arithmetic to logic (a program that of course eventually failed with the discovery of Russell's contradiction).

Despite the tenuousness of his status as a "philosopher of language" in the strict sense defined above, Frege did make extremely important contributions to the philosophy of language. Salient among these are certain distinctions that he drew clearly for the first time in the area of what we generally think of as "meaning." While the exact ways in which he drew these distinctions are questionable in certain respects, it seems beyond doubt that the distinctions are valid and important in *some* form:

(a) In *On Sense and Reference* Frege famously draws a sharp distinction between a referring-term's *reference* [*Bedeutung*] and its *sense* [*Sinn*] (a distinction which he had himself failed to observe in earlier work). His main argument for this distinction turns on the fact that we can make, not only true *un*informative identity-statements such as "The Morning Star = The Morning Star," but also true *informative* identity-statements such as "The Morning Star = The Evening Star." This fact only seems explicable on the assumption that the referring-terms involved possess different senses in addition to their identical referents.

Frege also points out in the essay that we sometimes encounter referring-terms which lack referents but which do nonetheless have senses (e.g. "the least rapidly convergent series"). This suggests a further argument for the distinction: referring-terms often have senses despite lacking referents (or despite their referents having ceased to exist). Several commentators have indeed taken this to be Frege's main argument for the distinction. It is actually a very compelling argument for it. But it did not play a major role for Frege, and there is an interesting reason why not which well illustrates the distinctive character of his philosophy, the extent to which it is oriented to a scientific purpose and in particular to the development of an ideal logical language: In Frege's view, a proper scientific language will not contain any referring-terms that lack referents, because such terms undermine science's concern with truth and make logic inapplicable. How so? According to Frege, this is due to the fact that it is a precondition of a proposition's having a truth-value that its referring-terms really refer, so that any proposition that contains referring-terms which fail to refer will ipso facto both lack a truth-value and in consequence also fail to conform to such logical laws as the law of bivalence or excluded middle. By contrast, science *cannot* dispense with informative identity statements, which in particular play an essential role in mathematics, so that appealing to *these* as a reason for drawing the distinction between sense and reference is acceptable.[36]

(b) Frege in *On Sense and Reference, The Thought*, and elsewhere also draws a sharp distinction between sense and what he variously calls mere "coloring," "ideas," etc.—by which he means mere psychological accompaniments of sense. This is another vitally important distinction, which any plausible account of meaning seems bound to preserve in *some* form.

However, there are several problems with the *particular way* in which Frege draws the distinction: (i) He conceives it as dividing two sharply separate ontological realms: the Platonic realm of eternal, mind-independent senses, on the one hand, and the psychological realm, on the other. Clearly, if one is skeptical about his Platonism (as one should be) one will have to recast this aspect of the distinction. Indeed, in light of the Herder-Hamann *meaning-word* and especially *meaning-sensation principles*, it may well be that sense really includes a psychological aspect, so that the distinction needs to be reconceived as one which (at least in part) falls *within* the psychological. (ii) Frege draws the distinction in a way that classifies as mere differences of coloring rather than of sense many differences which by intuitive lights would seem clearly to be differences of sense. For example, in *The Thought* he classifies the difference between "and" and "but" as merely one of coloring, not of sense. Such oddities result from the fact that he uses as the criterion of sameness of word-sense *interchangeability-in-sentences-without-change-of-truth-value* (except, of course, in cases where mere mention or homonymy is involved)—together with his conviction that this criterion is satisfied by such word pairs as "and" and "but." However, the oddities only result from his use of this criterion under a certain further assumption. Someone might urge that the criterion is a valid one but that, *pace* Frege, it in fact yields the intuitive answer for cases like "and" and "but," namely that they *differ* in sense. Cannot, for example, the sentence "Smith said/believed that Jones was good-natured *and* foolish" be true while the sentence "Smith said/believed that Jones was good-natured *but* foolish" is false (and vice versa)? What blocks this reasoning for Frege, and leads him to his counterintuitive conclusion for cases like "and" and "but," is an assumption that in such contexts of indirect speech, belief-reporting, etc. words do not have their usual senses—specifically, he holds that they *refer* to their usual senses and that they do so by means of senses which are different from their usual ones—so that such contexts are no more relevant to the criterion in question than would be contexts in which normal homonymy occurs. However, this assumption itself seems very dubious. For it is surely quite implausible to say that, for example, "but" has two different senses in "Jones is good-natured but foolish" and "Smith said that Jones was good-natured but foolish." It is therefore in the end attractive to suggest the following revision of Frege here: while interchangeability-in-sentences-without-change-of-truth-value is indeed a valid criterion of sameness of word-sense, it needs to be applied in a way that *includes* sentences containing indirect speech, belief-reports, etc.[37] We thereby free ourselves *both* from Frege's implausible assumption that words change their senses when they enter such contexts *and* from his counterintuitive conclusion that such differences as that between "and" and "but" are merely ones of coloring rather than sense. (iii) Frege tends to lump together as mere "coloring" or "ideas" a number of things that really need to be distinguished. These include what Grice calls "conversational implicatures," i.e. roughly, propositions which, though not part of the sense of a form of words (not implications), are such that any competent user of a language will associate them with the use of that form of words in a particular context; propositions which individuals associate with a form of words in a merely idiosyncratic way; attitudes or sensations not actually expressed but nonetheless conventionally communicated by a form of words (e.g. in the case of "After you!" respect); and attitudes or sensations which individuals associate with a form of words in a merely idiosyncratic way. (iv) Frege tends to regard all "coloring" or "ideas" as radically private, i.e. unshareable and incommunicable. This is clearly untrue of at least some of the items just listed (e.g. conversational implicatures), and indeed arguably of them all.[38]

(c) A third vitally important distinction which Frege draws, especially in *The Thought*, is that between a *thought* or sentential-sense, on the one hand, and the *force* with which it is used (e.g. assertion or question), on the other. One area in which this distinction had not been properly observed before Frege was formal logic. Logicians such as Kant had conceived propositional logic as concerned exclusively with "judgments." This in effect amounted to assuming, falsely, that all (logically treatable) thoughts occur as (mental or verbal) *assertions*. To the extent that this assumption was taken seriously, it precluded not only the exploration of logical relations involving thoughts which occur within other types of force (e.g. questions), but also the analysis of even *asserted* compound thoughts into component thoughts which occur within them but without themselves being asserted (e.g. "p" and "q" within "If p then q").[39] Frege's distinction has since been extended and refined by some of the most important twentieth-century work in the philosophy of language, especially the theory of "locutionary" versus "illocutionary" force developed by Austin, Searle, and others.

Turning now to another topic, Mill and Frege both advance important but conflicting theories about the nature of proper names (i.e. names such as "Barack Obama" and "Japan"—not what Frege *himself* calls "proper names," which includes *all* singular referring-terms).

Mill argues that, unlike general names (e.g. "geese," "men"), proper names have only denotation, not connotation (or in Frege's terminology: only reference, not sense). According to Mill, they function like mere labels.

Prima facie at least, this theory is implausible. Proper names certainly *seem* to have connotation for anyone competent in their use—e.g. anyone competent in using the name "Barack Obama" must at least know that he is a man, anyone competent in using the name "Japan" that it is a country. Also, since proper names are not *literally* labels, it is unclear how on such a theory they could succeed in picking out an object. Also, how could such a theory account for the informativeness of identity statements involving proper names (e.g. "Cicero is Tully")? And so forth.

Frege offers a much more promising-looking theory: Like other referring-terms, proper names have not only a reference but also a sense, and they succeed in picking out the former by means of the latter. More specifically, the sense of a proper name is a definite description (i.e. a uniquely referring expression of the form "the such-and-such"). This theory was subsequently taken over by Russell. It also formed the starting-point for an important variant theory first developed by Wittgenstein and then adopted by Searle, Strawson, and others which identifies the sense of a proper name, not with a *single* definite description, but rather with a *cluster* of definite descriptions understood to be, not necessarily all, but *mostly* true of some single object. This variant theory has certain advantages over the original theory. In particular, it seems truer to the usual psychological condition of competent users of proper names. And it is better able to cope with the objection to the original theory that it is normally possible to deny any given definite description of the bearer of a proper name without self-contradiction (e.g., while it is indeed false, it does not seem actually self-contradictory to deny that Barack Obama is the current president of the U.S.A.).[40]

Finally, Frege also advanced several further theses which would later play important roles in twentieth-century philosophy of language, either as inspirations or as targets of attack: (i) It was mainly he who was responsible for introducing the idea, subsequently fundamental to much twentieth-century philosophy of language, that the sentences and sub-sentential components of ordinary language are often misleading in their grammatical appearance—that they often have a quite different implicit structure, which can be spelled out by a logical language. For example, according to Frege's *Begriffsschrift* (1879) sentences such as "All men are mortal" and "Some men are mortal," which appear to be subject-predicate in form, turn out not in fact to be so. This idea subsequently gained ground with Russell's analysis of definite descriptions (and of ordinary proper names in terms of them), as well as with Wittgenstein's *Tractatus*, and continues to be influential in some recent philosophy of language (e.g. Davidson).

(ii) In *The Foundations of Arithmetic* (1884) Frege famously espouses a principle "never to ask for the meaning of a word in isolation, but only in the context of a sentence/proposition" (this is sometimes known as the *context principle*). As Hans Sluga points out, this principle was not entirely new with Frege; versions of it already occur in Kant (who was probably its original source), Gruppe, Trendelenburg, Lotze, and (one might add) Humboldt. However, its exact meaning in Frege is by no means transparent. In particular, he seems to have at least two different rationales for it which lend it two different meanings: (a) According to one rationale, it is the fundamental function of language, and a function on which all linguistic meaning (i.e. what Frege will eventually distinguish as "sense") consequently depends, to state *truths*; the smallest linguistic unit that can state a truth is the sentence/proposition; and word-meanings therefore consist in words' contributions to the truth-conditions of the many sentences/propositions in which they can occur. (b) According to another rationale, found in the essay *On the Law of Inertia* (1885), terms such as "mass" and "force" only receive their senses from the law of inertia, and moreover it is a mistake to consider this law and the other laws of motion "in separation from one another" because they "have a meaning only as a whole." Here the point seems to be the quite different one that a commitment to the truth of a certain set of sentences/propositions in which a word occurs (and by implication, to the falsehood of another set) is internal to its meaning. These two different rationales and meanings of the context principle may perhaps be compatible, but they are quite distinct. Be this as it may, versions of the context principle would subsequently play central roles in Wittgenstein's philosophy of language (both early and late), as well as in much other twentieth-century philosophy of language.

(iii) Frege insists that genuine concepts must have *sharp boundaries*, i.e. that every object must determinately either instantiate them or not. His reason for this insistence is similar to his reason for outlawing empty names in an ideal language, namely that a language which fails to conform to it will contain sentences that are neither true nor false, and will therefore also fail to conform to logical laws such as the law of bivalence or excluded middle. This insistence would later be subjected to a sustained attack by Wittgenstein in the *Philosophical Investigations* (1953).

(iv) Frege normally holds that thoughts and senses are of their very nature such that they can be *shared* by different people (this constituting for him one of the main features which distinguish thoughts and senses from mere coloring or ideas). However, in his late paper *The Thought* he makes a point which conflicts with that principle: he argues that when I think or speak about myself for my own purposes (i.e. rather than for purposes of communicating with others) the sense of "I" is given by "a special and primitive way" in which I am presented to myself but "to no-one else," and that it is only when I need to communicate with others, and therefore need to use a sense which they can grasp as well, that I switch to a sense for "I" which we can all grasp, such as "he who is speaking to you at this moment." This strange theory was probably the main catalyst and target for Wittgenstein's "private language argument" in the *Philosophical Investigations*, which can thus be seen as, in effect, defending Frege's normal insistence on the shareability of all senses against this incompatible theory.

## 6. Conclusion

Following its establishment by Herder and Hamann in the eighteenth century, the philosophy of language continued to flourish in the nineteenth century, and has done so ever since. As we have seen, the Herder-Hamann tradition from which it was born strongly influenced its subsequent forms. Moreover, having drifted some distance from the hearth of that tradition's principles during the late nineteenth and early twentieth centuries—especially in Nietzsche, Mauthner, Frege, Russell, and the early Wittgenstein—it more recently circled round into renewed proximity to them with the later Wittgenstein.

## Notes

1. I am here presupposing an assessment of their relative importance for which I have argued elsewhere. See *After Herder*, Essays 2 and 9.
2. For example, besides those discussed in this and the next two sections (Hegel, Schleiermacher, Friedrich Schlegel, and Wilhelm von Humboldt), also Fichte, Bernhardi, and the later Reinhold.
3. Interpretations such as Derrida's "The Pit and the Pyramid" which focus on Hegel's later *Encyclopedia* (1817–30) therefore fail to encounter his views about language at their most interesting.
4. For a fuller discussion of Hegel's philosophy of language, see Essay 5.
5. A move towards semantic holism is one of the most original and striking features of nineteenth-century philosophy of language generally. We will encounter several further representatives and forms of such a holism in the course of this article.
6. The suggestion in some of the secondary literature that Schleiermacher thinks such knowledge *irrelevant* to interpretation is absurd.
7. The widespread notion in the secondary literature that "divination" is for Schleiermacher a process of psychological self-projection into texts is basically mistaken. Like Herder, because of the *diversity principle*, he is rather concerned to *discourage* interpreters from assimilating the outlooks of people they interpret to their own.
8. This principle to some extent rests on but also goes far beyond Schleiermacher's *semantic* holism.
9. See esp. Herder's *On Thomas Abbt's Writings* (1768) and *On the Cognition and Sensation of the Human Soul* (1778).

10. For the emphasis in question, see especially Herder's *This Too a Philosophy of History for the Formation of Humanity* (1774), for the solution in question his *Critical Forests* (1769).

    It is also worth noting that Friedrich Ast (1778–1841) in a work concerned with hermeneutics titled *Basic Elements of Grammar, Hermeneutics, and Criticism* which he published in 1808 likewise borrowed from Herder in the two general ways just mentioned, i.e. complementing linguistic with psychological interpretation and insisting on holism in interpretation.

11. For further discussion of Schleiermacher's hermeneutics, see *After Herder*, Essays 4 and 11, and in the present volume Essay 9.

12. Schleiermacher sometimes implies a similar-looking position, most famously in his doctrine that the interpreter should aim to understand an author better than he understood himself. But that in fact turns out to mean something rather tame, namely that the interpreter should achieve an explicit grasp of grammatical and lexical rules which the interpretee only grasped implicitly. Whereas Schlegel's position is much more radical—envisaging, indeed, an "infinite depth" of meaning largely unknown to the author.

13. For a fuller discussion of Schlegel's hermeneutics, see Essay 2.

14. For instance, faced with the Homeric color word *chlôros*, which Homer sometimes applies to things that we would classify as green (e.g. healthy foliage) but at other times to things that we would classify as yellow (e.g. honey), a translator might attempt to capture its intension by reproducing its extension through the paraphrase "green or yellow." However, in doing so he would sacrifice the original intension in other ways—since Homer did not *have* the concept green or the concept yellow (only the concept *chlôros*), and for Homer *chlôros* was not a *disjunctive* concept.

15. Consider, for example, such a translator faced with the task of translating Homer's ethical word *aretê* into English. He will recognize that nothing in existing English exactly expresses this concept. He will therefore judge that the best way to convey it in English is to modify existing English usage in a systematic way over the course of the translation in order thereby to mimic Greek usage and hence meaning. He will begin by taking the word from existing English which already comes closest to *aretê* in meaning, say the word *virtue*. However, he will recognize that the rule for use which governs this word in existing English is still very different from that which governs Homer's word *aretê*, so that the two words are still quite sharply different in meaning—that, for instance, the descriptive component of the rule which governs the word *virtue* in existing English

makes it a solecism to ascribe *virtue* to a habitual liar or a pirate, but quite proper under certain circumstances to ascribe it to a physically weak man, whereas just the converse rule governs the word *aretê* in Homer. What therefore will he do? He will not simply resign himself to this discrepancy. Instead, for the duration of the translation he will modify the rule that governs the word *virtue* in order to make it resemble that which governs Homer's word *aretê*. For instance, he will drop the descriptive rule governing the word *virtue* that was just mentioned and switch to its converse instead, consequently for the duration of the translation writing quite happily of certain habitual liars and pirates as having *virtue* (e.g. Odysseus and Achilles, respectively), but scrupulously avoiding describing any physically weak man as having it. He will thereby succeed in expressing (or at least come close to expressing) the meaning of Homer's word *aretê* in English.

16. For instance, to continue with the preceding note's example, the reader of such a translation of Homer will find himself faced with jarring descriptions of habitual liars and pirates as possessing *virtue*.

17. Schleiermacher's ultimate picture of translation—as of interpretation—is therefore that it is a matter of striving for an ideal which is never fully attainable, though striving for it nonetheless remains very valuable and important. This is a characteristically Romantic model.

18. For a fuller discussion of Schleiermacher's theory of translation, see *After Herder*, Essay 12. Besides Friedrich Schlegel and Boeckh, another important figure from this period who is in broad agreement with Schleiermacher's theories of interpretation and translation is Wilhelm von Humboldt (whom we are about to consider in another connection). For example, concerning interpretation, like Schleiermacher, Humboldt argues in his Kawi-introduction of 1836 that not only nations but also individuals within nations are always deeply different linguistically and conceptually-intellectually so that "all understanding is always at the same time a misunderstanding." And concerning translation, he argues in the introduction to his translation of Aeschylus' *Agamemnon* (1816) for an approach to translation that is virtually identical to Schleiermacher's.

19. For example, they both subscribe to the naturalistic account of the origin of language that Herder had given in his *Treatise on the Origin of Language* (1772), according to which language is interdependent and coeval with human awareness [*Besonnenheit*] (Schlegel restricting this to Sanskritic languages, however). Also, Humboldt strongly emphasizes a version of the *language-sociality* principle, the principle that language is fundamentally social in nature. Also, Humboldt is developing a version of the *principle of*

*indirect reference* derived from Herder's *Ideas for the Philosophy of History of Humanity* (1784–91) when he argues in the Kawi-introduction that referring-terms never refer directly but only through the mediation of general concepts: "Even for [external physical objects] the word is not the equivalent of the object that hovers before the sense, but rather the conception thereof through language-production at the moment of finding the word. This is a notable source of the multiplicity of expressions for the same objects; and if in Sanskrit, for example, the *elephant* is now called the twice-drinking one, now the two-toothed one, and now the one equipped with a single hand, as many different concepts are thereby designated, though always the same object is meant." (This position anticipates, and may well have influenced, a position of Frege's to be discussed later in this essay.)

20. As we saw previously, Schleiermacher likewise embraces versions of doctrines (a)–(c) at about the same period.

21. Some examples are the expression of relations by inflection, a clear morphological or syntactic distinction between verb and noun, a sharp distinction between word and sentence, and even the placement of the verb between the subject and the object.

22. For example, in *On the Dual Form* (1827) Humboldt implicitly criticizes in this spirit native languages in which the third-person singular pronoun always specifies posture or distance from the speaker—which invites the response that such an economical inclusion of this sort of information might be very useful to a society living by hunting or warfare.

23. See e.g. *On the Diversity of Human Language Structure* (1827–9) and *On the Language of the South Sea Islands* (1828).

24. Another, even more factually and morally dubious example of normative theorizing about language from the period should perhaps be mentioned here as well. Fichte in his *Speeches to the German Nation* (1808) draws a sharp normative distinction between the Romance languages and German, arguing that because the former are based on a different parent-language, Latin, they are not properly understood by their users, and so produce intellectual unclarity; whereas German, as an *original* language, is linguistically transparent, and therefore produces intellectual clarity. This argument is again factually flawed—both because it underestimates the extent of German's own indebtedness to other languages such as Latin and, perhaps more importantly, because it disregards an important principle which had already been established by earlier theorists such as Ernesti and Herder: that what determines a word's current meaning is not its *historical etymology* but its *current use*. Moreover, Fichte's argument is again morally objec-

tionable as well, in that it encourages an invidious ranking of peoples. And it is less easy to excuse Fichte in this respect than Schlegel and Humboldt. For, while it could be said in his defense that, like them, he had been a cosmopolitan earlier in his career, and that he was only provoked to adopt this position through Germany's occupation by the French under Napoleon, this very same fact also shows that, unlike them, he embraced it out of hatred for another people.

25. For a fuller discussion of Friedrich Schlegel, Humboldt, and the birth of modern linguistics, see Essay 4.

26. These three thinkers were also influenced—as indeed were Herder and Hamann themselves—by the British Empiricists, especially Bacon, Locke, and Hume.

27. Similarly, a little later Marx would criticize Hegel on the basis of a misconception that Hegel had a conventional dualistic conception of the relation of the mind to physical nature, whereas Hegel had in fact, again largely under Herder's influence, moved to a physical-behavioristic conception of the mind.

28. Note that he here implicitly re-etymologizes the word "metaphor" a little to mean "carrying over," and hence lends it a somewhat broader sense than usual.

29. For example, since Mauthner was already committed to a conception that although all (philosophical) language is profoundly flawed, certain forms of it are more revealing than others, the "resolute" reading of the *Tractatus* recently championed by Cora Diamond and her followers is probably anachronistic.

30. One small but revealing symptom of the depth of Mauthner's impact on both the early and the late Wittgenstein is a plethora of metaphors which they share in their discussions of language: long before Wittgenstein, Mauthner had already described (his philosophical) language as a "ladder" eventually to be kicked away, called language a "tool," spoken of its "game-rules," likened it to a "river" or "river-bed," compared it to an "old city," etc.

31. M. Dummett, "Was Frege a Philosopher of Language?" in his *The Interpretation of Frege's Philosophy* (Cambridge, Mass.: Harvard University Press, 1981). It is reasonable to assume that the—by this period pervasively influential—Herder-Hamann tradition was a significant influence on Frege here. However, the situation is complicated. The Herder-Hamann tradition was itself ultimately indebted for the *thought-language principle* to Leibniz (see esp. Leibniz's *Dialogue on the Connection between Things and Words* [1677]). And Frege probably absorbed the doctrine not only from

the Herder-Hamann tradition but also in more direct ways from Leibniz (e.g. through Trendelenburg).

32. His main argument for this Platonism is the rather dubious one that unless thoughts had such a character—if instead they were somehow created by human beings—there could be no timeless truths or truths concerning times prior to human existence.

33. One can more readily persuade oneself of this by contrasting their positions with those of eighteenth-century counterparts such as Hume and Kant respectively, which were more radically non-linguistic.

34. It is, of course, absurd to claim, as Dummett and Kenny do, that Frege *began* the philosophy of language.

35. Therefore, when M. Dummett argues in his essay "The Relative Priority of Thought and Language," in his *Frege and Other Philosophers* (Oxford: Oxford University Press, 1991), that Frege had not yet recognized our modern distinction between the meaning of an expression in the common language and an individual's grasp of it, he in effect misrepresents as Frege's ignorance of a position that had not yet been developed what was in reality Frege's reaction against a position with which he was already very familiar in an extreme form.

36. To be a little more precise: For Frege identity statements play an indispensable role in both arithmetic and geometry. Arithmetic he considers *analytic* a priori, in virtue of his logicism. That might seem to imply that all true arithmetical identity statements are uninformative, but in fact he denies this. Geometry he considers predominantly *synthetic* a priori, so that true geometrical identity statements are for him even more obviously in some cases informative. It is therefore not an accident that in giving his argument for the sense-reference distinction from informative identity statements in *On Sense and Reference* he uses a mathematical, and more specifically a geometrical, example.

37. It has sometimes been questioned whether even this version of the criterion would be strictly correct. For example, S. Blackburn in *Spreading the Word* (Oxford: Clarendon Press, 1984) questions this on the grounds that despite the fact that "widow" means the same as "person who had a husband who died while still married to her, and has not since remarried," we may on occasion correctly describe someone as puzzling whether all and only widows are people who had a husband etc., but not as puzzling whether all and only widows are widows (since everyone knows that). However, I would suggest that such apparent counterexamples can in fact be coped with—for instance, in this case by noting that

when it is correct to report that someone is puzzling whether all and only widows are people who had a husband etc., this is possible because the report involves a disguised (degree of) *mention* of "widow" rather than a (pure) *use* of it.

38. On the other hand, (iii) and (iv) are only *tendencies* in Frege. For his work does also contain small hints of different, more nuanced, and better positions. For example, at one point in *On Sense and Reference* he recognizes a class of "overtones of subsidiary *thoughts*, which are however not explicitly expressed and therefore should not be reckoned in the sense" (emphasis added).

39. Kant had attempted to avoid such disastrously restrictive consequences by invoking a class of "problematic judgments." However, this arguably amounted less to a solution than to an implicit self-contradiction. (A more charitable reading, recently championed by Béatrice Longuenesse for example, would in effect *make* a Kantian "judgment" a Fregean thought.)

40. Frege's theory and this variant theory have in more recent years been subjected to a subtle critique by S.A. Kripke in *Naming and Necessity* (Oxford: Blackwell, 1980). (Kripke instead prefers an account closer to Mill's.) However, it seems very doubtful that Kripke's critique succeeds.

Kripke's case mainly turns on two points: (i) Proper names are "rigid" (i.e. pick out the same referent in all possible worlds), whereas definite descriptions are "non-rigid," so that it cannot be true that the latter constitute the sense of the former. (ii) People who use a proper name are in some cases unable to provide any definite description that might uniquely pick out its referent at all (e.g. someone may use the name "Cicero" without knowing more than that he was a Roman orator), and in other cases the only definite descriptions they associate with the name turn out to be false of the referent (e.g. it is probably not in fact true that Jonah was "the ancient Israelite who was swallowed and then regurgitated by a whale," for, although it is likely that he is a historical figure, that story is probably a mere legend).

Neither of these points seems compelling on reflection. Point (i) loses its force when one realizes that definite descriptions can be used *rigidly* as well as non-rigidly—that someone can, for example, use the definite description "the current president of the U.S.A." in the sense "the current president of the U.S.A., *that very man.*" (Kripke is himself skeptical that a rigid use of definite descriptions occurs, but his skepticism seems implausible.) Hence a Fregean can cope with argument (i) by identifying the sense of a proper name with a *rigid* definite description (or a cluster of such definite descriptions).

Point (ii) loses its force when one realizes that the definite descriptions that constitute the sense of a proper name for a particular user might include such definite descriptions as "the ancient Roman whom most classical scholars refer to as 'Cicero'" and "the man whom the authors of the Bible refer to as 'Jonah.'" Kripke is aware of the possibility of this sort of response, and tries to counter it, but his counterarguments are not convincing. First, he places much weight on a danger of vicious circularity that he sees in invoking descriptions which themselves employ the notion of reference in this way. However, vicious circularity would only arise here if the claim were that *all* (clusters of) relevant descriptions were of this sort, or that *all* (clusters of) descriptions relevant to some particular name which succeeds in referring were of this sort, whereas a sensible version of the response in question can easily avoid making or implying any such claim, while still leaving a large role for this sort of description, and in particular a large enough role to answer point (ii) effectively. Second, Kripke objects that the sort of parasitism in the use of definite descriptions that would often be involved according to such an account—e.g. Smith's taking "Fido" to mean the creature Jones refers to as "Fido," while Jones in turn takes it to mean the content of some other definite description—brings with it a possibility that, unbeknownst to them, the people in question may fail to refer to any object at all—e.g. if the vicious-circularity scenario is realized, Jones's definite description happening to be "the creature Smith refers to as 'Fido.'" But surely, it is no duty of a correct account of proper names to exclude such a possibility; on the contrary, any account that *did not* make room for the possibility that people might unknowingly be using a proper name that failed to refer for reasons such as this would ipso facto be unacceptable. Third, Kripke focuses on a specific version of this idea of parasitic reference by means of definite description that was championed by Strawson, and Kripke objects that it implies that the parasitic user of a proper name would have to be able to identify the person whose reference he intended to replicate and that this is an unrealistic requirement. But this is no more than an ad hominem point against Strawson, who just happens to put the general idea in terms of parasitism on a *particular individual's* reference. As two of the examples given above already illustrate, there is no reason why the parasitism in question could not instead be on the reference achieved by some vaguely specified general group (e.g. "most classical scholars").

In sum, it looks as though a theory in the spirit of Frege's can well withstand Kripke's critique. On the other hand, his critique does help to bring out the fact that certain closer specifications of such a theory may be necessary: in particular (a) an identification of the senses of proper names with (clusters of) *rigid* definite descriptions, and (b) an assignment of an important role among the relevant definite descriptions to the sort of parasitic description just discussed.

# 9

# Hermeneutics

For the purpose of this essay, "hermeneutics" means the theory of interpretation, i.e. the theory of achieving an understanding of texts, discourse, and so on (it does *not* mean a certain twentieth-century philosophical movement). Hermeneutics in this sense has a long history, reaching back at least as far as ancient Greece. However, new focus was brought to bear on it in the modern period, in the wake of the Reformation with its displacement of responsibility for interpreting the Bible from the Church to individual Christians generally. This new focus on hermeneutics occurred especially in Germany.[1]

Two fairly common but competing pictures of the course of modern hermeneutics in Germany are that it began with a fumbling germination in the eighteenth century and then flowered in the systematic hermeneutics of Friedrich Daniel Ernst Schleiermacher in the early nineteenth century,[2] or that it began with a fumbling germination in the late eighteenth and early nineteenth centuries and then eventually flowered in the philosophical hermeneutics of Martin Heidegger and Hans-Georg Gadamer in the twentieth century (hence the very word "hermeneutics" is today often treated as virtually synonymous with "Gadamer's philosophy").[3]

I take both of these pictures to be deeply misguided (especially the latter). What I would like to substitute for them in the present essay is something more like the following picture: There has indeed been impressive progress in hermeneutics since the eighteenth century. However, this progress has consisted, not in the attainment of a hermeneutic system or a philosophical hermeneutics, but instead in the gradual accumulation of particular insights, both into the very nature of interpretation itself and into the scope and significance of interpretation. And the thinkers who have contributed most to this progress have not been the ones who are most likely to spring to mind at the mention of the word hermeneutics (for example, Schleiermacher and Gadamer), but instead certain thinkers less commonly fêted in this connection (especially, Johann August Ernesti, Johann Gottfried Herder, Friedrich Schlegel, Wilhelm Dilthey, Friedrich Nietzsche, and more recently John Langshaw Austin and Quentin Skinner).

With a view to establishing this picture, the present essay will attempt to provide a reasonably comprehensive survey of the field of modern hermeneutics, focusing on the ideas of its most prominent representatives more or less in chronological sequence, and providing some critical assessment of them along the way.[4] The essay will conclude with some suggestions for new horizons in hermeneutics.

## 1. Ernesti

A seminal figure in the development of modern hermeneutics in Germany was Johann August Ernesti (1707–81). Ernesti's *Institutio interpretis Novi Testamenti* [*Instruction for the Interpreter of the New Testament*] of 1761 constitutes an important transition from a hermeneutics focused exclusively on the Bible towards a more general hermeneutics. The work was greatly respected by, and strongly influenced, important immediate successors in the German hermeneutic tradition such as Herder and Schleiermacher. It makes many points which can still be read with profit today.

Ernesti in particular takes five vitally important steps in hermeneutics. First, he argues that the Bible must be interpreted in just the same way as any other text.[5] He does not follow through on this principle fully or consistently. For, while he does indeed forgo any reliance on a divine inspiration of the interpreter, he assumes that, as the word of God,[6] the Bible must be true and hence also self-consistent throughout,[7] which is not something that he would assume in connection with profane texts. However, Herder and Schleiermacher would soon go on to embrace this principle in a full and consistent way.

Second, Ernesti identifies the following twofold obstacle that he sees facing interpretation in many cases: (1) different languages possess markedly different conceptual resources;[8] and (2) an author's concepts often diverge significantly from those of his background language.[9] The conception that interpreters in many cases face such a twofold obstacle would subsequently be taken over by Herder and Schleiermacher, who would indeed make it even more fundamental to their theories. In particular, principle (1) is the source of an acute awareness they both share of an ever-present danger in interpretation of falsely assimilating the concepts (and beliefs, etc.) expressed by a text to one's own, or to others with which one happens already to be especially familiar. And principle (2) grounds an intuition they both share that *linguistic* interpretation needs to be complemented by a side of interpretation that focuses on the author's *psychology*, namely in order to make it possible to penetrate the author's individuality in conceptualization.

Third, Ernesti argues that the *meaning* of words depends on *linguistic usage* [*usus loquendi*], so that interpretation is fundamentally a matter of determining the linguistic usage of words.[10] This is another vitally important move. It would eventually lead, in Herder, Johann Georg Hamann, and Schleiermacher, to a stronger version of the same thesis which grounded it in the further, revolutionary claim that it is true because meaning *is* word-usage.[11] Ernesti's thesis also formed a sort of base line from which such successors would later set out to look for *additional* tasks that interpretation needs to accomplish as well (for example, determining aspects of the author's psychology).

Fourth, Ernesti insists—in opposition to a tradition of exclusively text-focused reading of the Bible that was still very much alive in his day—[12] that interpretation must deploy a detailed knowledge of a text's historical, geographical, etc. context.[13] Subsequently, Herder, Schleiermacher, and August Boeckh would all take over this position in their hermeneutic theories.[14]

Fifth, Ernesti insists on various forms of holism in interpretation:[15] in particular, the parts of a text must be interpreted in light of the whole text;[16] and both of these in light of an author's broader corpus and other related texts.[17] Such holism is especially necessary in order to acquire sufficient evidence to be able to pin down word-usages, and hence meanings.[18] This principle of holism would subsequently be taken over and developed further by successors such as Herder, Friedrich Ast, and Schleiermacher. Herder in particular already placed greater emphasis on it,[19] as well as expanding it to include consideration of the author's whole historical context,[20] and of his whole psychology.[21] Such a principle of holism leads to the notorious problem of a "hermeneutic circle" (later highlighted by Dilthey among others). For example, if interpreting parts of a text requires interpreting the whole of the text, then, given that interpreting the whole obviously also requires interpreting the parts, how can interpretation ever be achieved at all? Herder in the *Critical Forests* already anticipates that problem, and also develops a plausible solution to it: since understanding is not an all-or-nothing matter but instead something that comes in *degrees*, it is possible to interpret the parts of a text in sequence with at least some measure of success, thereby achieve a measure of understanding of the whole text, then deploy that measure of understanding of the whole text in order to refine one's understanding of the parts, thereby refining one's understanding of the whole text, and so on (in principle, indefinitely). Schleiermacher subsequently took over this solution.

## 2. Herder

Another very important early contributor to the development of hermeneutics was the man already mentioned, Johann Gottfried Herder (1744–1803). In addition to taking over and developing the five principles just described, Herder also made several further significant moves.

Perhaps the most important of these was to set hermeneutics on the foundation of a new, and moreover arguably correct, philosophy of language. In particular, Herder grounded hermeneutics in the following three principles: (1) Meanings are—not, as many philosophers have supposed, referents, Platonic forms, subjective mental ideas, or whatnot, but instead—word-usages. (2) Because of this, all thought (as essentially articulated in terms of meanings, or concepts) is essentially dependent on and bounded by the thinker's capacity for linguistic expression—i.e. a person can only think if he has a language and can only think what he can express linguistically. (3) Meanings are also essentially grounded in (perceptual and affective) sensations—either directly (as with the "in" of "The dog is in the garden," for example) or via a sort of metaphorical extension (as with the "in" of "Jones is in legal trouble," for example).[22] Principles (1) and (2) essentially established modern philosophy of language in one fell swoop, and would still be widely accepted in some form by philosophers of language today. The quasi-empiricist principle (3) would meet with much more skepticism among contemporary philosophers of language, but may well be correct too (contrary to first appearances, it need not conflict with principle (1); and the widespread anti-psychologism concerning meaning due to Gottlob Frege and Ludwig Wittgenstein that is likely to make it seem dubious to philosophers of language today is arguably itself mistaken).

Now these three principles all carry important consequences for interpretation. Principle (1) grounds at a deeper level Ernesti's thesis that it is an essential task of interpretation to determine linguistic usage and hence meaning. Principle (2) implies that in order to discover an author's thoughts an interpreter must explore the author's language, and ensures that there is no danger that an author's thoughts will transcend his language (i.e. his capacity for linguistic expression). The quasi-empiricist principle (3) implies that interpretation requires the interpreter to perform some sort of imaginative reproduction of an author's meaning-internal sensations (this is an important aspect of Herder's notorious thesis that interpretation requires *Einfühlung*, "feeling one's way in").[23] Versions or variants of these three principles, and of their consequences for interpretation, would subsequently be taken over by Schleiermacher.[24]

Herder also took a number of further important steps in his theory of interpretation. One of these was to argue for the need to complement the focus on language that Ernesti had already championed with a focus on the author's *psychology*.[25] Herder has several reasons for making this move. A first is the idea just mentioned that interpretation requires an imaginative recapturing of certain of the author's sensations. A second is the idea that it is often necessary to consider features of the author's psychology in order to resolve ambiguities in his text. A third is the idea that a focus on the author's psychology is an important means for penetrating his conceptual-linguistic individuality. Schleiermacher would subsequently take over Herder's principle of complementing linguistic with psychological interpretation, and especially the third of the rationales for doing so just mentioned (which he also elaborated significantly). Indeed, one way of characterizing the development of hermeneutics after Herder more generally is as a sort of progressive confirmation of Herder's thesis that linguistic interpretation needs to be complemented with a focus on the author's psychology.[26] This progressive confirmation took the form of an identification of more precise and additional reasons why that is so. Examples of this trend are, besides Schleiermacher's elaboration of Herder's third rationale, a novel point of Schlegel's that texts often express thoughts not explicitly in any of their parts but instead implicitly and holistically, and Austin and Skinner's novel assignment of an essential role in interpretation to the identification of illocutionary force or intention.[27]

Herder also argues that interpretation, especially in its psychological aspect, requires the use of what he calls "divination," by which he essentially means (not some sort of divinely guided insight or infallible intuition, but instead much more reasonably) a method of fallible, corrigible hypothesis based on but also going well beyond the relatively meager linguistic and other behavioral evidence available.[28] Schleiermacher would again subsequently take over this principle, similarly holding that a method of "divination" predominates on the psychological side of interpretation, and similarly conceiving this as a method of fallible, corrigible hypothesis based on but also going well beyond the meager empirical evidence available.[29]

Another of Herder's vital contributions to the theory of interpretation is his emphasis on the essential role played in interpreting a work by a correct identification of its *genre*, and on the difficulty of achieving such a correct identification in many cases. Herder conceives of a genre as consisting in a general purpose together with certain rules of composition which serve it.[30] He implies that correctly identifying a work's genre is crucial for properly interpreting the work not only because such an identification of genre is itself an essential constituent of fully comprehending a work (very much in the same way that correctly identifying the illocutionary force of a sentence is itself an essential constituent of fully comprehending the sentence), but also because the genre often carries meanings which are not explicitly articulated in the work itself, and because a proper grasp of the genre is moreover essential for correctly interpreting many of the meanings which *are* explicitly articulated in the work. This much would probably have been accepted by several of Herder's forerunners in the theory of genre (for example, Aristotle and Herder's contemporary

Gotthold Ephraim Lessing). But Herder adds an important new twist: Just as concepts often vary in subtle ways across historical periods and cultures, and even between individuals within a single period and culture, thereby complicating the task of interpretation, in particular by creating ever-present temptations falsely to assimilate the concepts found to ones with which the interpreter is already familiar (especially when they are expressed by the same word), so likewise the task of identifying a genre correctly is complicated by the fact that genres often vary in subtle ways across historical periods and cultures, and even between authors working within a single period and culture, indeed sometimes even between different works seemingly in the same genre by a single author,[31] so that in particular the interpreter faces ever-present temptations falsely to assimilate an encountered genre to one that is already familiar to him (especially when they share the same name).[32] In addition, Herder applies this whole position concerning genre not only to linguistic works but also to non-linguistic art.[33] Herder's insight into the vital role that identifying genre plays in interpretation, and into the difficulty of accomplishing this task properly, would subsequently be taken over by Friedrich and August Wilhelm Schlegel and by Boeckh (in contrast, Schleiermacher emphasizes this much less). Boeckh was perhaps the first to add a further important point here: that the vital role and the difficulty in question are by no means confined to works of linguistic and non-linguistic art, but also apply to texts and discourse generally.[34]

The points discussed so far have all been concerned with the question of the very nature of interpretation itself, but Herder also makes several important contributions concerning the question of the scope and significance of interpretation. One contribution which straddles both questions has to do with non-linguistic art (for example, sculpture, painting, and instrumental music). Herder's views on this subject underwent a dramatic evolution early in his career. In the *Critical Forests* he was initially inclined to suppose that principles (1) and (2) in his philosophy of language precluded non-linguistic art expressing meanings and thoughts, and he therefore took the position that it did not. However, in the course of writing the *Critical Forests* he came to recognize the (on reflection, rather obvious) fact that non-linguistic art often *does* express meanings and thoughts, and he came to realize that this is not inconsistent with principles (1) and (2) after all, provided that the meanings and thoughts in question are ones which the artist possesses *in virtue of his linguistic capacity*. This was henceforth Herder's considered position. This position entailed two important consequences for interpretation: first, that non-linguistic art often requires interpretation, just as linguistic texts and discourse do (this constitutes a sort of broadening of the scope of interpretation); and second, that its interpretation needs to proceed via interpretation of the artist's language (this can be seen as a further insight into the very nature of interpretation itself). One of the most interesting and contested questions in modern hermeneutics is whether this position of Herder's is correct. For, while Herder's attribution of meanings and thoughts to non-linguistic art seems beyond serious dispute, and has been accepted by most hermeneutic theorists since (for example, by Georg Wilhelm Friedrich Hegel, Dilthey, and Gadamer), his further thesis that such meanings and thoughts are always parasitic on the artist's linguistic capacity is far more controversial, and has been contradicted by several prominent theorists (including Hegel and Dilthey). I have argued elsewhere that this further Herderian thesis *is* in fact correct, though.[35]

Herder also effects another sort of broadening of the scope of interpretation. He recognizes that many animals have mental lives even without possessing any proper language. But he also holds, plausibly, that once language is acquired it transforms the character of a person's whole mental life, so that for example even the person's perceptual and affective sensations become implicitly linguistically articulated.[36] This position implies that properly identifying a mature person's mental states requires interpreting his language—an implication which constitutes a further sort of broadening of the scope of interpretation. Hegel would subsequently take over this position.[37] It also reappears in Heidegger's famous thesis in *Being and Time* that *Dasein*, or Man, is of its/his very nature an interpretive being, a being possessed of an understanding of meanings, even for example in its/his perceptual sensations.[38]

These two steps of broadening the scope of interpretation began an important trend in hermeneutics which continued after Herder. For example, Hegel not only follows these two steps (as has already been mentioned), but he also identifies a range of *socio-political institutions* which he calls "Objective Spirit" as expressions of meanings and thoughts, and therefore as requiring interpretation, and he notes that human *actions*, since they essentially express human mental life (in particular, beliefs and desires), which is essentially imbued with meanings and thoughts, can only be properly understood with the aid of interpretation as well. Dilthey subsequently takes over this even broader conception of the role of interpretation from Hegel.[39] As we shall see in the course of this essay, further forms of broadening have occurred since Herder as well (for example, in connection with such seemingly meaningless behaviors as acts of forgetting and slips of the tongue, and in connection with animals).

In addition, Herder makes several seminal moves concerning the *significance* of interpretation. One of these lies in his assignment to interpretation of a central role in the discipline of history. He argues for this on the grounds that historians should focus less on the history of political and military events than they usually do, and more on the history of culture, where interpretation plays a paramount role.[40] However, the sort of broadening of interpretation to cover human mental life generally, socio-political institutions, and actions which Herder himself began and Hegel extended implies a central role for interpretation even in the historian's treatment of political and military events. And accordingly, Hegel would go on to assign it a central role across the whole range of the historian's work, political and military as well as cultural. Subsequently, Dilthey would generalize this idea that interpretation plays the central role in history to include the human sciences more generally (as distinguished from the natural sciences, whose main task is rather causal explanation). He would thereby provide a plausible solution to two vexed questions concerning the human sciences: first, the question of what their appropriate method is, and second, the question of how they can claim the status of genuine sciences. (Concerning this, more anon.)

Herder also introduces the vitally important insight that interpreting, or coming to understand, historical and cultural Others is essential for achieving a proper *self*-understanding. There are two main reasons why, in his view. First, it is only by interpreting historical and cultural Others and thereby arriving at a knowledge of the nature of their concepts, beliefs, etc. that one can come to see what is universal and what by contrast distinctive in one's own concepts, beliefs, etc. Second, it is only by interpreting historical Others in one's own cultural tradition who were one's own cultural forerunners that one can come to see how one's own concepts, beliefs, etc. arose over time, this insight in itself constituting an important contribution to the deeper comprehension of them (this is Herder's justly famous "genetic method"). This whole position has been central to much historically and hermeneutically oriented philosophical thought since Herder. For example, it plays a vital role in Hegel, Friedrich Nietzsche, and Michel Foucault (all of whom are in particular strongly committed to increasing our self-understanding by means of versions or variants of Herder's "genetic method").[41]

Herder also develops several further compelling ideas concerning the significance of interpretation, especially in cases involving historical or cultural distance. One of these is the idea that (once we drop the naive and narcissistic assumption that we represent a sort of historical and cultural pinnacle) it turns out that we have a lot to *learn* from the sources in question, for example in relation to ethical and aesthetic ideals.[42]

Another is the idea that accurate interpretation of (historical and especially) cultural Others is important for the ethico-political good of promoting intercultural respect: accurate interpretation of such Others both expresses and encourages this sort of respect, whereas sheer neglect or careless interpretation expresses and encourages depreciation, and hence supports disrespectful treatment.[43]

In sum, Herder makes a number of vitally important contributions to hermeneutics, both concerning the very nature of interpretation and concerning its
scope and significance.

## 3. Schleiermacher

One of the best known theorists of hermeneutics is Friedrich Daniel Ernst
Schleiermacher (1768–1834), who developed his views on the subject in lectures delivered during the first third of the nineteenth century.[44] Schleiermacher
is indeed commonly regarded as the father of modern hermeneutics. I would
suggest, however, that such a title may more properly belong to one of his
predecessors.

Like Herder, Schleiermacher grounds hermeneutics in a philosophy of language (indeed, one very similar and heavily indebted to Herder's)—in particular, the doctrines that (1) meaning consists in "the unity of the word-sphere," (2)
thought is identical with language (or inner language), and (3) meanings are
constituted by empirical schemata, or rules for the production of images (à la
Kant).

Schleiermacher is especially famous for insisting on the following points: that
hermeneutics should be a universal discipline, applicable to all types of interpretation alike; that, contrary to a common assumption that "understanding
occurs as a matter of course," in fact "misunderstanding occurs as a matter of
course, and so understanding must be willed and sought at every point"; that
interpretation needs to proceed holistically; that interpretation needs to complement a linguistic (or "grammatical") focus with a psychological (or "technical") focus; that while a "comparative" (i.e. plain inductive) method should
predominate on the linguistic side, a "divinatory" (i.e. hypothetical) method
should predominate on the psychological side; that an interpreter ought to
understand an author better than the author understood himself; and that interpretation is an art rather than a science.[45]

I would suggest, though, that there has been a tendency in some of the literature to exaggerate Schleiermacher's importance for the development of hermeneutics, and that his contribution, while significant, was fairly modest.

To begin with the negative side of this assessment, when one views
Schleiermacher's theory against the background of Ernesti and Herder's, it
turns out that much of what is good in it is not new, much of what is new not
good, and that it omits much that was good in the preceding theories.

*Much of what is good in it is not new.* This applies to the philosophy of language
on which Schleiermacher founds his theory of interpretation, which to a great

extent repeats Herder's. It also applies to Schleiermacher's complementing of linguistic with psychological interpretation, and even to his main justification of this in terms of the need to penetrate the author's individuality in conceptualization—both moves which, as we saw, Herder had already made. It also applies to Schleiermacher's conception that the predominant method on the psychological side of interpretation should be "divination," in the sense of fallible, corrigible hypothesis based on but also going well beyond the meager empirical evidence available—a conception which, as we saw, Herder had already introduced. And it also applies to Schleiermacher's insistence on various sorts of holism in interpretation, and to his conception that, contrary to first appearances, such holism does not make interpretation impossible because understanding comes in degrees and so can be achieved by means of a provisional understanding of parts which then affords a provisional understanding of a whole, which can then in turn be used to refine the understanding of the parts, and so on—a position which, as we saw, Ernesti and especially Herder had already developed.

*Much of what is new in it is not good:* This applies to Schleiermacher's modification of Herder's doctrine of thought's essential dependence on and boundedness by language into a doctrine of their outright identity (on reflection, this turns out to be philosophically untenable). It also applies to Schleiermacher's modification of Herder's quasi-empiricism about meanings into an equation of meanings with empirical schemata à la Kant, for the sharply dualistic way in which Kant had conceived schemata, namely as related to language only contingently, leads to an inconsistency here with Schleiermacher's equation of meanings with rules of word-usage, or "the unity of the word-sphere." It also applies to Schleiermacher's transformation of Ernesti and Herder's plausible *empirically grounded rule of thumb* that authors *often* conceptualize in idiosyncratic ways into an *a priori principle allegedly grounded in the very nature of reason* that people *always* do so, so that *exact understanding of another person is never possible*—a principle which is implausible in its very a priori status, in the specifics of its a priori argument concerning the nature of reason, and in its highly counterintuitive implication that people never exactly understand each other. It also applies to Schleiermacher's novel closer specification of the central function of psychological interpretation as one of discovering an author's "seminal decision [*Keimentschluß*]" and how this unfolds itself in a necessary manner into his whole work (for how many works are actually written in such a way?). It also applies to Schleiermacher's restriction of the empirical evidence that can be adduced in order to arrive at an estimation of an author's psychology to *linguistic* evidence, rather than, as Herder had held, behavioral evidence more generally (for cannot non-linguistic behavior constitute just as valid and important evidence for relevant psychological traits as linguistic behavior?). Finally, it also applies to Schleiermacher's argument, contradicting Herder's normal tendency in works such as *On Thomas Abbt's Writings* to treat interpretation as a science rather like the natural sciences, that due to the role of "divination," or hypothesis, in interpretation, interpretation is not a science but an art (for have we not since Schleiermacher's day come to recognize that hypothesis is on the contrary a *paradigm* of natural scientific method?).

*It omits much that was good in the preceding theories*: This arguably applies to Schleiermacher's omission of Herder's conception that *Einfühlung*, "feeling one's way in," has an essential role to play in interpretation. It also applies to Schleiermacher's relative neglect, in comparison with Herder, of the importance to interpretation of determining *genre*, and of the serious difficulties that often stand in the way of doing so.

Turning now to the more positive side of my assessment, Schleiermacher's real achievement in hermeneutics seems to me to consist mainly in four things. First and foremost, he draws together in an orderly way many of the important ideas about interpretation that had already been developed by Ernesti and Herder before him (Herder in particular had left his own contributions to the subject scattered throughout a large number of works, moreover ones largely devoted to other subjects). This process would subsequently be carried still further by Schleiermacher's pupil and follower August Boeckh (1785–1867) in his *Encyclopedia and Methodology of the Philological Sciences* (1877), which distinguishes four fundamental types or aspects of interpretation that need to be undertaken: historical, linguistic, individual (i.e. what Herder and Schleiermacher had characterized as psychological), and generic.

Second, Schleiermacher's philosophy of language takes one important step beyond Herder's, in that Schleiermacher introduces several forms of semantic holism (as distinct from—though no doubt also constituting one reason for— interpretive holism): (i) a doctrine of "the unity of the word sphere," which basically says that the several different usages and hence meanings which typically belong to a single word (and which will be distinguished by a good dictionary entry) are essentially interdependent; (ii) a doctrine that the usages and hence meanings of cognate words in a language are likewise essentially interdependent; and (iii) a doctrine that the distinctive *grammar* of a language is internal to the usages and hence meanings of the particular words in the language.[46] These several forms of semantic holism entail corresponding tasks for an interpreter (and furnish one specific rationale or set of rationales for holism in interpretation).

Third, as I already mentioned, Schleiermacher espouses the project of a *universal* hermeneutics, a single theory of interpretation that will apply to all types of interpretation alike—as much to the interpretation of sacred works as to that of profane, as much to the interpretation of modern works as to that of ancient, as much to the interpretation of oral discourse as to that of written texts, and so on. The idea of such a project already had certain precedents earlier in the hermeneutic tradition,[47] and Herder had recently in effect erased the sacred/profane and modern/ancient divisions in particular. But Schleiermacher's explicit commitment to this project still arguably constitutes a significant contribution. (His idea of applying general hermeneutic principles to the interpretation of oral discourse is perhaps especially striking and noteworthy.)

Fourth, Schleiermacher elaborates on Herder's idea that one reason why linguistic interpretation needs to be complemented with psychological interpretation is that the latter is required in order to penetrate an author's conceptual-linguistic individuality. Schleiermacher sees this, more specifically, as due to the fact that where an author's rules of word-use and hence meanings are idiosyncratic, rather than shared in common with a whole linguistic community, the relevant actual uses of a word which are available to serve the interpreter as his evidential basis for inferring to the rule of word-use that governs them will usually be poor in both number and contextual variety, so that the interpreter will need to have recourse to a further source of guidance, namely a general knowledge of the author's distinctive psychology.[48]

## 4. Friedrich Schlegel

A figure of at least equal, and probably in fact greater, importance for the development of hermeneutics is Friedrich Schlegel (1772–1829). During the late 1790s, the period when they both began working intensively on hermeneutics (as well as translation-theory), Schlegel and Schleiermacher were close friends and collaborators, even sharing accommodation in Berlin for a time, and there is therefore a serious question as to which of them can claim the greater credit for the ideas which Schleiermacher eventually articulated in his hermeneutics lectures.[49] However, Schlegel's claim to importance in the development of hermeneutics does not, I think, mainly turn on that question. Instead, it mainly turns on five contributions he made which are not really to be found in Schleiermacher.

First, Schlegel (together with his older brother August Wilhelm) continues Herder's emphasis on the importance for interpretation of identifying genre and the difficulty of doing so. He also applies this point in some original and important ways, for example in developing the distinction between "classical" and "romantic" literature, and in overturning Aristotle's authority concerning the genre of ancient tragedy.

Second, Schlegel makes the point that texts sometimes express meanings and thoughts, not explicitly in any of their parts, but instead through their parts and the way in which these are put together to form a whole.[50] Schlegel apparently believes that this feature is especially characteristic of ancient texts,[51] though not exclusive to them.[52] This point is basically correct and extremely important.[53] Consider, for example, *Iliad*, book 1. There Homer communicates something like the following message, not by explicitly stating it anywhere, but instead by artfully juxtaposing and contrasting, on the one hand, the quarrel between the mortals Agamemnon and short-lived Achilles (which Nestor attempts to mediate), with all its grandeur, passion, and seriousness, and, on the other hand, the structurally similar but parody-like quarrel between the immortals Zeus and Hera (which Hephaistos attempts to mediate), with all its ultimate triviality and even ludicrousness:

You may well have supposed that the immortality and the other apparent advantages enjoyed by the gods would be a huge boon to any being who possessed them, raising their lot far above that of mere mortals like us, as indeed the gods' traditional epithet "blessed" implies. But in fact, if you think about it, since nothing would ever be seriously at stake for such beings as it is for us mortals, and in particular they could never really acquire honor by risking their lives, their existence would be reduced to a sort of endless meaninglessness and triviality, so that our lot is in a very real sense the better one.[54]

(Notice that this point of Schlegel's provides an additional reason why, or sense in which, Herder was correct in thinking that linguistic interpretation needs to be complemented with psychological interpretation.)

A third important contribution of Schlegel's concerns the role of *unconscious* meanings and thoughts in texts, and hence in their interpretation. The general idea that unconscious mental processes occur already had a long history in German philosophy by Schlegel's day: it had been a commonplace among the Rationalists, Kant had been strongly committed to it as well, and so too had Herder, who had moreover discussed it in close connection with questions of interpretation in *On the Cognition and Sensation of the Human Soul* (1778). However, it is above all Schlegel who develops this idea into a principle that the interpreter should penetrate beyond an author's conscious meanings and thoughts to include his unconscious ones as well: "Every excellent work ... aims at more than it knows";[55] "In order to understand someone who only partially understands himself, you first have to understand him completely and better than he himself does."[56] This is a very important idea.[57] It was subsequently pursued further by Nietzsche, then by Freud and his followers. Nietzsche's pursuit of it is impressive. However, Freud and his followers' pursuit of it has perhaps done less to realize its full potential than to reveal its epistemological hazardousness, its encouragement of arbitrariness due to the fact that the appropriate criteria for imputing unconscious meanings and thoughts are even less clear than those for imputing conscious ones.[58] Developing a proper methodology for, and application of, this aspect of interpretation arguably remains a work in progress.[59] (Notice that this third point again tends to vindicate Herder's intuition that linguistic interpretation needs to be complemented with psychological.)

A fourth important contribution made by Schlegel is as follows. Already before Schlegel, Ernesti had encouraged the imputation of inconsistencies and other forms of confusion to profane texts where appropriate, and Herder had extended that principle to sacred texts as well. Schlegel emphasizes and develops this principle still further, not only stressing the importance of acknowledging the presence of confusion in texts when it occurs, but also insisting that in such cases the interpreter must seek to understand and explain it.[60] This principle is valid and important.[61] It is particularly valuable as a corrective to certain misguided ideas about the need for "charity" in interpretation which have become widespread in recent Anglophone philosophy. Some recent theorists of hermeneutics who, by contrast, are in substantial and commendable agreement with Schlegel in insisting on a principle of this sort are Jacques Derrida and Skinner.[62]

A fifth important contribution Schlegel makes to hermeneutics concerns non-linguistic art (music, sculpture, painting, architecture, etc.). He recognizes very clearly that like linguistic texts and discourse non-linguistic art communicates meanings and thoughts, and that it therefore stands equally in need of interpretation. Moreover, he develops a very sophisticated set of principles for accurately interpreting it.[63]

## 5. Hegel

Another thinker who is sometimes held to have played an important role in the development of hermeneutics is Georg Wilhelm Friedrich Hegel (1770–1831). As in the case of Schleiermacher, however, the picture turns out to be equivocal.

Hegel can certainly claim considerable credit for taking over and further developing some of Herder's most important principles concerning the scope and significance of interpretation. As has already been mentioned: He takes over Herder's principles that non-linguistic art (architecture, sculpture, painting, instrumental music, etc.) often expresses meanings and thoughts, and hence stands in need of interpretation; and that the whole mental life of a mature human being is implicitly linguistically articulated, and hence stands in need of interpretation as well. He adds the principles that the socio-political institutions which he calls "Objective Spirit" express meanings and thoughts and hence stand in need of interpretation, and that human actions, as expressions of a mature human being's mental life, do so too. And he accordingly espouses a richer version of Herder's principle that the central task of the discipline of history is an interpretive one. In addition, he adopts a form of Herder's principle that interpreting historical and cultural Others is essential for full *self*-comprehension, both because it makes possible insight into what is distinctive and what by contrast universal in one's own outlook, and because it enables one to understand one's outlook's historical emergence.

But Hegel might also be thought to have achieved important progress on the question of the very nature of interpretation itself. For he makes two moves in this area which sharply contradict previous theorists of hermeneutics and which have exerted strong influence on subsequent theorists (especially Dilthey and Gadamer):

(1) Prior to Hegel hermeneutic theorists assumed that the meaning of a text or discourse was as objective a matter as any other, in particular that it was independent of whatever interpretations of the text or discourse might have taken place since—and that the interpreter's task was therefore to recapture such an original meaning, which in particular required resisting frequent temptations falsely to assimilate it to his own (or other more familiar) meanings and thoughts. Hegel often seems to hold otherwise, however, to *embrace* the assimilation of past meanings to one's own meanings and thoughts. And this Hegelian position has been warmly praised and imitated by Gadamer.[64]

(2) As we have seen, Herder had argued that the expression of meanings and thoughts by non-linguistic art is always in fact parasitic on the artist's capacity to express them linguistically. Hegel denies this, however—in particular arguing that ancient Egyptian architecture and ancient Greek sculpture already expressed meanings and thoughts (of a broadly religious nature) which were not yet linguistically expressible by the cultures in question.[65] This position of Hegel's was subsequently taken over by the later Dilthey (who, having begun his career more favorable to a position like Herder's, apparently absorbed Hegel's position while working on his classic study of the young Hegel, *Die Jugendgeschichte Hegels* [1905]).

Exciting as these two moves are, and influential as they have been, I strongly suspect that they are both errors. Having argued for this view at some length elsewhere,[66] I shall here limit myself to a few brief remarks.

Concerning move (1), Hegel seems to rest his case for this on three main arguments:

(a) All past meanings and thoughts, when interpreted strictly, turn out to be implicitly self-contradictory and hence false, so that we may as well undertake to interpret them charitably as approximate expressions of self-consistent, true Hegelian meanings and thoughts instead.

(b) All past meanings and thoughts can be seen to have been implicitly teleologically directed towards the eventual achievement of Hegelian meanings and thoughts in the modern world.

(c) All mental conditions, including in particular all acts of meaning, are constituted by physical behavior (including linguistic behavior), but in an openended way such that it is always possible, at least as long as a person is alive, for his "past" mental conditions, or acts of meaning, to be modified by his future behavior. Furthermore, meaning is essentially constituted by the linguistic behavior, not merely of an individual, but of a community or communal tradition to which he belongs. Putting these two principles together, it therefore seems that even the acts of meaning of a dead individual from the past are always in principle open to subsequent modification by his communal tradition.

However, these arguments are quite problematic. Note, to begin with, that they seem to be inconsistent with each other. In particular, (a) and (b) seem to be inconsistent with (c), for whereas (a) and (b) presuppose that there *is* such a thing as a determinate original meaning (the point being merely that it always turns out to be self-contradictory, and to be teleologically directed towards the achievement of another, consistent meaning), (c) implies that there is *not*.

But in addition, the arguments face separate problems. For one thing, it surely seems very unlikely in the end that all past (i.e. pre-Hegelian) meanings and thoughts really have been self-contradictory, or that they really have been teleologically directed towards the achievement of Hegelian meanings and thoughts, as (a) and (b) assert. For another thing, both the open-ended behaviorism and the social theory of meaning which serve as the premises in argument (c) turn out to be very dubious. They both conflict sharply with commonsense intuitions. For example, the former (the open-ended behaviorism) conflicts with a commonsense intuition that particular mental conditions sometimes occur which receive no behavioral manifestation at all; with a commonsense intuition that, once a mental condition occurs, its character at the time to which one normally assigns it is then fixed, immune to alteration by whatever behavior may take place subsequently; and with a commonsense intuition that mental conditions cause behavior (rather than being constituted by it). And the latter (the social theory of meaning) conflicts with a commonsense intuition that if, for example, a cosmic Robinson Crusoe, existing all alone in the universe, were to start using chalk marks in a systematic fashion on his cave wall in order to keep a record of his goats and their numbers, then those marks would have meanings. Moreover, the predecessor in the hermeneutic tradition with whom Hegel is most taking issue in (1), namely Herder, had already provided a plausible alternative theory of the nature of mental conditions, including acts of meaning, which, unlike Hegel's theory, can do justice to all of the commonsense intuitions just mentioned: mental conditions, including acts of meaning, are real "forces [*Kräfte*]," i.e. conditions of a subject that are apt to produce certain patterns of behavior but without being reducible to them (hence the "real"). In other words, they are what a philosopher today might call real "dispositions" to behavior.

Concerning move (2), Hegel's evidence for his thesis that certain forms of non-linguistic art express meanings and thoughts which are not yet linguistically articulable by the artist turns out to be dubious on closer inspection. In particular, while Hegel seems clearly right to think that ancient Egyptian architecture expressed religious meanings and thoughts, his conviction that the architects or artists involved were not yet able to express those meanings and thoughts linguistically seems to be little more than an error due to the fact that Hegel and his contemporaries were not yet able to identify any ancient Egyptian linguistic means for expressing them because Egyptian hieroglyphics had not yet been properly deciphered (Champollion only published his pathbreaking *Dictionnaire* and *Grammaire* in 1832, the year after Hegel's death).[67] And Hegel's conviction that Greek sculpture expressed meanings and thoughts that were not yet linguistically expressible flies in the face of a very plausible point which Herder had already made forcefully: that the meanings and thoughts that it expressed were in fact drawn from past poetry, myth, and legend (i.e. from linguistic sources).

In sum, while Hegel makes significant contributions to the question of the scope and significance of interpretation, his more dramatic ideas concerning the very nature of interpretation itself arguably turn out to be misguided.

## 6. Dilthey

Another important theorist of hermeneutics is Wilhelm Dilthey (1833–1911). Like Hegel, Dilthey fails to make progress on the question of the nature of interpretation itself, but he does make a very important contribution to the understanding of its scope and significance.

Dilthey's interest in hermeneutics, especially in Schleiermacher's version of it, began early (his study *Schleiermacher's Hermeneutical System in Relation to Earlier Protestant Hermeneutics* dates from 1860) and remained pronounced throughout his career (for example, his classic essay *The Rise of Hermeneutics* is from 1900).[68]

Ironically, though, both Dilthey's conception of Schleiermacher's theory of interpretation, and his own conception of the nature of interpretation, turn out to be rather naive and unsatisfactory.[69]

Where Dilthey really comes into his own is instead in connection with the question of the *significance* of interpretation. He identifies interpretation as the central task of the human sciences [*Geisteswissenschaften*]—including not only history, but also such further disciplines as literary studies, classical scholarship, anthropology, and art history.[70] His rationale for this position has two sides—one negative, the other positive. Negatively, he is skeptical of the alternative accounts of the main task of the human sciences that have been proposed. In particular, he believes that the scope for *discovering causes and causal laws* in these disciplines is severely limited;[71] and he believes that grand systems which purport to *discover an overall meaning in history* (Hegel's system, for example) are little more than misguided afterechoes of a superseded religious outlook.[72] This leaves the task of interpretation as a sort of default. More positively, Dilthey also argues that the intellectual need for (interpretive) narration is more fundamental than that for (causal) explanation;[73] and that the interpretive achievements of the disciplines in question can enrich our drab lives by acquainting us with types of mental experience that are very different from our own.[74] (This whole rationale for considering interpretation the central task of the human sciences is heavily indebted to one that can already be found scattered throughout Herder's works.[75])

In addition, Dilthey argues—in opposition to Schleiermacher's view that interpretation is not a science but an art—that this interpretive function warrants a claim that the disciplines in question have the status of genuine *sciences*, like the natural sciences. His line of thought here does not usually involve questioning Schleiermacher's position that the method of interpretation is sharply different from that of the natural sciences. Instead, it is usually that, *despite* the difference in method, interpretation can still claim the status of a science, namely for the following two reasons: (1) Its subject-matter, namely the meaning of "expressions," is as objective as that dealt with by the natural sciences (like virtually everyone else in his day, Dilthey takes this for granted).[76] (2) Due to the sorts of deep variations in concepts, beliefs, etc. between different historical periods, cultures, and even individuals that predecessors such as Herder and Schleiermacher had already emphasized, interpretation turns out to be a very *challenging task*, requiring very *rigorous methods*—just like natural science.[77] However, Dilthey also sometimes modifies this usual position in a significant way, *downplaying* the difference in methods between interpretation and the natural sciences, in particular suggesting that induction and hypothesis are central to both.[78] This position is arguably more correct, and furnishes yet a *third* good reason for allowing interpretation the status of science alongside the natural sciences.

## 7. Marx, Nietzsche, Freud: The Hermeneutics of Suspicion

A further important development in hermeneutics that occurred during roughly the same period was the emergence of what Paul Ricoeur has aptly called a "hermeneutics of suspicion," exemplified by Karl Marx (1818–83), Friedrich Nietzsche (1844–1900), and Sigmund Freud (1856–1939).[79] This can be seen as a project of *deepening* the task of interpretation in a certain way, adding new levels to it.

The defining feature of a hermeneutics of suspicion can reasonably be characterized as a thesis that the evident *surface* meanings and thoughts that a person expresses (and perhaps in addition certain aspects of his behavior which at first sight seem meaningless, for example bodily posture or slips of the tongue or pen) often serve as representative-but-also-masking proxies for *deeper* meanings and thoughts which are in some degree hidden (even from the person himself), which are quite different from and indeed often quite contrary to the surface meanings and thoughts involved, and which the person has some sort of motive for concealing in this way (both from others and from himself).

Three examples of such a position are Marx's theory that ideologies are rooted in class interests; Nietzsche's theory that Christian morality, with its overt emphasis on such ideals as "love" and "turning the other cheek," is in fact motivated by hatred and resentment [*Ressentiment*]; and Freud's theory that a broad range of both apparently meaningful and apparently meaningless behaviors express unconscious motives and meanings.

What warrants classifying such theories as forms of *hermeneutics* is the fact that in each case they offer not only deeper *explanations* of the surface meanings and other phenomena involved but deeper explanations in terms of underlying *meanings*.

These theories constitute a major development in the field of hermeneutics— indeed, one too large and important to be dealt with in any detail here. I shall therefore confine myself to making just a few remarks about them.

Marx's commitment to a hermeneutics of suspicion in the sense described above is perhaps the least obvious among the three thinkers mentioned. For Marx usually casts his theory of ideology in terms of underlying *socio-economic contradictions*, or the underlying interests of *socio-economic classes*. However, even so cast, the theory's reference to underlying *interests*—i.e. to something psychological and meaning-laden—already provides at least some basis for classifying it as a hermeneutics of suspicion. Moreover, since, on reflection, it seems plausible to say that class interests cannot be coherently conceived as sharply independent of the interests and motives of the individuals who compose the classes in question, the theory arguably also carries implications concerning the interests and motives of *individuals*.[80] And this points towards a dimension of the theory which makes it even more clearly a hermeneutics of suspicion.

Consider, for example, what for Marx is the very paradigm of an ideology, namely (Christian) religious belief. Marx's account of religious belief is roughly as follows: religious belief serves ruling class interests by defusing the dissatisfactions of the working class on whose oppression the ruling class depends; it does so, in particular, by (1) representing the working class's degraded condition and dissatisfactions in this world as natural and inevitable, part of the very order of things,[81] and (2) providing illusory compensations in the form of fictitious satisfactions in a fictitious other world. It seems to be an implication of this account of religious belief that a hermeneutics of suspicion applies at the level of at least many individual religious believers: that at least in many cases when members of the ruling class hold religious beliefs they do so in part from an underlying, unacknowledged, and rather contrary wish thereby to promote a mechanism which serves their own socio-economic interests at the expense of others'; and that at least in many cases when members of the working class hold religious beliefs they do so in part from an underlying, unacknowledged, and rather contrary wish thereby to see their own socio-economic dissatisfactions palliated.

Turning to Nietzsche, a preliminary point to note is that there is a certain tension in Nietzsche's position on interpretation generally. His usual position, which reflects his own background as a classical philologist, is a conventional assumption that texts mean certain things but not others, and that there is therefore a clear distinction between good and bad interpretation. This is the Nietzsche who in *The Antichrist* (1888) champions "philology" in the sense of "the art of reading well—of reading facts without falsifying them by interpretation, without losing caution, patience, delicacy, in the desire to understand,"[82] and who claims such philology for himself and certain other critics of Christianity,[83] but denies it to Christian theologians.[84] However, there are also some strands in Nietzsche which seem to point towards a much less conventional position—for example, his early hostility to careful philology in *On the Use and Disadvantage of History for Life* (1873) on the grounds that it is inimical to life, and his general perspectivist thesis that "facts is precisely what there is not, only interpretations" (which presumably implies that in particular there are no facts about meanings).[85] In my view, Nietzsche's former position is his better one.[86]

Now to our main topic, Nietzsche's hermeneutics of suspicion. In works such as *The Gay Science* (1882) and *On the Genealogy of Morals* (1887) Nietzsche prominently develops all the central theses of a hermeneutics of suspicion: that beneath a person's superficial conscious meanings (and other behaviors) there lie deeper unconscious meanings; that his superficial conscious meanings (and other behaviors) function as representative-but-also-masking proxies for those deeper unconscious meanings; that the latter are moreover typically contrary to the former; and that the person involved has motives for thus "repressing" or concealing the latter (even from himself).[87]

Furthermore, Nietzsche applies this general model in some very plausible and interesting specific ways. For example, in *On the Genealogy of Morals* he argues that Jesus' explicit, conscious message of love and cheek-turning in fact concealed and represented at a deeper, less conscious level a quite contrary motive of hatred and revenge directed against an oppressive Greek and Roman imperial order, which he shared with his Jewish forebears and contemporaries—[88] a thesis which close scrutiny of the New Testament shows to be highly plausible.[89]

Finally, a few observations about Freud. As I have already implied, Freud's hypothesis of the unconscious, and even of unconscious meanings, was by no means new with him (nor, in fairness, did he claim that it was).[90] Indeed, as we just saw, even the additional features of his theory that turn it into a real hermeneutics of suspicion—his theses that superficial conscious meanings (and other behaviors) function as representative-but-also-masking proxies for those deeper unconscious meanings; that the latter are moreover typically contrary to the former; and that the person involved has motives for thus "repressing" or concealing the latter—had already been developed by Nietzsche.[91] So Freud's claim to real importance in this area largely turns on the plausibility of his specific explanations. (The worry, to put it pointedly, would be that he has merely added to a generic theory inherited from predecessors a lot of false specificity.)

In that connection, the picture is in fact very mixed. Generally speaking, the more ambitious Freud's theory becomes, either in terms of the universality of its claims or in terms of their surprise, the less plausible it tends to be. For example, his position in *The Interpretation of Dreams* (1900) that *all* dreams are explicable as wish-fulfillment seems very implausible indeed.[92] So does his similar position concerning *all* poetry in *The Relation of the Poet to Day-Dreaming* (1908). So does his position in *The Interpretation of Dreams* and elsewhere that an "Oedipus Complex" plays a pervasive role in human psychology.[93] So does his position in *The Future of an Illusion* (1927) that all religion arises from an infantile longing for a protective father. So does his position in *Moses and Monotheism* (1939) that the Judeo-Christian tradition in particular arose out of, and replays, the trauma of a pre-historical murder of a "primal father" by other male members of his tribe.

By contrast, where Freud's theory becomes more flexible and intuitive in character—for example, in *The Psychopathology of Everyday Life* (1901), where his explanations of "parapraxes" such as slips of the tongue or pen and acts of forgetting are quite various in nature, and usually rather intuitive (for instance, in terms of repressed sexual impulses and feelings of aggression)—they are proportionally more plausible.

So much for Freud's attempts to *deepen* interpretation in a hermeneutics of suspicion. Another aspect of Freud's position deserves emphasis here as well, though. This is its *broadening* of interpretation to include, not only phenomena that are usually regarded as expressing meanings and thoughts and hence as interpretable (for example, literature), but also many phenomena that are not usually seen in such a light at all (for example, neurotic behaviors, parapraxes, and what we would today call body language), or which are at least usually seen as expressing meanings and thoughts only in an obvious and trivial way and hence as scarcely requiring or deserving interpretation (for example, dreams and jokes).[94] This move seems very plausible. It significantly extends a broadening trend in hermeneutics which we have already encountered in such predecessors as Herder and Hegel.

## 8. Heidegger

At this point in history, namely the early twentieth century, real progress in hermeneutics virtually comes to an end in Germany, and indeed in continental Europe as a whole, it seems to me (in keeping with a precipitous decline in the quality of German philosophy generally at the time).[95] However, there are several further continental thinkers who are commonly *thought* to have made major contributions to the subject, including three who are bound together by ties both of influence and of shared views: Martin Heidegger (1889–1976), Hans-Georg Gadamer (1900–2002), and Jacques Derrida (1930–2004). One fundamental view which they all share, and which they can be commended for sharing, is a—probably correct—conviction, continuous with Herder and Schleiermacher, that all meaning and thought are essentially dependent on language.

Martin Heidegger has undoubtedly had a strong influence on the course of hermeneutics in the twentieth century. But the value of his contributions to the subject has been greatly exaggerated, in my view.

One of Heidegger's key ideas, developed in *Being and Time* (1927), paragraphs 31–4, is that the understanding of meanings, and hence also the possession of language, are fundamental and pervasive modes of the existence of *Dasein*, or Man. However, as we have already seen, this (certainly very plausible and important) point essentially just repeats an insight that was originally developed by Herder in his *Treatise on the Origin of Language* and elsewhere, and then taken over by Hegel.

Another of Heidegger's key ideas, found in the same paragraphs of *Being and Time*, develops an aspect of that first idea in a more specific way: fundamental and pervasive in *Dasein*, or Man, is a sort of "pre-understanding [*Vorverständnis*]" that essentially underpins explicit linguistic understanding, and that is involved, for example, even in cases of perceptual or active engagement with the world in which explicit linguistic articulation is absent. Versions or variants of this idea have been fundamental to other twentieth-century German hermeneutic theories related to Heidegger's as well, in particular those of Rudolf Bultmann and Gadamer.

Now it seems likely that this principle is correct in some form, and also important. In particular, as I hinted earlier in this essay, I think that one should be skeptical about what is likely to be the main source of theoretical resistance to it, especially in the Anglophone world, namely a Fregean–Wittgensteinian tradition of anti-psychologism about meaning, which denies that psychological states or processes play any essential role in semantic understanding, on the grounds that semantic understanding instead consists purely in grasping a quasi-Platonic sense (Frege) or in possessing linguistic competence (later Wittgenstein).[96]

However, Heidegger's principle is again much less original than it may seem. In particular, it is quite similar to Herder's quasi-empiricist principle in the philosophy of language (described above). Its claim to novelty as compared to Herder's principle rests mainly on two features: (1) Heidegger, and following him Gadamer, would be loath to equate pre-understanding with something as subjective as the possession of sensations, since it is an essential goal of their philosophies to overcome the subject-object dichotomy (in a *Dasein* or a "Life World" that bridges and transcends it). (2) Heidegger, and following him Gadamer, would claim that pre-understanding is more fundamentally a matter of active engagement with the world than of theoretical contemplation of it, more fundamentally a matter of the world being "ready-to-hand [*zuhanden*]" than of its being "present-at-hand [*vorhanden*]"—

which might seem to contrast sharply with Herder's conception in his *Treatise on the Origin of Language* that an attitude of theoretical detachment, which he calls "awareness [*Besonnenheit*]" or "reflection [*Reflexion*]," is fundamental to and distinctive of human language.[97] However, it is quite doubtful that these two features really constitute a large difference from and advance over Herder. Note to begin with that they would at least leave Heidegger and Gadamer's position belonging to the same general family as Herder's, constituting only a sort of family dispute within it. Moreover, feature (1) rests on a very questionable philosophical theory. And feature (2) is arguably much closer to Herder's position than it may seem. For, on closer inspection, Herder's position in the *Treatise on the Origin of Language* in fact appears to be the very similar one that the detached "awareness" or "reflection" that is fundamental to and distinctive of human language emerges from a background of active engagement with the world which human beings share in common with the animals.

Finally, Heidegger is also famous for espousing a principle that, especially when interpreting philosophy, "every interpretation must necessarily use violence."[98] This principle hovers between two points, one of which is valid and important, the other of which is more questionable, but neither of which is original. One thing Heidegger has in mind here is a version of Schlegel's insight that texts often convey meanings and thoughts which they do not express explicitly.[99] That is a valid and important point, but unoriginal. Another thing Heidegger has in mind, though, is something more like the idea that one should interpret texts in the light of what one takes to be the correct position on the issues with which it deals and as attempting to express that position, even if there is no real textual evidence that the author had the meanings or thoughts in question in mind, and indeed even if there is textual evidence that he did not. This idea is again unoriginal—in particular, earlier versions of it can already be found in Kant,[100] and in Hegel (as discussed above). Concerning its value, much depends on exactly how it is conceived, and exactly how implemented. Provided that it is not meant to exclude more textually scrupulous forms of interpretation, that the person who applies it is clear about what he is doing (both in general and at specific points in his interpretation), that he makes this equally clear to his readers, and that the quality of his own opinions concerning the subject-matter involved is sufficiently high to make the exercise worthwhile, then there is probably no harm in it, and there may even be a little good.[101] However, in practice these conditions are rarely met, and in particular it is far from clear that Heidegger himself meets them.

## 9. Gadamer

The most influential twentieth-century German theorist of hermeneutics, though, was Heidegger's student Hans-Georg Gadamer. Gadamer's discussions of hermeneutics in *Truth and Method* (1960) and elsewhere are certainly learned and thoughtful, and can be read with profit. But what is distinctive in his position is, I think, misguided and indeed baneful.

Gadamer rejects the traditional assumption that texts have an original meaning which is independent of whatever interpretations of them may have occurred subsequently, and which it is the interpreter's task to recapture. Instead, Gadamer conceives meaning as something that only arises in the interaction between texts and an indefinitely expanding and changing interpretive tradition. Consequently, he denies that interpretation should seek to recapture a supposed original meaning, and instead holds that it must and should incorporate an orientation to distinctive features of the interpreter's own outlook and to the distinctive application that he envisages making of the text in question.

Despite the strong generic similarity between this position and the Hegelian one discussed earlier, which Gadamer holds up as its inspiration, Gadamer's arguments for it are different from Hegel's.

A central part of Gadamer's case consists in a large family of exhortations that we should assimilate interpretation, in the sense of achieving *understanding* of a text, discourse, etc., to various other sorts of activities from which, prima facie at least, and almost certainly also in fact, it is crucially different—in particular, *explicating* or *applying* a text, discourse, etc.; *translating* it into another language; *conversation* aimed at achieving agreement; *legal "interpretation"*; and *re-presenting* a work of (theatrical or musical) art. These Gadamerian exhortations hardly amount to an argument, however. Rather, they are just invitations to a nest of serious confusions—and should be firmly refused.

Gadamer does also offer several somewhat more substantial arguments, though, in particular the following four:

(a) Both in the case of linguistic and non-linguistic art and in the case of linguistic texts and discourse more generally, interpretations change over time, and these changing interpretations are internal to the meaning of the art, text, or discourse in question, so that there is after all no such thing as an original meaning independent of these changing interpretations.[102]

(b) The original meaning of artistic and linguistic expressions from the past is always strictly speaking unknowable by us due to the essential role played in all understanding by a historically specific form of "pre-understanding" or "prejudice" which one can never entirely escape.[103]

(c) The original meaning is something "dead," something no longer of any possible interest to us.[104]

(d) *All* knowledge is historically relative, so interpretive knowledge is so in particular.[105]

But how convincing are these arguments? A first point to note is that arguments (a)–(c) seem to be inconsistent with each other: argument (a) says that there is no such thing as an "original meaning," whereas arguments (b) and (c) imply that there is (but that it is unknowable and "dead"); argument (b) says that it is unknowable, whereas argument (c) implies that it is knowable (but "dead," of no possible interest to us). However, since the arguments also face separate problems, I shall not here dwell any further on this problem of their mutual inconsistency.

Argument (a) seems to be implicitly incoherent. Consider the case of texts, for example. To say that interpretations of a text change over time is presumably to say, roughly, that the author of the text meant such and such, that there then arose an interpretation A which meant something a bit different from that, that there then arose a further interpretation B which meant something a bit different again, and so on. In other words, the very notion of changing interpretations *presupposes* an original meaning (indeed, a whole *series* of original meanings, one belonging to the text, and then one belonging to each of its subsequent interpretations).[106] Moreover, as far as I can see, Gadamer has no real argument to begin with for his surely very counterintuitive claim that subsequent (re)interpretations are internal to an author's meaning. In particular, the mere facts (both emphasized by Gadamer in this connection) that (re)interpretations occur, and that authors often expect and even welcome this, by no means suffice to justify it.

Argument (b) runs into an epistemological problem. For if one were always locked into a modifying pre-understanding, then how could one even know that other perspectives undergoing modification existed?[107] Moreover, as I have argued elsewhere, this sort of epistemological problem eventually leads to a conceptual one as well: a problem about whether in that case it would even make *sense* to speak of such perspectives.[108] Furthermore, Gadamer's assumption that pre-understanding is internal to understanding and that it is always historically specific in an epistemically insurmountable way is very questionable to begin with. One objection to it which many Anglophone philosophers are likely to find attractive is that the conception that pre-understanding is internal to understanding violates an anti-psychologistic insight about meaning and understanding which we owe to Frege and Wittgenstein. But, as I have already mentioned, such anti-psychologism in fact seems quite dubious on reflection, so it is not on *this* ground that I would question Gadamer's assumption. Nor would I question its idea that pre-understandings are historically specific (that too seems true). Rather, I would suggest that what is really wrong with it is its implication that such historical specificity is epistemically insurmountable, that it is impossible to abstract from one's own specific pre-understanding and recapture the specific pre-understanding of a historical Other. Indeed, I would suggest that Herder's conception that *Einfühlung* ("feeling one's way in") plays an essential role in the interpretation of texts from the past already quite properly pointed towards an ability that we possess to perform just this sort of imaginative feat, and towards the essential contribution that exercising this ability makes to our attainment of an exact understanding of past texts' original meanings.

Argument (c) is one of the weakest parts of Gadamer's case. Far from inevitably being "dead," or of no possible interest to us, the original meanings of texts and discourse from the past, and from contemporary Others, can be of *great* interest to us, and for *many* different reasons (a number of which had already been pointed out by Gadamer's predecessors). One reason (which Herder and Dilthey had already noted) is simply that the discovery of such meanings and of the views they articulate satisfies our intellectual curiosity and enriches our experience. Another reason (again already important to Herder) is that it expresses our respect and sympathy for Others and promotes the same attitudes among our contemporaries. Another reason (again already important to Herder) is that it promises to acquaint us with concepts, convictions, values, techniques, and so on which can help us to improve our own in various ways. Another reason (again already important to Herder) is that it makes an essential contribution to our *self*-understanding, both by enabling us to see our own perspective in a comparative light and by enabling us to understand how it arose. And no doubt there are many further good reasons as well.[109]

Finally, argument (d) is unconvincing as well. One problem with it lies in the well-known fact that the thesis of relativism seems to run into problems of self-contradiction in connection with the awkward question of whether this thesis is *itself* of merely relative validity. Gadamer touches on this problem at various points, but his answers to it are naive and unconvincing. In one place he concedes that a self-contradiction arises here, but responds that this merely shows the weakness of the sort of "reflection" that reveals this and objects to it![110] In another place he argues that the thesis of relativism is not "propositional" but merely something of which one has "consciousness," so that it and its own subject-matter are "not at all on the same logical level."[111] But surely, the alleged circumstance that what is involved here is merely a consciousness that relativism is true, rather than, say, an explicit assertion that it is true, would not diminish either the fact or the unacceptability of the self-contradiction one whit.

Another problem with the argument is that, contrary to Gadamer's clear wish to claim that meaning's relativity to interpretations makes it distinctive in comparison with other subject-matters, such as those dealt with by the natural sciences, and consequently resistant to the sorts of methods that can legitimately be used in connection with other subject-matters, in particular the "positivist," or objectivity-presupposing, methods of the natural sciences, this argument would leave meaning *no less (if also no more) objective than anything else.*

In short, Gadamer fails to provide any good argument at all for his surely very counterintuitive position.[112] The position is therefore in all probability false. Moreover, if it *is* false, then it is so in a way that is likely to prove baneful for interpretive practice. For it actively encourages (as allegedly inevitable and hence appropriate) just the sort of assimilation in interpretation of the meanings and thoughts of (historical or cultural) Others to the interpreter's own that it was one of the most important achievements of earlier theorists of hermeneutics such as Herder and Schleiermacher to identify as a constant temptation and to outlaw.[113] (A similar point applies to conceptions in recent Anglophone philosophy—for example, the work of Donald Davidson—that it is necessary to use "charity" in interpretation.[114])

## 10. Derrida

Another twentieth-century continental thinker who has been very influential in hermeneutics is the French philosopher Jacques Derrida.[115] However, here again performance falls some way short of promise.

Derrida encapsulates his theory of meaning and interpretation in such concepts as those of an open-ended "iterability"—a word which he uses in the double sense of *other* and *again*—and "difference"—a word which he uses in the double sense of *differing* and *deferring*.[116] In its former, synchronic aspect, this is largely just a cryptic way of repeating Saussure's important point that meaning only arises through a system of linguistic oppositions.[117] In its latter, diachronic aspect, it is largely just a cryptic way of repeating Gadamer's conception that meaning is something that only arises through an open-ended process of (re) interpretation.[118] Derrida provides even less of an argument for this surely very counterintuitive conception than Gadamer does, however (and as we have seen, Gadamer's own arguments for it are woefully inadequate).[119]

Derrida also has a number of more interesting ideas about interpretation, though. One of these is a thesis that texts, especially philosophical texts, typically contain hidden contradictions, which interpretation should reveal (Derrida famously calls this revelation "deconstruction," and practices it on many philosophers from the tradition, including for instance Rousseau and Hegel).[120] This thesis is true of many texts, including philosophical ones, and is important. The thesis is not new; in particular, Schlegel had already articulated it, and had indeed already applied it to philosophers. But Derrida's commitment to it is at least superior to dubious contrary ideas about the need to exercise interpretive "charity," and in particular to avoid imputing logical inconsistencies to texts, which are currently widespread among Anglophone philosophers and historians of philosophy.[121]

Another interesting idea of Derrida's (shared with several other French theorists who are similarly influenced by structuralist linguistics, including Roland Barthes and Michel Foucault) concerns what is sometimes called the "death of the author," or in other words the alleged erroneousness of imputing what is expressed in a text to an individual author and his intentions.[122] This idea involves a huge exaggeration, for much of what is expressed in texts *is* imputable to authors and their intentions. But it is at least a useful counterweight to equally one-sided author-centered positions which ignore the large role played in texts by inherited linguistic conventions, borrowed formulas and tropes, and so on. Avoiding both the Scylla and the Charybdis here—or in other words, recognizing that texts involve neither just "individuality" nor just "universality," but a *synthesis* of the two—had in fact already been a driving and noteworthy ambition behind Schleiermacher's position in hermeneutics.[123]

Finally, Derrida is also significant for advocating "decentering" in interpretation. He evidently means different things by this in different contexts. Sometimes he merely means acknowledging the (alleged) situation that there is never a discrete, pre-given meaning to interpret due to the sort of situation that Saussure and Gadamer had described.[124] But sometimes he rather means reading texts with a focus on aspects which the texts themselves present as of only marginal importance (for example, aspects that carry an implicit political or social ideology).[125] Such readings can indeed sometimes be legitimate and illuminating.

## 11. Austin and Skinner

A far more important contribution to the development of hermeneutics than any made by Heidegger, Gadamer, or Derrida is due to several recent theorists from the Anglophone world, especially John Langshaw Austin (1911–1960)[126] and Quentin Skinner (1941–present).[127] Their contribution lies in recognizing the central role that *illocutionary force* plays in texts and discourse, and hence in their interpretation.[128] (This role can be seen as a further vindication of Herder's basic intuition that linguistic interpretation needs to be complemented with psychological interpretation.)

In order to see that interpretation requires the identification not only of linguistic meaning but also of something like illocutionary force, consider the following example (loosely borrowed from Skinner). If I encounter a stranger by a frozen lake who says to me "The ice is thin over there," I may understand the meaning of his words perfectly, and yet still not fully comprehend what he has said—for in order to do so I would in addition need to know whether he was simply informing me, warning me, joking (for example, by stating the obvious), threatening me (for example, by alluding to the expression "You're skating on thin ice"), or whatnot.

I say "something like" illocutionary force because in order usefully to employ this concept originally introduced by Austin,[129] one probably needs to drop from it certain implications that he built into it. In particular, one probably needs to drop his restriction of it to cases where there are corresponding "performatives" (it does not seem helpful to include here only such linguistic acts as promising, telling, and commanding, but to exclude such linguistic acts as joking and insinuating, simply on the grounds that one can promise, tell, and command by saying "I promise," "I tell [you]," and "I command [you]" but one cannot joke by saying "I joke" or insinuate by saying "I insinuate").[130] And one probably also needs to drop his inclusion of "uptake" by other people in his definition of an illocutionary act (there is indeed a sense of, for example, "to tell" in which it is a success word, so that one only tells someone if he actually hears and understands what one tells him, but there is surely also another and equally important sense of the word in which one may tell someone even if he fails to hear and/or fails to understand).[131] The really crucial point is just that there are clearly aspects of any intelligible writing or discourse which are additional to its linguistic meaning, and which must be identified as well in order for full comprehension of the writing or discourse in question to occur (aspects which can at least be defined by giving examples, such as the ones already mentioned in passing—informing, warning, etc.).

However, there are also some important further features of this situation which have been overlooked or even denied by the theorists mentioned and their followers, and which complicate the interpreter's task here still more. One of these is the fact that—despite Austin's, and especially John Searle's, resistance to the point,[132] but in accordance with a hint of Wittgenstein's—[133] the number of possible different illocutionary forces seems to be indefinitely large.[134] This raises the prospect, and the potential challenge, for an interpreter that he may on occasion encounter an illocutionary force with which he is unfamiliar, and which he therefore needs not merely to select correctly from a range of already understood types but to interpret in the first place in order for its selection to become possible.

A second further feature of the situation which complicates the interpreter's task here is that in some cases the divergence of a newly encountered illocutionary force from any with which he is yet familiar may take the more specific and subtler form of similarity to one with which he is already familiar but with significant differences (so that he might eventually be inclined to say, not that the alien people involved employ an entirely unfamiliar type of illocutionary force, but rather that they, for example, have a somewhat different practice and concept of "assertion" than ours).[135] In its own way, this situation may be even more challenging for an interpreter than the former one, because it insidiously tempts him falsely to assimilate the illocutionary force in question to one with which he is already familiar.

These two additional challenges facing the interpreter in connection with illocutionary forces are precisely analogous to ones which Herder and Schleiermacher already identified as facing him in connection with *concepts* and *genres*.

## 12. Some New Horizons

The points just made constitute a potential new horizon for hermeneutics. Let me conclude this article by briefly mentioning two more.

The linguist Roman Jakobson has written that "a faculty of speaking a given language implies a faculty of talking about this language...a 'metalinguistic' operation."[136] This is probably not *strictly* correct; in particular, "implies" seems too strong a word, since one can at least coherently imagine forms of language-use which lack a metalinguistic component.[137] However, as an empirical matter language-use does usually include such a component. And this fact is important and interesting.

Discourse and texts often make *explicit* use of semantic terms: we talk or write about the specific meanings of words, about words being meaningful rather than meaningless, about words sharing the same meaning (being synonyms) rather than having different meanings, and so on. But this is only the explicit tip of a much larger iceberg, for semantic concepts also play a large implicit role in the construction of discourse and texts, and (at the receiving end) in their interpretation. One example of this is the common occurrence of puns and other word-plays in texts such as Homer's *Odyssey* (with its famous "Nobody [*Outis*]" episode, for instance) or Shakespeare's *Romeo and Juliet*. In order to compose such features of a text the author needs to think fairly consciously about the meanings of the words involved *as such*, and in order fully to understand him an interpreter needs to recapitulate those thoughts. Another example is texts governed by a strong aesthetic of avoiding unmotivated word-repetitions (Shakespeare's plays are again a case in point). In order to compose such a text, an author frequently needs to look for (near-)synonyms so as to avoid word-repetitions, and in order to interpret such a text accurately an interpreter needs to recognize that this is what is going on, and that, for instance, the author's shift in two adjacent lines from one word to another, nearly synonymous word therefore primarily has this sort of aesthetic significance rather than a semantic one. Another example is virtually any discourse or text that strives for a high degree of semantic or poetic precision (Shakespeare's plays are again a case in point). For this requires the author to reflect on, and compare, the semantic properties of various alternative words which are available to him, and full interpretation of such a text requires the interpreter to recapitulate those reflections and comparisons to a significant extent.

Now if there were just a *single* concept of meaning, meaningfulness/meaninglessness, sameness of meaning/difference of meaning, etc. common to all historical periods and cultures, then this situation would present only a modest challenge to an interpreter. But such concepts in fact vary significantly from period to period, culture to culture, and perhaps even individual to individual.[138] And this makes the situation a lot more challenging. For it raises the prospect that, besides the sort of first-order incommensurability between the explicit conceptual subject-matter of a discourse or text and the closest concepts initially available to the interpreter which has been recognized as a major challenge for interpretation at least since Ernesti, there will also sometimes be a sort of hidden second-order incommensurability concerning the semantic concepts which implicitly articulate the discourse or text. Consequently, in order fully to understand the alien discourse or text in such cases, the interpreter will need (in addition to his other tasks) to recapture the author's distinctive semantic concepts and then construe the author's implicit (as well as explicit) deployments of them accordingly.

Another new (or at least somewhat new) horizon for hermeneutics involves a further expansion of the *scope* of interpretation, namely beyond its traditional focus on human language-use. So far this article has been exclusively concerned with human beings. But what about animals? In recent years a wealth of fascinating research has been done into animal language-use, which turns out to be surprisingly extensive and sophisticated, both among certain animals in their natural state (for example, vervet monkeys with their differentiated alarm cries)[139] and among certain animals trained in language-use by human beings (for example, bonobo apes).[140] Philosophers have for the most part been slow and reluctant to recognize this situation, tending instead (in continuity with a long philosophical tradition that was originally rooted in religious assumptions) to look for reasons to deny that animal language is real language, or at least to claim that it is essentially different from human language.[141] However, the reasons they have given have not been very convincing (most of the criteria they have proposed in order to justify the discrimination turn out to be either arbitrary-looking or in fact satisfied by at least some animal language-use or in many cases both). We therefore probably need to recognize that some animals do indeed use language.[142] And that of course implies a corresponding task of *interpreting* it. Nor should it be assumed that the fact that animal language-use is going to be in some sense more "primitive" than ours ensures that such a task will be an easy or trivial one. As can be seen from anthropologists' attempts to interpret more "primitive" language-use by other *human beings*, if anything the opposite may well turn out to be the case.

Reflection on the case of animals also suggests the need for another sort of broadening of the scope of interpretation, and perhaps a modest modification in the very nature of interpretation. Animals' capacities for classifying perceptual experiences and for certain sorts of intellection (for instance, recognizing predators or prey) often far outstrip their capacities for linguistic expression (even when they do happen to use language), instead finding manifestation in other forms of behavior.[143] A similar point applies to human infants (as Jean Piaget and his followers have shown). We should arguably resist the temptation to describe such cases as involving meaning or thinking in the strict sense (thereby avoiding a conflict with Herder's first two principles in the philosophy of language). But, if so, we at least need to acknowledge that they are very similar to meaning and thinking, and moreover that they constitute the evolutionary and individual foundations for these (we might therefore describe them as proto-meaning and proto-thinking). Accordingly, they also call for a type of *interpretation* (or if one prefers to reserve this term for the identification of meanings and thoughts proper, then "interpretation") in many ways similar to that which we apply to language. For example, if a certain animal's regular behavior of fleeing at the sight of predators provides evidence of its possession of some sort of proto-concept of a predator, then questions can be pursued concerning the more exact nature of that proto-concept, for instance concerning its exact extension (precisely which types of animals, or which types of animals in which types of situations, provoke this flight response and which not?). And a similar point applies to human infants.

The Ernesti-Herder-Schleiermacher tradition in hermeneutics can be helpful in this area. For example, the tradition's core procedure of accumulating actual uses of a word in order to infer from these to the rule for use that is governing them would be applicable to animal language-use, and would also have a close analogue in the sort of non-verbal case just described. And a version of the tradition's warning against falsely assimilating alien concepts to superficially similar ones with which the interpreter happens already to be familiar would be salutary in both of these sorts of cases as well.

In sum, the development of hermeneutics—both as it concerns the nature of interpretation itself and as it concerns the scope and significance of interpretation—is still very much an ongoing process.

## Notes

1. Concerning the history of hermeneutics in general, and the role of the Reformation in particular, see W. Dilthey, *Schleiermacher's Hermeneutical System in Relation to Earlier Protestant Hermeneutics* (1860) and *The Rise of Hermeneutics* (1900), both in his *Hermeneutics and the Study of History* (Princeton, NJ: Princeton University Press, 1996).

2. This is roughly the view held by the German scholar of hermeneutics Manfred Frank, for example.

3. This is roughly the view held by Gadamer himself. It is also reflected in such works as R.E. Palmer, *Hermeneutics* (Evanston, Ill.: Northwestern University Press, 1969).

4. One of the more unusual and confusing features of modern hermeneutics lies in the fact that many of its most prominent thinkers tend to suppress rather than to celebrate the intellectual influences on them. Accordingly, one of the tasks of this essay will be to try to bring some of these influences to light—in particular, Herder's influence on Schleiermacher, Nietzsche's on Freud, Nietzsche's on Gadamer, and Gadamer's on Derrida.

5. *Ernesti's Institutes*, ed. C.H. Terrot (Edinburgh: Thomas Clark, 1832), 1:30–2, 127. A step of this sort was also taken at around the same time by other progressive Bible scholars in Germany, such as Michaelis, Semler, and Wettstein.

6. Ibid., 2:1–4.

7. Ibid., 1:36, 38.

8. Ibid., 1:56–7.

9. Ibid., 1:63–4. Ernesti identifies the language of the New Testament as a good example of this (cf. 1:121–3).

10. Ibid., 1:27, 63.

11. Ernesti did not himself go this far. Instead, he still conceived meaning, in continuity with the tradition of British Empiricism (especially Locke), as a matter of a regular connection between words and *ideas* (see e.g. ibid., 1:15–17, 27).

12. See on this Dilthey, *Schleiermacher's Hermeneutical System*, pp. 67, 73–4.

13. *Ernesti's Institutes*, 1:210, 2:260–2. This move was again shared by other progressive Bible scholars in Germany from the period, for example Semler and Michaelis.

14. Hermeneutics threatened to go full circle on this issue in the first half of the twentieth century with the de-contextualizing position of the New Critics. But fortunately that particular piece of retrograde foolishness has receded into abeyance again.

15. This principle was not altogether new with Ernesti.

16. *Ernesti's Institutes*, 1:70–1.

17. Ibid., 1:74.

18. Ibid., 1:70–1.

19. See esp. his early works on biblical interpretation and his *Critical Forests* (1769).

20. See esp. his *This Too a Philosophy of History for the Formation of Humanity* (1774).

21. See esp. his *On Thomas Abbt's Writings* (1768) and *On the Cognition and Sensation of the Human Soul* (1778).

22. Herder also in a way believes the converse. For he holds that the sensations of a mature human being are essentially grounded in meanings, and hence in language. This, together with his idea of metaphorical extensions, distinguishes his position in principle (3) from that of a traditional empiricist like Hume. I shall therefore describe it as quasi-empiricist.

23. For some further details concerning these three principles and their consequences for interpretation, see *After Herder*, Essays 1, 2, and 4.

24. Schleiermacher's debt is most straightforward in connection with (1) and (2). His variant of (3) lies in his mature theory that concepts consist in empirical schemata, or rules for the production of images.

25. See esp. Herder's *On Thomas Abbt's Writings* and *On the Cognition and Sensation of the Human Soul*.

26. *Pace* recent French theories of "the death of the author."

27. With just a little interpretive charity, Herder and Schleiermacher can indeed be seen as already hinting at these two additional rationales. For example, Herder arguably anticipates the idea of implicit holistic meanings in the *Critical Forests*. And Schleiermacher arguably anticipates that of illocutionary force or intention (see F.D.E. Schleiermacher, *Hermeneutics*

*and Criticism* [Cambridge: Cambridge University Press, 1998], pp. 229, 254, as discussed in *After Herder*, Essay 11).

28. See esp. *On Thomas Abbt's Writings* and *On the Cognition and Sensation of the Human Soul*.

29. As a linguistic clue to understanding Herder and Schleiermacher's conception of "divination," the French verb *deviner* (to guess, to conjecture) is more helpful than the Latin adjective *divinus* (of a god, prophetic).

30. This conception arguably requires a little modification. For example, sometimes a genre is constituted by *multiple* purposes. See *After Herder*, Essay 5.

31. For example, ancient Greek "tragedy" is not really the same genre as Shakespearean "tragedy," Shakespeare's "tragedy" not quite the same genre as Ben Jonson's "tragedy," and indeed the genre of "tragedy" even varies between some of Shakespeare's own "tragic" works. Herder also countenances the possibility of a genre being found in just a single work by an author. That might seem incoherent at first sight, but it is in fact not. For, as Boeckh would later go on to point out explicitly, what is essential to a genre is not multiple instantia*tion*, but only multiple instantia*bility*.

32. See on all this esp. Herder's classic essay *Shakespeare* from 1773 (in its several drafts).

33. See, for example, his discussion of ancient Egyptian vs. ancient Greek portrait sculpture in *This Too A Philosophy of History for the Formation of Humanity*.

34. Boeckh thus includes generic interpretation among the four fundamental types or aspects of interpretation that he distinguishes (along with historical, linguistic, and individual [i.e. what Schleiermacher called psychological] interpretation). Boeckh seems to credit the Schlegels as the main innovators in this area. But Herder has a stronger claim to such a title.

35. See *After Herder*, Essay 3 and in the present volume Essays 6 and 7.

36. See esp. *Treatise on the Origin of Language* and *On the Cognition and Sensation of the Human Soul*.

37. See e.g. Hegel, *Encyclopedia* (1830), pars. 2, 24 (Zusatz 1), and 462 (Zusatz), which argue that all human mental life is imbued with thought and that thought is impossible without language; also, and especially, the preface to the 1832 edition of the *Science of Logic*.

38. See M. Heidegger, *Being and Time* (Oxford: Blackwell, 1978), pars. 31–4. Reading through *Being and Time*, one might initially wonder whether Heidegger considers the understanding of meanings in question here essentially to involve language, for his opening discussion of the matter at pars. 31–2 focuses on understanding and meaning alone. However, he goes

on at par. 34 to make it clear that language *is* essentially involved (and the later Heidegger is even more emphatic on this point).

39. For a little more discussion of this whole subject, see Essay 7.

40. For some more details, see *After Herder*, Essay 1.

41. For more on this subject, see my "Genealogy and Morality."

42. This is a prominent theme in the *Fragments on Recent German Literature* (1767–8), for example.

43. This is a prominent theme in the *Popular Songs* [*Volkslieder*] (1774/8), for example.

44. F.D.E. Schleiermacher, *Hermeneutics and Criticism* and *Hermeneutics: The Handwritten Manuscripts* (Atlanta: Scholars Press, 1986).

45. These doctrines can all be found in the two works cited in the previous note.

46. Doctrine (i) is prominent in the hermeneutics lectures; doctrines (ii) and (iii) are especially prominent in Schleiermacher's essay *On the Different Methods of Translation* (1813). Note that Friedrich Schlegel had already developed a version of doctrine (iii) in his seminal work *On the Language and Wisdom of the Indians* (1808).

47. See on this K. Vorländer, *Geschichte der Philosophie* (Hamburg: Felix Meiner, 1975), 3/1:58–9.

48. For further discussion of Schleiermacher's hermeneutics, see *After Herder*, Essays 10 and 11.

49. Concerning this question, see J. Körner, "Friedrich Schlegels 'Philosophie der Philologie,'" and H. Patsch, "Friedrich Schlegels 'Philosophie der Philologie' und Schleiermachers frühe Entwürfe zur Hermeneutik."

50. *Athenaeum Fragments* (1798–1800), in F. Schlegel, *Philosophical Fragments*, no. 111: "The teachings that a novel hopes to instill must be of the sort that can be communicated only as wholes, not demonstrated singly and not subject to exhaustive analysis" (cf. no. 325).

51. Schlegel writes, loosely quoting a famous fragment from Heraclitus: "But Apollo, who neither speaks nor keeps silent but intimates, no longer is worshipped, and wherever a Muse shows herself, people immediately want to carry her off to be cross-examined" (ibid., no. 325).

52. See Schlegel's reference to modern novels in the note before last.

53. It is a further question whether or not the meanings and thoughts involved *could* in principle have been linguistically expressed by the artist in the usual way. In the passage quoted a few notes back from *Athenaeum Fragments*, no. 111 Schlegel seems to imply that at least sometimes they could not have been. But if so, then this is really a further thesis on his part. Hence this point *need* not stand in any tension with Herder's doctrines

that meaning is word-usage and that thought is essentially dependent on and bounded by language. Nor is it clear that insofar as such a tension does arise it need amount to a contradiction.

54. That this message is not merely being read into the text here but is intended by the poet is confirmed by a famous episode in *Odyssey*, book 5 in which the fair nymph Calypso invites Odysseus to stay with her as her consort and become immortal as she is, but he (the most intelligent man in all of Homer, note!) declines the invitation, choosing instead to return to Ithaca and his aging wife Penelope as a mere mortal and eventually to die.

55. *On Goethe's Meister* (1798), in *Friedrich Schlegel 1794–1802. Seine prosaischen Jugendschriften*, 2:177.

56. *Athenaeum Fragments*, no. 401. Schleiermacher uses the formula of understanding an author better than he understands himself as well, but he means something much less ambitious by it than Schlegel—roughly, just that the sorts of rules of word-usage and grammar which the native speaker of a language masters implicitly should be known explicitly by his interpreter—and is in general relatively reluctant to impute unconscious mental processes to people.

57. Schlegel has certain specific ways of developing it which are more questionable, though. In particular, he conceives this situation less as a matter of properties that belong to an author than as a matter of ones that belong to his text (a position which would no doubt find favor with recent French theorists of "the death of the author," but perhaps not correctly), and that are moreover "infinite" or divine in nature. (See Patsch, "Friedrich Schlegels 'Philosophie der Philologie,'" pp. 456–9.)

58. Derrida has aptly criticized certain Freudian readings of literature on the score of such arbitrariness. For a helpful discussion of his criticisms, see Matthew Sharpe's treatment in *Understanding Derrida*, pp. 67 ff.

59. As in the case of Schlegel's second point, it might be thought that this third point stands in tension with Herder's principles in the philosophy of language that meaning is word-usage and that thought is essentially dependent on and bounded by language. However, once again this at least need not be the case. For it could be that the unconscious meanings and thoughts in question are always ones that an author has the linguistic capacity to express (as Lacan seems to hold).

60. Schlegel already writes in about 1797: "In order to understand someone, one must first of all be cleverer than he, then just as clever, and then also just as stupid. It is not enough that one understand the actual sense of a confused work better than the author understood it. One must also oneself

be able to know, to *characterize*, and even *construe* the confusion even down to its very principles" (KFSA 18:63).

61. More questionable, though, is a philosophically ambitious general explanation which Schlegel sometimes gives for the presence of, and consequent need to recognize, confusion in texts, namely that this is due to the chaotic nature of the *reality* that texts aim to characterize: "Is this infinite world [of the texts of science and art] not formed by the understanding out of unintelligibility or chaos?"; "It is a high and perhaps the final step of intellectual formation to posit for oneself the sphere of unintelligibility and confusion. The understanding of chaos consists in recognizing it" (*On Incomprehensibility* [1800], in *Friedrich Schlegel 1794–1802*, 2:393; KFSA 18:227).

62. Derrida's commitment to such a principle will be discussed later in this essay. For Skinner's, see his "Meaning and Understanding in the History of Ideas."

63. For a fuller discussion of Schlegel's hermeneutics, see Essay 2.

64. See H.-G. Gadamer, *Truth and Method*, esp. pp. 165–9. As Gadamer notes, Hegel holds this position in the "Religion" chapter of his *Phenomenology of Spirit* (1807), for example.

65. See esp. *Hegel's Aesthetics*.

66. See Essays 6 and 7.

67. Hegel does mention Champollion's work in his *Lectures on the Philosophy of History*, but presumably only knew Champollion's preliminary publications and those not very deeply.

68. In the interim, he published the first volume of *Das Leben Schleiermachers* in 1870, and continued working on volume two (eventually published posthumously in 1922). This material contains further discussions of Schleiermacher's hermeneutics.

69. For example, Dilthey's account of Schleiermacher's theory of interpretation, and his own theory of interpretation, tend to emphasize the psychological over the linguistic aspect of interpretation to an extent that is unfaithful both to Schleiermacher's theory and to the actual nature of interpretation. Again, Dilthey conceives the "divinatory" method which according to Schleiermacher's theory predominates on the psychological side of interpretation as a sort of psychological self-projection by the interpreter onto the author or his text (see, for instance, *The Rise of Hermeneutics*, pp. 248–9)—a conception which, while not *entirely* without a textual basis in Schleiermacher (see *Hermeneutics and Criticism*, pp. 92–3), fails to do justice to Schleiermacher's strong and quite proper emphasis, continuous with Herder's, on the need in interpretation to resist a pervasive temptation

falsely to assimilate the concepts, beliefs, etc. expressed by texts (from the remote past, for instance) to one's own (see ibid., p. 23). Again, Dilthey construes Schleiermacher's theory as one that advocates omitting the consideration of historical context from interpretation (*Schleiermacher's Hermeneutical System*, p. 217)—which is an extraordinary misunderstanding of Schleiermacher's principle that consideration of historical context needs to precede interpretation proper (see e.g. *Hermeneutics: The Handwritten Manuscripts*, p. 104), a principle whose real point was in fact exactly the opposite, namely to emphasize that the consideration of historical context is a *conditio sine qua non* of any interpretation worthy of the name taking place at all. More promising-looking at first sight is the mature Dilthey's shift in his own theory of interpretation away from an exclusive focus on linguistic texts and discourse towards focusing on a broader class of "expressions" (see e.g. W. Dilthey, *The Formation of the Historical World in the Human Sciences*, pp. 168, 173, 230–1). However, the aspect of this shift that is clearly correct, namely its insistence that not only linguistic texts and discourse but also, for instance, architecture, sculpture, painting, and instrumental music express meanings and thoughts requiring interpretation, was not new, having already been emphasized by Herder and Hegel (as previously mentioned). And the aspect of it that is more novel, namely the claim, taken over from Hegel but with modification (unlike Hegel, who focuses on architecture and sculpture in this connection, Dilthey focuses especially on instrumental music—see ibid., p. 245), that the additional forms of expression in question are in some cases autonomous of language, arguably turns out to be mistaken in the end (for an argument to this effect, see Essay 6).

70. Over the course of his career Dilthey vacillates somewhat between assigning this role to interpretation/hermeneutics and assigning it to psychology. However, because of the prominence of psychology in his conception of interpretation itself, this is less of a vacillation than it may seem.

71. See, for example, W. Dilthey, *Introduction to the Human Sciences* (Princeton, NJ: Princeton University Press, 1989), pp. 88–9. Dilthey has a variety of specific reasons for this pessimism.

72. See e.g. ibid., pp. 145–7.

73. See e.g. *Hermeneutics and the Study of History*, pp. 261–2.

74. See e.g. *Dilthey: Selected Writings*, pp. 228, 247, 257.

75. Concerning this, see *After Herder*, Essay 1.

76. Note that I say "*as* objective," not simply "objective." This is because in his conception of the subject-matters of both interpretation and the natural sciences Dilthey is strongly influenced by Kant's Copernican Revolution.

77. Thus in his *Introduction to the Human Sciences* Dilthey's avowed aim is to provide a methodology for the "Historical School" (including Herder, the Romantics, and Boeckh) which "considered spiritual life as historical through and through" (p. 48). And in *The Rise of Hermeneutics* he writes: "Interpretation and its codification entered a new stage with the Renaissance. Because one was separated by language, living conditions, and nationality from classical and Christian antiquity, interpretation became even more than in ancient Rome a matter of transposing oneself into an alien spiritual life through linguistic, factual, and historical studies" (p. 242).

78. See e.g. *Schleiermacher's Hermeneutical System*, pp. 98, 158; *The Rise of Hermeneutics*, pp. 253–7.

79. P. Ricoeur, *Freud and Philosophy: An Essay on Interpretation* (New Haven and London: Yale University Press, 1970).

80. Cf. J.-P. Sartre, *Search for a Method* (New York: Vintage, 1968), who argues persuasively that Marxism needs to bridge the gap between socio-economic classes and individuals, and that in order to do so it should call on such auxiliary disciplines as psychoanalysis.

81. This side of Marx's theory ultimately owes much to the "Unhappy Consciousness" section of Hegel's *Phenomenology of Spirit*.

82. *The Portable Nietzsche*, ed. W. Kaufmann (New York: Penguin, 1976), p. 635.

83. Ibid., pp. 600, 627–8.

84. Ibid., p. 635.

85. F. Nietzsche, *The Will to Power* (New York: Vintage, 1968), par. 481.

86. I shall not argue the case for this here. However, some hints as to why I find the latter position unattractive can be gleaned from my criticisms of Gadamer later in this essay.

87. See esp. F. Nietzsche, *The Gay Science*, pars. 333, 354; *On the Genealogy of Morals*, pp. 57–8, 84–5.

88. Ibid., pp. 34–5.

89. For example, as Nietzsche points out, Jesus's ideal of love and cheek-turning can plausibly be seen as part of a broad systematic inversion of Greek and Roman values that he undertakes (for instance, in the Sermon on the Mount). And at Mark 7:27 Jesus contrasts Jews and Greeks as respectively children and dogs.

90. For Freud's explicit recognition of forerunners, see e.g. S. Freud, *The Interpretation of Dreams* (New York: Avon, 1965), pp. 650 ff.

91. Freud does not acknowledge this intellectual debt to Nietzsche. However, it seems quite clear. Cf. the evident indebtedness of Freud's critique of

morality in *Civilization and Its Discontents* (1929) as aggression re-directed against the self to Nietzsche's critique of morality in *On the Genealogy of Morals*.

92. Freud does recognize the most obvious class of prima facie counterexamples: anxiety dreams. But his attempts to explain these in conformity with his theory—see *The Interpretation of Dreams*, pp. 168 ff., 595–6—are unconvincing. And as Jonathan Lear points out, he seems eventually to have conceded that such dreams constitute genuine exceptions (J. Lear, *Freud* [New York and London: Routledge, 2005], pp. 110, 154 ff.). A less obvious, but no less important, class of prima facie counterexamples consists of what one might call neutral dreams: dreams which seem not to relate to wishes either positively or negatively in any deep way.

93. Cf. Lear, *Freud*, pp. 180–3. It seems to me that Freud's theory of the "Oedipus Complex" probably in the end tells us a lot more about Freud's own troubled relations with his parents than about the human condition generally.

94. Concerning jokes, see Freud's *The Joke and Its Relation to the Unconscious* (1905).

95. "German" in this parenthetical remark excludes Austrian.

96. While the later Wittgenstein's arguments that psychological states and processes are never *sufficient* for semantic understanding are extremely strong, his arguments that they are never *necessary* are far weaker.

97. See *Treatise on the Origin of Language*, in *Herder: Philosophical Writings*, esp. pp. 87–9.

98. M. Heidegger, *Kant and the Problem of Metaphysics* (1929) (Bloomington: Indiana University Press, 1997), p. 141.

99. See ibid., pp. 140–1.

100. For example, this is the force of Kant's famous remark in the *Critique of Pure Reason* concerning the interpretation of Plato that we often "understand an author better than he has understood himself" (A314). (This slogan would subsequently be taken over by Schlegel and Schleiermacher, but in each case with a significant modification of its meaning.)

101. For some similar thoughts delivered with greater enthusiasm, see R.B. Brandom, *Tales of the Mighty Dead* (Cambridge, Mass.: Harvard University Press, 2002), esp. ch. 3.

102. See e.g. Gadamer, *Truth and Method*, pp. 339–40, 388.

103. See e.g. ibid., pp. 246 ff., 293, 301–2, 265–307; also, Gadamer, *Gesammelte Werk*, 2:475, 8:377.

104. See e.g. *Truth and Method*, p. 167; *Gesammelte Werke*, 8:377. Gadamer sometimes alludes in this connection to Nietzsche's famous argument along

similar lines in *The Use and Disadvantage of History for Life* (see e.g. *Truth and Method*, p. 304; *Gesammelte Werke*, 4:326, 8:377). The debt to Nietzsche here is indeed probably much greater than Gadamer lets on—being downplayed by him, not so much from a wish to seem more original than he is (he is often generous in crediting influences, for example Hegel and Heidegger), but rather from embarrassment over Nietzsche's association with Nazism. (As we shall see, Derrida subsequently repays Gadamer in kind for this obfuscation of an intellectual influence.)

105. See e.g. *Truth and Method*, pp. 199–200, 230 ff. Here again there may well be a suppressed debt to Nietzsche, namely to his perspectivism. Anglophone interpreters have tended, misleadingly, to deny or downplay this relativistic aspect of Gadamer's position (see, for instance, several of the articles in *The Cambridge Companion to Gadamer*).

106. Gadamer's strange suggestion at one point that the interpreter's contribution always gets reabsorbed into the meaning and so vanishes (*Truth and Method*, p. 473) is evidently a symptom of this incoherence in his position. What he is really trying to say here is that there both is and is not a reinterpretation involved, but he masks this contradiction from himself and his readers by casting it in the less transparently self-contradictory form of a process of precipitation followed by reabsorption.

107. In one formulation of his position which especially prompts this sort of objection, Gadamer writes that "the discovery of the historical horizon is always already a fusion of horizons" (*Gesammelte Werke*, 2:475). My brief statement of the objection here is meant to be suggestive rather than probative. For a fuller statement of an objection of this sort against a relevantly similar position of Wittgenstein's, see my *Wittgenstein on the Arbitrariness of Grammar*, pp. 168–72.

108. See ibid., esp. pp. 169–83. The argument is complicated (in particular it does not, and should not, rest on an easy appeal to verificationism), so I shall not go into it here.

109. Insofar as Nietzsche's case from *The Use and Disadvantage of History for Life* lies behind Gadamer's argument here, a fuller response might also include some additional points (for example, concerning the actual twentieth-century results of the attempt to enliven German culture by sacrificing scrupulous human science in favor of new mythologies).

110. *Truth and Method*, p. 344.

111. Ibid., p. 448.

112. Despite widespread assumptions to the contrary. See e.g. recently R.B. Pippin, "Gadamer's Hegel," p. 236.

113. It should be mentioned here that the late Heidegger's continued commitment to the principle of doing "violence" to texts, Gadamer's denial to texts of an original meaning and consequent encouragement of interpretations which adapt them to the interpreter's own purposes, and the similar position held by the deconstructionist Paul de Man have a much more sinister aspect as well. All of these men were Nazis or Nazi collaborators who had left a trail of embarrassing pronouncements behind them during the Nazi period. How convenient that they developed general methodologies of interpretation that warranted the reinterpretation of such pronouncements to their own current advantage and taste!

114. For a critique of Davidson's conception of the need for "charity" in interpretation, see my "On the Very Idea of Denying the Existence of Radically Different Conceptual Schemes."

115. One of Derrida's most explicit general discussions of interpretation is "Structure, Sign, and Play in the Discourse of the Human Sciences," in J. Derrida, *Writing and Difference* (Chicago: University of Chicago Press, 1978). However, many of his other works bear on this subject as well.

116. For the concept of "iterability," see esp. the essay "Signature, Event, Context," in J. Derrida, *Margins of Philosophy*. For the concept of "différance," see especially the essay "Différance," in the same volume and J. Derrida, *of Grammatology* (Baltimore and London: Johns Hopkins University Press, 1974).

117. See esp. *Writing and Difference*, p. 280.

118. See esp. *Of Grammatology*, pp. 66–7, 163, 296, 304, 311–14. Although it is usually overlooked, there can be no doubt about Derrida's intellectual debt to Gadamer here: like Gadamer, Derrida stresses the open-endedness of this process (p. 163), takes the re-presentation of such things as theatrical works as a model (p. 304), even has a version of Gadamer's strange idea that the interpreter's contribution always gets reabsorbed into the meaning and so vanishes (pp. 313–14), and also in effect repeats Gadamer's sharp contrast between this whole model of interpretation and Romantic hermeneutics' allegedly misguided contrary conception of interpretation as the recapturing of an original meaning (*Writing and Difference*, p. 292). This raises an ugly question of plagiarism. For, to my knowledge, Derrida nowhere acknowledges this intellectual debt to Gadamer. One might have been tempted to ascribe that sin of omission charitably to a political motive, namely aversion to Gadamer's conservatism and association with Nazism. However, this explanation seems implausible, given that Derrida is far from shy about giving credit to Heidegger, a figure who is even more conservative-reactionary and tainted by Nazism.

119. This state of affairs also carries negative consequences for Derrida's central thesis in *Of Grammatology* that *writing is primordial*. This thesis is far more ambitious than just the sound and important point that the introduction of writing not only itself involved significant novelties, such as the spacing of words, but also thereby affected speech. And its greater ambition makes it prima facie absurd. How does Derrida propose to defuse this prima facie absurdity? One strategy to which he resorts is that of more or less completely redefining "writing" (see, for example, pp. 54–5 on "writing in the colloquial sense," "a vulgar concept of writing," as contrasted with Derrida's "reform[ed]...concept of writing," which he sometimes calls arche-writing). But this strategy is altogether intellectually boring, rendering the thesis that writing is primordial merely a gratuitously confusing way of saying something quite different and much less surprising. However, a more sophisticated strategy to which Derrida sometimes appeals is rather to exploit Gadamer's theory about the nature of meaning and interpretation: since we end up in history with writing and speech influenced by writing, this retroactively becomes internal to the nature of all *earlier* language use as well (see esp. pp. 314–15). But if Gadamer's theory is mistaken, then even this more interesting of Derrida's two strategies for defending his prima facie absurd thesis that writing is primordial fails.

120. For examples of this approach at work, see *Of Grammatology, Margins of Philosophy*, and *Writing and Difference*.

121. Such ideas in the Anglophone tradition often stem from a sort of double error: a principle, espoused by many philosophers in one version or another (including Aristotle, Kant, the early Wittgenstein, and Quine), to the effect that it is impossible to think inconsistently; plus an inference from that principle to the inevitable erroneousness of imputing inconsistencies to texts. This is a double error because, first, the principle in question turns out to be mistaken (see my *Wittgenstein on the Arbitrariness of Grammar*, ch. 5), and second, even if it were true, it would only plausibly apply to *explicit* inconsistencies, whereas the ones that need to be imputed to texts are normally just *implicit* ones.

122. See e.g. *Writing and Difference*, pp. 226–7.

123. See on this M. Frank, *Das individuelle Allgemeine*. The title of Frank's book reflects this project of Schleiermacher's.

124. See esp. "Structure, Sign, and Play in the Discourse of the Human Sciences."

125. Closely related to this strategy (or perhaps really just a special form of it) is Derrida's strategy in the interpretation of visual art of focusing on such

seemingly marginal features of an artwork as the "subjectile" (i.e. the material medium), the "trait" (e.g. the brushstroke), and the "parergon" (e.g. the frame, the title, or the signature). For a good account of this, see J. Wolfreys' discussion of Derrida's theory of art in *Understanding Derrida*, ch. 10.

126. See J.L. Austin, *How to Do Things with Words* (1955) (Cambridge, Mass.: Harvard University Press, 1975).

127. See Skinner's essays in *Meaning and Context: Quentin Skinner and His Critics*.

128. The division of labor here was roughly that Austin invented the concept of "illocutionary force" and saw its relevance for interpretation in a general way, whereas Skinner then brought it to bear on the interpretation of historical texts in particular.

129. Austin, *How to Do Things with Words*.

130. For a similar point, cf. J.R. Searle, "A Taxonomy of Illocutionary Acts," in his *Expression and Meaning: Studies in the Theory of Speech Acts* (Cambridge: Cambridge University Press, 1979), p. 7. It may not therefore after all be necessary to invoke additional categories such as Skinner's "oblique strategies" in order to cover cases like irony which fail Austin's performative litmus test (in my broader sense of the term, these too can qualify as examples of illocutionary force).

131. For a similar point, cf. P.F. Strawson, "Intention and Convention in Speech Acts," in his *Logico-linguistic Papers* (Bristol: Methuen, 1977), p. 156.

132. See Austin, *How to Do Things with Words*; and esp. Searle, "A Taxonomy of Illocutionary Acts."

133. L. Wittgenstein, *Philosophical Investigations*, par. 23.

134. For a defense of Wittgenstein's position on this subject against Searle's attack on it, see my "A Wittgensteinian Anti-Platonism."

135. For an argument that this situation in fact occurs historically, see ibid., where I draw in this connection on some of my work in ancient philosophy concerned with the nature of Pyrrhonism.

136. R. Jakobson, "On Linguistic Aspects of Translation," in *The Translation Studies Reader*, ed. L. Venuti (London and New York: Routledge, 2000), p. 115.

137. Think, for example, of some of the later Wittgenstein's more primitive language-games in the *Philosophical Investigations*.

138. For an elaboration of this point, see my "A Wittgensteinian Anti-Platonism," where I draw in this connection on some of my work in ancient philosophy concerned with the Platonic dialogues.

139. See D.L. Cheney and R.M. Seyfarth, *How Monkeys See the World* (Chicago: University of Chicago Press, 1990).

140. See S. Savage-Rumbaugh, S.G. Shanker, T.J. Taylor, *Apes, Language, and the Human Mind* (Oxford: Oxford University Press, 1998).

141. Two recent examples of this attitude are Jonathan Bennett and Charles Taylor.

142. For a little more discussion of this subject, see *After Herder*, Essay 3.

143. For a broad-ranging and rich discussion of both linguistic and non-linguistic cases, see D.R. Griffin, *Animal Thinking* and *Animal Minds*.

# Select Bibliography

## Friedrich Schlegel

### Primary texts

The standard German edition of Schlegel's works is:

*Kritische Friedrich Schlegel Ausgabe*, E. Behler et al. (eds.), Munich: F. Schöningh, 1958– . (*On the Language and Wisdom of the Indians* is in vol. 8.)

*Friedrich Schlegel 1794–1802. Seine prosaischen Jugendschriften*, 2 vols., J. Minor (ed.),Vienna: Carl Konegen, 1882.

Friedrich Schlegel, *Literary Notebooks (1797–1801)*, H. Eichner (ed.), Toronto: University of Toronto Press, 1957.

"Friedrich Schlegels 'Philosophie der Philologie' mit einer Einleitung herausgegeben von Josef Körner," *Logos*, 17 (1928).

*Friedrich Schlegels philosophische Vorlesungen aus den Jahren 1804 bis 1806*, C.J.H. Windischmann (ed.), Bonn: Eduard Weber, 1846.

### Translations

*On the Study of Greek Poetry*, S. Barnett (ed.), Albany, NY: State University of New York Press, 2001.

*Philosophical Fragments*, P. Firchow (ed.), Minneapolis: University of Minnesota Press, 1991. (Includes the "*Athenaeum* fragments.")

*Classic and Romantic German Aesthetics*, J.M. Bernstein (ed.), Cambridge: Cambridge University Press, 2003. (Includes "On Goethe's *Meister*," "On Incomprehensibility," and several other pieces.)

*German Romantic Criticism*, A.L. Willson (ed.), New York: Continuum, 1982. (Includes long excerpts from the "Dialogue on Poetry.")

*Lectures on the History of Literature*, London: Bell and Daldy, 1873.

*The Philosophy of Life and the Philosophy of Language*, A.J.W. Morrison (ed.), London: H.G. Bohn, 1859.

### General treatments

Behler, E., *Friedrich Schlegel in Selbstzeugnissen und Bilddokumenten*, Reinbek: Rowohlt, 1966. (Short but extremely informative and helpful.)

Eichner, H., *Friedrich Schlegel*, New York: Twayne, 1970. (Very helpful.)

Haym, R., *Die Romantische Schule*, 1870; 4th edn., Berlin: Weidmann, 1920. (Still well worth reading.)

*Works on Schlegel's philosophy of language*

Fiesel, E., *Die Sprachphilosophie der Deutschen Romantik*, Tübingen: J.C.B. Mohr, 1927.

Gipper, H., and Schmitter, P., *Sprachwissenschaft und Sprachphilosophie im Zeitalter der Romantik*, Tübingen: Gunter Narr, 1985. (Excellent on Schlegel as well as other subjects.)

Körner, J., "Friedrich Schlegels 'Philosophie der Philologie' mit einer Einleitung herausgegeben von Josef Körner." (Körner helpfully discusses Schlegel's hermeneutics in relation to Schleiermacher's and Boeckh's.)

Nüsse, H., *Die Sprachtheorie Friedrich Schlegels*, Heidelberg: Carl Winter, 1962.

Patsch, H., "Friedrich Schlegels 'Philosophie der Philologie' und Schleiermachers frühe Entwürfe zur Hermeneutik," in *Zeitschrift für Theologie und Kirche*, 63 (1966). (Very good on Schlegel's hermeneutics.)

Szondi, P., "Friedrich Schlegel's Theory of Poetical Genres: A Reconstruction from the Posthumous Fragments," in his *On Textual Understanding and Other Essays = Theory and History of Literature*, vol. 15, Manchester: Manchester University Press, 1986.

——"Von der normativen zur spekulativen Gattungspoetik," in his *Poetik und Geschichtsphilosophie II*, Frankfurt am Main: Suhrkamp, 1974. (Szondi's pieces provide a very informative and thoughtful treatment of Schlegel's theory of genre.)

*Literature on other topics*

Behler, E., *German Romantic Literary Theory*, Cambridge: Cambridge University Press, 1993. (Largely concerned with Schlegel, and very helpful.)

Beiser, F.C., *German Idealism*, Cambridge, Mass.: Harvard University Press, 2002, pt. 3, ch. 4. (Helpful on Schlegel and his relation to German Idealism in the areas of metaphysics and epistemology.)

——*Enlightenment, Revolution and Romanticism: The Genesis of Modern German Political Thought 1790–1800*, Cambridge, Mass.: Harvard University Press, 1992, chs. 9–10. (Excellent on Schlegel's early political philosophy.)

——*The Romantic Imperative*, Cambridge, Mass.: Harvard University Press, 2003. (Very helpful on Schlegel's aesthetics.)

Eichner, H., "Friedrich Schlegel's Theory of Romantic Poetry," *Proceedings of the Modern Language Association*, 71 (1956).

——"The Supposed Influence of Schiller's *Über naive und sentimentale Dichtung* on F. Schlegel's *Über das Studium der griechischen Poesie*," *Germanic Review*, 30 (1955).

Frank, M., *Unendliche Annäherung*, Frankfurt am Main: Suhrkamp, 1998. (Helpful on Schlegel's metaphysics and epistemology.)

——*Einführung in die frühromantische Ästhetik*, Frankfurt am Main: Suhrkamp, 1989. (Helpful on Schlegel's aesthetics.)

Lovejoy, A.O., "The Meaning of 'Romantic' in Early German Romanticism," "Schiller and the Genesis of German Romanticism," and "On the Discrimination of Romanticisms," all in his *Essays on the History of Ideas*, 1948; repr. New York: Capricorn

Books, 1960. (These are seminal essays concerning the origin and nature of "Romanticism," especially in Schlegel.)

## Wilhelm Von Humboldt

### Primary texts

The following is the standard German edition of Humboldt's works:

*Wilhelm von Humboldts Gesammelte Schriften*, A. Leitzmann et al. (eds.), Berlin: B. Behr, 1903– .

*Wilhelm von Humboldts Briefe an Karl Gustav Brinkmann*, A. Leitzmann (ed.), Leipzig: Hiersemann, 1939.

*Der Briefwechsel zwischen Friedrich Schiller und Wilhelm von Humboldt*, S. Seidel (ed.), Berlin: Aufbau, 1962.

### Translations

*On Language: On the Diversity of Human Language-Structure and its Influence on the Mental Development of Mankind*, trans. P. Heath, introd. H. Aarsleff, Cambridge: Cambridge University Press, 1988. (This translation was subsequently reissued by the same publisher with a slightly modified title and an introduction by M. Losonsky instead of H. Aarsleff in 1999.)

*Essays on Language*, T. Harden and D. Farrelly (eds.), Frankfurt am Main: Peter Lang, 1997.

*Translation/History/Culture*, A. Lefevere (ed.), London: Routledge, 1992. (Includes part of Humboldt's introduction to his translation of Aeschylus' *Agamemnon* from 1816, which is concerned with translation theory.)

*The Limits of State Action*, J.W. Burrow (ed.), Cambridge: 1969. (This is a translation of Humboldt's *Ideas towards an Attempt to Fix the Limits of the State's Operation* from 1791.)

### General treatments

Haym, R., *Wilhelm von Humboldt. Lebensbild und Charakteristik*, Berlin: Gaertner, 1856. (Not as good as some of Haym's other works but still useful.)

Sweet, P.R., *Wilhelm von Humboldt: A Biography*, 2 vols., Columbus: Ohio State University Press, 1978. (An excellent, detailed biography.)

### Works on Humboldt's theory of language

Aarsleff, H., "Guillaume de Humboldt et la pensée linguistique des idéologues," in A. Joly and J. Stéfanini (eds.), *La Grammaire générale: Des modistes aux idéologues*, Lille: Presses Universitaires de Lille III, 1977.

—— *From Locke to Saussure: Essays on the Study of Language and Intellectual History*, Minneapolis: University of Minnesota Press, 1982.

Aarsleff, H. Introduction to Wilhelm von Humboldt, *On Language* (cited above).

Brown, R.L., *Wilhelm von Humboldt's Conception of Linguistic Relativity*, The Hague/Paris: Mouton, 1967. (A helpful treatment.)

Cassirer, E., *The Philosophy of Symbolic Forms*, New Haven: Yale University Press, 1953, vol. 1.

Chomsky, N., *Cartesian Linguistics*, New York/London: Harper and Row, 1966.

—— *Current Issues in Linguistic Theory*, The Hague/Paris: Mouton, 1964. (The former is especially helpful. Chomsky's work is highly controversial both in its reading of Humboldt and in its own position, but is essential reading.)

Coseriu, E., "Semantik, innere Sprachform und Tiefenstruktur," *Folia Linguistica*, 4 (1970). (Largely devoted to a critique of Chomsky. Not especially illuminating.)

Fiesel, E.; *Die Sprachphilosophie der Deutschen Romantik.*

Gipper, H., *Wilhelm von Humboldts Bedeutung für Theorie und Praxis moderner Sprachforschung*, Münster: Nodus, 1992. (An excellent collection of essays.)

Gipper, H., and Schmitter, P., *Sprachwissenschaft und Sprachphilosophie im Zeitalter der Romantik.* (Excellent on Humboldt as well as other subjects.)

Manchester, M.L., *The Philosophical Foundations of Humboldt's Linguistic Doctrines*, Amsterdam/Philadelphia: John Benjamins, 1985. (Informative and helpful.)

Oesterreicher, W., "Wem gehört Humboldt?" in *Logos Semantikos: Studia Linguistica in Honorem Eugenio Coseriu 1921–1981*, Berlin/New York: de Gruyter, 1981. (Another attack on Chomsky.)

Scharf, H.-W., *Das Verfahren der Sprache: Humboldt gegen Chomsky*, Paderborn: F. Schöningh, 1994. (The most extensive attempt to refute Chomsky's interpretation of Humboldt and to defend Humboldt's position against Chomsky's. Not especially rewarding.)

Trabant, J., *Apeliotes oder der Sinn der Sprache. Wilhelm von Humboldts Sprachbild*, Berlin: Akademie Verlag, 1986. (Along with Gipper's works, the best recent German treatment of Humboldt's theory of language.)

### Literature on other topics

Beiser, F.C., *Enlightenment, Revolution and Romanticism*, ch. 5. (Helpful on Humboldt's political philosophy.)

Bunzl, M., "Franz Boas and the Humboldtian Tradition: From *Volksgeist* and *Nationalcharakter* to an Anthropological Concept of Culture," in *Volksgeist as Method and Ethic*, G.W. Stocking Jr. (ed.), Wisconsin: University of Wisconsin Press, 1996. (Bunzl's article is a very thorough and informative treatment of Humboldt's role in the development of American anthropology.)

Kaehler, S., *Wilhelm von Humboldt und der Staat*, Göttingen: Vandenhoeck and Ruprecht, 1963.

Müller-Vollmer, K., *Poesie und Einbildungskraft: Zur Dichtungstheorie Wilhelm von Humboldts*, Stuttgart: Metzler, 1967.

# Hegel

## Primary texts

The German edition of Hegel's works most commonly used is:

G.W.F. Hegel, *Werke*, E. Moldenhauer and K.M. Michel (eds.), Frankfurt am Main: Surhkamp, 1970.

G.W.F. Hegel, *Jenaer Systementwürfe I*, Hamburg: Felix Meiner, 1986.

G.W.F. Hegel, *Jenaer Realphilosophie* (1805–6), Hamburg: Felix Meiner, 1969.

*Dokumente zu Hegels Entwicklung*, J. Hoffmeister (ed.), Stuttgart: Frommann, 1936.

## Translations

*Phenomenology of Spirit*, A.V. Miller (ed.), Oxford: Oxford University Press, 1977.

*Hegel's Logic*, W. Wallace (ed.), Oxford: Clarendon Press, 1975. (This is a translation of the Logic from the *Encyclopedia* of 1830.)

*Hegel's Philosophy of Mind*, W. Wallace and A.V. Miller (eds.), Oxford: Clarendon Press, 1971. (This is a translation of the Philosophy of Mind from the *Encyclopedia* of 1830.)

*Science of Logic*, A.V. Miller (ed.), New York: Humanities Press, 1976.

*Hegel's Aesthetics*, T.M. Knox (ed.), 2 vols., Oxford: Clarendon Press, 1998.

*Lectures on the History of Philosophy*, 3 vols., E.S. Haldane and F.H. Simson (eds.), Atlantic Highlands, NJ: Humanities Press, 1974.

*Lectures on the Philosophy of World History: Introduction*, H.B. Nisbet (ed.), Cambridge: Cambridge University Press, 1980.

*On Art, Religion, Philosophy*, J.G. Gray (ed.), New York: Harper Torchbooks, 1970. (Contains Hegel's introductions to the three lecture series in question.)

*Early Theological Writings*, T.M. Knox (ed.), Philadelphia: University of Pennsylvania Press, 1981.

*Hegel's System of Ethical Life and First Philosophy of Spirit*, H.S. Harris and T.M. Knox (eds.), Albany, NY: State University of New York Press, 1979. (Includes Hegel's *First Philosophy of Spirit* from 1803–4.)

## General treatments

Inwood, M., *Hegel*, London: Routledge and Kegan Paul, 1983. (An excellent treatment; interpretively scrupulous, philosophically sophisticated, and thorough.)

Pinkard, T., *Hegel: A Biography*, Cambridge: Cambridge University Press, 2000. (A good, readable biography.)

Taylor, C., *Hegel*, Cambridge: Cambridge University Press, 1975. (A classic broad treatment of Hegel's thought which develops many new interpretive insights.)

## Works on Hegel's philosophy of language

Bodammer, T., *Hegels Deutung der Sprache*, Hamburg: Felix Meiner, 1969. (The best book on Hegel's philosophy of language.)

Brandom, R.B., *Tales of the Mighty Dead*, Cambridge, Mass.: Harvard University Press, 2002. (A stimulating and thought-provoking discussion by a contemporary philosopher of language.)

Bubner, R., and Hindrichs, G. (eds.), *Von der Logik zur Sprache*, Stuttgart: Klett-Cotta, 2007.

Cook, D.J., *Language in the Philosophy of Hegel*, The Hague/Paris: Mouton, 1973. (Informative and helpful.)

Coseriu, E., "Zu Hegels Semantik," *Kwartalnik neofilologiczny*, 24 (1977).

Derrida, J., "The Pit and the Pyramid: Introduction to Hegel's Semiology," in his *Margins of Philosophy*, Chicago: University of Chicago Press, 1982. (A famous and thought-provoking treatment.)

Forster, M.N., *Hegel's Idea of a Phenomenology of Spirit*, Chicago: University of Chicago Press, 1998.

Freyer, H., "Sprache und Kultur," *Die Erziehung* (1928).

Hahn, S., "Hegel on Saying and Showing," *The Journal of Value Inquiry*, 28/2 (1994).

Hoffmeister, J., "Hegels erster Entwurf einer Philosophie des subjektiven Geistes," *Logos*, 20 (1931).

Inwood, M., *A Hegel Dictionary*, Oxford: Blackwell, 1992. (Helpful on Hegel's views about language generally and especially on his philosophical terminology.)

Koyré, A., "Note sur la langue et la terminologie hégéliennes," *Revue philosophique de la France et de l'Étranger*, 112 (1931).

Redding, P., *Hegel's Hermeneutics*, Cornell: Cornell University Press, 1996. (Helpful especially on Hegel's relation to Gadamer.)

Simon, J., *Das Problem der Sprache bei Hegel*, Stuttgart: Kohlhammer, 1966.

Surber, J.O. (ed.), *Hegel and Language*, Albany NY: State University of New York Press, 2006.

*Works on Hegel's philosophy of art (especially music)*

Bungay, S., *Beauty and Truth*, Oxford: Oxford University Press, 1984.

Hanslick, E., *On the Musically Beautiful*, Indianapolis: Hackett, 1986.

Heimsoeth, H., "Hegels Philosophie der Musik," *Hegel Studien*, 2 (1963).

Moos, P., *Moderne Musikästhetik in Deutschland*, Berlin: Hermann Seemann Nachfolger, 1902, pp. 18 ff.

Nowak, A., *Hegels Musikästhetik*, Regensburg: G. Bosse, 1971.

*Additional literature on Hegel*

Beiser, F.C. (ed.), *The Cambridge Companion to Hegel*, Cambridge: Cambridge University Press, 1993.

—— *The Cambridge Companion to Hegel and Nineteenth-century Philosophy*, Cambridge: Cambridge University Press, 2008.

Dilthey, W., *Die Jugendgeschichte Hegels*, in his *Gesammelte Schriften*, Stuttgart: B.G. Teubner and Göttingen: Vandenhoeck and Ruprecht, 1914–, vol. 4.

Forster, M.N., *Hegel and Skepticism*, Cambridge, Mass.: Harvard University Press, 1989.

——"Das geistige Tierreich," in *Hegels Phänomenologie des Geistes*, K. Vieweg and W. Welsch (eds.), Frankfurt am Main: Suhrkamp, 2008.

Haering, T., *Hegel: sein Wollen und sein Werk*, 2 vols., Leipzig/Berlin: B.G. Teubner, 1929–38.

Harris, H.S., *Hegel's Development: Toward the Sunlight 1770–1801*, Oxford: Oxford University Press, 1972.

Rosenkranz, K., *Hegels Leben*, 1844; repr. Darmstadt: Wissenschaftliche Buchgesellschaft, 1977.

Schwarz, J., *Hegels philosophische Entwicklung*, Frankfurt am Main: Klostermann, 1938.

Taylor, C., "Hegel's Philosophy of Mind," in his *Human Agency and Language: Philosophical Papers I*, Cambridge: Cambridge University Press, 1996.

Vieweg, K., and Welsch, W., (eds.), *Das Interesse des Denkens — Hegel aus heutiger Sicht*, Munich: Wilhelm Fink, 2003.

——*Hegels Phänomenologie des Geistes*.

## And Beyond

This section of the Bibliography roughly follows the order of treatment of subjects in the last two essays of the volume, Essays 8 and 9.

### The development of nineteenth-century linguistics

Fiesel, E., *Die Sprachphilosophie der Deutschen Romantik.*

Foucault, M., *The Order of Things*, London: Tavistock, 1970, ch. 8.

Gipper, H., and Schmitter, P., *Sprachwissenschaft und Sprachphilosophie im Zeitalter der Romantik.*

Pedersen, H., *The Discovery of Language: Linguistic Science in the 19th Century*, Bloomington: Indiana University Press, 1962.

### Gruppe

Gruppe, O.F., *Antäus. Ein Briefwechsel über spekulative Philosophie in ihrem Konflikt mit Wissenschaft und Sprache*, Berlin: Nauck, 1831.

——*Wendepunkt der Philosophie im neunzehnten Jahrhundert*, Berlin: G. Reimer, 1834.

——*Gegenwart und Zukunft der Philosophie in Deutschland*, Berlin: G. Reimer, 1855.

Sluga, H.D., *Gottlob Frege*, London: Routledge and Kegan Paul, 1980, esp. pp. 19–26.

### Nietzsche

Nietzsche, F., *Sämtliche Werke: Kritische Studienausgabe in 15 Einzelbänden*, G. Colli and M. Montinari (eds.), Munich/Berlin: Deutscher Taschenbuch/de Gruyter, 1988.

——"On Truth and Lies in a Nonmoral Sense," in *Philosophy and Truth: Selections from Nietzsche's Notebooks of the Early 1870's*, D. Breazeale (ed.), Atlantic Highlands, NJ: Humanities Press, 1979. (Breazeale's introduction is also helpful.)

Nietzsche, F., *Friedrich Nietzsche on Rhetoric and Language*, S.L. Gilman, C. Blair, D.J. Parent (eds.), Oxford: Oxford University Press, 1989.
—— *The Birth of Tragedy and The Case of Wagner*, W. Kaufmann (ed.), New York: Vintage, 1967.
—— *The Gay Science*, W. Kaufmann (ed.), New York: Vintage, 1974.
—— *Beyond Good and Evil*, W. Kaufmann (ed.), New York: Vintage, 1989.
—— *The Will to Power*, W. Kaufmann and R.J. Hollingdale (eds.), New York: Vintage, 1968.
—— *The Portable Nietzsche*, W. Kaufmann (ed.), New York: Penguin, 1976.

Clark, M., *Nietzsche on Truth and Philosophy*, Cambridge: Cambridge University Press, 1990, esp. ch. 3.
Danto, A.C., *Nietzsche as Philosopher*, New York: Columbia University Press, 1980.

## Mauthner

Mauthner, F., *Beiträge zu einer Kritik der Sprache*, 1902; 3rd edn., Berlin: Felix Meiner, 1923.
—— *Die Sprache*, Frankfurt am Main: Ruetten and Loening, 1906.
—— *Wörterbuch der Philosophie*, Munich and Leipzig: Georg Müller, 1910.

Janik, A., and Toulmin, S., *Wittgenstein's Vienna*, New York: Simon and Schuster, 1973, esp. pp. 121–33.
Sluga, H.D., *Gottlob Frege*, esp. pp. 74–6, 183–6.
Weiler, G. "Mauthner, Fritz," in *The Encyclopedia of Philosophy*, P. Edwards (ed.), New York: Macmillan, 1972.
—— *Mauthner's Critique of Language*, Cambridge: Cambridge University Press, 1970.

## Frege

Frege, G., *Collected Papers on Mathematics, Logic, and Philosophy*, B.F. McGuinness (ed.), Oxford: Blackwell, 1984.
—— *The Foundations of Arithmetic*, J.L. Austin (ed.), Evanston, Ill.: Northwestern University Press, 1968.

Baker, G.P., and Hacker, P.M.S., *Frege: Logical Excavations*, Oxford: Oxford University Press, 1984. (Highly critical but thought-provoking.)
Blackburn, S., *Spreading the Word*, Oxford: Oxford University Press, 1984. (Good on Frege and on the philosophy of language generally.)
Dummett, M., "Frege, Gottlob," in *The Encyclopedia of Philosophy*, P. Edwards (ed.).
—— *Frege: Philosophy of Language*, Cambridge, Mass.: Harvard University Press, 1981.
—— *The Interpretation of Frege's Philosophy*, Cambridge, Mass.: Harvard University Press, 1981.
—— *Frege and Other Philosophers*, Oxford: Clarendon Press, 1991. (Dummett's is some of the most important work that has been done on Frege.)
Kenny, A., *Frege*, London: Penguin, 1995. (A helpful concise treatment.)
Kripke, S.A., *Naming and Necessity*, Oxford: Blackwell, 1980. (A critical engagement with some of Frege's ideas by an outstanding philosopher.)

Sluga, H.D., *Gottlob Frege*. (Historically and interpretively painstaking; a good counter-weight to Dummett's work.)

Weiner, J., *Frege in Perspective*, Ithaca: Cornell University Press, 1990.

——"Has Frege a Philosophy of Language?" in *Early Analytic Philosophy: Frege, Russell, Wittgenstein—Essays in Honor of Leonard Linsky*, W. W. Tait (ed.), Chicago: Open Court, 1997.

## *Wittgenstein*

Wittgenstein, L., *Tractatus logico-philosophicus* (1921), D.F. Pears and B.F. McGuinness (eds.), London: Routledge, 1961.

——*Philosophical Investigations*, G.E.M. Anscombe (ed.), 1953; 2nd, rev. edn., Oxford: Blackwell, 1958.

——*Wittgenstein's Lectures: Cambridge 1932–1935*, A. Ambrose (ed.), Chicago: University of Chicago Press, 1982.

——*The Blue and Brown Books*, Oxford: Blackwell, 1975.

——*Zettel*, G.E.M. Anscombe (ed.), Oxford: Blackwell, 1967.

——*Remarks on the Philosophy of Psychology*, 2 vols., G.E.M. Anscombe et al. (eds.), Chicago: University of Chicago Press, 1980.

Fogelin, R.J., *Wittgenstein*, London: Routledge and Kegan Paul, 1976. (A helpful treatment of Wittgenstein both early and late.)

Forster, M.N., *Wittgenstein on the Arbitrariness of Grammar*, Princeton, NJ: Princeton University Press, 2004.

Hacker, P.M.S., *Insight and Illusion*, 1972; rev. edn., Bristol: Thoemmes, 1997. (Still the best book on Wittgenstein both early and late.)

Janik, A., and Toulmin, S., *Wittgenstein's Vienna*.

Kripke, S.A., *Wittgenstein on Rules and Private Language*, Cambridge, Mass.: Harvard University Press, 1982. (A brilliant elaboration of Wittgenstein's ideas concerning rule following and the impossibility of a private language.)

Monk, R., *Ludwig Wittgenstein: The Duty of Genius*, New York: Penguin, 1991. (An excellent biography.)

## *Dilthey*

Dilthey, W., *Gesammelte Schriften*, Stuttgart: B.G. Teubner and Göttingen: Vandenhoeck and Ruprecht, 1914– .

——*Dilthey: Selected Writings*, H.P. Rickman (ed.), Cambridge: Cambridge University Press, 1979.

——*Introduction to the Human Sciences*, R.A. Makkreel (ed.), Princeton, NJ: Princeton University Press, 1989.

——*Hermeneutics and the Study of History*, R.A. Makkreel (ed.), Princeton, NJ: Princeton University Press, 1996.

——*The Formation of the Historical World in the Human Sciences*, R.A. Makkreel (ed.), Princeton, NJ: Princeton University Press, 2002.

Dilthey, W., *Poetry and Experience*, R.A. Makkreel (ed.), Princeton, NJ: Princeton University Press, 1985.

Makkreel, R.A., *Dilthey: Philosopher of the Human Studies*, Princeton, NJ: Princeton University Press, 1975. (Learned and helpful.)

Palmer, R.E., *Hermeneutics: Interpretation Theory in Schleiermacher, Dilthey, Heidegger, and Gadamer*, Evanston, Ill.: Northwestern University Press, 1969, ch. 8.

Rickman, H.P., *Wilhelm Dilthey: Pioneer of the Human Studies*, Berkeley and Los Angeles: University of California Press, 1979. (A helpful study.)

### Heidegger

Heidegger, M., *Gesamtausgabe*, Frankfurt am Main: Klostermann, 1975– .

—— *Being and Time*, J. Macquarrie and E. Robinson (eds.), Oxford: Blackwell, 1978.

—— *Kant and the Problem of Metaphysics*, R. Taft (ed.), Bloomington: Indiana University Press, 1997.

Dreyfus, H., *Being-in-the-world: A Commentary on Heidegger's Being and Time, Division I*, Cambridge, Mass.: MIT Press, 1991. (A classic treatment by a sophisticated philosopher.)

Inwood, M., *Heidegger*, Oxford: Oxford University Press, 1997. (A very helpful short treatment.)

—— *A Heidegger Dictionary*, Oxford: Blackwell, 1999. (Philologically and philosophically sophisticated. Very helpful as a guide through Heidegger's obscurities.)

Palmer, R.E., *Hermeneutics*, chs. 9–10.

### Gadamer

H.-G. Gadamer, *Gesammelte Werke*, Tübingen: J.C.B. Mohr, 1993.

—— *Truth and Method*, J. Weinsheimer and D.G. Marshall (eds.), New York: Continuum, 2002.

*The Philosophy of Hans-Georg Gadamer*, L.E. Hahn (ed.), Chicago: Open Court, 1997.

*The Cambridge Companion to Gadamer*, R.J. Dostal (ed.), Cambridge: Cambridge University Press, 2002.

Palmer, R.E., *Hermeneutics*, chs. 11–12.

# Index